Social Welfare
in Transition

Social Welfare in Transition

SELECTED ENGLISH DOCUMENTS, 1834–1909

Edited by Roy Lubove

Introductory Essays by John Duffy and Samuel Mencher

UNIVERSITY OF PITTSBURGH PRESS

Library of Congress
Catalog Card Number 66-12679
Copyright © 1966, University of Pittsburgh Press
Manufactured in the
United States of America

Preface

ROY LUBOVE

Each of the documents included in this collection represents a landmark in the history of social welfare. Taken together, they illustrate changing conceptions of health and poverty, and of the role of the state in dealing with these issues.

The Chadwick *Report* of 1842 was instrumental in the emergence of health administration and urban sanitary control. Public health, in turn, led to new views of the governmental welfare function. One of the most perplexing problems of the modern industrial era has been to define the areas of public intervention, and to work out the appropriate administrative techniques. Classic liberalism, as represented by Adam Smith and his successors, confused the issue considerably. In their revolt against mercantilist theory and policy, they tended to reduce the interventionist and planning role of government to a minimum. This may have been necessary to clear away the ideological and institutional debris inherited from the medieval era, but the economists and Social Darwinists failed to ask the right question. It should not have been whether public or private decision-making was preferable, but which activities were properly public in character, which were private, which were private but necessitating public regulation, and which were mixed. At a comparatively early date, health problems forced a more realistic consideration of the public planning and control functions. One of the most significant roots of the modern day welfare states lies in the relationship between government and health. It led to the discreditation of extreme philosophies of public nonintervention, and a significant expansion of municipal service and welfare functions. In this context the Chadwick *Report* represents a turning point in social welfare as well as public health policy.

The 1834 *Report of the Royal Poor Law Commission* shaped public welfare institutions for nearly a century. Inspired, in part, by utilitarianism, classical economics, and Malthusian population doctrine, it epitomized a punitive attitude toward poverty. The Poor Law reformers of 1834 sought to insure that public assistance would not enable individuals to escape their responsibilities as productive members of the working force. They applied the utilitarian pleasure–pain principle to charity— that the condition of the public assistance recipient should be made less palatable than that of the lowest–paid, but independent laborer. However, the *Report* did lead to a greater measure of administrative centralization on the local and national levels, a necessary prerequisite to future improvement of the welfare machinery.

In comparing the *Report* of 1834 with that of 1909, it is possible to trace the evolution of the Poor Law and efforts to adapt it to changing conditions. The Majority of the Royal Commission of 1909 attempted to modify rather than overturn entirely the "principles of 1834." The *Majority Report* is particularly interesting for its efforts to define the role of private, voluntary welfare organizations and their relationship to the public sector. Both in England and the United States, this became an increasingly significant issue as public agencies in the twentieth century assumed many of the responsibilities once considered the prerogative of voluntary groups. The Minority of the 1909 Commission, led by Beatrice Webb, sought to discredit the "principles of 1834" in favor of a new approach. It recommended the "break–up" of the Poor Law and the transfer of responsibility to divisions of local government such as health and education. The Poor Law, the Minority emphasized, was already breaking up as local authorities assumed increasing responsibility for various categories of the poor, and it aspired to hasten the process in the name of efficiency and greater opportunities to prevent dependency: *"What is demanded by the conditions is not a division according to the presence or absence of destitution, but a division according to the services to be provided."* In fact, there was considerable agreement between Majority and Minority on major issues—administrative centralization, a public assistance system geared to prevention and rehabilitation, and the transfer of numerous functions from destitution authorities to other agencies—but the Minority seemed more radical in seeking a swifter, more complete, and decisive rationalization.

In seeking the breakup of the Poor Law the Minority (and to some extent the Majority) operated on the presumption of the Webbs that "when a Destitution Authority departs from the simple function of providing bare maintenance under deterrent conditions, *it finds it quite impossible to mark off or delimit its services from those which are required by, and provided for, the population at large."* This point of view, implying the creation of universal, tax–supported services in lieu of a separate tier of welfare services whose availability was contingent upon a degrading means test, anticipated features of the twentieth-century welfare state. In this and other respects, the *Report of the Royal Commission* of 1909 retains considerable timeliness.

* * *

The major editorial decision made in preparing this collection of documents was to offer longer selections from a few strategic documents rather than a large number of snippets. This policy, it is believed, allows for better understanding of the issues raised. In line with this policy, the largest segment is drawn from both *Reports* of the Royal Commission of 1909, which offer a sweeping overview of contemporary welfare organization and problems, as well as considerable historical perspective. Furthermore, the 1909 Commission took the "principles of 1834" and their evolution as the point of reference, and devoted much attention to health and medical matters, thus providing continuity and integration for all the documents.

The selections are drawn from the following original sources:

1. *Report from the Poor Law Commissioners on an Inquiry Into the Sanitary Condition of the Labouring Population of Great Britain*, pp. 279-80, 282, 287-88, 308, 340-44, 348-57, 364-66, 368-72.

2. *Report for Inquiring Into the Administration and Practical Operation of the Poor Laws* (1834), pp. 55-56, 66, 74, 99-100, 127-28, 146-48, 152-76, 180, 183-85, 189-92, 202, 204-05.

3. *Report of the Royal Commission on the Poor Laws and Relief of Distress* (1909):

   a) *Majority Report,* pp. 596-645

   b) "Introduction" to *Minority Report,* Part 1, from Sidney and Beatrice Webb, *The Break-up of the Poor Law* (London: Longmans, 1909), pp. ix-xvii.

   c) *Minority Report,* Part 1, pp. 999-1031

   d) "Introduction" to *Minority Report,* Part 2, from Sidney and Beatrice Webb, *The Public Organisation of the Labour Market* (London: Longmans, 1909), pp. ix-xii

   e) *Minority Report,* Part 2, pp. 1179-1215

Except for minor typographical changes, and the elimination of most footnotes (particularly in the *Report* of the 1909 Commission), the text is identical with the original documents.

* * *

I wish to thank the University of Pittsburgh's Graduate School of Social Work for giving financial aid toward the publication of this book.

Contents

Report of the Royal Commission on the Poor Laws
and Relief of Distress (1909): Minority Report

Social Welfare
in Transition

Introduction
to the Sanitary Report
of 1842

JOHN DUFFY

L ATE in the summer of 1842 the
British government published Edwin Chadwick's *Report on the Sanitary
Condition of the Labouring Population of Great Britain*. Probably no
single document so profoundly affected the development of public health
as this grim, detailed account of the incredible filth in England's slums.
For almost a century drastic changes in agriculture, transportation, and
industry had been adding to England's wealth. During this time, food
supplies and productive capacity outstripped the multiplying population,
resulting in a gradual rise in the standard of living and a slow but steady
decrease in the death rate. But the rapidity with which the change from a
rural to an urban-industrial society took place found British society ill-
prepared to deal with the sanitary needs of their exploding population.
Between 1800 and 1830 many British towns doubled and tripled in size.
It was bad enough when thousands of jerry-built structures brought an
urban sprawl, but it was a rare town where building kept pace with the
growing population. Generally, the working classes were simply jammed
into already crowded areas. Run-down mansions, warehouses, and other
undesirable structures soon became warrens in which one or more families

1

often occupied a single room, and back-to-back houses became common as every available square foot of space was utilized by landlords seeking to provide high-rent housing for low-income people.

The already bad sanitary conditions soon became atrocious. Sewers existed in only a few cities, and these were designed primarily to drain surface water rather than carry sewage. Privies were the order of the day. Their construction varied, but all had to be cleaned by hand and the contents carted away. As long as towns were small and fecal matter had value as a fertilizer, this primitive system worked fairly well. With the emergence of large metropolitan areas, transportation costs made the price of cleaning privies prohibitive for the lower income groups. To complicate matters, often ten, twenty, or thirty families shared one privy. Under these circumstances every court, alley, and vacant space became a foul and loathesome mire.

The few private water companies were content to supply the homes of the well-to-do at high rates and let the poor take care of themselves. As the streams, rivers, and shallow wells became contaminated beyond use, clean water became almost unobtainable in the slum areas.

This was the situation which Edwin Chadwick brought to the attention of the English middle and upper classes. He was not the first to describe these social evils, but he was a forceful and dedicated individual who pressed his points home with incredible tenacity. Moreover, his investigations came at a time when the truths he was demonstrating were becoming all too self-evident. Chadwick, however, did much more than awaken the public conscience; the solutions he embodied in his celebrated report of 1842 set the pattern of public health in Western Europe and North America for the rest of the century. Indeed, the principles he set forth have validity today.

Chadwick, like many single-minded reformers, was humorless, dogmatic, egotistical, and intolerant of all who disagreed with him. Ironically, his faults arose from his virtues, for it was precisely these qualities which enabled him, in spite of constant frustration, to keep fighting against stupidity, apathy, greed, and economic waste. At the same time, these personal characteristics constantly frustrated his own career and deprived him of the high office which he should rightfully have held. On the credit side, he enjoyed warm relationships with his family and friends, and his impatience and intolerance of social evils—and for those who tolerated them—can scarcely be counted a fault.

Edwin Chadwick was born in 1800, the eldest son of an English middle-class family.[1] In 1812 his father became editor of *The Statesman*, a spokesman for the Radicals. His family connections with the leading English Radicals undoubtedly provided intellectual stimulation, but they were no asset to a government career in the highly stratified English society. After an excellent private education, young Chadwick decided to study law. During the long years of legal training he, like many law students, supplemented his income by working as a newspaper reporter, a much despised profession in those days. This experience proved a revelation to him, and he soon acquired a firsthand knowledge of the courts, jails, workhouses, and fever-ridden slums of London. During these years he came to the attention of Jeremy Bentham, who was much taken by this earnest young man. Through the Benthamite circle, Chadwick soon came to know many of the prominent intellectuals. These contacts proved valuable, for Chadwick's career as a lawyer ended almost as soon as it began. In the process of defending his first client, he discovered the man was guilty and threw up the case in disgust—never to practice again.

In the meantime he continued with his newspaper work and, during the last year of Bentham's life, served as his private secretary. In 1832 the door was opened to a career in government service and Chadwick found his niche. This first break came when he was appointed an assistant commissioner on a newly created Royal Commission established to study the Poor Laws. The Poor Laws, a hodge-podge of measures dating back to the Elizabethan period, left matters largely to the discretion of local authorities. For almost three hundred years local officials had been interpreting the regulations to suit themselves, while a succession of new laws and amendments added continuously to the confusion. Chadwick was, above all, a man with a practical and orderly turn of mind. His legal training and years as a newspaper man made him ideally suited for studying social problems. In making his investigation of the Poor Laws he had no intention of sitting in some remote government office evaluating second-hand information. Wherever possible, he visited the slum areas and talked with the poor. His personal knowledge of the evils he exposed undoubtedly strengthened his firm opposition to what he considered human wastage.

[1] For general information about Chadwick I have relied upon two first-class studies: S. E. Finer, *The Life and Times of Sir Edwin Chadwick* (London, 1952); and R. A. Lewis, *Edwin Chadwick and the Public Health Movement, 1832–1854* (London, 1952).

While he did not quickly jump to conclusions, once he had studied a situation and arrived at his decisions, Chadwick brooked no opposition. Supremely confident of his judgment, he maintained his position despite all odds.

Chadwick's energy and ability pushed him to the forefront of the Poor Law Commission, and his ideas became embodied in its findings and eventually into the Poor Law Act of 1834. Like many of his contemporaries, he was convinced of the efficacy of unrestricted private enterprise. The existing Poor Laws, by supporting the poor in idleness, had kept them from productive labor. He proposed to drive the able-bodied laborers into useful work by making relief as unpleasant as possible. Recognizing that elected officials could scarcely be expected to put the harsh provisions of the new measure into practice, he proposed a powerful central agency to administer the act. In essence, the main proposals of Chadwick were accepted, but many of his suggestions, which might have mitigated some of the worst effects of the law, were neglected.

When it came time to appoint the three commissioners to whom the administration of the Poor Law had been given, Chadwick suffered the first of a series of disappointments. He had played a key role in drawing up the commission report and in securing passage of the act, but in mid-nineteenth-century Britain to give a high government position to an individual with neither family background nor money was unthinkable. He was consoled by an appointment as secretary to the commissioners, a position which enabled him to be largely responsible for the operation of the law. Since the Poor Law brought incredible hardship to thousands of English workers, Chadwick's name became almost an anathema. Moreover, the limitations on his authority combined with his personal clashes with Commissioner Thomas Frankland Lewis and his son George Cornewall Lewis, who succeeded his father in 1839, eventually caused Chadwick to be deprived of all duties and responsibilities.

For once the English political system worked to Chadwick's benefit. Since political offices, once granted, were considered virtually private property, Chadwick was left free to his own devices. In the unpublished sections of the Poor Law Report of 1834 he had already investigated the relationship between poverty and health, particularly noting the connection between poor housing and high morbidity and mortality rates. In the intervening years he had served on Royal Commissions studying factory laws and police regulations. In the course of these activities Chadwick had gained an almost unrivaled knowledge of the English legal system and, more significantly, of the way in which it functioned.

Whether contemplating the condition of paupers, criminals, or factory children, Edwin Chadwick was always preoccupied with preventing rather than mitigating social evils. For example, in his report on police laws, he constantly stressed that the main function of the police was to prevent crime rather than to punish evil-doers. As he worked with the Poor Laws, Chadwick was struck by the interrelationship between pauperism, sickness, and unsanitary conditions. Whereas he had formerly subscribed in general to the thesis that the poor were largely responsible for their own degradation, Chadwick gradually came to realize that environmental conditions were a major determining factor. A sick and debilitated people could scarcely be effective workers. As a Utilitarian, Chadwick was always appalled at economic waste. He did not accept Ricardo's Wages Fund Thesis—that the amount of money available for labor was limited—but had become convinced that production was the key to economic progress. Unnecessary deaths from fevers and disease cut down the amount of labor available. If sickness could be eliminated or reduced, the output of economic goods would increase, and a major cause of poverty could be eliminated.

In 1837–38 a series of influenza and typhoid epidemics ravaged London. Chadwick seized this opportunity to urge an investigation by the Poor Law Commission into the causes of sickness, arguing that epidemics contributed directly to increasing poverty and raising the poor rates. At his instigation in 1838 three medical investigators, Drs. Neil Arnott, J. Kay-Shuttleworth, and Southwood Smith, were appointed to make a special investigation of the fever districts in London. They were asked to determine whether the habits and morals of the poor were responsible for the horrible and degrading conditions in which they lived. The three men concluded that the environment was even more important in determining their way of life than personal habits. Surrounded by foul miasmas, deprived of fresh air and water, and living in the midst of overflowing cesspools and privies, even those who wished could scarcely follow a life of prudence. Adequate building regulations, proper sewage and water facilities, and an adequate street-cleaning system could remove the most objectionable features.

The shocking reports of the three medical men aroused indignation among middle- and upper-class Englishmen and led Chadwick to press for a further inquiry. To gain public support, Chadwick circulated seven thousand copies of the special investigators report. In August of 1839 Lord John Russell ordered the Poor Law commissioners to look into the matter. Although preoccupied with other matters during most of 1839, Chadwick was able to devote full time to the project for the next two years. He gathered material from all over Britain and then turned to the writings of Continental authorities. The more he studied the situation, the more he became convinced of the necessity for a comprehensive sanitary program. Whereas he had previously urged building regulations to improve houses and dwellings, he now came to the conclusion that these measures were useless by themselves. While he was writing his *Report*, Lord Normanby, who had become a convert to Chadwick's views, introduced a series of bills embodying his earlier ideas on building regulations and sanitation. Chadwick publicly repudiated Normanby's measures, and by so doing he almost prevented the publication of his *Report*, since Normanby was outraged at Chadwick's seeming inconsistency. Despite a series of difficulties (including Chadwick's faculty for antagonizing his own supporters), the commissioners agreed to publication of the study in July of 1842. Even at the last moment, however, a problem occurred. Commissioner Lewis felt that the *Report*'s bitter attack upon the Metropolitan Commission of Sewers and the private water companies, as well as the slighting references to the medical profession and to responsible local officials, would outrage public opinion. Fortunately for Chadwick, the commissioners compromised by publishing the results under his name, unwittingly giving him full credit for his great work.

The *Report* was detailed and specific, pinpointing streets and areas. The great urban centers had no monopoly on misery and degradation because these conditions could be found in rural communities as well as towns and cities. Chadwick's concern was not simply to expose the slums to public view, but rather to demonstrate the tremendous economic loss they entailed. As he saw it, the slums undermined the morale of their occupants, thus pushing them into crime, apathy, and intemperance. Even more disastrous was their impact upon health and life expectancy. To demonstrate this latter fact, Chadwick compiled statistics showing the average age at death for various social classes. His figures showed that laborers had a life expectancy of less than half that of the gentry and professional classes.

Creating a public awareness of social evils was only part of Chadwick's task. Having posed the problem, he then sought to provide an answer. As a pragmatic individual, he was convinced that the same engineering techniques that had revolutionized the English economy could be applied to social problems. The medical profession, which in this prebacteriological era was still desperately searching for an adequate rationale, offered Chadwick little hope. Aside from the bitter wrangles within the ranks of the doctors, he considered their aims to be curative, whereas he was convinced that the real answer lay in prevention. Accepting the miasmatic or pythogenic theory of disease, he believed the solution lay in preventing the accumulation of dirt and filth. While searching for some means to achieve this end, he encountered Joe Roe, a civil engineer who, as a surveyor for one of the sewer commissions, had introduced a number of innovations. With Chadwick's backing, Roe began a series of experiments to determine the best size, shape, materials, and method for constructing sewers.

Encouraged by Roe's findings, Chadwick's grand design gradually evolved. Basic to his plan was the universal use of the water closet and the elimination of privies and cesspools. All water closets were to be connected with underground sewers which would quickly carry excreta out of the town as soon as toilets were flushed. The sewers were to be made of smooth glazed material and designed in an oval shape, thus insuring a maximum current of water to carry the solid particles away. All sharp corners were to be eliminated and hydraulic principles were to be applied in order to achieve a maximum water flow. A constant pressure was to be maintained in the sewers strong enough not only to carry away sewage but sufficient to handle street dirt and the waste products from stores, trades, and industries. Since the flow of sewage lines should follow the natural drainage to take advantage of gravity flow, sewage districts were to encompass natural geographic basins rather than to follow local political boundaries.

The proposed sewer system was predicated on the assumption that ample quantities of water could be supplied to every house or building on a twenty-four-hour-a-day basis. Because it was believed, probably with some justification, that the wooden pipes that carried the water would not stand up under constant use, most water companies maintained pressure for only one or two hours a day. The *Report* criticized the niggardliness, lack of initiative, and poor administration of the private water companies and recommended that the government take over this essential function.

A coordinated water and sewage system could be counted on to remove sewage, but what was to be done with the sewage water? Soil chemistry and scientific agriculture, which were beginning to come into their own, supplied Chadwick with the answer: It was to be piped into the country-side to be used for fertilizing and irrigating the fields.

Even if the government was willing to accept his proposals, Chadwick realized that the multitude of conflicting local authorities and elected officials would ruin any chance of success. He proposed therefore two radical innovations: a highly centralized administrative system and the employment of well–trained professional officials. It speaks well for Chadwick that, although a firm believer in private initiative, he was not so blindly committed to an economic theory or doctrine to prevent him from seeking the necessity for governmental action in certain spheres.

According to one of Chadwick's biographers, the appearance of the *Report* in 1842 created a sensation and was acclaimed by newspapers and the public alike.[2] There can be no question that it had a major impact on leading intellectual and political circles, nor that it enjoyed a wider distri-bution than any preceding governmental publication. Yet no mention was made of it in such leading journals as the *Edinburgh Review, Blackwood's Magazine,* and the *Gentlemen's Magazine.* While its publication came toward the end of the Parliamentary Session, one might reasonably expect some member to have raised his voice either for or against it, but *Hansard's Parliamentary Debates* give no hint of such action. *The Times* did not even deign to notice it until December, when it damned the *Report* with faint praise. After mentioning that it had been published the previous July, *The Times* editorialist added condescendingly: "Excellent report we believe them to be; but unfortunately extending to a length, and filled with an accumulation of details, which renders it impossible for any person with only a moderate share of leisure to give them even a cursory perusal." More or less as an afterthought, he added: "We call attention at this moment to their existence for no other purpose than to show the various subjects with which the Poor Law Commissioners have been recently intermeddling. . . ."[3]

There can be no gainsaying, however, that Chadwick's findings proved

---

[2] Finer, *Chadwick*, p. 210.

[3] *The Times*, December 15, 1842. I made no attempt to examine all contemporary newspapers or journals, but I did carefully check *Hansard's Parliamentary Debates* and the three magazines noted above.

a real shock to the English middle and upper classes, and that they made public health a major political issue for several years. The widespread circulation of Chadwick's views and the rising interest in public health forced the British government in 1843 to respond to the *Report* by appointing a Health of Towns Commission. Although not officially a member, Chadwick virtually took charge. In his initial *Report*, he had been concerned primarily with directing public attention to social evils and had stated his proposed remedies only in general terms. The *Report* of the Health of Towns Commission, which was hammered out between 1843 and 1845, refined Chadwick's original proposals and recommended specific legislation. An intensive political campaign followed which culminated in the Public Health Act of 1848. While it was far short of what Chadwick would have wished, it did establish a central board and began Great Britain on the long and slow process toward an effective public health administration.

Although two wars had left a considerable residue of bitterness, the United States still looked to England for intellectual and cultural leadership. For Americans with a social conscience, Chadwick's findings helped crystalize their own awareness of what was happening in the burgeoning American towns. It was more than a coincidence that John H. Griscom, a major public figure in New York, copied the title of Chadwick's report almost verbatim when Griscom published in 1845 his celebrated study, *The Sanitary Condition of the Laboring Population of New York*. Influenced both by Chadwick and Griscom, five years later Lemuel Shattuck issued his classic work on the health needs of Boston. Meanwhile, in Louisiana, men such as Edward H. Barton and J. C. Simonds were encouraged by Chadwick's work to press for public health reforms in New Orleans.

One might well call Chadwick the father of sanitary reform in the nineteenth century, but it would be only a half truth. The need for reform was becoming all too apparent when he came on the scene, and many able and articulate spokesmen were beginning to raise their voices in protest on both sides of the Atlantic. Most of the ideas Chadwick set forth had already been expressed, and the developments in engineering and technology which were to make effective public sanitation a reality arose independently from what Chadwick may have written. It was Chadwick's destiny—and good fortune—to be able to mobilize his evidence so conclusively that no one could deny his findings. He was an untiring advocate and a forceful polemicist, and it was this which enabled him, in a day when individual initiative was considered the prime motivating factor and the prerogatives of local government were zealously cherished, to be able to convince the English ruling class of the need for strong, centralized action in the public health area. Had Chadwick been a retiring individual, content to study social conditions and submit his findings, his *Report* might well have gathered dust. His greatness lay in the fact that, having identified the problem and arrived at a solution, he entered the political arena and waged incessant war against ignorance, apathy, and self-interest. More than any other individual in Britain he made public health a major issue. Even had he lost his fight to obtain the Public Health Act of 1848, the defeat would have been only temporary. The stark facts he had set before the British public could not be glossed over, and the problems themselves were demanding attention. Nevertheless, it was Chadwick who first awakened the public conscience and pointed the direction in which the British and other governments, however reluctantly, were forced to go.

Report on the Sanitary Condition of the Labouring Population of Great Britain

(1842)

Recognised Principles of Legislation and State of the Existing Law for the Protection of the Public Health

The evidence already given will, to some extent, have furnished answers to the question—how far the physical evils by which the health, and strength, and morals of the labouring classes are depressed may be removed, or can reasonably be expected to be removed by private and voluntary exertions. I now submit for consideration the facts which serve to show how far the aid of the legislature, and of administrative arrangements are requisite for the attainment of the objects in question.

It will have been perceived, that the first great remedies, external arrangements, *i. e.* efficient drainage, sewerage and cleansing of towns, come within the acknowledged province of the legislature. Public opinion has of late required legislative interference for the regulation of some points of the internal economy of certain places of work, and the appointment of special agents to protect young children engaged in certain classes of manufactures from mental deterioration from the privation of the advantages of education, and from permanent bodily deterioration from an excess of labour beyond their strength. Claims are now before Parliament for an extension of the like remedies to other classes of children and to young persons, who are deemed to be in the same need of protection. The legislature has interfered to put an end to one description of employment which was deemed afflicting and degrading, *i. e.* that of climbing-boys for sweeping chimneys, and to force a better means of performing by machinery the same work. It will be seen that it has been the policy of the legislature to interfere for the public protection by regulating the structure of private dwellings to prevent the extension of fires; and the common law has also interposed to protect the public health by preventing overcrowding in private tenements. The legislature has recently interfered to direct the poorer description of tenements in the metropolis to be properly cleansed. On considering the evidence before given with relation to the effects of different classes of buildings, the suggestion immediately arises as to the extent to which it is practicable to protect the health of the labouring classes by measures for the amendment of the existing buildings, and for the regulation of new buildings in towns in the great proportion of cases where neither private benevolence nor enlightened views can be expected to prevail extensively.

It will have been perceived how much of the existing evils originate from the defects of the external arrangements for drainage, and for cleansing, and for obtaining supplies of water. Until these are completed, therefore, the force of the evils arising from the construction of the houses could scarcely be ascertained.

* * *

It has been shown that the cheapest mode of street cleansing is by supplies of water, which it would be necessary to use from standing pipes. By the Street Act, the parish officers are directed to provide standing pipes for the supply of engines in case of fire. This regulation is declared to be almost a dead letter. The only means to obtain supplies of water in the case of fire are from the plugs provided by the water companies themselves for cleansing the pipes by occasionally allowing the water to flow into the streets. It has been proved to be practicable without any considerable cost to keep up, at all times, such a pressure of water as on putting on a hose on any standing pipe connected with the service, to enable the water to be thrown over the highest houses. The fronts of houses in London have, in some instances, been washed by this means, and in one instance it was immediately and successfully applied to extinguish a fire.

* * *

All the information as to the actual condition of the most crowded districts is corroborative of the apprehensions entertained by witnesses of practical experience, such as Mr. Thomas Cubitt and other builders, who are favourable to measures for the improvement of the condition of the labouring classes, that anything of the nature of a Building Act that is not equally and skillfully administered will aggravate the evils intended to be remedied. To whatever districts regulations are confined, the effect proved to be likely to follow will be, that the builder of tenements which stand most in need of regulation will be driven over the boundary, and will run up his habitations before measures can be taken to include them. The condition of the workman will be aggravated by the increased fatigue and exposure to weather in traversing greater distances to sleep in a badly-built, thin, and damp house. An increase of distance from his place of work will have the more serious effect upon his habits by rendering it impracticable to take his dinner with his family, compelling him either to take it in some shed or at the beer shop. It is also apprehended that anything that may be done to increase unnecessarily or seriously the cost of new buildings, or discourage their erection, will aggravate the horrors of the over-crowding of the older tenements; at the same time, the certain effect of an immediate and unprepared dislodgement of a cellar population, would be to overcrowd the upper portions of the houses where they reside. It would indeed often be practicable to make those cellars as habitable as are the cellars inhabited by servants in the houses of the middle and higher classes of society. The difficulties which beset such regulations do not arise from the want of means to pay any necessary increase of rents for increased accommodation, but in the very habits which afford evidence of the existence of the sufficiency of the means of payment.

* * *

The most important immediate general measure of the nature of a Building Act, subsidiary to measures for drainage, would be a measure for regulating the increments of towns, and preventing the continued reproduction in new districts of the evils which have depressed the health and the condition of whole generations in the older districts. Regulations of the *sites* of town buildings have comparatively little effect on the cost of construction, and it may in general be said that a Building Act would effect what any enlightened owner of a district would effect for himself, of laying it out with a view to the most permanent advantage; or what the separate owners would effect for themselves if they had the power of co-operation, or if each piece of work were governed by enlarged public and private views. Had Sir Christopher Wren been permitted to carry out his plan for the rebuilding of London after the great fire, there is little doubt that it would have been the most advantageous arrangement for rendering the whole space more productive, as a property to the great mass of the separate interests, by whom the improvement was defeated. The most successful improvements effected in the metropolis by opening new lines of street, and the greater number of the openings projected are approxima-tions at an enormous expense to the plan which he laid down. The larger towns present instances of obstructions of the free current of air even through the principal streets, and of deteriorations which a little foresight and the exercise of an impartial authority would have prevented. In one increasing town, a builder made a successful money speculation by pur-chasing such plots of ground as would enable him to erect impediments and extort compensation for their removal from the path of improvements in building. The improvements affecting whole towns are also frequently frustrated by the active jealousies of the occupants of rival streets. It would appear to be possible to provide an impartial authority to obtain and, on consultation with the parties locally interested, to settle plans for regulating the future growth of towns, by laying down the most advanta-geous lines for occupation with due protection of the landowners' interest. The most serious omissions in the building of common houses are so frequently oversights as to make it probable, that if it were required that a plan of any proposed building should be deposited with a trustworthy officer, with a specification of the arrangements intended for the attain-ment of the essential objects, such as cleansing and ventilation, the mere preparation of the document would of itself frequently lead to the detection of grievous defects.

* * *

Some of the most important improvements that might be accomplished in the poorer and most infected districts of the larger towns by pulling down the present tenements and erecting tenements of a superior order, would, there is little doubt, amply repay any large capitalist or single proprietor. In the course of our examination of the most wretched and overcrowded wynds of Glasgow and Edinburgh, we were informed by persons apparently of competent local information that, if they could be purchased at a fair price for the public to be pulled down, there would be a gain in the prevention of the charges of sickness and crime arising from them; and that if they were simply rebuilt on a good plan, the necessary outlay would be repaid by the improved rental from the superior order of tenements. Each flat or story, however, frequently belonged to a different owner, and the property in which the most afflicted classes lived appeared to be extensively subdivided amongst persons of different interests, of different degrees of permanency, and with no power of co-operation, and with little or no capital.

* * *

In reports and communications, the institution of district Boards of Health is frequently recommended, but in general terms, and they nowhere specify what shall be their powers, how they shall seek out information or receive it, and how act upon it. The recommendation is also sanctioned by the committee which sat to inquire into the health of large towns; and the committee state that "the principal duty and object of these boards of health would be precautionary and preventive, to turn the public attention to the causes of illness, and to suggest means by which the sources of contagion might be removed." "Such board would probably have a clerk, paid for his services, whose duty it would be to make minutes of the proceedings, and give such returns in a short tabular form as might be useful for reference, and important, as affording easy information on a subject of such vital interest to the people."

I would submit that it is shown by the evidence collected in the present inquiry, that the great preventives—drainage, street and house cleansing by means of supplies of water and improved sewerage, and especially the introduction of cheaper and more efficient modes of removing all noxious refuse from the towns—are operations for which aid must be sought from the science of the civil engineer, not from the physician, who has done his work when he has pointed out the disease that results from the neglect of proper administrative measures, and has alleviated the sufferings of the victims. After the cholera had passed, several of the local boards of health that were appointed on its appearance continued their meetings and made representations; but the alarm had passed, and although the evils represented were often much greater than the cholera, the representations produced no effect, and the boards broke up. In Paris a Board of Health has been in operation during several years, but if their operations, as displayed in their reports, be considered, it will be evident that, although they have examined many important questions and have made representations, recommending for practical application some of the principles developed in the course of the present inquiry; still as they had no executive power, their representations have produced no effect, and the labouring population of Paris is shown to be, with all the advantages of climate, in a sanitary condition even worse than the labouring population of London. In the Appendix I have submitted a translation of a report descriptive of the labours of the Conseil de Salubrité, in Paris. From this report it will be seen that they have few or no initiative functions, and that they are chiefly called into action by references made to them by the public authorities to examine and give their opinion on medical questions that may arise in the course of public administration as to what manufacturing or other operations are or are not injurious to the public health.

The action of a board of health upon such evils as those in question must depend upon the arrangements for bringing under its notice the evils to be remedied. A body of gentlemen sitting in a room will soon find themselves with few means of action if there be no agency to bring the subject matters before them; and an inquiring agency to seek out the evils from house to house, wherever those evils may be found, to follow on the footsteps of the private practitioner would be apparently attended with much practical difficulty.

The statements of the condition of considerable proportions of the labouring population of the towns into which the present inquiries have been carried have been received with surprise by persons of the wealthier classes living in the immediate vicinity, to whom the facts were as strange as if they related to foreigners or the natives of an unknown country. When Dr. Arnott with myself and others were examining the abodes of the poorest classes in Glasgow and Edinburgh, we were regarded with astonishment; and it was frequently declared by the inmates, that they had never for many years witnessed the approach or the presence of persons of that condition near them. We have found that the inhabitants of the front houses in many of the main streets of those towns and of the metropolis, have never entered the adjoining courts, or seen the interior of any of the tenements, situate at the backs of their own houses, in which their own workpeople or dependents reside.

The duty of visiting loathsome abodes, amidst close atmospheres compounded of smoke and offensive odours, and everything to revolt the senses, is a duty which can only be expected to be regularly performed under much stronger motives than can commonly be imposed on honorary officers, and cannot be depended upon even from paid officers where they are not subjected to strong checks. The examination of loathsome prisons has gained one individual a national and European celebrity. Yet we have seen that there are whole streets of houses, composing some of the wynds of Glasgow and Edinburgh, and great numbers of the courts in London, and the older towns in England, in which the condition of every inhabited room, and the physical condition of the inmates, is even more horrible than the worst of the dungeons that Howard ever visited. In Ireland provisions for the appointment of Boards of Health have been made, but they appear to have failed entirely. One of the medical practitioners examined before the Committee of the House of Commons was asked, in respect to the operation of these provisions:

3297. "But in ordinary times, when the fever is not of very great intensity, and is confined to the dwellings of the humbler classes, there is no such provision put into force?—No, but then there is another provision which may be put into force; this Act provides, that 'whenever in any city, town, or district, any fever or contagious distemper shall prevail, or be known to exist, it shall and may be lawful for any one or more magistrates, upon the requisition of five respectable householders, to convene a meeting of the magistrates and householders of such city, town, or district, and of the medical practitioners within the same, in order to examine into the circumstances attending such fever or contagious distemper.' There is another Act of 59 Geo. III., c. 41, which enables the parishes to appoint officers of health; that is, a permanent power. Those officers have very considerable authority; they can assess a rate.

3298. "Are they appointed?—They are appointed, I think, in all the parishes in Dublin except two; but they are inoperative: they are unpaid, and it is a very disgusting duty. They can be made to serve, but there is no control as to the amount of service they perform; so that the provision is quite inoperative, unless an alarm exists.

3299. "Do you not think the appointment of some such officers, properly appointed, properly paid, and having reasonable power, for the purpose of suggesting and enforcing such measures as shall be beneficial, would be highly valuable?—I am sure it would, and it would save an amazing quantity of expenditure to the country."

It has only been under the strong pressure of professional duties by the physicians and paid medical and relieving officers responsible for visiting the abodes of the persons reduced to destitution by disease that the condition of those abodes in the metropolis have of late been known; and I believe that it is only under continued pressure and strong responsibilities and interests in prevention that investigation will be carried into such places, and the extensive physical causes of disease be effectually eradicated.

Whilst experience gives little promise even of inquiries from such a body as Boards of Health without responsibilities, still less of any important results from the mere representations of such bodies separated from executive authority, I would submit for consideration what appears to me a more advantageous application of medical science, viz., by uniting it with boards having executive authority.

Now, the claim to relief on the ground of destitution created by sickness, which carries the medical officer of the union to the interior of the abode of the sufferer, appears to be the means of carrying investigation precisely to the place where the evil is the most rife, and where the public intervention is most called for. In the metropolis the number of cases of fever alone on which the medical officers were required to visit the applicants for relief, at their own residences, amounted during one year to nearly 14,000. The number of medical officers attached to the new unions throughout the country, and engaged in visiting the claimants to relief on account of sickness, is at this time about 2300.

Were it practicable to attach as numerous a body of paid officers to any local Boards of Health that could be established, it would scarcely be practicable to insure as certain and well directed an examination of the residences of the labouring classes as I conceive may be ensured from the medical officers of the unions. In support of these anticipations of the efficiency of the agency of the medical officers when directed to the formation of sanitary measures, I beg leave to refer to the experience of a partial trial of them under a clause of the recent Metropolitan Police Act, by which it is provided, that if the guardians of the poor of an union or parish, or the churchwardens and overseers of the poor of any parish within the Metropolitan Police district, together with the medical officer of any such parish or union, shall be of opinion, and shall certify under the hands of two or more of such guardians, churchwardens, and overseers, and of such medical officer, that any house, or part of any house, is in such a filthy unwholesome condition that the health of the inmates is thereby endangered, then the magistrates may, after due notice to the occupiers, cause the house to be cleansed at his expense.

The defects of the provision are, that it only authorizes cleansing and not providing for the means of cleansing and personal cleanliness, by directing supplies of water to be laid on; that it does not extend to the alterations of the external condition of the dwelling; that the immediate expense falls upon the occupier, who is usually in so abject a state of destitution as to serve as a barrier to any proceeding apparently tending to any penal infliction. With all these disadvantages, its working may be submitted to show the general eligibility of the medical officers of unions as officers for the execution of sanitary measures. The following account is given by the clerk to the Board of Guardians of Bethnal Green of the working of the provision in that part of the metropolis:

Mr. William Brutton—We have taken prompt measures to execute the clause of the Metropolitan Police Act, and the Commissioners' recommendations upon it, in our parish, and the effect produced has already been beneficial. For example, the medical officer recently reported, through me, to the Board of Guardians, that fever had arisen in certain small tenements in a court called Nicholl's Court, and that it was likely to spread amongst the poorer classes in the district. He reported that others of the houses than those in which fever existed (and the inmates) were in a filthy condition, and that, unless measures were taken for cleansing them properly, fever must necessarily ensue. The Board, on receiving this communication, desired me to proceed instantly, and take such measures as appeared to me to be necessary for the abatement and prevention of the evil. I immediately obtained a summons from the magistrates for the attendance of the owner of the houses. He came directly, and stated that he was not aware that the premises were in the condition in which our medical officer had found them; and he promised that measures should be taken for proper cleansing. Those measures were taken: the furniture of the houses was taken out and washed; the houses were lime-washed. Some of those who were ill died, but the progress of the fever was certainly arrested.

The Board followed up these proceedings by circulating the Commissioners' instruction and form of notification in every part of the parish.

* * *

It may therefore be submitted as an eligible preliminary general arrangement, that it shall be required of the medical officer as an extra duty, for the due performance of which he should be fairly remunerated, that on visiting any person at that person's dwelling, on an order for medical relief, he shall, after having given such needful immediate relief as the case may require, examine or cause to be examined any such physical and removable causes as may have produced disease or acted as a predisposing cause to it; that he shall make out a particular statement of them, wherein he will specify any things that may be and are urgently required to be immediately removed. This statement should be given to the relieving officer, who should thereupon take measures for the removal of the nuisance at the expense of the owner of the tenement, unless he, upon notice which shall be given to him, forthwith proceed to direct their removal. Except in the way of appeal by the owner against the proceedings of either officer, or where a higher expense than 5*l*., or a year's rent of the tenement, were involved by the alterations directed by the medical officer, it appears to be recommended that no application to the Board of Guardians or the magistrates should be required in the first instance, as it frequently happens that the delay of a day in the adoption of measures may occasion the loss of life and the wide spread of contagious disease; and an application to the Board of Guardians or to the petty sessions would usually incur delay of a week or a fortnight. To repeat the words of Blackstone, "The security of the lives and property may sometimes require so speedy a remedy, as not to allow time to call on the person on whose property the mischief has arisen to remedy it." When any tenement is in a condition to endanger life from disease, as it comes within the principle of the law, so it should be included within its provisions, and should be placed in the same condition as a tenement condemned as being ruinous and endangering life from falling.

The instances above given of the working of the provisions of the Metropolitan Police Act for the cleansing of filthy tenements are, however, instances of zealous proceedings taken by competent officers in unions, where the attention of the guardians was specially called to the subject, and where there were no opposing interests. But several other instances might be presented, where the execution of the law is as much needed, but where it is already as dead as any of the older laws for the public protection, and the reason assigned is, that the local officers will not, for the sake of principle and without manifest compulsion, enter into conflicts by which their personal interests may be prejudiced. Medical officers, as private practitioners, are often dependent for their important private practice, and even for their office, on persons whom its strict performance might subject to expense or place in the position of defendants. Under such circumstances it is not unfrequent to hear the expression of a wish from these officers, that some person unconnected with the district may be sent to examine the afflicted place, and initiate the proper proceedings. The working of the provisions of the Factory Act for the limitation of the hours of labour of children has been much impeded by the difficulty of obtaining correct certificates of age and bodily strength from private medical practitioners. On this topic a large mass of evidence might be adduced, showing the unreasonableness of expecting private practitioners to compromise their own interests by conflicts for the public protection with persons on whom they are dependent.

Cases of difficulty requiring superior medical experience and skill occur frequently amongst the paupers. For general supervision as well as for the elucidation of particular questions, the Board have proved the practicability of obtaining for the public service the highest medical skill and science. They have availed themselves of more various acquirements than would be found in any standing *conseil de salubrité*. On questions respecting fever they have availed themselves of the services of the physician of the London Fever Hospital; on questions of vaccination they have consulted the Vaccine Board of London, and the authorities on the same question in Scotland. On questions as to ventilation they have availed themselves of the services of Dr. Arnott; and on the general questions affecting the sanitary condition of the population they have consulted that gentleman and Dr. Kay, and Dr. Southwood Smith, and others who could be found to have given special attention to the subject. When serious epidemics have broken out in particular unions the central Board has dispatched physicians to their aid, or suggested to the guardians that they should have recourse to the services of physicians in the neighbourhoods. The services of Dr. Arnott, Dr. Kay, and Dr. Southwood Smith were thus directed in aid of the medical officers of the eastern districts of the metropolis; and their reports first developed to the public and the legislature the evils which form the subject of the extended inquiry, and that might otherwise have continued without chance of notice, or mitigation or removal, to have depressed the condition of the labouring classes of the population. But the results of such occasional visits appear to prove the necessity and economy of an increase of the permanent local medical service, and to establish a case for the appointment of a superior medical man for a wider district than an ordinary medical officer, for the special aid and supervision of the established medical relief.

It will frequently be found that there is the like need of immediate local inspection of the medical treatment of the destitute that there is of a grade of inspecting surgeons for the military hospitals. It cannot be otherwise than that amidst a numerous body of men there must be much error and neglect in the treatment of the destitute, in the absence of immediate securities against neglect. The most able of the guardians would confess that if they are not entirely incompetent to surpervise medical service, they are at the best but imperfectly qualified for such a task, and the medical officers would act with more satisfaction to themselves from the supervision of officers from whom they might derive aid and confidence.

But besides the medical treatment of the inmates of the workhouses and prisons, there are other cases within most districts which need the preventive service of a superior medical officer for the protection of the public health.

First, in the cases where the poorer classes are assembled in such numbers as to make the assemblages *quasi* public, and afford facilities for medical inspection, as in schools.

Secondly, also in places of work and in workmen's lodging-houses. The occasional visits of a district officer, for the prevention of disease would lead to the maintenance of due ventilation, and to the protection of the workpeople on such points as are already specified as injurious to the health, and that arise simply from ignorance, and are not essential to the processes. An examination of such places, if only quarterly, would lead to the most beneficial results.

So far as I have observed the working of the Factory Act, it appears to me that the duties now performed by the sub-inspectors of factories might be more advantageously performed by superior medical officers, of the rank of army surgeons, who are independent of private practice.

I am confirmed in this view by the following evidence of *Mr. Baker*, surgeon of Leeds, the only factory inspector who has such qualifications:

"Have you, as a surgeon, whilst visiting the factories as an inspector, had occasion to exercise your professional knowledge?—Frequently; during my service I have turned out great numbers of children with scald-heads, which they were apt to propagate amongst the rest of the children; some with phthisis, whose subsequent death was more than probable; some with scrofulous ulcers; a great many with extreme cases of ophthalmia; probably I may have removed a thousand of these cases altogether. I rarely go to a mill where I do not see a case of scald-head.

"Have you ever had occasion to interpose in respect to ventilation?—Frequently in extreme cases of variable temperature, also in cases of offensive privies, which I find attended by dysenteric affections; and also where there has been offensive water from neglected sewers. I have also endeavoured to enforce personal cleanliness on the children through the instrumentality of overlookers and parents. One practice amongst the children in all kinds of mills is to wear handkerchiefs on the head, by which the neglect of personal cleanliness was concealed. Under these handkerchiefs were most of the cases of scald-head, in a state of filthiness not easily describable. I have assured the operatives that by the Act I had the power to direct measures for the protection of their health as well as labour; and I have established in many places the rule that the children shall come with the faces clean, and the hair combed, and without handkerchiefs whilst at work.

"By such inspection of workpeople in the places of work do you conceive it would be practicable to influence largely the sanitary condition of the labouring population without inspection of the private houses?—Yes; for the ill health which was occasioned by the state of their houses or other places, would of course be visible on such inspection. If they were removed from their places of employment on the presentation of such appearances, the inattention which had occasioned it would be removed too.

"What length of time do you find such inspection would require each time, say in a mill of about 1000 persons, and how frequent should such inspection be?—On the average about two hours; to a practised eye the symptoms of indisposition are discernable almost in walking through a room. Under some circumstances an inspection of once in three months would suffice.

"Are there masters in your district who are aware of the interest they have in the health of their workpeople?—Yes; there are many who pay particular attention. I might mention two where a surgeon is specially employed to take care of their workpeople. When persons are ill, they are listless and sleepy, and negligent; there is also more waste made in the processes of manufacture."

The superior economy of preventive services by such inspection as that above displayed will scarcely need elucidation.

From a consideration of such opportunities of inspection it will be perceived that the enforcement of sanitary regulations on such inspection by superior and independent officers, qualified by previous examination, as in the army, would be a wise economy. By such arrangements efficient medical superintendence would be provided for the independent labourer employed in crowded manufactures, as well as for the soldier and the sailor, not to speak of the pauper or the criminal. One such officer would be able so to inspect and keep under sanitary regulations the places of work, the schools and all the public establishments of such a town as Leeds, which would bring under view perhaps the greater proportion of the lower classes of the population. There would still remain, however, those of the labouring classes who do not work or lodge in large numbers, or work in a quasi-public manner, to bring them within the means of convenient inspection. There would also remain without protection the cases of persons of the middle classes.

To meet these cases, I would suggest that the information brought to the superintendent registrar as to the cause of death, imperfect and hearsay as it yet is, may serve as the most accurate index to the direction of the labours of a district officer appointed to investigate the means of protecting the health of all classes. Having suggested the registration of the causes of death (under medical superintendence), a head of information not contained in the original draught of the Deaths' Registration Bill, I would guard against an over-estimate of the importance of that provision; but I feel confident it would be found, when properly enforced, one of the most important means of guiding preventive services in an efficient direction. For example, wherever, on the examination of these registries, deaths from fever or other epidemics were found to recur regularly, and in numbers closely clustered together, there will be found, on examination, to be some common and generally removable cause in active operation within the locality. Amongst whatsoever class of persons engaged in the same occupation deaths from one disease occur in disproportionately high numbers or at low ages, the cause of that disease will generally be found to be removable, and not essential to the occupation itself. The cases of the tailors, miners, and dressmakers, and the removable circumstances which are found to govern the prevalence of consumption amongst them, I adduce, as examples of the importance of the practical suggestions to be gained from correct and trustworthy registries of the causes of death occurring in particular occupations as well as in particular places. When a death from fever or consumption occurs in a single family, in the state of isolation in which much of the population live in crowded neighbourhoods, they have rarely any means of knowing that it is not a death arising from some cause peculiar to the individual. Even medical practitioners who are not in very extensive practice may have only a few cases, and may be equally unable to see in them, in connexion with others, the operation of an extensive cause or a serious epidemic. The registration of the causes of death, however, presents to view the extent to which deaths, from the same disease, are common at the same age, at the same time, or at the same place, or in the same occupation.

One of the most important services, therefore, of a superior medical officer of a district would be to ensure the entries of the causes of death with the care proportioned to the important uses to be derived from them. The public should be taught to regard correct registration as being frequently of as much importance for the protection of the survivors as a post-mortem examination is often found to be.

The mortuary registries and the registration of the causes of death are not only valuable as necessary initiatives to the investigation of particular cases, but as checks for the performance of the duty. The system of registration in use at Geneva, combining the certificate and explanation of the private practitioners and the district physician, corresponds with a recommendation originally made for the organization of the mortuary registries in England, and the experience of that country might, perhaps, be advantageously consulted.

It would be found that the appointment of a superior medical officer independent of private practice, to superintend these various duties, would also be a measure of sound pecuniary economy.

The experience of the navy and the army and the prisons may be referred to for exemplifications of the economy in money, as well as in health and life, of such an arrangement. A portion only of the saving from an expensive and oppressive collection of the local rates would abundantly suffice to ensure for the public protection against common evils the science of a district physician, as well as the science of a district engineer. Indeed, the money now spent in comparatively fragmentitious and unsystematized local medical service for the public, would, if combined as it might be without disturbance on the occurrence of vacancies, afford advantages at each step of the combination. We have in the same towns public medical officers as inspectors of prisons, medical officers for the inspection of lunatic asylums, medical officers of the new unions, medical inspectors of recruits, medical service for the granting certificates for children under the provisions of the Factory Act, medical service for the post-mortem examinations of bodies, the subject of coroners' inquests, which it appears from the mortuary registries of violent deaths in England amount to between 11,000 and 12,000 annually, for which a fee of a guinea each is given. These and other services are divided in such portions as only to afford remuneration in such sums as 40*l.*, 50*l.*, 60*l.*, or 80*l.* each; and many smaller and few larger amounts.

Whatever may be yet required for placing the union medical officers on a completely satisfactory footing, the combination of the services of several parish doctors in the service of fewer union medical officers will be found to be advances in a beneficial direction. The multiplication or the maintenance of such fragmentitious professional services is injurious to the public and the profession. It is injurious to the profession by multiplying poor, ill-paid, and ill-conditioned professional men.[1] Although each may be highly paid in comparison with the service rendered, the portions of service do not suffice for the maintenance of an officer without the aid of private practice; they only suffice, therefore, to sustain needy competitors for practice in narrow fields. Out of such competition the public derive no improvements in medical science, for science comes out of wide opportunities of knowledge and study, which are inconsistent with the study to make interests and the hunt for business in poor neighbourhoods.

A medical man who is restricted to the observation of only one establishment may be said to be excluded from an efficient knowledge even of that one. Medical men so restricted are generally found to possess an accurate knowledge of the morbid appearances, or of the effects amongst the people of the one establishment, but they are frequently found to be destitute of any knowledge of the pervading cause in which they are themselves enveloped, and have by familiarity lost the perception of it. Thus it was formerly in the navy that medical officers on board ship, amidst the causes of disease, the filth, and bad ventilation, and bad diet, were referring all the epidemic disease experienced exclusively to contagion from some one of the crew who was discovered to have been in a prison. We have seen that local reports present similar examples of similar conclusions from the observation of single establishments in towns, in which reports effects are attributed as essential to labour, of which effects that same labour is entirely divested in establishments in the county, or under other circumstances which the practitioners have had no means of observing and estimating. The various contradictory opinions on diet, and the older

---

[1] The parish doctors in England were often paid only 20*l.* per annum for attendance in parishes of considerable extent. The payments to medical officers who have their private practice are generally quadrupled, as compared with the parish doctors. The medical arrangements in Glasgow will illustrate the frequent state of the existing arrangements in Scotland. The burgh of Glasgow, exclusive of the suburbs, is divided into 12 districts, to each of which a medical practitioner is appointed, who is paid for his services out of the poor's rates. Dr. Cowan stated of them in his report: "The duties of the district surgeons are laborious and dangerous. Nearly all of them take fever, which involves a heavy pecuniary loss. Their salary is less than 21*l.* per annum, being less than 1*s.* for the treatment of each case." For an equivalent district in population under the New Poor Law in England, namely, in Lambeth, there are four out-door medical officers, at salaries of 107*l.* each, and two in-door medical officers, at salaries of 128*l.* each. They have in addition their private practice and fees for vaccination, and special cases. The usual rate of medical allowance to the resident medical officers of dispensaries, who are excluded from private practice, has been from 60*l.* to 70*l.* per annum.

views on the innocuousness of miasma, are commonly referable to the circumstances under which the medical observers were placed; and examples abound in every district of the errors incidental to narrow ranges of observation in cases perplexed by idiosyncracies, and by numerous and varying antecedents. It should be understood by the public that the value of hospital and dispensary practice consists in the range of observation they give; and that the extent of observation or opportunities of medical knowledge are influenced or governed by administrative arrangements. In several of the medical schools of the metropolis, however, the opportunities of knowledge are dependent on the cases which may chance to arise there. Fortunate administrative arrangements have, in Paris, greatly advanced medical knowledge, by bringing large classes of cases under single observation. The most important discoveries made with respect to consumption, those made by M. Louis, were based on the results of the post-mortem examinations of nearly 1300 cases by that one practitioner. Nearly all the important conclusions deduced from this extensive range of observations were at variance with his own previous opinions and the opinions that had prevailed for centuries. The later and better knowledge of the real nature of fever cases has been obtained by a similar range of observation gained from the cases in fever hospitals. Applications have been several times made to the Commissioners by medical men engaged in particular researches to aid them in the removal of the impediments to extended inquiry, by collecting the information to be derived from the sick-wards of the workhouses and the out-door medical relief lists.

The highest medical authorities would agree that, whatsoever administrative arrangements sustain narrow districts, and narrow practice, sustain at a great public expense, barriers against the extension of knowledge by which the public would benefit, and that any arrangements by which such districts or confined practice is newly created, will aggravate existing evils. An examination of the state of medical practice divided amongst poor practitioners in the thinly populated districts shows that, but for the examinations, imperfect though they be, as arrangements which sustain skill and respectability, a large part of the population would be in the hands of ignorant bone-setters.

On a full examination of the duties which are suggested for a district physician, or officer of public health, that which will appear to be most serious is not the extent of new duties suggested, but the extent of the neglect of duties existing. The wants, however, which it is a duty to represent and repeat, as the most immediate and pressing, for the relief of the labouring population, are those of drainage, cleansing, and the exercise of the business of an engineer, connected with commissions of sewers, to which the services of a board of health would be auxiliary. The business of a district physician connects him more immediately with the boards of guardians, which, as having the distribution of medical relief, and the services of medical officers, I would submit, may be made, with additional aid, to do more than can be done by any local boards of health of the description given, separated from any executive authority or self-acting means of bringing information before them.

I have submitted the chief grounds on which it appears to me that whatever additional force may be needed for the protection of the public health it would everywhere be obtained more economically with unity, and efficiency, and promptitude, by a single securely-qualified and well-appointed responsible local officer than by any new establishment applied in the creation of new local boards. Including, as sanitary measures, those for drainage and cleansing, and supplies of water as well as medical appliances, I would cite the remarks on provisions for the protection of the public health, made by Dr. Wilson at the conclusion of a report on the sanitary condition of the labouring population of Kelso. After having noted some particular improvements which had taken place, as it were, by chance, and independently of any particular aids of science directed to their furtherance, he remarks that "it is impossible to avoid the conclusion that much more might still be accomplished, could we be induced to profit by a gradually extending knowledge, so as to found upon it a more wisely directed practice. When man shall be brought to acknowledge (as truth must finally constrain him to acknowledge) that it is by his own hand, through his neglect of a few obvious rules, that the seeds of disease are most lavishly sown within his frame, and diffused over communities; when he shall have required of medical science to occupy itself rather with the prevention of maladies than with their cure; when governments shall be induced to consider the preservation of a nation's health an object as important as the promotion of its commerce or the maintenance of its conquests, we may hope then to see the approach of those times when, after a life spent almost without sickness, we shall close the term of an unharassed existence by a peaceful euthanasia."

Common Lodging-Houses

A town may be highly advanced in its own internal administration, its general drainage, and its arrangements for house and street-cleansing may be perfect, and they may be in complete action, and yet if the police of the common lodging-houses be neglected, it will be liable to the continued importation, if not the generation, of epidemic disease by the vagrant population who frequent them. I have reserved the evidence respecting them in order to submit it for separate consideration, because they may apparently be better considered independently of the administrative arrangements which affect the resident population of the labouring classes.

From almost every town from whence sanitary reports have been received that have been the results of careful examinations, the common lodging-houses are pointed out as *foci* of contagious disease within the district. These houses are stages for the various orders of tramps and mendicants who traverse the country from one end to the other, and spread physical pestilence, as well as moral depravation. The evidence everywhere received distinguishes them prominently as the subjects of immediate and decidedly strong legislative interference for the public protection.

The following extract from the Report of *Mr. E. W. Baines*, the medical officer of the Barnet union, is submitted as an example of the information received respecting them from the rural unions:

The lodging-houses for trampers are a prolific source of disease, and productive of enormous expense to the parish in which they may be situate; from one I have within this week sent into the union workhouse six cases, namely, two of fever, three of itch and destitution, and one of inflammatory dropsy. These unhappy beings are boarded and bedded in an atmosphere of gin, brimstone, onions, and disease, until their last penny be spent, and their clothes pledged to the keeper of the house, when they are kicked out and left to the mercy of the relieving officer.

* * *

It appears that, on the several grounds of public expediency, for the preservation of the public health, and for the preservation of the public peace, all common lodging-houses—all places which are open for the reception of strangers, travellers, and wayfarers by the night, and houses laid out and provided for numbers of lodgers, should be subjected to regulations for the protection of the inmates as well as the public at large. This appears, indeed, to be consistent with the ancient police of the country. By narrowing the definition of the places for which licences were rendered necessary to those where spirits or fermented liquors are sold to be drunk on the premises (as if a revenue were the only proper object of their government), it appears that there has been a mischievous dereliction of the ancient and sound policy of the law which subjects the "victualler" as well as the keeper of the hostel, inn, or lodging-house to responsibilities for the protection of the inmates, and the convenience of the inhabitants in the neighbourhood where such houses may be situate. The common lodging-house keeper is in fact an inferior victualler, but evading the licence and the responsibilities of the victualler, by sending out for the fermented liquors which are consumed by the lodgers.

It appears, from various portions of evidence, that the occupation of a lodging-house keeper is a profitable one: instances are given from various parts of the country where the keepers of such houses have accumulated property; and whilst the keepers of public-houses, however small, or of beer-shops, are subjected to the necessity of taking out licences, there is no apparent reason for the exemption of lodging-house keepers from that charge by reason of poverty; neither should I consider that it would be a disadvantage, but the contrary, if the proper regulation of such houses were effected at some increase of the price of the lodgings. On examination of the description of persons accommodated in such houses (whilst there is a public provision for those who are really in a state of destitution, and means are provided for removing them to their places of settlement when it is necessary), I find no class whose migration is entitled to any encouragement by any diminution of the charge of providing proper lodgings. Another topic of consideration in connexion with houses of this class, is the tendency of the degraded accommodation to degrade the classes of the population who have recourse to it. I would therefore submit for consideration, whether all common lodging-houses should not be required by law to take out licences in the same manner as public-houses; and that, as the condition of holding such licences, they be subjected to inspection by the medical officers of the union (or the district medical officer), and bound to conform to such sanitary regulations in respect to cleanliness, ventilation, and numbers proportioned to the space, as he may be authorized to prescribe for the protection of the health of the inmates: and also that all such lodging-houses shall be subjected to the regulations of the magistrates, and shall be open to the visits and inspection of the police, for the enforcement of duly authorized regulations, without any search-warrant or other authority than that necessary for their entrance into any house belonging to a licensed victualler.

It may further be submitted for consideration that, by the beneficial progress made in the habits of temperance in some districts, the disuse of spirituous or fermented liquors may enable the proprietors of houses of a higher order of resort than those in question to convert them into coffee-houses or victualling-houses, and at the same time dispense with the expense of the licence, and avoid also the responsibilities for the protection of the public which the law has attached to licensed houses of resort for travellers.

From the reports received from the more populous towns, it would appear that there are few houses which are let for the accommodation of large numbers of regular lodgers which might not be benefited by the inspection of a medical officer. I believe it would be more beneficial to the public to extend than to narrow the definition of the places which should be subjected to regulations as lodging-houses; and that a discretion as to the description of house which shall be included might be safely confided to the magistrates who have local charge of the public peace and the public economy of the towns.

* * *

Recapitulation of Conclusions

The last cited instance of the practical operation of measures for the abatement of the nuisances attendant on common lodging-houses may also be submitted as an instance of the advantages derivable from the extension of such fields of inquiries as the present. On each of the chief points included in it there would have been a loss of what I hope will be deemed valuable corroborative information, had the inquiry been confined either to England or to Scotland. The observation of the important productive use of the refuse of the city of Edinburgh would have been of comparatively little value as evidence leading to practical applications, apart from the observation of what is accomplished by the practical application of science to sewerage and drainage for the immediate and cheapest removal of all the refuse of towns by water through closed drains afforded by the operation in the Holborn and Finsbury division of the metropolis.

It may be stated confidently that, if the inquiry could conveniently have had still further extension as to time and place, the information would have been strengthened and rendered more complete. From incidental facts I have met with, I am led to believe that the whole of the effects which are the subject of the present report would have been still more strikingly displayed in many parts of Ireland.

After as careful an examination of the evidence collected as I have been enabled to make, I beg leave to recapitulate the chief conclusions which that evidence appears to me to establish.

First, as to the extent and operation of the evils which are the subject of the inquiry:

That the various forms of epidemic, endemic, and other disease caused, or aggravated, or propagated chiefly amongst the labouring classes by atmospheric impurities produced by decomposing animal and vegetable substances, by damp and filth, and close and overcrowded dwellings prevail amongst the population in every part of the kingdom, whether dwelling in separate houses, in rural villages, in small towns, in the larger towns —as they have been found to prevail in the lowest districts of the metropolis.

That such disease, wherever its attacks are frequent, is always found in connexion with the physical circumstances above specified, and that where those circumstances are removed by drainage, proper cleansing, better ventilation, and other means of diminishing atmospheric impurity, the frequency and intensity of such disease is abated; and where the removal of the noxious agencies appears to be complete, such disease almost entirely disappears.

That high prosperity in respect to employment and wages, and various and abundant food, have afforded to the labouring classes no exemptions from attacks of epidemic disease, which have been as frequent and as fatal in periods of commercial and manufacturing prosperity as in any others.

That the formation of all habits of cleanliness is obstructed by defective supplies of water.

That the annual loss of life from filth and bad ventilation are greater than the loss from death or wounds in any wars in which the country has been engaged in modern times.

That of the 43,000 cases of widowhood, and 112,000 cases of destitute orphanage relieved from the poor's rates in England and Wales alone, it appears that the greatest proportion of deaths of the heads of families occurred from the above specified and other removable causes; that their ages were under 45 years; that is to say, 13 years below the natural probabilities of life as shown by the experience of the whole population of Sweden.

That the public loss from the premature deaths of the heads of families is greater than can be represented by any enumeration of the pecuniary burdens consequent upon their sickness and death.

That, measuring the loss of working ability amongst large classes by the instances of gain, even from incomplete arrangements for the removal of noxious influences from places of work or from abodes, that this loss cannot be less than eight or ten years.

That the ravages of epidemics and other diseases do not diminish but tend to increase the pressure of population.

That in the districts where the mortality is the greatest the births are not only sufficient to replace the numbers removed by death, but to add to the population.

That the younger population, bred up under noxious physical agencies, is inferior in physical organization and general health to a population preserved from the presence of such agencies.

That the population so exposed is less susceptible of moral influences, and the effects of education are more transient than with a healthy population.

That these adverse circumstances tend to produce an adult population short-lived, improvident, reckless, and intemperate, and with habitual avidity for sensual gratifications.

That these habits lead to the abandonment of all the conveniences and decencies of life, and especially lead to the overcrowding of their homes, which is destructive to the morality as well as the health of large classes of both sexes.

That defective town cleansing fosters habits of the most abject degradation and tends to the demoralization of large numbers of human beings, who subsist by means of what they find amidst the noxious filth accumulated in neglected streets and bye-places.

That the expenses of local public works are in general unequally and unfairly assessed, oppressively and uneconomically collected, by separate collections, wastefully expended in separate and inefficient operations by unskilled and practically irresponsible officers.

That the existing law for the protection of the public health and the constitutional machinery for reclaiming its execution, such as the Courts Leet, have fallen into desuetude, and are in the state indicated by the prevalence of the evils they were intended to prevent.

Secondly, as to the means by which the present sanitary condition of the labouring classes may be improved:

The primary and most important measures, and at the same time the most practicable, and within the recognized province of public administration, are drainage, the removal of all refuse of habitations, streets, and roads, and the improvement of the supplies of water.

That the chief obstacles to the immediate removal of decomposing refuse of towns and habitations have been the expense and annoyance of the hand labour and cartage requisite for the purpose.

That this expense may be reduced to one-twentieth or to one-thirtieth, or rendered inconsiderable, by the use of water and self-acting means of removal by improved and cheaper sewers and drains.

That refuse when thus held in suspension in water may be most cheaply and innoxiously conveyed to any distance out of towns, and also in the best form for productive use, and that the loss and injury by the pollution of natural streams may be avoided.

That for all these purposes, as well as for domestic use, better supplies of water are absolutely necessary.

That for successful and economical drainage the adoption of geological areas as the basis of operations is requisite.

That appropriate scientific arrangements for public drainage would afford important facilities for private land-drainage, which is important for the health as well as sustenance of the labouring classes.

That the expense of public drainage, of supplies of water laid on in houses, and of means of improved cleansing would be a pecuniary gain, by diminishing the existing charges attendant on sickness and premature mortality.

That for the protection of the labouring classes and of the ratepayers against inefficiency and waste in all new structural arrangements for the protection of the public health, and to ensure public confidence that the expenditure will be beneficial, securities should be taken that all new local public works are devised and conducted by responsible officers qualified by the possession of the science and skill of civil engineers.

That the oppressiveness and injustice of levies for the whole immediate outlay on such works upon persons who have only short interests in the benefits may be avoided by care in spreading the expense over periods coincident with the benefits.

That by the combinations of all these arrangements, it is probable that outlay for drainage might be saved, which on an estimate of the expense of the necessary structural alterations of one-third only of the existing tenements would be a saving of one million and a half sterling, besides the reduction of the future expenses of management.

That for the prevention of the disease occasioned by defective ventilation, and other causes of impurity in places of work and other places where large numbers are assembled, and for the general promotion of the means necessary to prevent disease, that it would be good economy to appoint a district medical officer independent of private practice, and with the securities of special qualifications and responsibilities to initiate sanitary measures and reclaim the execution of the law.

That by the combinations of all these arrangements, it is probable that the full ensurable period of life indicated by the Swedish tables; that is, an increase of 13 years at least, may be extended to the whole of the labouring classes.

That the attainment of these and the other collateral advantages of reducing existing charges and expenditure are within the power of the legislature, and are dependent mainly on the securities taken for the application of practical science, skill, and economy in the direction of local public works.

And that the removal of noxious physical circumstances, and the promotion of civic, household, and personal cleanliness, are necessary to the improvement of the moral condition of the population; for that sound morality and refinement in manners and health are not long found co-existant with filthy habits amongst any class of the community.

I beg leave further to suggest, that the principles of amendment deduced from the inquiry will be found as applicable to Scotland as to England; and if so, it may be submitted for attention whether it might not be represented that the structural arrangements for drainage would be most conveniently carried out in the same form as in England, that is by commissions, of the nature of commissions of sewers adapted, as regards jurisdiction to natural or geological areas, and including in them the chief elected officers of municipalities, and other authorities now charged with the care of the streets and roads or connected with local public works.

The advantages of uniformity in legislation and in the executive machinery, and of doing the same things in the same way (choosing the best), and calling the same officers, proceedings, and things by the same names, will only be appreciated by those who have observed the extensive public loss occasioned by the legislation for towns which makes them independent of beneficent, as of what perhaps might have been deemed formerly aggressive legislation. There are various sanitary regulations, and especially those for cleansing, directed to be observed in "every town except Berwick and Carlisle"; a course of legislation which, had it been efficient for England, would have left Berwick and Carlisle distinguished by the oppression of common evils intended to be remedied. It was the subject of public complaint, at Glasgow and in other parts of Scotland, that independence and separation in the form of general legislation separated the people from their share of the greatest amount of legislative attention, or excluded them from common interest and from the common advantages of protective measures. It was, for example, the subject of particular complaint, that whilst the labouring population of England and Ireland had received the advantages of public legislative provision for a general vaccination, the labouring classes in Scotland were still left exposed to the ravages of the small-pox. It was also complained by Dr. Cowan and other members of the medical profession, that Scotland had not been included in the provisions for the registration of the causes of death which they considered might, with improvements, be made highly conducive to the advancement of medical science and the means of protecting the public health.

I have the honour to be,

Gentlemen,

Your obedient servant,

EDWIN CHADWICK

Introduction
to the Poor Law Reports
of 1834 and 1909

SAMUEL MENCHER

1834

THE Report of the Poor Law Commission of 1834 had a tremendous impact on the poor law administration of its period and a continuing influence on British and American poor law policy into the twentieth century. In contrast to the next major evaluation of poor law policy in 1909, the Commission's recommendations were relatively free of controversy, provided a simple set of principles for relieving the poor, and were readily translated into implementing legislation.

The Report was prepared by a Royal Commission, an independent body whose members were nominated by the Crown in 1832 for the purpose of conducting an unbiased inquiry. Among the members of the Commission were some of the leading authorities on the poor law, including the indefatigable Chadwick, who was to play a central role in carrying out the Commission's recommendations. Apart from the prestige of the Commission itself, the Report was impressive because of the mass of evidence, some twelve volumes collected by a team of Assistant Commissioners to support the conclusions of their superiors. This evidence was the result of a survey conducted with the aid of an enormously lengthy and detailed questionnaire in selected areas throughout the country. It was in accord with the new spirit of science in public administration introduced by Jeremy Bentham and his followers, of whom Chadwick was the most earnest, and may be considered a landmark in the application of research to social problems. However, the results of the survey and the conclusions reached were largely predictable in view of the preconceptions of the Commission and its assistants and the persons interviewed in the study.

The timeliness of the Commission's Report and its concurrence with the dominant opinions and trends of the period heavily accounted for its influence. Pressures for the reform of the poor law had become increasingly strong since the beginning of the nineteenth century. Criticism of the poor law administration was focused around the practice of supplementing wages known as the Speenhamland policy. The Speenhamland magistrates had introduced the policy of making up roughly the difference between the cost of living of an agricultural worker's family and his employer's wage. The end of the eighteenth century and the beginning of the nineteenth century were particularly difficult for agricultural laborers. The uncertainties of the Napoleonic wars and their aftermath exacerbated economic conditions generally. On the other hand, the fear of the radical ideas of the French Revolution and the need for the support of the yeomanry during the struggle against Napoleon led no doubt to greater tolerance by the upper classes of a more generous poor law policy.

However, following the defeat of Napoleon the growing commercial and industrial interests desired a return to "normalcy." The poor law was viewed as the source of most, if not all, social and economic evils of the period. It was generally believed that the poor law was responsible for everything from low wages to illegitimacy. It was alleged that the poor law caused low wages, discouraged migration from depressed areas, lowered agricultural production through high taxes and inefficient labor, favored the idle at the expense of the industrious, and encouraged both illegitimacy and the marriage of young people before they were ready to undertake independently their household responsibilities.

The Report of the Commission confirmed all these suspicions with vivid case material, and the effects ascribed to the poor law became accepted doctrine. Both in Britain and America the findings and conclusions of the Commission were quoted as authoritative in all discussions of poor law policy. Although there had been no Speenhamland policy in America, the thinking on poor law matters closely paralleled the Commission's. The

Yates and Quincy reports of New York and Massachusetts, which predated the English Commission by a few years, reached much the same conclusions and recommended the substitution of in-door or almshouse care for all other forms of help. Only at the end of the nineteenth century was some skepticism displayed at the inordinate significance accorded the effects of poor law policy at the beginning. It is noteworthy that despite the absence of any political concern about the implications of the 1834 reforms, contemporary scholars still find the state of the poor law preceding the Commission's recommendations a controversial subject.

The inefficiency of the local poor law administration and the riots in agricultural districts following refusal of further aid of the Speenhamland type created a sense of immediate urgency for reform. However, major changes in society and its dominant ideologies were the fundamental sources of dissatisfaction. The mercantilist nation for which the Elizabethan poor law had been designed had given way to a laissez-faire society. Paternalism and local responsibility had been replaced by the nexus of free and unlimited exchange. Traditional restrictions to trade and industry must be removed. The poor law as well as other measures which represented anachronistic mercantilist ideas and the dominance of the old landed aristocracy would undergo radical changes under the pressure of the rising business classes.

The ideology of the new leadership was a combination of classical economics and Utilitarianism. Adam Smith had emphasized that enlightened self-interest and unfettered relationships were the core of the economic system and that intervention by the state could only be harmful. Malthus documented this by pointing out the disastrous results of the poor law in stimulating population increase at the cost of thrift and prudence. The eighteenth-century belief in natural law and the distrust by the Utilitarians of the clumsy functioning of government resulted in a widespread move to restrict the power of the state. The general conclusion was that unless the poor law was reformed and the state's interference in economic life reduced the nation could not prosper.

The recommendations of the Commission of 1834 must, therefore, be seen in the light of its attempt, first, to restore the conditions of a free labor market, and second, to provide an effective administrative structure to insure the implementation of its policies. The Commission's concern about the role of the poor law in the labor market was indicated by the report's almost exclusive attention to the able-bodied worker. The "impotent poor"

—the unemployable—were assumed to receive necessary public care. The main goal was to keep the able-bodied worker off relief and in the labor market. For this there was enunciated the principle of "less eligibility" which, according to the pleasure-pain psychology of the Benthamites, would so operate as to make work more pleasurable than idleness. The condition of the unemployed worker would never be as eligible as the employed and would therefore be an inducement to remain in or accept employment.

The "workhouse test" was to be the instrument of this policy since it was assumed that no worker who could obtain employment would undergo in preference the rigors of the workhouse. The workhouse also appealed to the Benthamites as an institution for controlling and disciplining the inmates much along the lines of Bentham's Panopticon. The poor could not, as they might if left in the community, engage in vice and idleness, and they would be kept continually ready for employment.

The Commission sought as well to reform the administration of the law. Its survey had turned up instances of both corruption and inefficiency. The Commission's recommendations included the creation of a national board to advise and supervise the local authorities and to arrange the grouping of parishes into larger units or Unions for administering the law. The central body would insure the enforcement of national policy, and the Unions would provide better financed and organized programs on the local level.

The Commission's recommendations represented a radical departure from the administration of the poor laws since the Elizabethan period. The Commissioners maintained that they were returning to the true spirit of the original act, which, in their opinion, had been distorted and all but destroyed in the intervening years. Whatever its rationale, the Report of the Poor Law Commissioners of 1834 was the beginning of a new era of poor law policy, and in many respects redefined the responsibility of society for poverty. In England, it was not until the Minority Report of the 1905-1909 Commission that the principles of 1834 were fully challenged, and it was the Beveridge Report and the major health and welfare measures after World War II which led to the final dissolution of the policies introduced in 1834. In the United States, policies reflecting the philosophy of 1834 have been of longer duration, and the Social Security Act of 1935 was the first important break with the restrictive nature of the nineteenth-century poor laws.

1905-1909

The Royal Commission of 1905 was appointed to appraise the poor law founded on the principles of the 1834 Report. Some thirty-eight months and fifty volumes later the Commission completed its work and returned a divided report. From the start there was little question that this would be a Commission in controversy. As the Webbs, who were intimately connected with its functioning, commented, it was "the exact antithesis of its famous predecessor," the Commission of 1832-1834. There was no popular demand for reform in 1905. The policies of 1834, which guided the administration of the law, still represented the dominant elements in the poor law administration. While there were critics, they differed so much among themselves as to prevent any unified attack on the existing system. To a great extent the deliberations of the Commission reflected the anomalous situation surrounding its origin.

Although the Commission in 1834 had presented a unified set of recommendations, the administration of the act never completely fulfilled its expectations. Out-door relief and lenient behavior toward the able-bodied and their families continued to irritate the central government boards responsible for poor law administration. They exhorted the local authorities and pointed to the numbers on poor relief as validation of their concern. Thus among the pressures for a Royal Commission was the desire of the central government officials for the strict enforcement of the established policy.

At the other extreme were the Fabian Socialists who wanted to replace the old poor law with an entirely new system of economic assistance and social services. On the scene also, and by no means passively standing by, were the leaders of the Charity Organisation Society and of the growing movement of "scientific" social work. They were dissatisfied with the state of public relief generally and considered themselves to possess the only true gospel of charitable endeavor.

The Commission represented all these points of view. In addition to senior poor law officials, the Commission included such prominent social workers from the voluntary societies as Charles S. Loch, Helen Bosanquet, and Octavia Hill. The radicals, who were to author the Minority Report, were led by Beatrice Webb, Fabian Socialist, social researcher, and activist reformer par excellence.

With this cast the stage was set for full-scale debate. The deliberations of the Commission were marked by bitterness from the start. The Minority group did not trust the Majority's evidence and conducted its own research. However, despite overt conflict, what has impressed most commentators on the work of the Commission has been the relatively moderate differences in the final Majority and Minority Reports after the dust of controversy had been allowed to settle.

The main disagreements were not so much in substance as in spirit. Neither Report favored a reestablishment of the principles of 1834, and both reflected the social and economic changes which had occurred in British society since the beginning of the nineteenth century. It was apparent that the difficulties noted by the central government officials were not alone due to administrative carelessness. The temper of the times had radically changed, and even so conservative a group as the Majority commissioners had more in common with contemporary radicals than with their counterparts of 1834.

Both the Majority and Minority reports agreed on the abolition of the old poor law structure. The poor law guardians would be replaced by the elected local authority councils. The deterrent principles of 1834 were not to be applied to unemployable persons. In general, both Majority and Minority accepted a positive or constructive approach to relief and the social services, and each suggested a variety of institutions and services for "preventive, curative, and restorative" action. The Majority, however, still reflected the thinking of 1834 with respect to the causes and responsibility for poverty, still largely viewed as an individual phenomenon brought on by the habits and attitudes of the lower classes. For the most part, the Majority group was skeptical about the possibility of rehabilitating the chronically destitute and recommended that they be relieved by the relatively harsh measures of the local authorities while the sympathetic and more generous efforts of voluntary aid would be reserved for the "worthy" poor. The Minority group differed strongly with this view of the causes of poverty. Its members viewed poverty as socially caused and as the function of society to prevent. The Minority report preferred to emphasize preventive programs rather than merely to classify the more rehabilitable among those already suffering from poverty.

This conflict reflected the clash of philosophies between the Protestant ethic of liberal capitalism and the Fabian socialists. The latter viewed the individual as primarily determined by his social and economic environment. The Majority considered the individual as a unique entity struggling to refine his character against the temptations of his environment, and the good society as a consummation of individual victories. For the Majority, poverty was a transient and individual phenomenon while for the Minority it was a continuing consequence of an irrational and unhealthy social order. In the beginning the Fabians doubted whether unemployment and poverty could be prevented under a capitalist order. By 1909, however, they concluded that preventive measures could be applied even in a predominantly laissez-faire society. The Minority recommended the regular planning of public expenditures and public works as a normal part of the economy. The Majority, while accepting the need for public action, viewed public planning as an emergency rather than routine measure.

Apart from ideological conflicts, the most pronounced and publicized differences centered around the administrative structure of the poor law system. The Majority favored the reform of the existing organization, but the Minority pressed for its total replacement by a variety of specialized authorities which would minister to rich and poor alike without the stigma of the old poor law. The Majority group, impressed with the burgeoning casework of the voluntary societies and desirous of limiting dependence on public aid, favored a focal role for voluntary bodies in the administration of relief. The Minority group, and particularly Beatrice Webb and her Fabian friends, were strongly opposed to what they considered paternalistic charity and the delegation of public responsibility to the voluntary societies. Not that the Minority believed that assistance should be granted as a guaranteed right. If anything, the Minority recommendations indicated greater controls over the individual in the interests of his social rehabilitation, but these controls would be exercised in the first resort by specialized authorities in their areas of competence. The "break-up of the old poor law" became the rallying cry of the Minority supporters. The pertinence of their movement was greatly weakened when Lloyd George introduced his social insurance reforms in 1911, and the dissolution of the poor law was begun under official auspices.

The Minority recommendations became gradually adopted as British welfare policy. Many of the next generation of government leaders were Fabians or, like Beveridge, had been influenced by them. The old poor law guardians eventually gave way to the National Assistance Board, the National Health Service, and the several local authority departments concerned with housing, child welfare, the aged, the handicapped, health, and education. The goals of the Minority were achieved, and the prestige of the Minority Report in time far overshadowed the work of the Majority. It was not, as already suggested, that the Majority Report was relatively so deficient, but rather the energy, propaganda, and influence of the Minority leaders accounted in large measure for the difference in fame.

Only the significance of the social insurances eluded the Minority commissioners. They were doubtful about the administrative practicality of the insurances and did not see them as preventive in the same sense as the projected social services. Prevention was the crux of the Minority's recommendations, and they envisaged a welfare service for society as a whole, neither discriminating against the poor or the more well-to-do.

The Minority goal was the establishment of the general conditions for healthy living. The Majority approach, on the other hand, gave greater attention to the problem of individual failure. In time both approaches have tended to coalesce as greater balance in the social services has permitted the consideration of individual as well as social factors. The Majority and Minority Reports, in addition to setting forth dramatically the issues of social welfare at the beginning of the twentieth century, provided a broad framework for their resolution. In contrast to 1834, the Reports of 1909 encompassed the basic causes and consequences of poverty rather than concentrating on the narrow issue of pauperism and its relation to the system of relief. Thus poverty as a broad social and economic problem was firmly introduced as a matter for public concern and policy.

Report for Inquiring into the Administration and Practical Operation of the Poor Laws

(1834)

The Overseers

As the law now stands the overseers are able to make, assess, collect and distribute the fund for the relief of the poor. They are to decide in the first instance what amount of money is wanted, what persons are to pay it, and in what proportions; they are to enforce payment of it from those persons, and they are to dole it out to those whom they think proper objects of relief so as to satisfy what they think the necessities of those objects. Where a Select Vestry exists, they are desired by the 59 Geo. III, c. 12, to conform to the directions of that vestry, but as the Act does not put an end to their responsibility or enact any penalty for their non-conformance, this clause, though productive of important results in practice, appears to want legal sanction.

The office is annual and sometimes lasts only six or four, or even three months, it being in some places the practice to appoint two or three, or even four every year, each of whom serves for only half a year or four months, or only three. The persons appointed are in general farmers in country places, and shopkeepers or manufacturers in towns.

If they refuse or neglect to serve they may be indicted or fined, but they receive no remuneration for serving.

Such agents must often be prevented by their other avocations, from giving the time necessary to the vigilant and effectual performance of their duties; neither diligence nor zeal are to be expected from persons on whom a disagreeable and unpaid office has been forced, and whose functions cease by the time that they have begun to acquire a knowledge of them, and even when zealous and diligent they must often fail from want of experience and skill. To these sources of maladministration may be added the danger of the parochial fund being misapplied either in the way of actual embezzlement, or what is more frequent, through jobbing or partiality and favouritism, or through the desire of general popularity, or through the fear of general unpopularity, or of the hostility of particular individuals.

The only checks then on their profusion or partiality, or fraud, are the share which they bear as rate-payers in the burthen, and the necessity of annually submitting their accounts to the vestry, and having them allowed by the magistrates.

With respect to the former check, it is to be observed, first, that the increase or diminution of the rates of the whole parish, which one overseer can affect during his year, or half year, or three months of office, is in general so small, and his own individual share of that increase or diminution so trifling as to be an insufficient motive for making any real sacrifice or encountering any real danger; and secondly, that if, as an immediate employer of labour, he is interested in keeping down its price, he may gain, or think that he gains more by the reduction of wages than he loses by the rise of rates. With respect to the latter check, that arising from the necessity of having the accounts passed, it is to be observed that no form is prescribed for keeping these accounts, that sometimes they are merely entered on loose paper, and that in most cases they consist of a mere day book of receipt and expenditure without any statement of the grounds on which relief has been afforded, and often without stating even the names of the persons relieved. Such accounts afford clues by which a person devoting himself to their investigation might in time ascertain the mode in which the fund had been administered, but on a cursory examination they tell nothing, and we shall see that they do receive only a cursory examination from the vestry of which the overseers themselves form a part, and are then passed as a matter of course by the justices.

On the other hand, if the overseers refuse relief or grant less than the applicant thinks himself entitled to, they may be summoned before the

justices to defend themselves against the charge of inhumanity and oppression, and if they do not comply with the magistrates' order, they are
punishable by indictment or fine, and unhappily the applicant who has
been refused relief has frequently recourse to a much more summary
remedy than the interference of the magistrates. The tribunal which en-
forces it sits not at the petty sessions but at the beer shop. It compels
obedience not by summons and distress, but by violence and conflagration.
The most painful and the most formidable portion of our evidence consists
of the proof that in many districts the principal obstacle to improvement
is the well founded dread of these atrocities.

* * *

Magistrates

We have seen that the early statutes of Elizabeth gave extensive powers
to the justices. The 5 Elizabeth enabled them to tax an obstinate person
according to their good discretion. The 14th directed them to select the
objects of relief, to tax all the inhabitants in their divisions, and to appoint
collectors to make delivery of the contributions according to the discretion
of the justices. This discretionary power, however, did not long continue.
The 39 Eliz. c. 3, and the 43 Eliz. c. 2, which in this respect as in most
others merely repeats the 39 Elizabeth, after having directed the justices
to appoint overseers, impose on the overseers the whole business of raising
and distributing relief, and give to the justices no further authority than
that which is implied by the direction that the overseers, in certain parts
of their duty, shall act "by and with the consent of two or more justices."
A direction which appears to give to the justices only a negative authority:
an authority to forbid but not to command. Nearly a century elapsed
before their power was enlarged; and it may be a question whether the
3 & 4 Will. & Mary, c. 11, which is the foundation of their present power
to order relief, was intended to produce any such result. The object of that
statute was to check parochial profusion.

* * *

But though the scale is the worst form in which the influence of magistrates can be exerted, great evils arise from their interference even when
less systematically exercised. In the first place, the very mode in which
their jurisdiction is enforced seems intended to destroy all vigilance and

economy on the part of those who administer relief, and all sense of degradation or shame on the part of those who receive it. The overseer is summoned perhaps six or seven miles from his business or his farm to defend himself before the tribunal of his immediate superiors against a charge of avarice or cruelty. He seldom has any opportunity to support his defence by evidence; the pleadings generally consist of the pauper's assertions on the one side, and the overseer's on the other. The magistrate may admit or reject the evidence of either party at his pleasure; may humiliate the overseer in the pauper's presence with whatever reproof he may think that his frugality deserves, and finally pronounces a decree, against which, however unsupported by the facts of the case or mischievous in principle, there is no appeal. It must be remembered, too, that the pauper has often the choice of his tribunal. The clause of the 3 & 4 W. & M. c. 11, which confined the jurisdiction to a justice of the peace residing within the parish, or, *if none be there dwelling*, in the parts near or next adjoining, was disregarded at the unfortunate period to which we have referred. The 36 Geo. III, c. 23, gives its discretionary powers to any of His Majesty's justice or justices of the peace for any county, city, town or place usually acting in or for the district wherein the same shall be situated. And though the 59 Geo. III, c. 12, s. 5, has required the concurrence of two justices to an order for relief, yet this restriction, as is the case with many other wisely intended clauses in the Act, is neutralized by a proviso enabling one justice to make an order in case of emergency; an emergency of which *he* is the judge. All the overseers of a district are therefore at the mercy of any two magistrates, and to a considerable degree at the mercy of any one. The pauper may select those magistrates whom misdirected benevolence, or desire of popularity, or timidity, leads to be profuse distributors of other people's property, and bring forward his charges against the overseer, secure of obtaining a verdict. He appears in the character of an injured man dragging his oppressor to justice. If he fails he loses nothing, if he succeeds he obtains triumph and reward. And yet we find persons expressing grave regret that the parochial fund is wasted, that relief is claimed as a right, and that pauperism has ceased to be disgraceful. The subject of regret is, either that the existing system is suffered to continue, or that such is the constitution of human nature, that a vigilant administration of public money is not to be expected from those on whom we have heaped every motive to extravagance and every obstacle against economy; that what the magistrate awards is considered a right, and that the exercise of an acknowledged right is not felt a degradation.

Most of our preceding remarks apply not to the magistrates personally, but to the jurisdiction exercised by them respecting relief, and would be applicable to any tribunal invested with similar powers; to any tribunal, in short, which should be empowered to enforce charity and liberality by summons and fine. But supposing that such a power ought to exist, there are strong grounds for thinking that the present magistrates are not the best persons to be entrusted with it. In the first place, they are men of fortune, unacquainted with the domestic economy of the applicants for relief, and as unfit from their own associations "to settle what ought to be the weekly incomes of the industrious poor," as the industrious poor would be to regulate the weekly expenditure of the magistrates.

* * *

National Charge

We have now reported the result of our inquiry into the practical operation of the Laws for the Relief of the Poor, and into the mode in which those laws are administered; and we proceed to the performance of the remaining part of our duty, that of reporting what alterations, amendments or improvements may be beneficially made in the said laws, or in the mode of administering them, and how the same may be best carried into effect.

We shall preface this part of our Report by a short statement of the principal amendments which have been suggested to us, and to which we cannot add our recommendation.

Many persons, for whose opinion we have a great respect, have proposed that the relief of the poor should be made a national instead of a parochial charge, and be both provided and administered under the direction of the government.

The advantages of making it a national charge would be great and immediate.

It would put an end to settlements. With settlements would go removals, labour-rates, and all the other restrictions and prohibitions by which each agricultural parish is endeavouring to prevent a free trade in labour, and to insulate itself by a conventional cordon as impassable to the unsettled workman as Bishop Berkeley's wall of brass. There would be no longer a motive for preferring in employment the men with large families to those with small, the married to the unmarried, the destitute to those who have saved, the careless and improvident to the industrious and enterprising. We should no longer have these local congestions of a surplus, and therefore a half employed dissolute population, *ascripta glebæ*, some driven, not by the hope of reward but by the fear of punishment to useless occupation, and others fed on condition of being idle; character would again be of some value to a labouring man. Another advantage much smaller than the first, but still considerable, would be the diminution of expense; a considerable sum would be instantly saved in litigation and removals, and we might hope to save a still larger sum by substituting the systematic management of contractors and removeable officers, for the careless and often corrupt jobbing of uneducated, unpaid and irresponsible individuals.

It may be added, that there is no change that would have so numerous and so ardent a body of supporters; all the heavily burdened parishes, and all those which, though still in a tolerable state, foresee, from the annual increase of their expenditure, the ruin that is creeping on them, all the rate-payers who are hesitating between a voluntary exile from the homes to which they are attached, and remaining to witness vice and misery, and encounter loss and perhaps danger, would hail with transport the prospect of such a relief. Other changes may be submitted to; this alone would have enthusiastic partizans.

Still admitting the force of all these arguments in favour of a national charge we do not recommend one.

In the first place, it is objectionable in principle. To promise, on the part of the government, subsistence to all, to make the government the general insurer against misfortune, idleness, improvidence and vice, is a plan better perhaps than the parochial system, as at present administered; but still a proposal which nothing but the certainty, that a parochial system is unsusceptible of real improvement, and that a national system is the only alternative against immediate ruin, the only plank in the shipwreck, could induce us to embrace.

It is probable, indeed it is to be expected, that at first it would work well; that there would be a vigilant and uniform administration, a reduction of expenditure, a diminution of pauperism, an improvement of the industry and morality of the labourers, and an increase of agricultural profit and of rent. But in this case, as in many others what was beneficial as a remedy might become fatal as a regimen. It is to be feared, that in time the vigilance and economy, unstimulated by any private interest, would be relaxed; that the workhouses would be allowed to breed an hereditary workhouse population, and would cease to be objects of terror; that the consequent difficulty of receiving in them all the applicants would occasion a recurrence to relief at home; that candidates for political power would bid for popularity, by promising to be good to the poor; and that we should run through the same cycle as was experienced in the last century, which began by laws prohibiting relief without the sanction of the magistrates; commanding those relieved to wear badges, and denying relief out of the workhouse; and when by these restrictions the immediate pressure on the rates had been relieved, turned round, and by statutes, with preambles, reciting the oppressiveness of the former enactments, not only undid all the good that had been done, but opened the flood-gates of the calamities which we are now experiencing. If we ought to be on our guard against the unforeseen effects of any untried institution, even when its obvious consequences appear to be beneficial, how much more is there to dread from one that in itself is obviously injurious, and is recommended only as less mischievous than what exists. If a national system had been adopted 100 years ago, it is probable that our present situation would have been worse than we now find it; that the mischief would have been still more general, and the remedy still more difficult. Another objection is the difficulty of providing the necessary funds. In Guernsey the poor are provided for by one general fund; but even in that island, one of the most flourishing parts of the empire, it is found necessary to provide for it by a general income tax of not less than three per cent. A property tax would be called for, for that purpose, in England. But all those who are domiciliated in Ireland and Scotland must be exempted from it, as respects their personal property. How should we be able to distinguish between the English, Irish and Scotch funded property, even if the claim of fundholders to immunity from direct taxation were abandoned? And if funded property were exempted, how could we assess personal property of any other description? If personal property is exempted, and the assessment confined to lands and houses, how bitter would be the complaints of those whose rates are now below what would then be the general average?

* * *

Remedial Measures

The most pressing of the evils which we have described are those connected with the relief of the Able-bodied. They are the evils, therefore, for which we shall first propose remedies.

If we believed the evils stated in the previous part of the Report, or evils resembling or even approaching them, to be necessarily incidental to the compulsory relief of the able-bodied, we should not hestitate in recommending its entire abolition. But we do not believe these evils to be its necessary consequences. We believe that, under strict regulations, adequately enforced, such relief may be afforded safely and even beneficially.

In all extensive communities, circumstances will occur in which an individual, by the failure of his means of subsistence, will be exposed to the danger of perishing. To refuse relief, and at the same time to punish mendicity when it cannot be proved that the offender could have obtained subsistence by labour, is repugnant to the common sentiments of mankind; it is repugnant to them to punish even depredation, apparently committed as the only resource against want.

In all extensive civilized communities, therefore, the occurrence of extreme necessity is prevented by alms giving, by public institutions supported by endowments or voluntary contributions, or by a provision partly voluntary and partly compulsory, or by a provision entirely compulsory, which may exclude the pretext of mendicancy.

But in no part of Europe except England has it been thought fit that the provision, whether compulsory or voluntary, should be applied to more than the relief of *indigence*, the state of a person unable to labour, or unable to obtain, in return for his labour, the means of subsistence. It has never been deemed expedient that the provision should extend to the relief of *poverty*; that is, the state of one, who in order to obtain a mere subsistence, is forced to have recourse to labour.

From the evidence collected under this Commission, we are induced to believe that a compulsory provision for the relief of the indigent can be generally administered on a sound and well defined principle; and that under the operation of this principle, the assurance that no one need perish from want may be rendered more complete than at present, and the mendicant and vagrant repressed by disarming them of their weapon, the plea of impending starvation.

It may be assumed, that in the administration of relief, the public is warranted in imposing such conditions on the individual relieved, as are conducive to the benefit either of the individual himself, or of the country at large, at whose expense he is to be relieved.

The first and most essential of all conditions, a principle which we find universally admitted, even by those whose practice is at variance with it, is, that his situation on the whole shall not be made really or apparently so eligible as the situation of the independent labourer of the lowest class. Throughout the evidence it is shown, that in proportion as the condition of any pauper class is elevated above the condition of independent labourers, the condition of the independent class is depressed; their industry is impaired, their employment becomes unsteady, and its remuneration in wages is diminished. Such persons, therefore, are under the strongest inducements to quit the less eligible class of labourers and enter the more eligible class of paupers. The converse is the effect when the pauper class is placed in its proper position, below the condition of the independent labourer. Every penny bestowed, that tends to render the condition of the pauper more eligible than that of the independent labourer, is a bounty on indolence and vice. We have found, that as the poor's rates are at present administered, they operate as bounties of this description, to the amount of several millions annually.

The standard, therefore, to which reference must be made in fixing the condition of those who are to be maintained by the public, is the condition of those who are maintained by their own exertions. But the evidence shows how loosely and imperfectly the situation of the independent labourer has been inquired into, and how little is really known of it by those who award or distribute relief. It shows also that so little has their situation been made a standard for the supply of commodities, that the diet of the workhouse almost always exceeds that of the cottage, and the diet of the gaol is generally more profuse than even that of the workhouse. It shows also, that this standard has been so little referred to in the exaction of labour, that commonly the work required from the pauper is inferior to that performed by the labourers and servants of those who have prescribed it: So much and so generally inferior as to create a prevalent notion among the agricultural paupers that they have a right to be exempted from the amount of work which is performed and indeed sought for by the independent labourer.

We can state, as the result of the extensive inquiries made under this

Commission into the circumstances of the labouring classes, that the agricultural labourers when in employment, in common with the other classes of labourers throughout the country, have greatly advanced in condition; that their wages will now produce to them more of the necessaries and comforts of life than at any former period. These results appear to be confirmed by the evidence collected by the Committees of the House of Commons appointed to inquire into the condition of the agricultural and manufacturing classes, and also by that collected by the Factory Commissioners. No body of men save money whilst they are in want of what they deem absolute necessaries. No common man will put by a shilling whilst he is in need of a loaf, or will save whilst he has a pressing want unsatisfied. The circumstance of there being nearly fourteen millions in the savings banks, and the fact that, according to the last returns, upwards of 29,000 of the depositors were agricultural labourers, who, there is reason to believe, are usually the heads of families, and also the fact of the reduction of the general average of mortality, justify the conclusion that a condition worse than that of the independent agricultural labourer, may nevertheless be a condition above that in which the great body of English labourers have lived in times that have always been considered prosperous. Even if the condition of the independent labourer were to remain as it now is, and the pauper were to be reduced avowedly below that condition, he might still be adequately supplied with the necessaries of life.

But it will be seen that the process of dispauperizing the able-bodied is in its ultimate effects a process which elevates the condition of the great mass of society.

In all the instances which we have met with, where parishes have been dispauperized, the effect appears to have been produced by the practical application of the principle which we have set forth as the main principle of a good Poor Law administration, namely, the restoration of the pauper to a position below that of the independent labourer.

The principle adopted in the parish of Cookham, Berks, is thus stated:

As regards the able-bodied labourers who apply for relief, giving them hard work at low wages by the piece, and exacting more work at a lower price than is paid for any other labour in the parish. In short, to adopt the maxim of Mr. Whately, to let the labourer find that the parish is the hardest taskmaster and the worst paymaster he can find, and thus induce him to make his application to the parish his last and not his first resource.

In Swallowfield, Berks, labour was given "a little below the farmers' prices."

The principle adopted by the Marquis of Salisbury, in Hatfield, Herts, is set forth in the following rules:

All persons, except women, employed by the parish, under the age of fifty, shall be employed in task work. The value of the work done by them shall be calculated at *five-sixths* of the common rate of wages for such work. Persons above the age of fifty may be employed in such work as is not capable of being measured, but the wages of their labour shall be *one-sixth* below the common rate of wages.

* * *

From the above evidence, it appears, that wherever the principle which we have thus stated has been carried into effect either wholly or partially, its introduction has been beneficial to the class for whose benefit Poor Laws exist. We have seen that in every instance in which the able-bodied labourers have been rendered independent of partial relief, or of relief otherwise than in a well regulated workhouse—

1. Their industry has been restored and improved.
2. Frugal habits have been created or strengthened.
3. The permanent demand for their labour has increased,
4. And the increase has been such, that their wages, so far from being depressed by the increased amount of labour in the market, have in general advanced.
5. The number of improvident and wretched marriages has diminished.
6. Their discontent has been abated, and their moral and social condition in every way improved.

Results so important would, even with a view to the interest of that class exclusively, afford sufficient ground for the general introduction of the principle of administration under which those results have been produced. Considering the extensive benefits to be anticipated from the adoption of measures, founded on principles already tried and found beneficial, and warned at every part of the inquiry by the failure of previous legislation, we shall, in the suggestion of specific remedies, endeavour not to depart from the firm ground of actual experience.

We therefore submit, as the general principle of legislation on this subject, in the present condition of the country:

That those modes of administering relief which have been tried wholly or partially, and have produced beneficial effects in some districts, be introduced, with modifications according to local circumstances, and carried into complete execution in all.

The chief specific measures which we recommend for effecting these purposes are—

FIRST, THAT EXCEPT AS TO MEDICAL ATTENDANCE, AND SUBJECT TO THE EXCEPTION RESPECTING APPRENTICESHIP HEREINAFTER STATED, ALL RELIEF WHATEVER TO ABLE-BODIED PERSONS OR TO THEIR FAMILIES, OTHERWISE THAN IN WELL-REGULATED WORKHOUSES (*i. e.* PLACES WHERE THEY MAY BE SET TO WORK ACCORDING TO THE SPIRIT AND INTENTION OF THE 43d OF ELIZABETH) SHALL BE DECLARED UNLAWFUL, AND SHALL CEASE, IN MANNER AND AT PERIODS HEREAFTER SPECIFIED; AND THAT ALL RELIEF AFFORDED IN RESPECT OF CHILDREN UNDER THE AGE OF 16, SHALL BE CONSIDERED AS AFFORDED TO THEIR PARENTS.

It is true, that nothing is necessary to arrest the progress of pauperism, except that all who receive relief from the parish should work for the parish exclusively, as hard and for less wages than independent labourers work for individual employers, and we believe that in most districts useful work which will not interfere with the ordinary demand for labour may be obtained in greater quantity than is usually conceived. Cases, however, will occur where such work cannot be obtained in sufficient quantity to meet an immediate demand; and when obtained, the labour by negligence, connivance or otherwise, may be made merely formal, and thus the provisions of the legislature may be evaded more easily than in a workhouse. A well-regulated workhouse meets all cases, and appears to be the only means by which the intention of the Statute of Elizabeth, that all the able-bodied shall be set to work, can be carried into execution.

The out-door relief of which we have recommended the abolition, is in general partial relief, which as we have intimated, is at variance with the spirit of the 43d of Elizabeth, for the framers of that Act could scarcely have intended that the overseers should "take order for setting to work" those who have work, and are engaged in work; nor could they by the words: "all persons using *no* ordinary and daily trade of life to get their living by," have intended to describe persons "who *do* use an ordinary and daily trade of life."

Wherever the language of the legislature is uncertain, the principle of administration, as well as of legal construction, is to select the course which will aid the remedy; and with regard to the able-bodied, the remedy set forth in the statute is to make the indolent industrious. In proposing further remedial measures we shall keep that object steadily in view.

And although we admit that able-bodied persons in the receipt of outdoor allowances and partial relief, may be, and in some cases are, placed in a condition less eligible than that of the independent labourer of the lowest class; yet to persons so situated, relief in a well regulated workhouse would not be a hardship: and even if it be, in some rare cases, a hardship, it appears from the evidence that it is a hardship to which the good of society requires the applicant to submit. The express or implied ground of his application is, that he is in danger of perishing from want. Requesting to be rescued from that danger out of the property of others, he must accept assistance on the terms, whatever they may be, which the common welfare requires. The bane of all pauper legislation has been the legislating for extreme cases. Every exception, every violation of the general rule to meet a real case of unusual hardship, lets in a whole class of fraudulent cases, by which that rule must in time be destroyed. Where cases of real hardship occur, the remedy must be applied by individual charity, a virtue for which no system of compulsory relief can be or ought to be a substitute.

The preceding evidence as to the actual operation of remedial measures, relates principally to rural parishes. We shall now show, from portions of the evidence as to the administration of relief upon a correct principle in towns, that by an uniform application of the principle which we recommend, or, in other words, by a recurrence to the original intention of the Poor Laws, other evils produced by the present system of partial relief to the able-bodied will be remedied. The principal of the further evils which it would extirpate is, the tendency of that system to constant and indefinite increase, independently of any legitimate causes, a tendency which we have shown to arise from the irresistible temptations to fraud on the part of the claimants. These temptations we have seen are afforded—

First. By the want of adequate means, or of diligence and ability, even where the means exist, to ascertain the truth of the statements on which claims to relief are founded:

Secondly. By the absence of the check of shame, owing to the want of a broad line of distinction between the class of independent labourers and the class of paupers, and the degradation of the former by confounding them with the latter:

Thirdly. By the personal situation, connexions, interests, and want of appropriate knowledge on the part of the rate distributors, which render the exercise of discretion in the administration of all relief, and especially of out-door relief, obnoxious to the influence of intimidation, of local partialities, and of local fears, and to corrupt profusion, for the sake of popularity or of pecuniary gain.

1. The offer of relief on the principle suggested by us would be a self-acting test of the claim of the applicant.

It is shown throughout the evidence, that it is demoralizing and ruinous to offer to the able-bodied of the best characters more than a simple subsistence. The person of bad character, if he be allowed anything, could not be allowed less. By the means which we propose, the line between those who do, and those who do not need relief is drawn, and drawn perfectly. If the claimant does not comply with the terms on which relief is given to the destitute, he gets nothing; and if he does comply, the compliance proves the truth of the claim, namely, his destitution. If, then, regulations were established and enforced with the degree of strictness that has been attained in the dispauperized parishes, the workhouse doors might be thrown open to all who would enter them, and conform to the regulations. Not only would no agency for contending against fraudulent rapacity and perjury, no stages of appeals (vexatious to the appellants and painful to the magistrates) be requisite to keep the able-bodied from the parish, but the intentions of the statute of Elizabeth in setting the idle to work, might be accomplished, and vagrants and mendicants actually forced on the parish; that is, forced into a condition of salutary restriction and labour. It would be found that they might be supported much cheaper under proper regulations, than when living at large by mendicity or depredation.

Wherever inquiries have been made as to the previous condition of the able-bodied individuals who live in such numbers on the town parishes, it has been found that the pauperism of the greater number has originated in indolence, improvidence or vice, and might have been averted by ordinary care and industry. The smaller number consisted of cases where the cause of pauperism could not be ascertained rather than of cases where it was apparent that destitution had arisen from blameless want. This evidence as to the causes of the pauperism of the great mass of the able-bodied paupers, is corroborated by the best evidence with relation to their subsequent conduct, which has corresponded in a remarkable manner with the effects produced in the dispauperized parishes of the rural districts. Ill-informed persons, whose prepossessions as to the characters of paupers are at variance with the statements of witnesses practically engaged in the distribution of relief, commonly assume that those witnesses form their general conclusions from exceptions, and that their statements are made from some small proportion of cases of imposture; but wherever those statements have been put to a satisfactory test, it has appeared that they were greatly below the truth. The usual statements of the permanent overseers in towns are, that more than one half or two-thirds of the cases of able-bodied paupers are cases of indolence or imposture; but it rarely appears that more than five or six in a hundred claimants sustain the test of relief given upon a correct principle.

* * *

Under the present system it is found, that wherever relief is permitted to remain eligible to any except those who are absolutely destitute, the cumbrous and expensive barriers of investigations and appeals erected to protect the rates, serve only as partial impediments, and every day offer a more feeble resistance to the strong interests set against them. To permit this system to continue, to retain the existing permanent officers, and yearly to subject a larger and larger proportion of those who are pressed into the public service as annual officers, to a painful and inefficient struggle, in which they must suffer much personal inconvenience and loss, a loss which is not the less a public loss, because borne by only a few individuals, must excite great animosity against themselves, and ultimately be borne down in a conflict in which the ingenuity and pressing interests of a multitude of paupers, each having his peculiar case or his peculiar means of fraud, are pitted against the limited means of detection, and the feeble interests in the prevention of fraud of one or a few public officers.

In the absence of fixed rules and tests that can be depended upon, the officers in large towns have often no alternative between indiscriminately granting or indiscriminately refusing relief. The means of distinguishing the really destitute from the crowd of indolent impostors being practically wanting, they are driven to admit or reject the able-bodied in classes. Now however true it may be that the real proportion of cases which are found to have the semblance of being well founded, may not exceed three or four per cent. of the whole amount of claims, yet since each individual thus rejected may possibly be one of that apparently deserving minority, such a rejection, accompanied by such a possibility, is at variance with the popular sentiment; and it is found that the great body of the distributors of relief do prefer, and may be expected to continue to prefer, the admission of any number of undeserving claims, to encountering a remote chance of the rejection of what may be considered a deserving case.

On the other hand, the belief which prevails that under the existing system some claims to relief *are* absolutely rejected, operates extensively and mischievously. It appears that this belief, which alone renders plausible the idea of every mendicant (that he applied for parochial relief, and was refused) is the chief cause of the prevalence of mendicity and vagrancy, notwithstanding the existence of a system of compulsory relief; a system which, if well administered, must immediately reduce and enable a police ultimately to extirpate all mendicity. If merit is to be the condition on which relief is to be given; if such a duty as that of rejecting the claims of the undeserving is to be performed, we see no possibility of finding an adequate number of officers whose character and decisions would obtain sufficient popular confidence to remove the impression of the possible rejection of some deserving cases; we believe indeed, that a closer investigation of the claims of the able-bodied paupers, and a more extensive rejection of the claims of the undeserving, would for a considerable time be accompanied by an increase of the popular opinion to which we have alluded, and consequently by an increase of the disposition to give to mendicants.

We see no remedy against this, in common with other existing evils, except the general application of the principle of relief which has been so extensively tried and found so efficient in the dispauperized parishes. When that principle has been introduced, the able-bodied claimant should be entitled to immediate relief on the terms prescribed, wherever he might happen to be; and should be received without objection or inquiry; the fact of his compliance with the prescribed discipline constituting his title to a sufficient though simple diet. The question as to the locality or place of settlement, which should be charged with the expense of his maintenance, might be left for subsequent determination.

On this point, as on many others, the independent labourers may be our best teachers. We have seen, that in the administration of the funds of their friendly societies, they have long acted on the principle of rendering the condition of a person receiving their relief less eligible than that of an independent labourer. We have now to add, that they also adopt and enforce most unrelentingly the principle, that under no circumstances, and with no exceptions, shall any member of their societies receive relief while earning anything for himself. Mr. Tidd Pratt was asked whether, in the rules for the management of friendly societies framed by the labouring classes themselves, he had ever found any for the allowance of partial relief; such as relief in aid of wages, or relief on account of the number of a family? He answers—

"No, I never met with an instance.

"Then do the labouring classes themselves, in the rules submitted to you, reject all partial relief or relief on any other ground than the utter inability to work?—Invariably.

"By what penalties do they usually endeavour to secure themselves from fraud, on the part of persons continuing on the sick list after they have become able to work?—In all cases by utter expulsion and enforcement of the repayment of the money from the period at which it was proved the party was able to work.

"Does that utter expulsion take place whatever may have been the period at which the party had contributed towards the society?—Yes; and all his contributions are forfeited to the society; and so strict are they in the enforcement of these regulations, that I have known them expel a party for stirring the fire, or putting up the shutters of his window, these acts being considered by them evidence of the party being capable of going to work. A small shopkeeper has been expelled for going into his shop; and the only exception I have found in favour of such a rule is, that of a party being allowed to sign a receipt, or to give orders to his servant. They are perfectly well aware, from experience, that to give relief in an apparently hard case, would open the door to a whole class of cases which would ruin them. The other day the steward of a friendly society came to consult me as to the re-instatement of a member who had been expelled for having neglected to pay his quarter's subscription on the regular quarter night half an hour after the books were closed. The party had been a member 32 years, and during that time had received little or no relief. The case struck me as an extremely hard one, and I endeavoured to prevail on the steward to reinstate the member, but the steward stated to me so many facts, shewing that if they yielded to this one case, that it would determine a whole class of cases, and let in so much abuse, that I was ultimately forced to agree in the necessity of the decision of the society. These rules may appear to be capricious and arbitrary, but my observation leads me to believe that they are necessary to protect the society. Although there is an extremely severe enforcement of them, societies are seriously injured, and frequently ruined, by the frauds committed under this mode of relief, notwithstanding the incessant vigilance exercised against them.

"What description of vigilance is that?—It is generally provided by the rules that a domiciliary visit shall be paid by the stewards, or by a member, generally every day; these visits are to be paid at uncertain times, that they may increase the chances of detection. It is also usually provided that a sick member shall not leave his house before or after such an hour, and that on his leaving home at other times he shall leave word in writing where he has gone, by what line of road he has gone, and by what line he intends to return, in order that the stewards or members may track him. In some instances the members follow up these precautions by requiring a member, when he 'declares off' the box, to swear that he was unable to work during the whole time that he has been receiving relief of the society.

"Are these precautions effectual?—No; notwithstanding the utmost vigilance, serious frauds are committed, especially by the members of those trades who can work at piecework within doors; such, for example, as tailors, shoemakers, watchmakers and weavers. An operative of these trades keeps his door shut and works, and when the visitor comes, the work is put under the bed clothes or otherwise concealed, and he is found in bed apparently sick. I find that in those societies where the members' work is of a nature to render fraud liable to detection, such as painters, plumbers, glaziers, stone masons, carpenters, and any other occupation that takes a man out of his own room, the money paid for sickness in the course of a year is less than in societies composed of equal numbers of the class of members before mentioned. From the opportunities of fraud, I always judge of the certainty of fraud, and from those opportunities the certainty of the ruin of societies may be predicted."

This vigilance in the administration of out-door relief to the sick, a vigilance to which we have never found any parallel in the administration of the poors rates, would à fortiori, be requisite in the case of the administration of out-door relief to the able-bodied. But this is obviously impossible. No salaried officer could have the zeal or the knowledge of an inspector of a friendly society, who is always of the same class, and usually of the same trade as the claimant. And if it were possible, we believe that it would not be effectual. The labouring classes themselves find these daily visits and strict regulations inadequate substitutes for the means of supervision and prevention, which well-regulated workhouses afford, and which those classes, if their circumstances permitted, would doubtless adopt. In fact, the experiment has long and often been tried, and always with the same ill success. Visits are made to the claimants, their residences are inspected, and it appears that at these visits and inspections, false and fraudulent scenes are prepared with little more difficulty and much more effect than fraudulent stories, and that those who disregard all statements and trust only to what they call the evidence of their senses, are often the most completely deceived. The testimony of the most experienced and intelligent of our witnesses shews the extensive opportunities for fraud which the most rigid inspection leaves; and in the case of paupers much more than in the case of the sick members of friendly societies, from the extent of the opportunities may the extent of fraud be predicted. Mr. Pratt is asked—

"Have you as a barrister had much poor law practice?—Yes, I have practised 10 years at sessions, I have also edited Bott's Poor Laws and other works connected with the subject.

"Would you apply to the progress of out-door relief by parishes the same rules as are founded on the experience of the labouring classes in benefit societies?—Certainly, and considering a parish as a large friendly society (the members being mostly honorary, or persons who contribute without the intention of partaking of the benefits of the contribution, as the majority in most parishes are), I should look to them much more rigidly.

"If the regulations of a parish, or of a friendly society consisting of a parish, were brought to you to authorize under the statute of Elizabeth, would you certify them if you found in them rules for granting partial relief of any sort, or relief in aid of wages, or relief according to a bread money scale, or relief in proportion to the number of a family, or out-door relief of any description?—As a lawyer I should undoubtedly consider all such allowances entirely at variance with the spirit and intention of the statute of Elizabeth, and I should without hesitation reject them. My experience also derived from the observation of less dangerous regulations in friendly societies, would enable me to pronounce them to be mischievous and ruinous to whatever community adopted them. I am sure that no members of any benefit society, incomplete as their knowledge is, would ever frame rules upon such ruinous principles. The only definite ground of relief, as it appears to me, is utter inability to work, and so it appears to the labouring classes themselves, for whose benefit, and with whom I act, for their allowances are always made upon that ground.

"In what way do the members generally regard parochial assistance? As discreditable?—'In their rules it is generally provided, that in the case of the death of a member, notice be given to the treasurer, who summonses two of the stewards;' and, says the rule, 'They both shall attend such funeral, and see that the corpse is decently interred, *and free from parish grants*;' or it is expressed, as in the following rule: 'That the president and vice-president shall attend funerals of members and their wives, see they be decent, *and free from parochial assistance*; and if either of them neglect so to do, he shall be fined 5s. but for such attendance, each of them shall receive 2s. 6d. from the fund.' "

We believe that the following evidence expresses the sentiments of a large proportion of the most respectable mechanics:

Launcelot Snowdon examined—

"Are you acquainted with the operative class?—Yes, having been a journeyman printer 20 years, and one half of the time foreman, and having been in different situations in our own societies, as well as connected with various other societies of operatives, I believe I am well acquainted with them.

"In what way do they regard the fact of any one of their body receiving parochial relief?—I know that none but the worst characters would ever think of applying for parish relief; and that the respectable workmen consider it disgraceful. The other day, a list of those who received out-door parish relief was brought to a printing office to be printed. One of the men saw on the list the name and address of one of the journeymen in the same office. This man was challenged with the fact, which he did not attempt to deny. He had been receiving as much as 6s. or 8s. a week out-door relief, during two years, for four children, although he had been in receipt of 36s. a week steady wages, during the same time. The men stated the circumstance to the employer, and he was discharged.

"Did they request that he might be discharged?—The proceeding was tantamount to that, and of course the master acceded.

"Suppose the whole of the relief were regulated by an independent, or, say a Government authority, on a fixed rule, that of not rendering the condition of the pauper within the workhouse so good as that of the lowest class of workmen living by his labour out of the house?—That of course. No reasonable man would, I should conceive, expect to have his condition in the workhouse bettered. I think a Government authority would be much the best, as the parish officers are now, in ninety-nine cases out of a hundred, interested parties."

2. Little need be said on the next effect of the abolition of partial relief (even independently of workhouse regulations) in drawing a broad line of distinction between the paupers and the independent labourers. Experience has shown, that it will induce many of those, whose wants arise from their idleness to earn the means of subsistence; repress the fraudulent claims of those who have now adequate means of independent support, and obtain for others assistance from their friends who are willing to see their relations pensioners, but would exert themselves to prevent their being inmates of a workhouse.

3. It will also remove much of the evil arising from the situation of the distributors of relief.

It has been shown that destitution, not merit, is the only safe ground of relief. In order to enable the distributors to ascertain the indigence of the applicant, it has been proposed to subdivide parishes, and appoint to the subdivisions officers who, it is supposed, might ascertain the circumstances of those under their care. But when instances are now of frequent occurrence where a pauper is found to have saved large sums of money, without the fact having been known or suspected by the members of the same family living under the same roof, how should a neighbour, much less a parish officer, be expected to have a better knowledge of the real means of the individual? We are not aware that our communications display one instance of out-door pauperism having been permanently repressed by the mere exercise of individual knowledge acting on a limited area. What our evidence does show is, that where the administration of relief is brought nearer to the door of the pauper, little advantage arises from increased knowledge on the part of the distributors, and great evil from their increased liability to every sort of pernicious influence. It brings tradesmen within the influence of their customers, small farmers within that of their relations and connections, and not unfrequently of those who have been their fellow workmen, and exposes the wealthier classes to solicitations from their own dependents for extra allowances, which might be meritoriously and usefully given as private charity, but are abuses when forced from the public. Under such circumstances, to continue out-door relief is to continue a relief which will generally be given ignorantly or corruptly, frequently procured by fraud, and, in a large and rapidly increasing proportion of cases, extorted by intimidation—an intimidation which is not more powerful as a source of profusion than as an obstacle to improvement. We shall recur to this subject when we submit the grounds for withdrawing all local discretionary power, and appointing a new agency to superintend the administration of relief.

Many apparent difficulties in the proposed plan, will be considered, and we hope removed, in a subsequent part of this Report. One objection, however, we will answer immediately; and that is, that it implies that the whole, or a large proportion of the present paupers must become inmates of the workhouse. One of the most encouraging of the results of our inquiry is the degree in which the existing pauperism arises, from fraud, indolence or improvidence. If it had been principally the result of unavoidable distress, we must have inferred the existence of an organic disease, which, without rendering the remedy less necessary, would have fearfully augmented its difficulty. But when we consider how strong are the motives to claim public assistance, and how ready are the means of obtaining it, independently of real necessity, we are surprised, not at the number of paupers, but at the number of those who have escaped the contagion. A person who attributes pauperism to the inability to procure employment, will doubt the efficiency of the means by which we propose to remove it, tried as they have been, and successful as they have always proved. If such a person had been present when the 900 able-bodied paupers applied to the Maryle-bone officers, on the ground that they could find no work, he would have treated lightly the proposal of getting rid of them by the offer of wages and the stone-yard. He would have supposed that work must have been provided for the 900, not for the 85, who actually accepted it. If a workhouse had been offered, he would have anticipated the reception of the 900, not the 85, or rather, according to the opinion of the officer, the 10, who would probably have entered it. He would have come to the same conclusion respecting the 20 shoemakers, to whom relief was offered by

Mr. Hickson. We have seen that the test showed that among the 20 there was one deserving person: if the test had not been applied, and to meet the chance of there being one such person, the whole 20 had received out-door relief, even that person would have received relief instead of wages, and 19 persons, really capable of earning their support, would have been converted into permanent paupers, besides those whom the example would have attracted. Before the experiment had been tried, the 63 heads of pauper families at Cookham might have been confidently pronounced to be a surplus population, and emigration have been urged as the only remedy. "The low rate of wages," it might have been said, "proves the redundancy, and the certain effect of throwing upon the depreciated labour market nearly one-third more of competitors (rendered desperate by their privations) will be to increase the prevalent misery; the proposal to take them into the workhouse, which will require expensive preparations for the whole of them, is impolitic and indeed impracticable." Such, in fact, were the anticipations of persons deemed competent judges as to the number of the pauperized labourers who would remain permanently chargeable. It is stated in the Report from Cookham that "The work provided was trenching; an acre of hard gravelly ground was hired for the purpose. Some of the vestry at the outset considered that this quantity of land would be utterly inadequate. Many of the farmers thought the parish officers would have to trench the whole parish; but it turned out that not more than a quarter of an acre was wanted for the purpose." In several others of the dispauperized parishes, the erection of workhouses and other remedial measures were strongly and sincerely opposed on similar grounds. In answer to all objections founded on the supposition that the present number of able-bodied paupers will remain permanently chargeable, we refer to the evidence which shows the general causes of pauperism, and to the effects produced by administration on a correct principle, as guaranteeing the effects to be anticipated from the general application of measures which have been tried by so many experiments. But we cannot expect that such evidence will satisfy the minds of those who sincerely disbelieve the possibility of a class of labourers subsisting without rates in aid of wages; and we have found numbers who have sincerely disbelieved that possibility, notwithstanding they have had daily presented to their observation the fact that labourers of the same class, and otherwise no better circumstanced, do live well without such allowances; still less can we expect that such evidence will abate the clamours of those who have a direct interest in the abuses which they defend under the mask of benevolence.

Such persons will, no doubt, avail themselves of the mischievous ambiguity of the word *poor*, and treat all diminution of the expenditure for the relief of the poor as so much taken from the labouring classes; as if those classes were naturally pensioners on the charity of their superiors, and relief, not wages, were the proper fund for their support; as if the independent labourers themselves were not, directly or indirectly, losers by all expenditure on paupers; as if those who would be raised from pauperism to independence would not be the greatest gainers by the change; as if, to use the expression of one of the witnesses whom we have quoted, the meat of industry were worse than the bread of idleness.

We have dwelt at so much length on the necessity of abolishing out-door relief to the able-bodied, because we are convinced that it is the master evil of the present system. The heads of settlement may be reduced and simplified; the expense of litigation may be diminished; the procedure before the magistrates may be improved; uniformity in parochial accounts may be introduced; less vexatious and irregular modes of rating may be established; systematic peculation and jobbing on the parts of the parish officers may be prevented: the fraudulent impositions of undue burthens by one class upon another class—the tampering with the labour market by the employers of labour—the abuse of the public trust for private or factious purposes, may be corrected; all the other collateral and incidental evils may be remedied; but, if the vital evil of the system, relief to the able-bodied, on terms more eligible than regular industry, be allowed to continue, we are convinced that pauperism, with its train of evils, must steadily advance; as we find it advancing in parishes where all or most of its collateral and incidental evils are, by incessant vigilance and exertion, avoided or mitigated.

It has been strongly, and we think conclusively, urged, that all local discretionary power as to relief should be withdrawn. Mr. Mott, when he was examined on the subject of workhouse management, was asked, whether, under a well-regulated system, he thought that the local officers might be entrusted with the power of modifying the dietaries. He answers,

"I am decidedly of opinion that no such authority can be beneficially exercised, even by the local manager and superintendent of any place; whatever deviation there is in the way of extra indulgence has a tendency to extend and perpetuate itself which cannot be resisted. If you give to particular people an extra allowance on special grounds, all the rest will exclaim, 'Why should not we have it as well as they?' and too often they get it. That which was only intended to be the comfort of the few, and as an exception, at last, one by one being added to the list, becomes the general rule; and when once established, there are few annual officers who will interfere to abridge the accustomed allowance."

Thus uniformity of excess is produced; and then again, it is often deemed necessary to make distinctions, in the way of increase, which increase is again diffused, and the whole is again equalized to the profuse standard. Uniformity in the administration of relief we deem essential as a means, first, of reducing the perpetual shifting from parish to parish, and fraudulent removals to parishes where profuse management prevails, from parishes where the management is less profuse; secondly, of preventing the discontents which arise among the paupers maintained under the less profuse management, from comparing it with the more profuse management of adjacent districts; and thirdly, of bringing the management which consists in details, more closely within the public control. The importance of the last object will appear more clearly in our subsequent statement. The importance of uniformity in reducing removals appears throughout our evidence. We have found that the confirmed paupers usually have a close knowledge of the detailed management of various parishes (although the managers rarely have), and act upon that knowledge in their choice of workhouses. Many of the out-door paupers, when they have the means, avoid those parishes in which there are workhouses. The Rev. Rowland Williams, Vicar of Myfod, Montgomery, states in his communication—

It is notorious, that when paupers come to swear their settlements, they show a strong inclination to be removed to parishes where there are no workhouses. Those magistrates who are experienced in such removals exercise great caution in believing testimony given under such influence.

The next subject for consideration is the agency by which partial relief to the able-bodied may be abolished, and a continued administration of relief, on the principle suggested by us, maintained.

The simplicity of that principle, and the effects which it has produced, and apparently with ease, in the dispauperized parishes, naturally suggest to those who have observed only these striking instances, that the change may be effected by a single enactment. That there would be much able and correct administration of any law which the legislature might pass we entertain no doubt, since we find much ability, and often eminent ability, displayed in the administration of the existing system; neither do we doubt that the number of cases of voluntary improvement would greatly increase; for we have been informed of some instances where improvements have actually been commenced in consequence of the light thrown upon the subject by the published extracts from the Reports of our Assistant Commissioners; but the evidence collected under this Commission proves, that whilst the good example of one parish is rarely followed in the surrounding parishes, bad examples are contagious, and possess the elements of indefinite extension. The instances presented to us throughout the present inquiry of the defeat of former legislation, by unforeseen obstacles, and often by an administration directly at variance with the plainly expressed will of the legislature, have forced us to distrust the operation of the clearest enactments, and even to apprehend unforeseen mischiefs from them, unless an especial agency be appointed and empowered to superintend and control their execution.

While we find on the one hand that there is scarcely one statute connected with the administration of public relief which has produced the effect designed by the legislature, and that the majority of them have created new evils, and aggravated those which they were intended to prevent, we find on the other hand that the obstacles to the due execution by the existing functionaries of any new legislative measure are greater than they have ever been. The interests of individuals in mal-administration are stronger, the interests in checking abuses are proportionately weaker; and the dangers to person and property from any attempts to effect the intention of the statute of Elizabeth, are greater than any penalties by which the law might be attempted to be enforced. That the existing law admits of a beneficial administration of the provisions of that statute is proved by the instances of the dispauperized parishes, but those instances were produced by the circumstance of there being found within each of those parishes, an individual of remarkable firmness and ability, often joined with a strong interest in good administration, great influence to overcome opposition, and leisure to establish good management. In the majority of instances, the change originated with the clergyman or some of the largest holders of land within the parish. In the absence of these fortunate accidents the example has not been followed. In Cookham and White Waltham the benefits of the improved administration have been manifested since the year 1822, but manifested without imitation.

In Faringdon, Berks, which we have already cited as an instance of improvement, the governor of the workhouse was asked—

"Are the surrounding parishes aware of the effects produced in your parish by the change of system?—They are quite aware of them.

"If legislative measures were taken for the adoption of such a system as that adverted to by you, do you think that obstacles would be found to prevent their execution?—If the adoption of the measures were not enforced by some strong means, I do not believe they would be extensively carried into effect voluntarily.

"Are those parishes heavily or lightly burthened?—Most heavily burthened. Property is a great deal deteriorated in value in consequence of the progress of pauperism. One gentleman, the other day, mentioned to me that lately, in consequence of the heavy burthen of the poor's-rates, by which, for the last two or three years, he had lost upwards of a hundred a year upon the farm his family had held for upwards of two centuries, he had thrown up that farm, and gone to another parish, which was not yet so heavily burthened with poor's-rates. I know that in the surrounding parishes capital is fearfully diminishing, and property deteriorating.

"Are you aware of any steps being taken in those parishes to follow the example of your parish?—I am not aware of any steps being taken to follow the example. I have indeed heard some persons say they should be very glad to see the same system followed.

"What are the obstacles which stand in the way of their following it?— Partly fear, and partly the want of persons of influence and energy to come forward to take the first steps."

The Commissioner who examined Cookham, visited Bray, and made inquiries of persons connected with that and other adjacent parishes, why they did not adopt the means of reducing their heavy rates, which (as they were well aware) had been found so efficient and salutary in Cookham. The answers were usually to this effect: "The farmers are so disunited and unwilling to stir." "The members of the vestry are so jealous of each other, that they can do nothing." "We have no one to take the lead." "We have no one who will take upon himself the responsibility." "It never can be done, unless we have among us a man of the talent and influence of Mr. Whately."

Mr. Whately himself was asked—

"Do you think your example would be followed if extensively known?—I very much doubt it. I believe it is pretty extensively known, but it has been followed only in one or two solitary cases, so far as I am aware of.

"Are you aware that any pains have been taken by the neighbouring parishes to ascertain the nature of your system?—Yes; many have made themselves fully acquainted with it by personal application to me; but either through indolence or want of firmness, or some other cause, have not availed themselves of the information they have received; nor have I any reason to hope that a great national benefit can be effected by the personal exertions of individuals, who must necessarily expose themselves to considerable obloquy, if not to great loss of property, and who, in many cases, have no immediate personal interest.

"If you were to withdraw your exertions, do you think that the present system would be carried on in your parish?—Many of the principal ratepayers with whom I act, are of opinion that it would not."

In the communication of Messrs. Cameron and Wrottesley will be found an account of the ignorance and apathy prevalent amongst the rate distributors of the adjacent parishes, with relation even to the important pecuniary results of the change of system at Cookham. Mr. Whately having been prevented, by a severe illness from attending the vestry, the effects of his absence soon exhibited themselves in the management of the poor; and some of the members of the select vestry were convinced that the safety of the reformed system depended upon his restoration to health. It appears from Major Wilde's Report, that when the master of the workhouse at Southwell, who had long been accustomed to manage that establishment, under the admirable superintendence of Mr. Becher, went to another parish, he soon relapsed into the common habits. In Hatfield the management fell back during the short illness of the permanent overseer, who is a person excellently qualified; and it appears from various other instances, that the voluntary adoption and continuance of an improved system is dependent on obtaining, within each parish, an individual of great firmness, ability and disinterestedness, to originate it and carry it on; or in other words, that the good general administration of the existing system is dependent on a perpetual succession of upwards of fifteen thousand men of firmness and ability agreeing upon a system, and conducting it voluntarily.

We must again state that while there is no province of administration for which more peculiar knowledge is requisite than the relief to the indigent; there is no province from which such knowledge is more effectually excluded. The earlier part of our Report shows the consequences of acting upon immediate impressions, or upon conclusions derived from a limited field of observation. At present the experience which guides the administration of relief is limited to the narrow bounds of a parish, and to a year of compulsory service. The common administration is founded on blind impulse or on impressions derived from a few individual cases; where the only safe action must be regulated by extensive inductions or general rules derived from large classes of cases, which the annual officer has no means of observing. Capacity for such duties comes by intuition even to persons of good general intelligence as little as an intuitive capacity to navigate a ship or manage a steam engine. The influence of the information and skill which any officer may acquire, may be destroyed by other officers with whom his authority is divided, and even though he may prevail, it usually departs with him when he surrenders his office. The improvements which he may have introduced are not appreciated by his successor. In petty and obscure districts, good measures rarely excite imitation, and bad measures seldom yield warning. "I have seen," says Mr. Mott, "sets of officers succeed sets; I have seen a great many plans and systems suggested and tried; I have seen them tried by officers of the highest respectability and intelligence, and the little good derived from the practical operation of their plans utterly defeated by their successors, who, though equally honest, come into office with different opinions and views. Here and there an extraordinary man will come into office, and succeed very satisfactorily. But when he goes, there is generally an immediate relapse into the old system. His example works no permanent change in his own parish, still less is it attended to in the adjacent parishes. In short, I am quite convinced, from all my experience, that no uniform system can be carried into execution, however ably it may be devised; nor can any hopes of permanent improvement be held out, unless some central and powerful control is established."

Such being the qualifications essential to the performance of parochial offices, our evidence abounds with indications that in devising any new legislative measures it would be necessary to guard not only against adverse interests, but against the actual incapacity of the persons usually filling parochial offices. The following are instances from our communications:

The Rev. Robert Ellison, the rector of Slaugham in Sussex—

The accounts of eight or ten surrounding parishes should be audited by a person with a proper salary, resident in an adjoining town. It is difficult to get a proper person in villages to audit accounts. My vestry clerk is a pauper, and not a good character; the two last overseers could neither read nor write. Need I say more? The rates rose last year 9s. in the pound, which amounted to near £.700 additional. The poor cost upwards of £.1,600; the population not 800.

Major General Marriott, an acting magistrate of the Pershore division, containing sixty-six parishes, of Worcester, states that some of the overseers (small farmers)—

Can scarcely write their names, and few can keep accounts (witness the Returns made to Parliament), and are so ignorant or inattentive to the magistrates' orders, wishing to slip through their half year with as little trouble as possible, that many appeals against removals and other expenses are very unnecessarily incurred, which would have been saved to the parish by a regular assistant, and at a trifling expense. In the above sixty-six parishes there may be twelve or fifteen where gentlemen or clergymen reside, and take part in parish affairs; in most of the rest, I fear, I might draw too exact a picture by saying, their affairs are managed by some few principal farmers and landholders, generally at open variance, and formed into two inveterate parties; the poor parishioners are obliged to take one side or the other, and are favoured or oppressed as their party prevails. *Such are the persons for whom it is necessary to legislate (as well as for inhabitants of large towns) in making or altering laws for the poor.*

Although clear and often able replies to our queries have been received from the officers of the town parishes, some of the answers even from the metropolis, were evidently written by illiterate and ignorant men. One of the population returns from Middlesex, to which we had occasion to refer, was attested by the mark of the returning officer. The revision of the lists of votes under the Reform Act, however, brought to view, in some respects much more completely than the present inquiry, the qualifications of the general body of overseers; and it appears from the information of the revising barristers, that the inability of a large proportion of them was not confined to the comprehension of legal distinctions, but extended to the execution of the most simple directions.

The class of persons [says Mr. Moylan] whom I have seen in the office of overseer are generally men who, far from being able to fulfil the duties imposed upon them, seem unable to comprehend those duties. The general ignorance and stupidity of the overseers in country parishes with whom I came acquainted as Revising Barrister in Cheshire and Nottinghamshire, surpassed any thing which I could have previously conceived In some of the agricultural parishes we found a × substituted for the overseer's signature to the list of voters. Many lists were made out and signed by the village schoolmaster, or some other person who accompanied the overseer in attendance upon our court, and was alone competent to answer on his behalf any inquiries we deemed it requisite to make. In some cases where the overseer had not had recourse to the aid of others, his blunders were ludicrous. Instead of making the list a fair transcript of the claims, he would perhaps undertake to insert what he thought a more accurate description of the qualification, which would prove, in point of fact, no qualification at all.

In 1832 [says Mr. Maclean] I revised the list of voters for the Western Division of the county of Sussex, and in the present year I have revised the lists of the Northern Division of the county of Essex. In both counties I met with many overseers apparently perfectly unable to comprehend, from reading the Reform Act, what they were required to do. Many were unable to write at all, and others could with difficulty affix their names to the lists. Some appeared unable to copy accurately the schedule of the Act according to the form there given. Those lists which had any pretension to correction had been invariably written out by the parish schoolmaster, or under the advice and direction of some resident gentleman. Few were capable of furnishing any information, or of understanding that any distinction existed between a freehold and a leasehold qualification. Through ignorance or obstinacy, many had neglected several of the duties distinctly pointed out in the Act; such as to publish the names which were upon the register of the preceding year, or to sign the lists previous to affixing them on the church door. I met with few lists which did not require considerable alteration. Attempts at an alphabetical arrangement seemed to have completely failed. Several had omitted to make out lists at all. In one instance I was attended by a female overseer, and it is due to her to state, that the list furnished by her, and in her own handwriting, was one of the most correct I met with.

Mr. Flood, Revising Barrister for the Northern Division of the county of Leicester, states—

I found very great difficulty in revising the lists of voters, owing to the illiterate character of the overseers of many of the parishes. In one instance, where there were two overseers, one had not acted, and did not sign the list, though he was able to write; and a mark × was substituted for the signature of the other. There were, I think, three or four lists unsigned, none of the overseers being able to write, and about the same number only signed by one overseer. In about 16 or 18 lists the overseers had resorted to the assistance of the parish schoolmaster, or some other person, to assist them. In not more than 10 parishes did the overseers appear in the least to comprehend the duties they were required to perform. I found, however, the overseers of the parishes of Loughborough, Castle Donington, Melton Mowbray and Ashby-de-la-Zouch exceedingly intelligent men, while in the eastern side of the county, where the population is exclusively agricultural, I met with a degree of ignorance I was utterly unprepared to find in a civilized country.

Mr. Villiers, when acting as a Revising Barrister in North Devon, found that not less than one-fourth of the overseers were unable to read, and he mentions one overseer who had not that quailfication, and yet was intrusted with the distribution of rates to the amount of £.7,000 per annum.

Such being the *capacity* of a large proportion of the distributors, we shall find the state of their *motives* to either the commencement or the support of improvement equally unpromising. Persons engaged in trade have represented the management of parochial affairs to be analogous to the management of a bankrupt's estate by creditors, where, although each creditor has an interest in the good management of the estate, yet as the particular creditors who were appointed assignees had not an interest sufficient to incite them to exertions which necessarily interfered with their other and stronger interests, no estates were ever so extensively mismanaged, or so frequently abandoned to plunder until a special and responsible agency was appointed for their protection. The common fallacy in which the management by overseers, that is by two or three persons, is treated as a management by the people of the "people's own affairs," and an "attention to their own interests," meaning the affairs and interests of some hundreds or thousands of other persons, may be exposed by a slight examination of the evidence. It will be found that the private interests of the distributors of the rates are commonly at variance with their public duties, and that the few pounds, often the few shillings, which any parish officer could save to *himself* by the rigid performance of his duty, cannot turn the scale against the severe labour, the certain ill will, and now, in a large proportion of cases, the danger to person and property, all of which act on the side of profusion. And it must be recollected, that the consequences of a large proportion of the existing mismanagement do not fall on the parishes in which they have originated, but upon those against whom, under the present system of parochial warfare they are aimed, and that much of that mismanagement is, consequently, mismanagement by the officers and by the vestries, not of their own affairs, but of the affairs of other parishes, or of the public at large. Even if the whole power were left to the vestry, and the vestry were composed of the proprietors as well as of the occupiers, it could not be said, except in very small parishes, that the governing body were the managers of their own affairs. Numerous bodies are incapable of managing details. They are always left to a minority, and usually to a small minority; and the smaller that minority, the greater, of course, is the preponderance of private and interested motives.

It must be added, as indeed might have been expected, that as parochial duties become more arduous, as they require more leisure and ability, those who have that leisure and ability appear less and less inclined to undertake them. This is shown in the great falling off in the number of representative vestries, in consequence of the difficulty of obtaining the attendance of those who were the best qualified; although such vestries are amongst the best existing instruments for systematic management, with the least annoyance to those who perform the duties. It has been stated to us, that in one district where the income of the proprietors was reduced nearly one half, chiefly by the progressive increase of the rates, several of them declared that they would abandon the remainder rather than encounter the annoyance of having to contend against the system. The property of the whole parish of Cholesbury was abandoned to pauperism, apparently without a struggle.

We need only revert to the evidence quoted in the earlier part of our Report to mark the extent to which interests *adverse* to a correct administration prevail amongst those who are entrusted with the duties of distributing the fund for relief.

We must anticipate that the existing interests, passions, and local habits of the parish officers will, unless some further control be established, continue to sway and to vary the administration of the funds for the relief of the indigent; and that whatever extent of discretion is left to the local officers, will be used in conformity to those existing interests and habits. Wherever the allowance system is now retained, we may be sure that statutory provisions for its abolition will be met by every possible evasion. To permit out-door relief as an exception would be to permit it as a rule. The construction which has been put on the 59 Geo. III shows that every case would be considered "a case of emergency"; and under provisions directing that the able-bodied shall be relieved only in the workhouse, but allowing relief in money to be continued to the sick, we must be prepared to find allowances continued to many of the able-bodied, as belonging to the excepted class. We have had instances where, after the use of fermented liquors in workhouses had been forbidden, they were found in use in extraordinary quantities as medicines.

In addition to these strong elements for the perversion of any legislative measures, we cannot omit to notice again the comparatively new and still more powerful element of intimidation now openly avowed in the most pauperized districts.

The labouring men in a large proportion of the districts, where the allowance system prevails, must have seen and felt, what indeed the labourers who have been examined explicitly declare, that the discretion and irresponsible power allowed to the distributors of relief are often used prejudicially to them. We believe, however, that the acts of injustice properly imputed to those who have so exercised that power, bear no proportion to the injustice imagined, and erroneously attributed to them by the receivers, under the notion generated by the indefiniteness of the existing system of relief, that the poor's rates are an inexhaustible fund, from which all who call themselves poor are prevented drawing to the extent of their desires, only by the cupidity or partiality of parish officers.

However groundless this suspicion may be, its existence appears to us a sufficient reason for endeavouring to remove its pretext. Every man ought, in fact, to distrust his own judgment and his own actions in the affairs of others in proportion as his interests and affections are concerned. Our law, in its jealousy of the influence of similar interests, has rendered the taint of pecuniary interest a ground for incompetency in the case of a witness, and for exclusion from the execution of trusts, and in both cases to a degree which is very inconvenient. The powers vested in the overseers by the statutes of Elizabeth can only be accounted for on the supposition that the distribution of the poor's rates was little more than an occasional distribution of alms from the poor's box, too small in its amount and influence to be regarded. Not a century had elapsed, however, before the evils of the "unlimited power of the overseers" and their "giving relief upon frivolous pretences, but chiefly for their own private ends, to what persons and number they thought fit," had been stated and attempted to be remedied. The remedy however was, as we have seen, unsuccessful, indeed worse than unsuccessful. It gave, or was construed as giving, power to the justices, of which we have described the effects, and it does not, in practice, appear to check the powers of the overseers, powers which enable them to reduce the value of the labour, of which they themselves are the purchasers, and even to throw on others a part of its price, to increase the productiveness of their own property, and depreciate that of their neighbours, and generally to gratify their own feelings and promote their own interests at the expense of every other portion of the community.

Whatever may have been the various causes of the agricultural riots in various districts, whether the object was to force an increase of wages or a reduction of tithes or rent, the one effect has been to prove that the discretion exercised in the distribution of the poor's rates can be affected by intimidation, and the rate receivers every week show themselves more completely aware that intimidation may be made as efficient a means of producing mal-administration as the corrupt interests of the distributors. Various communications made to us in 1833, correctly anticipated the continuance of incendiarism, during the present winter. Intimidation is not unfrequently exercised in the town parishes, and the police called in for the protection of the distributors. To such an extent has it been carried in a large parish in the metropolis, that the officers thought it necessary for their safety to go armed to the vestry.

Under these circumstances, any discretionary power left to the local officers must be a source of suspicion, and so far as their persons or properties are obnoxious to injury, a bounty on intimidation. The ignorant rarely estimate, or even take into account the motives which lead men to pursue any line of conduct except the narrow track pointed out by their own immediate interest, and are prone to exaggerate any power that may be used against them, and to fear and hate those who exercise it. It is matter of common observation, that acts of incendiarism have been most frequently committed against persons who had done "nothing to excite animosity," or who were "distinguished for their kindness," or were "the last persons who would have been expected to become the victims of such revenge." We see no ground for expecting that any purity in act or intention in the distribution of rates will render the distributors less obnoxious to hatred, which is always the stronger as they are the more closely connected with the rate receivers. A refusal by a person who is nearly an equal, excites more animosity than one by a person who is comparatively a stranger and has greater authority. Can a farmer at a vestry be expected to refuse relief, and endanger his own property and person to save funds to which he is only one of many contributors, when, in proportion to his belief that the applicant is undeserving, must by his conviction of the capability of that applicant to resort to any criminal means of obtaining compliance with his demands, or of gratifying his revenge? But the immediate distributors of relief, are not the only persons obnoxious to such motives. Mr. Villiers states, that a magistrate declared to him that in his neighbourhood if a gentleman living upon his own property were strictly to perform his duty in a large proportion of the cases where paupers appealed from their overseers, he would be in danger of having his property destroyed. Such dangers, it is to be observed, are generally incurred by refusals to increase allowances, which are *now* wholly illegal, and, therefore, to expect the voluntary execution of new and strict regulations by persons placed under such circumstances, appears unreasonable. Mr. Day, the magistrate at Maresfield, to whose communication we have before referred, in the following passage forcibly expresses opinions, which we have reason to believe are entertained by a numerous class.

I must here guard against an impression that may be conveyed by these remarks, which might lead to a fatal disappointment. The workhouse system is at present legal, and funds for emigration many, in many instances, be raised by voluntary contributions. But were the plan, advocated by me, attempted to be put in execution at the mere instigation of an individual, or by a vote of vestry, it would probably induce an irritation that would lead to disastrous consequences. When in the parish of Mayfield it was rumoured that I intended interfering to reduce the rates, it was immediately suspected by the paupers that I was opposed to their interests. On the door of the first vestry I attended, I found affixed a notice, 'that they intended washing their hands in my blood.' In 1826, a threat of that kind was readily disregarded; at present it would be consummated in a riot or fire. But if the alteration be the act of the legislature, it assumes a different aspect. It comes with the sanction of the law, and however it may be murmured at, the odium is removed from the obnoxious vestryman, or the individual magistrate. The complaining pauper looks round to the adjacent parishes and the neighbouring benches. He sees his lot the lot of all; and is told that however he may meet with sympathy, there is no power of redress. He may hope to intimidate a vestry, but he cannot dare to oppose a government.

We believe however that general regulations made under the immediate control of the executive, would meet with comparatively ready obedience; not from despair of the success of resistance, but from confidence in the disinterestedness of the source from which the regulations emanated. We are happy in having found no distrust of the Government amongst the labouring classes in the pauperized districts: we rather apprehend that they entertain extravagant expectations of what can be accomplished by legislative interference. In the instructive letters from emigrants of the labouring classes to their friends in England, we see few traces of discontent with the political institutions, or the general government of their former country; few expressions of satisfaction that they now live under other institutions; but we do find in those letters, felicitations that they are no longer under local control or parochial management; "Here" say the labourers, in speaking of their new abodes, "there are no overseers to tread us under foot." Wherever in the course of this inquiry it has been deemed requisite to communicate directly with the labouring classes, the Commission appears to have been regarded with entire confidence. Our written communications from labouring men on the subject of the labour-rate are abundant; our Assistant Commissioners found their inquiries answered with alacrity by all the labourers who were examined. Under the conception that the Commissioners were invested with extraordinary powers, the labourers have appealed to us for interference against local malversations. One of the Sussex labourers was asked in the course of his examination—

"What alterations of the Poor Laws are talked about by the labourers?— They have hopes that Government will take it in hand, as they would then be contented with what was allotted to them; they would be sure that they would have what was right, and would not be driven about by the overseers.

"Are you sure that the labourers would be pleased to see the overseers deprived of their power?—Yes, that they would, for they often fail, and take the parishes in; and besides, all parish business now goes by favour. Many people do now say that they talk about reform in the Government, but there wants reform in the parish.

"Suppose that the workmen were deprived of the allowance in aid of wages, but deprived in such numbers that the farmers would be compelled to pay wages to the same amount, how do you think such a measure would be received by the workmen?—That would give a great deal more content, and I am sure that they would do the farmer more work. The parish money is now chucked to us like as to a dog."

The jealousy felt by the labourers towards the local authorities, from a suspicion of their being under the influence of adverse interests, combined with distrust of their possession of knowledge qualifying them to interfere with advantage, was strongly displayed in framing the present Act for the Regulation of Friendly Societies.

Dr. James Mitchell examined—

"We are informed that you have paid great attention to the formation of friendly societies, and the legislative proceedings with relation to them?—I have lectured and published works on the subject of benefit societies, and took an active part in assisting the delegates of the working men of the benefit societies in London in framing the present Act of Parliament under which benefit societies are regulated, and, as an actuary, I am very often consulted on the subject.

"Was the appointment of a central authority or control, under the authority of the Government, to revise the regulations of the benefit societies, and enforce conformity to the will of the Legislature, popular with the representatives of the working classes?—Yes; in order to prevent the capricious control of the various local authorities, each of whom had his own notions, which probably differed from the notions of every body else, and were formed from very limited experience and observation, and often from no observation whatever, the working men thought it would be very beneficial to get one person appointed to revise the rules of all the societies throughout the country, in order that their administration might be rendered uniform, and that the detailed regulations might be the result of more extended information. The chief object of the labouring men was to prevent capricious local interference, which might often be the interference of employers. The clause for the purpose was framed by the delegates themselves."

In the various dispauperized parishes, the enforcement of one inflexible rule of administering relief, prevented the exercise of any discretionary power by the employers of labour. The contentment which followed, is to a considerable extent attributable to this circumstance.

The circumstances which tend gradually to drive discreet and trust-worthy persons from voluntarily undertaking the management of the poor's rates, leave it in fact either to compulsory service, performed by officers whose authority is transient, who have no appropriate knowledge, and whose only interest is to get through their service with the least personal inconvenience to themselves, or to voluntary service by persons who have either a strong private interest, or who are actuated by ardent feelings. If those feelings are well directed they produce indeed the effects which have followed at Southwell, Bingham, Cookham and Farthingoe, but in ill disciplined minds they may be more injurious than the basest self interest. On these grounds many of the most respectable parochial officers who have been examined under this Commission have urged the necessity of withdrawing from themselves and from their associates and successors, all discretionary power in the distribution of relief. They implore even as a mere protection, that they may be released from that discretion, and declare that while it lasts they *dare* not pursue the course which they deem the most beneficial even to the paupers by whom the intimidation is exercised.

* * *

Witnesses, when speaking of the necessity of withdrawing all discretionary power from the distributors in their own parishes, usually express a hope that the relief may be fixed, and to the "smallest detail unalterably prescribed by the Legislature." The evidence, however, proves that little more reliance can be placed on the voluntary execution by the present agency of any regulations, than on their correct execution of any general principle of management prescribed to them.

It appears too that the actual condition of the pauperized districts does not admit of legislation in detail. The differences in the modes of administering the law in different districts have produced habits and conditions of the population equally different. The best-informed witnesses have represented that the measures applicable to adjacent districts are totally inapplicable to their own; and it appears to us, that measures which might be safely and beneficially introduced into the majority of parishes in a district might, if immediately introduced, be productive of suffering and disorder to the remainder. Even if the simultaneous and complete execution of so great a change of system throughout the country were practicable, we consider it desirable to avoid it.

It must be remembered that the pauperized labourers were not the authors of the abusive system, and ought not to be made responsible for its consequences. We cannot, therefore, recommend that they should be otherwise than gradually subjected to regulations which, though undoubtedly beneficial to themselves, may by any sudden application inflict unnecessary severity. The abuses have grown up in detail, and it appears from our evidence that the most safe course will be to remove them in detail. We deem uniformity essential; but in the first instance it is only an approximation to uniformity that can be expected, and it appears that it must be obtained by gradations in detail, according to local circumstances. And although uniformity in the amount of relief may be requisite, it may not be requisite that the relief should be invariably the same in kind. In Cumberland, and some others of the northern counties, milk is generally used where beer is used in the southern counties. The requisite equality in diet would probably be obtainable without forcing any class of the workhouses in the northern counties to take beer, or those of the southern counties to take milk.

The most practical witnesses concur with Mr. Mott in representing the voluntary adoption of detailed regulations hopeless, and legislation on details ineligible, if not impracticable. He is asked—

"Do you think it practicable to bring parishes to the voluntary adoption of any uniform regulation when their importance is proved to them?—He answers, I certainly do not think it practicable. I think it utterly impossible to bring the 14 or 15,000 parishes in England and Wales to one mind upon any one subject, however clear the evidence may be; much less so to act with uniformity in any one point. The Commissioners must be well aware, that great frauds are committed by paupers in the metropolis receiving relief from different boards on different board days. I have known instances of paupers receiving pensions from three or four different parishes. It was proposed some years ago, and it has been proposed from time to time to remedy this evil, which all the parishes are aware is very great, by one simple but effectual expedient, which it would be very easy to adopt, namely, by all the parishes paying on the same day; but they never could be got to do this. Individual conveniences prevented the remedy being applied, and the system of fraud still prevails, and will continue to prevail, so long as the present management prevails. Now, if the parishes in the metropolis cannot be got to act in concert for the suppression of an evil which affects only one part of the system, I think it will be seen that I am justified in my opinion, that any reform or cooperation in the country is quite hopeless without the establishment of a strong central management; nothing else will check the system.

"Might not such general regulations as those to which you have alluded be prescribed by Act of Parliament?—No, certainly not. The regulations of any system must be very numerous; and though they may be uniform, it would be necessary to vary them from time to time; and unless Parliament was to do nothing but occupy itself with discussions on details of workhouse management, it would be impossible to effect any great alteration in that way. Many regulations, however ably devised, must be experimental. Unforeseen and apparently unimportant details might baffle the best plans, if there were not the means of making immediate alteration. Suppose a general regulation were prescribed by Act of Parliament, and it was found to want alteration; you must wait a whole year or more for an Act of Parliament to amend it, or the law must be broken. A central authority might make the alteration, or supply unforeseen omissions in a day or two. Besides, a central board or authority might get information immediately on the matters of detail. If they had for instance to settle some uniform diet, they could at once avail themselves of the assistance of men of science, physicians or chymists; but you would find that Parliament, if it could really attend to the matter, and would do any thing efficient, must have almost as many committees as there are different details. If there was a central board established, and it were easily accessible, as it ought to be, persons in local districts would consult them or make suggestions, who would never think of applying to Parliament. Who would think of applying to Parliament to determine whether four or five ounces of butter should be used as a ration in particular cases, and whether the butter should be Irish or Dutch? or, if Irish, whether Cork or Limerick; or to determine whether the old women's under-petticoats should be flannel or baize, and how wide or how long? Yet on details of this sort, beneath the dignity of grave legislators, good or bad management would depend."

By many it is considered that the only means by which the system can be effectually amended, is the management of the whole Poor Law administration as a branch of the general Government. The advocates of a national rate, and those who are willing and desirous that the Government should take upon itself the whole distribution of the funds for the relief of the poor do not appear to have considered the expense and difficulties in the way of obtaining such an agency throughout the country.

We have received no definite plan for the purpose and have prepared none. We trust, that immediate measures for the correction of the evils in question may be carried into effect by a comparatively small and cheap agency, which may assist the parochial or district officers, wherever their management is in conformity to the intention of the legislature; and control them wherever their management is at variance with it. Subject also to this control, we propose that the management, the collection of the rates, and the entire supervision of the expenditure, under increased securities against profusion and malversation, shall continue in the officers appointed immediately by the rate-payers. This course we believe will be the most easily practicable, and will best accord with the recommendations of the majority of the witnesses, and with the prevalent expectation of the country.

The course of proceeding which we recommend for adoption, is in principle that which the legislature adopted for the management of the savings banks, the friendly societies and the annuity societies throughout the country. Having prescribed the outline and general principles on which those institutions should be conducted, a special agency (which in this instance was constituted by one barrister only) was appointed to see that their rules and detailed regulations conformed to the intention of the law. This agency we believe has accomplished the object effectually. From magistrates and clergymen, who act as trustees and managers of savings banks, we have learned, that it is found to work satisfactorily to them and to the members at large, because they are aware that the decision by which any regulation is established or disallowed is made on extended information derived from all similar institutions throughout the kingdom, instead of being made only on such as the neighbourhood might chance to afford. We believe that the control has also been found beneficial by the members of friendly societies, and has put a stop to many which were founded either ignorantly or dishonestly on principles fraught with ruin to the contributors. Since the adoption of this measure, there has been only one appeal against the barrister's decision, and that appeal was disallowed.

WE RECOMMEND, THEREFORE, THE APPOINTMENT OF A CENTRAL BOARD TO CONTROL THE ADMINISTRATION OF THE POOR LAWS, WITH SUCH ASSISTANT COMMISSIONERS AS MAY BE FOUND REQUISITE; AND THAT THE COMMISSIONERS BE EMPOWERED AND DIRECTED TO FRAME AND ENFORCE REGULATIONS FOR THE GOVERNMENT OF WORKHOUSES, AND AS TO THE NATURE AND AMOUNT OF THE RELIEF TO BE GIVEN, AND THE LABOUR TO BE EXACTED IN THEM, AND THAT SUCH REGULATIONS SHALL, AS FAR AS MAY BE PRACTICABLE, BE UNIFORM THROUGHOUT THE COUNTRY.

We have already recommended the abolition of partial relief to the able-bodied, and particularly of money payments. It appears to us that this prohibition should come into universal operation at the end of two years, and as respects new applicants, at an earlier period, and that the Board should have power, after due inquiry and arrangements, to shorten these periods in any district: one of their first proceedings should probably the gradual substitution of relief in kind for relief in money.

With such powers the Central Board might discontinue abusive practices, and introduce improvements gradually, detail after detail, in district after district, and proceed with the aid of accumulating experience.

Another advantage of this course, as compared with that of a simultaneous change is, that trouble and expense may be spared to all those parishes where abusive modes of administration do not exist.

The Commissioners would assist those who were willing to exert themselves in bringing about the change, and would exonerate from responsibility those who found it too heavy, or who could not sustain it beneficially. Since the Commissioners would have no local interests or affections, they would enforce the law without ill temper on their parts, and without exciting animosity. Unless those measures which have hitherto caused a decrease of pauperism, and diminished its pecuniary burthen, the only measures which it would be the duty of the Commissioners to enforce, should produce bad effects instead of good, the benefits of the change in the first districts in which it will be effected, must be such as to remove from the minds of the ill-informed or the timid all the undefined apprehensions which beset the subject, and suppress the interested opposition with which every such change will be assailed.

As one barrier to increase of expense in the detailed management, the Commissioners should be empowered to fix a maximum of the consumption per head within the workhouses, leaving to the local officers the liberty of reducing it below the maximum if they can safely do so.

The following are exemplifications of the regulations which might be transferred from district to district, when found applicable by the Commissioners. An officer of Whitechapel parish in London was asked,

"What sort of work have they in the workhouse?—They have various sorts of work in the workhouse. Out of the workhouse we employ them as general scavengers for cleansing the parish, contracting for carting only, and making the paupers cleanse all the lanes, alleys and streets, and fill the carts, giving them a small allowance.

"What has been the effect of this regulation?—It had been in operation some years before I came into office, and has been found very beneficial. The parish is much better cleansed, and is more healthy than if left to contractors only. The contractors generally shuffle off cleansing the alleys as they cannot get the cart up them, but we make our men take the wheelbarrows up the avenues. The paupers are by this system made spies to prevent any nuisances that may occasion them trouble. If they see any one throwing down filth, they fetch the superintendent and the party is made to take it up again. For this purpose we find that the paupers are better than the police. The efficiency of this system depends mainly on the superintendent, who is paid to attend to the labour of the paupers. The parish was fortunate in making choice of a proper officer."

In Mr. Codd's Report there is a similar instance. In the parish of St. Paul's Covent Garden, the able-bodied paupers were employed to cleanse the streets:

Our parishioners [the witness states] say that the streets were never kept so clean as they have been since the new system prevailed. The fact is, that it is the interest of the contractors to employ as few labourers in the work as possible, and to leave the streets until they are so dirty that large portions may be removed at once.

In the answer from Penrith, it is stated by the assistant overseer—

We have at present about 10 acres of land, two of which are planted with potatoes every year by the paupers, with the spade; the remainder is sown with corn and hay-grass. We also collect manure from the streets, which we farm of the Duke of Devonshire for that purpose, and for the sake of cleanliness and employment for the poor. The streets are kept clean by those in the work-house; and at times, when able-bodied out-door paupers apply for relief, we offer them work in the streets, which they invariably refuse. By this means, and that of spade husbandry, we get rid both of our male and female applicants.

Mr. Tweedy states, that at Huddersfield—

Two years ago a number of men (15) applied for relief as out of work, and were ordered to come next morning, and have employment in cleansing the streets. Of the 15, but one came the next morning, who said the others had got jobs elsewhere.

The same results may always be expected where the applicant cannot plead actual inability; and the labour of cleansing the streets can be offered in every town. The Reports of the various Local Boards of Health on the state of the densely peopled neighbourhoods, show how grievously this source of employment has been neglected. Even where it has been introduced, it has seldom been enforced with regularity and upon principle: even the success of the experiment does not ensure its repetition, still less its imitation.

Another instance is the mode in which the out-door paupers are paid in some of the large parishes in the metropolis. The vestry clerk of the parish of Saint Luke, Middlesex, states that—

For several years past a new system of paying the pensioners has been adopted in our parish. Formerly they came in crowds, the regular pensioners being then about 800, and were paid promiscuously on the presentation of their cards. It was found that some persons obtained payment twice over by getting other persons to present their cards after they had been once paid. The whole coming together, a large proportion of them was kept waiting a considerable time, and in addition to the time lost by the paupers, there was much mischief done by an extension of the opportunities of communication, and the formation of vicious acquaintances. The mothers of bastard children might form acquaintances with others still more depraved. The children of more creditable people became familiar with the confirmed paupers.

The improvement consisted in the pensioners being paid in sets of 100 each; each 100 is paid, and each payment entered within a quarter of an hour. Any person within the same 100 may be paid within the same quarter of an hour; the quarter of an hour, it may be observed, is printed on each ticket. If the party does not attend at the proper time their pension is suspended during the ensuing week. An hour and a half of the pauper's time is thus saved; and on an average, the crowd is reduced from 800 to 50, and the commission of fraud by repeated payments on the same ticket, is rendered impossible.

The regulation might probably be made much more efficient, but such as it is it appears to have been little imitated. The overseer of the adjacent parish of St. Matthew, Bethnal Green, states in his evidence—

There were 400 people with new faces for me to pay the first night I sat. I had no one to assist me or inform me, and I gave money away on the mere statements made to me; I am confident I paid some of the people twice over that night.

These crowds are kept often the whole day, and usually during several hours congregated together in the most corrupting state of idleness around the workhouse door. The conduct of these crowds is thus described by the governor of the St. Pancras workhouse.

Even this course has not entirely gotten rid of the evil; for while they are congregated round the workhouse doors, their language and conduct are so degrading and obscene, as to be a subject of heavy complaint with the neighbours and passengers; no decent female can approach them without being insulted; and I grieve to say, that the young women especially seem to have entirely lost all sense of propriety, or rather of common decency; it is no unusual sight to see them upon these occasions in situations of indecency that are most revolting.

These very shameful practices have not subsisted for more than five or six years; but they have increased in force and frequency within that time, and we have tried every means of prevention within our reach, without success. We have called in the aid of the police, have taken the parties before the magistrates, &c. but all to no purpose.

Other witnesses, whose own parishes are the boundaries of their knowledge, as well as of their experience on the subject, assert that such evils are incurable. One parish evinces perfect ignorance of regulations which have long been in force as efficient remedies in adjacent parishes. The instance mentioned at St. Pancras relates to a form of relief which we hope to see abolished; but during the period of its unavoidable continuance, provision should be made for the introduction of regulations by which its evils may be abated. Some valuable practical improvements of the existing system are found in the voluminous codes and by-laws under which incorporations are managed.

If the sum of the good regulations which are found in single and separate, and therefore partial operation, scattered amidst a multitude of parishes, were carried into complete execution in every parish or district to which they were found applicable, the improvement would probably be greater than can be hoped for from untried enactments. We recommend, therefore, that the *same* powers of making rules and regulations that are now exercised by upwards of 15,000 unskilled and (practically) irresponsible authorities, liable to be biassed by sinister interests, should be confided to the Central Board of Control, on which responsibility is strongly concentrated, and which will have the most extensive information. Even if the Board were to frame bad regulations (and worse regulations than those now in practice they could scarcely devise), it would be a less mischievous arrangement than the present, inasmuch as the chances of opposition to a pernicious measure would be increased in proportion to the extension of the jurisdiction, and success in such opposition would be success throughout the jurisdiction. Those who are now maintainers of their own errors would be vigilant and unsparing censors of the errors of a distant authority. Under the existing system, when opposition is made to the continuance of a bad practice, and the opposition is successful, the success is limited to one parish, or to one fifteen thousandth part of the whole field in which the practice may prevail. In the next parish, and in other parishes, the form of the abuse is generally varied, and requires a varied as well as a renewed opposition. These variations elude legislative enactments, and divide and weaken the force with which the opinion of the intelligent part of the community would act against them. But if a bad practice is rendered uniform, it becomes obnoxious, in proportion to its extent, to the full force of public opinion; the aggregate of its effects, immediate or collateral, which may appear insignificant, and unworthy of attention, in the single and obscure parish, or in any group of parishes, may be correctly estimated, and brought completely within the cognizance of the Legislature. For this purpose, therefore, in addition to the others which we have already laid down, we consider that uniformity of management would, in many cases, be essential to improvement, and to the permanency of any improved system. To the accomplishment of these objects, other measures, to which we shall shortly advert, appear to us to be requisite. By means, however, of the agency which we have proposed, by alterations of detail after detail, with which the Legislature could not occupy itself, bad practices may be weeded out of every district, good practices may be planted in every district. The precedent which we have adduced with relation to the control of savings banks and friendly societies illustrates this course of operations. Mr. Tidd Pratt states,

I invariably forward to all the institutions suggestions of the expediency of adopting rules which have been found to work beneficially; and I also warn them of mischievous results experienced from particular rules in other places. For example, with regard to the former, I found in one of the savings banks (the Exeter) a rule which allowed the trustees to apply to the member's benefit any portion of the deposits in case of insanity or imbecility; not one of the other savings banks possessed such a rule. The consequence was, that when a member became insane, they would have had no other mode to enable them to apply the member's money to his use than an application to the Lord Chancellor. Sometimes the sums to be applied were only 10*l*.: this rule I communicated by circular to the members of every savings bank, with a recommendation that it should be adopted: many of them have already adopted it; and I believe that in a short time it will be generally adopted. Where I find a good rule, I send it to all; and where I find a bad rule, I stop it in all, and the chances of finding good rules are just in proportion to the extent of the jurisdiction.

The central agency instituted by the Legislature for the control of the administration of the Poor Laws, would form a depositary of comprehensive information to guide the local officers in cases which, from their comparatively limited experience and knowledge, might appear to them to be, or which really were, anomalous. Applications in cases of this nature have already been made to the Commissioners. Their information would be received with the conviction of its being the best existing upon the subject. The last witness cited was asked, with reference to this point,

"Are you often consulted in cases of difficulty experienced by magistrates and others who are managers of the several societies within your supervision?—Yes; and by chairmen of quarter sessions, by Members of both Houses, under the supposition, as I conceive, that I am paid by salary, and that, being a servant of the Crown, they are entitled to apply to me in cases where they themselves feel difficulty. I invariably give the assistance asked, although it takes up a great deal of a professional man's time."

The chief remedy for the principal evil of the system, the increase of the number of the able-bodied paupers, having been shewn to be, their reception in a well-managed workhouse: we shall next consider by what means by which such workhouses can be provided, and the requisite management enforced.

The first difficulty arises from the small population of a large proportion of the parishes. Of the 15,535 parishes (including under that name townships maintaining their own poor) of England and Wales, there are 737 in which the population does not exceed 50 persons, 1,907 in which it does not exceed 100, and 6,681 in which it does not exceed 300. Few such parishes could support a workhouse, though they may have a poorhouse, a miserable abode, occupied rent free by three or four dissolute families, mutually corrupting each other. Even the parishes which are somewhat more populous, those containing from 300 to 800 inhabitants, and which amount to 5,353, in the few cases in which they possess an efficient management, obtain it at a disproportionate expense.

In such parishes, when overburthened with poor, we usually find the building called a workhouse occupied by 60 or 80 paupers, made up of a dozen or more neglected children (under the care, perhaps, of a pauper), about twenty or thirty able-bodied adult paupers of both sexes, and probably an equal number of aged and impotent persons, proper objects of relief. Amidst these the mothers of bastard children and prostitutes live without shame, and associate freely with the youth, who have also the examples and conversation of the frequent inmates of the county gaol, the poacher, the vagrant, the decayed beggar, and other characters of the worst description. To these may often be added a solitary blind person, one or two idiots, and not unfrequently are heard, from amongst the rest, the incessant ravings of some neglected lunatic. In such receptacles the sick poor are often immured.

In the former part of the Report we have given instances of the condition of the larger workhouses in the metropolis. The statements with respect to those in the provincial towns and in the rural districts, are equally unfavourable: we annex a very few instances.

Captain Pringle states that, in

Portsea Workhouse—In the women's yard all characters mix together, excepting that the very old have small rooms, in each room three or four; in these, and in the large day-room, in which were nurses with bastards, they had fires in August, and were cooking, making tea, &c. The general character of the house, both as to the persons of the paupers, their day-rooms and bed-rooms, is slovenly and dirty. The space so limited also, that in rooms containing from 20 to 30 beds, they were so close as merely to allow a person to pass between them.

In that at *Rumsey*, in which the inmates amounted to 48, they are farmed at the price of 3*s*. weekly, children included. There is no scale of diet, that being left to the farmer or contractor, who also employs the paupers where and how he pleases. The house was dirty, the old men particularly so; the younger men and boys were out at work. On inquiring for the boys' dormitory, I found they slept each with one of the men; the mistress said this was done to keep them quiet. The overseer, who accompanied me, and whose duty it was to inspect the house, stated that he was not aware of the placing men and boys to sleep together; that he never had any complaints either as to diet or beds, and he believed all were comfortable. And, as a further proof of the little attention paid by these constituted authorities to the duties confided to them, one of the girls, it appeared, had a child by the brother of the contractor. The overseer did not consider this as a circumstance of any importance. Nothing was said to the contractor, and his brother was still allowed to be about the house.

With regard to classification it may be observed, that in the small poor-houses, with the exception of Millbrook, I never found it more than nominal; and even in the larger poor-houses, classification and other regulations appeared never to be carried into effect in an efficient manner, for which the master was probably often less to blame than those under whose control he held his situation. The children are the sufferers from this neglect, as may be inferred from so large a portion turning out badly.

In the small agricultural parish of Tandridge, with a population of 478, a double tenement has been hired as a poor-house: in one of the rooms, in one bed, sleep the master with two boys, aged 15 and 12; in the other bed, a girl of 15 with a boy of 11; in another very small room, a man and wife and two children lie in one bed, and two children on the floor. The parish cage, the interior of which is about eight feet square, is used as the habitation of four persons, a man, his wife and two children; a grated opening in the wall admits light and air.

In Dover workhouse the number of inmates is 250; the average expense of diet 2*s*. 7¾*d*.; seven lunatics are confined here, two of whom are very dangerous, and are chained to their beds; one of them was lately at large in the yard, and had very nearly put one of the paupers to death, who was saved by the master coming in time to rescue him; in many workhouses in this county there are idiots and insane persons who are a great annoyance to the inmates in general; probably this nuisance will not exist much longer, as the asylum near Maidstone is nearly completed.

Mr. Osler, in his communication, gives the following instances of the condition of the workhouses in the vicinity of Falmouth:

Mabe House, a ruinous hovel, utterly unfit for the residence of a human being, two men, four women, three children; of whom four receive 8*s*. 9*d*.

weekly, and a man, his wife and three children have only shelter. A married couple occupy the same room with two women.

Mylor—Eight men, seventeen women, seven children, who are placed in the different rooms, supporting themselves either by an allowance of money from the parish, or by their own labour. A barber, who carries on business in the house, has his pole hung out at the door. No governor, or domestic authority of any description.

In such places when questions of the following tenor are put—Why is no labour found for the able-bodied? Why are not the children placed under proper tuition? Why is not proper care taken of the lunatic?—the usual answers are, "The parish is too poor to pay for a keeper;" "We cannot keep a schoolmaster for so few children;" "To provide a superintendent to keep half-a-dozen or a dozen of men at work would be too heavy a charge." Even the superintendence of the whole of these various classes, and the management of the house, is often found a pecuniary burthen disproportionately heavy; and the parish officers attempt to diminish it by confiding the whole to one who is in reality and sometimes avowedly a pauper.

Constantine House—Ten men, nineteen women, two children. The governor has been dismissed for the sake of economy, and an infirm old pauper regulates the diet and keeps the accounts. All rooms, except the kitchen, close, dirty and offensive. Bedsteads, clumsy wooden ones. Men's dormitory, their sitting-room, very low, with windows too small for ventilation; excessively dirty, and an abominable musty smell. The fish dinners are cooked here. House appeared not to have been white-washed from time immemorial. Two men slept in the women's rooms, but the new overseer expressed an intention to correct these evils.

The Rev. Peyton Blackiston, the curate of Lymington, Hants, states—

It appears to me that parochial workhouses are in most places very inefficient, owing to their want of a proper and extensive subdivision, so that the bad may be completely separated from the good. All the parish officers with whom I have conversed upon the subject have at once acknowledged the evil; but they say that the parishes could not afford the expense of such subdivisions.

The result of my inquiries and observations respecting the moral and religious education of the children in the parochial workhouses is, that it is greatly neglected. Even in the workhouse of Lymington there was no such instruction previous to the year 1831, with the exception of about an hour a day, in which the girl who cooked taught the children to read. This has also contributed to make them turn out badly. At this moment the generality of parochial workhouses in Hampshire do not supply any effective religious and moral instruction; the children cannot do even the coarsest needlework in a creditable manner, nor are they practised in that kind of work, which, as domestic servants, they would be required to perform. I dare say the parish officers will endeavour to gloss over the matter, and from shame would make it appear that the moral and religious instruction of the parish children was well attended to; but as an eye-witness of many parochial workhouses, and having conversed with many of my brother clergy on the subject, I can state that such is not the case. In the workhouse of Lymington parish, which is one certainly of the most improved provincial towns I know, a school was established in 1831, when an able woman was appointed to give instructions in reading and religious duties, and to teach and superintend needle work. The advantages were most striking. It is almost past belief, that about two months ago the vestry discontinued the schoolmistress, although her salary was only £.10. per annum and her dinner.

Even in the larger workhouses internal subdivisions do not afford the means of classification, where the inmates dine in the same rooms, or meet or see each other in the ordinary business of the place. In the largest houses, containing from eight hundred to a thousand inmates, where there is comparatively good order and, in many respects, superior management, it is almost impossible to prevent the formation and extension of vicious connections. Inmates who see each other, though prevented from communicating in the house, often become associates when they meet out of it. It is found almost impracticable to subject all the various classes within the same house to an appropriate treatment. One part of a class of adults often so closely resembles a part of another class, as to make any distinction in treatment appear arbitrary and capricious to those who are placed in the inferior class, and to create discontents, which the existing authority is too feeble to suppress, and so much complexity as to render the object attainable only by great additional expense and remarkable skill. Much, however, has been accomplished in some of the existing houses; but much more, it appears to us, may be effected and at a less expense by the measures which we proceed to suggest.

At least four classes are necessary—1. The aged and really impotent; 2. The children; 3. The able-bodied females; 4. The able-bodied males. Of whom we trust that the two latter will be the least numerous classes. It appears to us that both the requisite classification and the requisite superintendance may be better obtained in separate buildings than under a single roof. If effected in the latter mode, large buildings must be erected, since few of the existing buildings are of the requisite size or arrangement, and as very different qualities, both moral and intellectual, are required for the management of such dissimilar classes, each class must have its

separate superintendant. Nothing would be saved therefore in superintendance, and much expense must be incurred in buildings.

If, however, a separate building is assigned to each class, the existing
workhouses might, in most cases, be made use of. For this purpose the
parishes possessing these houses must, for certain purposes, be incorporated. By these means four parishes, each of which has at present no
means of classification, might at once obtain the means of the most effectual classification; and though so small a number of parishes as four might
be sufficient for an incorporation, it is obvious that a much larger number
might unite and obtain the advantages of wholesale management and good
superintendence, not only without any increase, but with a great diminution of expense.

The salary of the masters of separate workhouses in towns does not
usually exceed fifty or sixty guineas per annum; the aggregate expenses of
management of four such workhouses may be stated to be two hundred
or two hundred and forty guineas, and yet no special provision is usually
made for the superintendance of the labour of the able-bodied, nor for the
education of the children. Under a system of combined management a
less salary would probably suffice for the person who superintended the
poor-house or receptacle for the old, whilst a larger salary might be given
to a person of appropriate qualifications to act as taskmaster or superintendant of the workhouse, properly so called, for the reception of the
able-bodied, and also to a person properly qualified to act as a schoolmaster. Each class might thus receive an appropriate treatment; the old
might enjoy their indulgences without torment from the boisterous; the
children be educated and the able-bodied subjected to such courses of
labour and discipline as will repel the indolent and vicious. The principle
of separate and appropriate management has been carried into imperfect
execution, in the cases of lunatics, by means of lunatic asylums; and we
have no doubt that, with relation to these objects, the blind, and similar
cases, it might be carried into more complete execution under extended
incorporations acting with the aid of the central Board.

Apprehensions are frequently expressed of the evil consequences from
congregrating "large bodies of sturdy paupers together in workhouses."
Such consequences have not ensued in the instances of the dispauperised
parishes, and we believe that the most effectual means of preventing them
is the classification which we propose. It is natural, indeed, for those who

judge from the conduct of the able-bodied paupers in small classes under the existing system to anticipate that in larger classes their conduct will be proportionably worse, and that the difficulty of controlling them will be increased and could be overcome only in edifices constructed for the purpose. We should admit this opinion to have weight, if the able-bodied paupers were brought together in larger classes, without being placed under better management; the probable mischief of an *ill*-regulated and *idle* class being proportionate to the chances of there being found within the class persons able to give it a mischievous direction, and all other things remaining the same, these chances are of course increased by the increase of the class; but by good management those chances are almost annihilated. The evidence which we have received appears to establish that continued tumult on the part of able-bodied paupers is conclusive proof of inexperience or incapacity on the parts of those charged with their management. The testimony upon this subject of Mr. Mott, a witness of the most extensive practical experience of any witness examined under this Commission, is corroborated by that of others.

"The refractory poor," he states, "occasion great mischief and confusion in all workhouses; but the mischief arises more from the bad example of the *few*, than from the *many*, for all my experience has shown that the number of refractory paupers is not great, as compared with the gross number of paupers in any parish or district, perhaps not much above five per cent., certainly not ten per cent.; and the conduct even of persons of this class, must be attributed to the inducements offered by the present defective system, rather than to any innate disposition to act unlawfully. They know that their customary allowances and the rules of management are *discretionary* in the breasts of the parish officers; they have daily proof that the most refractory frequently obtain their ends, and get their condition 'bettered,' partly through the fear or dislike of the officers to come in contact with such characters, and partly from a desire of the stipendiary manager to save himself trouble, well knowing that a complaint to the magistrates is only a waste of time, because the punishment awarded is in fact no punishment whatever. These refractory characters are generally the most expert work-people (of those who apply for relief) under proper guidance. If I had a given quantity of work to get done in a certain time, by paupers, I should say to the parish officers, 'Let me have your most refractory characters;' as I find that with mildness and persuasion but with a determined conduct, constant superintendance, and suitable encouragement, they may be brought to do much more work than other paupers. They are not to be calculated upon as permanent paupers under a good system, and I do believe that to a man they would run to steady industry, if compelled by superior authority to conform to regulations rendering such industry preferable."

The success of the management of various institutions in the metropolis which give no partial relief, such as the Philanthropic Society, where the children of criminals are educated and brought up to useful trades; the Refuge for the Destitute, in which young persons who have been discharged from prison are supplied with the means of instruction and reformation; and the Guardian Society, in which females who have become outcasts from society are provided with a temporary asylum and suitable employment until their conduct affords assurances of their amendment, are instances of what might be done by the good management of separate classes of the existing paupers.

These societies take for their subjects persons trained up in vice, and are stated, in a large proportion of cases, to reclaim them. The children who enter an ordinary workhouse, quit it, if they ever quit it, corrupted where they were well disposed, and hardened where they were vicious.

The circumstances which appear to conduce to the success of the excellent institutions to which we have referred (and to which we might add the Asylums for the Indigent Blind, the Schools for the Deaf and Dumb, the Marine Society's Schools), appear to be—first, that by classification of the objects of relief, the appropriate course of treatment is better ascertained, and its application and the general management rendered less difficult: secondly, that the co-operation of persons of leisure and information is obtained. The institutions for females are generally superintended by ladies' committees.

The following extracts from some evidence given by Mrs. Park, wife of Mr. Adam Park, surgeon, Gravesend, the brother of the celebrated traveller, will serve to show that under good arrangements much voluntary service might be made available in a great proportion of the workhouses throughout the country.

"About two years ago the state of our workhouse attracted my attention, from the condition in which I learned that it was during my inquiries respecting Mr. Park's patients, he being then the surgeon of the parish. There were then fifty females in the workhouse. Of these, twenty-seven were young stout active women, who were never employed in doing any thing whatever. There were five of these young and able women who were accustomed to go to bed in the forenoon, solely to pass off the time. There was no separation of the sexes during the day, and the most frightful demoralization was the consequence. Four old females did the whole of the work of cooking, and cleaning the house.

"The younger females, the children, were brought up much in the same way; they were educated by an exceedingly ignorant, ill-conducted man, a pauper, who acted as the parish schoolmaster. These females were brought up in the same school with the boys, and very great disorders prevailed.

"The old females were also very ill regulated. I found that they made it a practice to send the children to the public-house for spirits. How they obtained the money was a mystery which I have never been able to penetrate. On the whole, the workhouse appeared to me, from all I saw and all I could learn, a frightful and increasing source of demoralization to the labouring classes, and of burthens to them in common with the higher classes.

"Seeing this, I got several ladies to form a committee, and we tendered our services to the churchwardens and the parish officers to educate the children, and to make the young and able-bodied paupers of our own sex work a certain number of hours a day, and conform to industrious and religious habits.

"The first object was to bring all the inmates to more industrious habits. Instead of four old persons always doing all the work in the house, our intention was, that the requisite number of persons should perform the cooking and other work in turn, so that these young women might learn household work, and form useful domestic habits, instead of bad habits and immorality."

The exertions of these ladies were greatly impeded by the parish officers; much good was nevertheless accomplished. The witness states, that

"The elder paupers were taught knitting stockings, and the younger females needlework. Before we went to the workhouse they were badly clothed, and some of them were almost in a state of rags and nakedness. We wished to have the whole clothed in one way, with gowns of blue linsey-woolsey, check aprons, dark handkerchiefs, and close white caps. After violent opposition from the mistress of the house and the females themselves, this was acceded to. Hitherto they had purchased the most gaudy prints for the females, and ready-made slop shirts for the men in the house, whilst the young women were lying in bed idle. One of the paupers, a girl of 18 years of age, who refused to work, was dressed in a dashing print-dress of red and green, with *gigot* sleeves, a silk band, a large golden or gilt buckle, long gilt earrings, and a lace-cap, turned up in front with bright ribbons, in the fashion of the day, and a high comb under the cap, and abundance of curls. A general order was given that the hair of the females should be braided, and put under their caps, and no curls or curl-papers seen. We got the whole of the young females clothed in the manner we designed in two months during the first year. This was done by their own labour, under the instructions we gave them. The benefit of this dress was, that whenever they went out of the workhouse they were known and liable to observation, and could not act as they had been accustomed to act when they could not be distinguished. In the next place, the parish saved money. They were thus clothed comfortably for 10s. each; the clothing consisting of one chemise, one apron, one cap, gown and petticoat, stockings, handkerchief, and all for 10s.

"After that we procured them needle-work, in which we had no difficulty, though we were opposed in the first instance, under the notion that we should injure the National School, where work is taken in. It was supposed also that it would injure industrious poor people in the neighbourhood. But according to the statements of the National School Society, the amount of the labour done was not diminished. Neither could we ascertain that any industrious people out of the house had been injured by it; we never had any complaint, nor ever heard of one from any industrious people. I believe the fact to be, that a great part of the work we procured was work created, or which would not have been done had it not been taken in at the workhouse. But it would have been much better that the work which might be done in wealthy families should be done in the workhouse, that these paupers should be occupied usefully, and instructed. The ladies paid great attention to the work, and employed one of the most intelligent and active of the inmates of the house as the general superintendant. The work was remarked for its neatness; no slovenly or indifferent work was permitted to go out; and the committee were so particular, that the instruction they received was necessarily much better than that which they would have obtained in the houses of their own parents. One effect of this partial discipline in the house was, that in almost two months about one-half of the workers left. Some of them called themselves widows; others said that they did not come in to work; they merely came in until they could accommodate themselves, until they could get themselves another situation; but they would not remain to work, indeed: that they would not; they would take a room and keep themselves when they were out of place sooner than put on a dress, and be made to work! One refractory person said, 'The poor were not going to be oppressed by work.'

"If you had been seconded in your exertions, and been allowed to carry into effect the alterations which you thought desirable, what further effects do you believe, judging from your experience, would have been practicable?— In the first place, we should have had the hours of work at least doubled. I am well convinced that the workhouse might, as regards females, be made a school of industry, and a place of wholesome restraint, instead of a school of vice. Whilst no one would come to it under the influence of the inducements afforded by indolence, those who must necessarily come there, orphans, and the great numbers of young people who have been born on the parish might be so instructed as to be made superior servants and good nurses, and superior wives of working men. In the first place, the workhouse affords the means of giving to females instruction in household work and in domestic economy, which at present is their great want, and which so frequently occasions the ruin and misery of labouring men when they take wives from this class. That which is done by the Guardian Society in London, might be done in every workhouse throughout the kingdom. If matrons, with proper qualifications, were appointed, they might conduct the system, and might obtain the assistance of the ladies of the vicinity. I was told at the outset that ladies could not be got to form a committee, but I found no difficulty whatever in getting a committee of the age and qualifications to command respect. The household work, scouring, cleaning, washing, plain cooking, needlework, knitting, mending and making up carpets, and economical industry might under such a system be taught in a much higher degree than they could be learned in a cottage, or even in the house of a person of the middle classes. They might also receive superior instruction in another respect; they might be well qualified to act as nurses when sickness occurred in the families of their employers or in their own families. There are always poor people sick in the workhouse, and they might be usefully taught to wait upon the sick people. There are very few females capable of acting as nurses; in fact, it requires good instruction of a nature which might be given by the physician who attends the workhouse. The ladies' committee might maintain a very high order of domestic instruction in these places; and the children of misfortune, who are now a prey to every vice, might be good servants, and in every respect good members of society. This is, in fact, accomplished by the ladies of the Guardian Society in London.

"Did you attempt to make any classification in the house?—In such a house classification was nearly impossible. We did on some occasions separate the very old from the young, which was deemed by the old a very great blessing. Some attempt was made to separate the very bad females from the others who were less depraved, but we never could effect it. In short, it appears to me that the only classification which could be made, would be by placing them in separate houses, which might be effected, I am sure, without any addition to the present number of houses. When I look at the parishes around here and their houses, I see no difficulty whatever in making a good classification of the inmates, provided they were under one general management. The persons who are placed as superintendants should have no local interests, and therefore should not be locally appointed. So surely as they are, so surely will there be disorder. The rules will not be so rigidly applied as they ought to be from the numbers in the house who are connected with them or known to them. The mischief which we find to result from this exercise of partiality goes beyond the violation of some rules, and the weakening of all others, in the ferment and discontent and disorder excited in the minds of the other paupers by the injustice done by the exercise of this partiality. If the class were large, as it would be for a time, from such a district, it might be worth while to employ as the superintendent of the house for the females a person of education and respectability. Such persons as the widows of non-commissioned officers would be extremely glad to accept such situations; and they might also be made acceptable to such persons as the widows of poor clergymen, and it would be cheap to the public in the end to obtain the services of such persons. They would be incapable of the low cunning and petty jobbing which exist at present."

The different effects of different modes of education and treatment upon the same descriptions of persons are strikingly exemplified in some portions of the evidence collected under this Commission, in which it is shown that whilst nearly the whole of the children of one parish where their education and training is neglected, become thieves or otherwise pests of society, nearly the whole of the children of another parish where better care of them is taken, are rendered industrious and valuable members of the community. In the latter case much of the beneficial results may be ascribed to the attention of persons of education who visited and superintended the schools. One great advantage of the classification obtainable by means of a combination of workhouses would be, that the aid of voluntary associations or local committees, of the class of persons who have conducted useful public institutions, might be more extensively obtained, to superintend the education of the workhouse children, as well as of the other classes of paupers adverted to by the lady whose testimony we have cited.

Although our evidence does not countenance the apprehension that, under a good system of management, a large proportion of the existing able-bodied paupers would continue permanently dependant on the poor rates, it appears that in the first instance the chief arrangements must be made with reference to this class of paupers. But we do not apprehend that in many instances new workhouses would be requisite for their reception. It is another of the advantages held out by the aggregation of paupers from a district for the purpose of classification, that the separate classes of the proper objects of relief might be accommodated temporarily in ordinary dwelling houses, and it is a fortunate district in which there are no empty tenements available for their reception. The tenements belonging to the parish might be rendered available for the separate accommodation of one class of paupers, and the poor-house itself for that of the able-bodied; and on the whole it appears from the evidence, that although a consider-able proportion of the parishes are without workhouses, there are few *districts* in which, by combined management, and under good regulations, the existing workhouse-room would not suffice.

By assigning one class of paupers to each of the houses comprehended in an incorporation, a greater number of persons might be received within each house. In small districts there are considerable fluctuations of the numbers of persons in each class; in the workhouse of a single parish the rooms appropriated for the reception of the sick must often be empty; in a house for the reception of the sick from a number of parishes, the absence of patients from one parish would be met by an influx from another, and a more steady average number maintained, and so with the other classes of inmates. The rooms left empty by these fluctuations or reserved for emergencies under the existing management, cannot without great incon-venience be immediately appropriated to the use of the redundant class. If any rooms on the female side of the house be left unoccupied, they can-not be readily appropriated to the use of an extra number of male paupers. The witness last cited states—

"In Lambeth, under the present arrangement, 800 is as great a number as we can reasonably calculate upon accommodating; whereas, if the whole workhouse was appropriated to the reception of only one class of persons, from 900 to 1,000 might be fairly accommodated. If you add to this the room that would be obtained by the discharge of those of the *present* inmates who *would not* submit to the restraint of strict workhouse regulations, I think ample accommodation might be made for all those who *would* avail themselves of the workhouse dietary and accommodation, when their money allowance was discontinued."

Although such is the general tenor of the evidence, we cannot state that there may not be some districts where new workhouses would be found requisite, but we have no doubt that where this does occur the erection of appropriate edifices though apparently expensive would ultimately be found economical. Under a system of district management the workhouses might be supplied under one contract at wholesale prices. Mr. Mott states, that if 500 persons cost £.10 per head, or £.5,000; 1,000 persons would cost only £.9 per head, or £.9,000. He also states, that there would be no more difficulty in managing five or six combined workhouses than five or six separate wards or rooms in one house. Considerable economy would also be practicable in combined workhouses, by varying the nature of the supplies. In the smaller workhouses the children receive nearly the same diet as the adults; if they were separated they might receive a diet both cheaper and more wholesome.

To EFFECT THESE PURPOSES WE RECOMMEND THAT THE CENTRAL BOARD BE EMPOWERED TO CAUSE ANY NUMBER OF PARISHES WHICH THEY MAY THINK CONVENIENT TO BE INCORPORATED FOR THE PURPOSE OF WORKHOUSE MANAGEMENT, AND FOR PROVIDING NEW WORKHOUSES WHERE NECESSARY, TO DECLARE THEIR WORKHOUSES TO BE THE COMMON WORKHOUSES OF THE INCORPORATED DISTRICT, AND TO ASSIGN TO THOSE WORKHOUSES SEPARATE CLASSES OF POOR, THOUGH COMPOSED OF THE POOR OF DISTINCT PARISHES, EACH DISTINCT PARISH PAYING TO THE SUPPORT OF THE PERMANENT WORKHOUSE ESTABLISHMENT, IN PROPORTION TO THE AVERAGE AMOUNT OF THE EXPENCE.

* * *

One of the most prominent suggestions of those who have written on Poor Law amendment, is compelling the adoption of a uniform and well arranged system of accounts, a provision which they often appear to consider a sufficient check on peculation. There can be no doubt that arrangements to insure completeness, clearness, uniformity and publicity of parochial accounts are as requisite in this as in any other department of public administration.

WE RECOMMEND, THEREFORE, THAT THE CENTRAL BOARD BE EMPOW-
ERED AND REQUIRED TO TAKE MEASURES FOR THE GENERAL ADOPTION OF
A COMPLETE, CLEAR, AND, AS FAR AS MAY BE PRACTICABLE, UNIFORM
SYSTEM OF ACCOUNTS.

* * *

WE FURTHER RECOMMEND . . . THAT THE CENTRAL BOARD BE EM-
POWERED TO INCORPORATE PARISHES FOR THE PURPOSE OF APPOINTING
AND PAYING PERMANENT OFFICERS, AND FOR THE EXECUTION OF WORKS
OF PUBLIC LABOUR.

We must not, however, conceal our fear, that the appointment of efficient permanent officers will be difficult. Those only who have a full knowledge of the peculiar nature of the duties to be performed, would be
qualified to judge of the fitness of the agents to perform them; a knowledge
which, as it does not influence the daily practice, can scarcely be presumed
to exist in the districts where abusive systems prevail. In the dispauperized
parishes the appointment of fitting officers was found to be attended with
great difficulty, and was rarely accomplished without opposition. The
person appointed as the permanent overseer and master of the workhouse
at Hatfield had been a drill-serjeant and paymaster-serjeant in the Coldstream Guards. One of the witnesses states—

"That the parish was entirely indebted for the change to the talents and personal energy applied to the work by the Marquis of Salisbury, and to the
peculiar personal qualifications of the person appointed by him to serve the
office of permanent overseer. This appointment would never have been made
had the matter been left in the hands of the rate-payers at large. Many of them
openly said that a stranger ought not to be brought into the parish; that they
ought to appoint a person from amongst themselves, some poor person, who
wanted a comfortable home; when the duties of the office required a person of
peculiar firmness and habits of command, and were such as ninety-nine out
of a hundred in the parish would have been unable to execute."

The success of this appointment occasioned similar appointments to
be made in some adjacent parishes where the larger proprietors attempted
to amend the administration. The Hon. and Rev. Robert Eden states,
that in Hertingfordbury,

"A permanent overseer was appointed, who was also to collect the rates in
the adjoining parishes of Bayford and Little Berkhampstead, and to keep the
accounts, and superintendent the men employed at parish work. He had been
a pay-serjeant in the Guards; his appointment was opposed chiefly on the
ground of his being a stranger."

The Rev. Ralph Clutton, the curate of Welwyn, states—

"A permanent overseer has been appointed, who is also the governor of the poor-house; he was serjeant in the Coldstream Guards, a married man, and not a parishioner. It is to the efficiency of himself and his wife that the success of the undertaking thus far must in a great measure be attributed. His chief qualifications are firmness, order, clearness and accuracy in his accounts, unconquerable resolution and integrity, and on the part of his wife, extraordinary cleanliness, and a sincere desire to better the condition of those (especially the young) under her care."

The wife herself stated "that the selection of her husband had excited great displeasure, because it was considered that none but a parishioner ought to have been appointed." In Watham, where some improvements were carried into effect—

"A permanent overseer has been appointed, who is also governor of the workhouse, but is not a parishioner; having been in the army, his qualifications for the discipline and management of the workhouse, by the aid of that order, regularity and system in which he had been there initiated, together with a perfect ability as to the arrangement and keeping of the accounts are his merits. Dissatisfaction was manifested to this appointment: the principal objections were his being a stranger, and not a parishioner."

The statement of Mr. Richard Gregory, of Spitalfields, is characteristic of the circumstances under which the permanent officers are frequently appointed in the town parishes:

"Might not paid and responsible officers be elected by the parishioners? He answers, No; I think you would never get such officers well filled unless it was by accident. The people have no conception of what sort of men are requisite to perform properly the duties of a parish officer. If such a situation were vacant, what sort of a man would apply for it? Why, some decayed tradesman; some man who had got a very large family, and had been 'unfortunate in business,' which, in ninety-nine cases out of a hundred, means a man who has not had prudence or capacity to manage his own affairs; and this circumstance is usually successful in any canvass for a parish situation to manage the affairs of the public. Men who have before been in office for the parish would obtain a preference. And what sort of men are those who would be likely to be at liberty to accept a vacant situation? The situations of overseer and church-warden are by some considered situations of dignity; and dignity always attracts fools. I have known numbers of small tradesmen who were attracted by 'the dignity of the office,' and succeeded in getting made overseers and church-wardens. Their elevation was their downfall. They have not given their minds to their own business as before. The consequence of this was that they have lost their business and have been ruined. Now and then a good man of business will be desirous of taking office when he thinks he is slighted, or has had an affront put upon him by being overlooked; but in general, any man in decent business must know, if he has the brains of a goose, that it will be much better for him, in a pecuniary point of view, to pay the fine than serve. I could name from fifteen to twenty people in our parish, who have been entirely ruined by being made churchwardens. These would be the people who would succeed best in parochial or district elections; for the people would say of any one of them, 'Poor man, he has ruined himself by serving a parish office, and the only recompense we can give him is to put him in a paid office.' This always has been the general course of parish elections, and I have no doubt would always continue to be so. There is infinitely more favouritism in parish appointments than in government appointments. In appointments by the government there is frequently some notion of fitness; but in the case of parish appointments, fitness is out of the question. When I was the treasurer of the watch department of the parish, I took great interest in the management of the police of the district, and determined to make it efficient. You would conceive that the inhabitants would have been so guided by their own apparent interests, as to get active men appointed, but I had solicitations from some of the first and most respectable houses in the parish to take their old and decayed servants and put them on the watch. I had also applications from the parish officers to put men upon the watch who were in the workhouse. As I was determined to make the police efficient, I resolutely resisted all these applications."

It is also clear that such officers should be selected as would not be biassed by local interests or partialities. The most fitting persons must often, as in the instances we have cited, be sought for in distant districts, and *cœteris paribus*, would be preferable to persons within the same districts.

These premises appear to lead to a conclusion that the Central Board ought to be empowered to appoint the permanent and salaried officers in all parishes, or at least in those which they should incorporate. But we do not venture such a recommendation. In the first place, because we doubt the power of a single Board to select a sufficient number of well-qualified persons; secondly, because such a duty would occupy too much of their time and attention; and, thirdly, because the patronage, though really a painful incumbrance to them, would be a source of public jealousy. But believing that, after all, more will depend, as more always has depended, on the administration of the law than on the words of its enactments, and that the good or bad administration will mainly rest on the selection of the inferior administrators, we think that no security for good appointments should be neglected, and no means of preventing the effects of bad appointments omitted. We think that the first object might be aided, if the Commissioners were directed to prescribe some general qualifications, in the absence of which no person should be eligible as a salaried officer, and we think that the number of competent persons who must in time come under their observation would enable them frequently to assist parishes and incorporations by recommending proper candidates; we also think that they might to a great degree both aid and support the well-disposed, and prevent the continuance in office of improper persons, if they were invested with the power of removing them. Some of the ablest of the permanent officers who have been examined under the authority of this Commission, have urged that they ought to be immediately responsible to the authority whose regulations they are to enforce; that it ought to be obvious that they really have no discretion, that the rule of duty is inflexible, and that, if they violate or neglect it, suspension or dismissal must be the consequence. If the permanent officers continue responsible only to the annual officers or to the vestry, a screen will be interposed between the Central Board and the actual administrators of relief, which will encourage and protect every form of malversation.

WE RECOMMEND, THEREFORE, THAT THE CENTRAL BOARD BE DIRECTED TO STATE THE GENERAL QUALIFICATIONS WHICH SHALL BE NECESSARY TO CANDIDATES FOR PAID OFFICES CONNECTED WITH THE RELIEF OF THE POOR, TO RECOMMEND TO PARISHES AND INCORPORATIONS PROPER PERSONS TO ACT AS PAID OFFICERS, AND TO REMOVE ANY PAID OFFICERS WHOM THEY SHALL THINK UNFIT FOR THEIR SITUATIONS.

* * *

A large proportion of those who become in any way chargeable to the parish, are incapable of self-control, or of altering their habits and making any reservation of money when once it is in their possession, although they acknowledge their obligations, and are satisfied to perform them.

It appears that from the Chelsea pensioners there are about 3,500 quarterly assignments or 14,000 annual assignments of pensions to parish officers, and 1,480 pensions annually claimed by virtue of magistrates' orders, in cases in which pensioners have allowed their wives or families to become chargeable to the parish; and that from the Greenwich out-pensioners, 1,200 pensions amounting to 12,530*l.* were attached and recovered last year. The parish officers examined upon this subject agree, that but for the provisions of the Act, the whole amount of these pensions would be lost to the parish, and would be injuriously wasted by the pensioners, from their incapacity to take care of large sums of money.

Any collection from the labourer himself must be weekly, and the labour of collecting these small instalments would often prevent its being undertaken; but if wages were attached in the hands of the master, the payments might be at longer intervals, or in liquidation at once of the whole demand.

Tradesmen declare that they should feel it no grievance to be compelled to make reservations of wages to satisfy such demands, and that whatever money was recovered, would be recovered from the gin shop. The more important object of the measure is the re-imposing motives to frugality on those who possess the means of being frugal; on this account we consider that it would be deserving of adoption, though the greater number of labourers defeated the claims upon them by absconding. By a tolerably vigilant administration of the proposed law, however, much money might be recovered from them. A large proportion of the labour of the classes in question is of a nature not to be found every where. A tailor may run away, but a brickmaker can only get work in the brick-fields, where he may be found. During the period when the labourer is in receipt of full wages, if he spend them he will have in prospect the necessity of absconding in search of work at the commencement of another season; and if subjection during the interval to strict workhouse regulation be comprehended in the view, there can be little doubt that he will often be impelled to have recourse to the savings banks to avoid the inconvenience.

It appears then that if power were given to parish officers of attaching wages, or of ordering the reservation of such instalments as they deemed expedient for the liquidation of debts due to the parish, a proportion of those debts would be recovered.

We are further of opinion that such a measure might be made still more useful if the principle on which the 29th, 30th, 31st, and 32d clauses of the 59 Geo. III, c. 12, are founded were acted on more extensively. The 29th clause enables the officer to whom it appears that the applicant for relief might, but for his extravagance, neglect, or wilful misconduct have been able to maintain himself or to support his family, to advance money to him weekly, or otherwise, by way of loan. It appears from our evidence that in some places this clause has been acted upon beneficially, but that in general little use is made of it, partly because a person who has not been guilty of extravagance, neglect, or wilful misconduct is excluded from its operation, and partly because the existence of the clause is not notorious. It appears to us advisable that, under regulations to be framed by the

Central Board, parishes should be empowered to treat any relief afforded to the able-bodied, or to their families, and any expenditure in the work-house or otherwise incurred on their account, as a loan, and recoverable, not only in the mode pointed out by the clause to which we have referred, but also by attachment of their wages, in a way resembling that in which the 30th, 31st, and 32d clauses of the same Act direct the attachment of pensions and seamen's wages.

WE THEREFORE RECOMMEND, THAT UNDER REGULATIONS TO BE FRAMED BY THE CENTRAL BOARD, PARISHES BE EMPOWERED TO TREAT ANY RELIEF AFFORDED TO THE ABLE-BODIED OR TO THEIR FAMILIES, AND ANY EXPENDITURE IN THE WORKHOUSES OR OTHERWISE INCURRED ON THEIR ACCOUNT, AS A LOAN, AND RECOVERABLE NOT ONLY BY THE MEANS GIVEN BY THE 29TH SECTION OF THE 59 GEO. III, C. 12, BUT ALSO BY AT-TACHMENT OF THEIR SUBSEQUENT WAGES, IN A MODE RESEMBLING THAT POINTED OUT IN THE 30th, 31st AND 32d SECTIONS OF THAT ACT.

In our recommendation of the prohibition of partial relief to the families of the able-bodied, we proposed that relief by apprenticing should, to a certain extent, be excepted from that prohibition. In the instructions given by us to our Assistant Commissioners, we directed them to ascer-tain "the practice in the different parishes as to the apprenticing of poor children, inquiring to what class of persons they are apprenticed, and whether such persons take them voluntarily or by compulsion, and if the latter, according to what principle they are distributed; whether any and what care is taken to see that they are well treated and taught; and whether there are any grounds for supposing that a power to bind for less than seven years would be expedient."

But we regret to say that we have received less information on this subject than on any other. The most important is that collected by Captain Chapman and Mr. Villiers, but even that is contradictory, and if it were consistent, too meagre to afford grounds for legislation. It is a mode of relief expressly pointed out by the 43d of Elizabeth, and so much inter-woven with the habits of the people in many districts, that we should hesitate, even if its evils were much more clearly ascertained, and even if we believed that those evils will not be much diminished by the alteration which we shall propose respecting settlement, to recommend its abolition until it has been made the subject of further inquiry, and until the effects of the measures now likely to be introduced have been ascertained by experience.

At the same time we think it probable, perhaps we might say certain, that further inquiry will show that the laws respecting the relief to be afforded by means of apprenticeship are capable of improvement, particularly those portions of them which render the reception of a parish apprentice compulsory.

WE RECOMMEND, THEREFORE, THAT THE CENTRAL BOARD BE EMPOWERED TO MAKE SUCH REGULATIONS AS THEY SHALL THINK FIT RESPECTING THE RELIEF TO BE AFFORDED BY APPRENTICING CHILDREN, AND THAT AT A FUTURE PERIOD, WHEN THE EFFECT OF THE PROPOSED ALTERATIONS SHALL HAVE BEEN SEEN, THE CENTRAL BOARD BE REQUIRED TO MAKE A SPECIAL INQUIRY INTO THE OPERATION OF THE LAWS RESPECTING THE APPRENTICING CHILDREN AT THE EXPENSE OF PARISHES, AND INTO THE OPERATION OF THE REGULATIONS IN THAT RESPECT WHICH THE BOARD SHALL HAVE ENFORCED.

On the subject of vagrancy a large mass of evidence is contained in the Appendix, particularly in the reports of Mr. Bishop, Mr. Codd, Capt. Chapman, and Mr. Henderson. It appears from this evidence, that vagrancy has actually been converted into a trade, and not an unprofitable one; and it also appears, that the severe and increasing burthen arises from the vagrants by trade, not from those on account of destitution. We state in proof of this, and the statement is more valuable as it points out the remedy as well as the cause of the evil, that in those few districts in which the relief has been such as only the really destitute will accept, the resort of vagrants has ceased, or been so much diminished as to become only a trifling inconvenience. But it appears vain to expect the remedy from detailed statutory provisions. The tendency of legislation respecting the poor to aggravate the evils which it was intended to cure, a tendency which we have so often remarked, is strikingly exemplified in that portion of it which respects vagrancy. The early statutes attempted to repress it by severity. "This part of our history," says Dr. Burn, "looks like the history of the savages in America. Almost all severities have been exercised against vagrants except scalping; and as one severity fell short, it seemed naturally to follow that a greater was necessary." But such was their effect that every successive preamble admits the inefficiency of the former law down to the 1 & 2 Geo. 4, c. 64, which recites, "that the provisions theretofore made, and then in force, relative to the apprehending and passing of vagrants, were productive of great expense, and that great frauds and abuses were committed in the execution thereof"; and to the 5 Geo. 4, c. 83, which declares that it is expedient to make further provision for the suppression of vagrancy. Nor has the last-mentioned Act been more successful than those which preceded it. As one among many instances in which its provisions have been perverted, we will mention the effect of the 15th clause, which allows the visiting justices of prisons to grant a certificate, or other instrument, enabling any person discharged from prison to receive relief on his route to his place of settlement. The intention of the clause was to enable prisoners, after having undergone their punishment or trial, to go *from* prison to their own homes without temptation to further crime. The effect has been "for the benefit of the pass" to convey *into* prisons paupers and families of paupers, as if the legislature intended that they and their children should have all the terrors of a prison obliterated from their minds, and receive instruction in the worst schools of vice; as if provision ought to be made to increase the stock of juvenile delinquents, already more numerous in England than in any other European country. By what foresight could the benevolent author of this clause have guarded against such an administration of the enactment as that which one of the witnesses, a gaoler thus describes?

"It is a melancholy thing that poor people are sent into prison as vagrants that they may be passed home. There is now a mother, a widow with five children under my care; the boys are from five to fifteen years of age. The mother was committed, not for any crime, but having been found sitting in the open air. Now what, I beg to ask, can be the effect of sending these children with their mother to a gaol? What can they not learn? In general vagrants are told that they are sent to prison, not for their punishment, but for their benefit. Prisons should not in any case, as I humbly conceive, be held out as places where people are to be *benefited*. They are now looked upon as places of *relief*, and the large class of vagrants are told that they are sent to prison avowedly for their advantage."

"When the law [says another witness] was made restricting pauper passes to Scotch and Irish, very few for a time came to Westmorland or Cumberland; but the vagrants soon found that they might easily resume their trade by swearing they belonged to those countries; and the expense became as large as ever. When this again was checked by making the contract for a fixed sum annually, to convey all paupers with passes by cart through the country, the number of vagrants calling themselves discharged prisoners (and therefore not subject to these regulations) began to increase, and has continued to do so progressively."

Feeling convinced that vagrancy will cease to be a burthen, if the relief given to vagrants is such as only the really destitute will accept; feeling convinced that this cannot be effected unless the system is general; and also convinced that no enactments to be executed by parochial officers will in all parishes be rigidly adhered to, unless under the influence of strict superintendence and control,

WE RECOMMEND THAT THE CENTRAL BOARD BE EMPOWERED AND DIRECTED TO FRAME AND ENFORCE REGULATIONS AS TO THE RELIEF TO BE AFFORDED TO VAGRANTS AND DISCHARGED PRISONERS.

We have now given a brief outline of the functions, for the due performance of which we deem a new agency, or central board of control to be requisite; and we have inserted none which the evidence would warrant us in believing attainable by any existing agency. The length of this Report precludes the statement, in further detail, of the powers and duties of the proposed board. The extent of those powers and duties must be measured by the extent and inveteracy of the existing evils, and by the failure, or worse than failure, of the measures by which their removal has been attempted. If for that purpose the powers which we have recommended are necessary, to withhold those powers is to decree the continuance of the evil. The powers with which we recommend that they should be invested, are in fact the powers now exercised by 15,000 sets of annual officers. By far the majority of those officers are ignorant of their duties, influenced by their affections, interests and fears, and restrained by scarcely any real responsibility. The Commissioners would act upon the widest information, under the direct control of the legislature and the supervision of the public, and under no liability to pecuniary or private bias, partiality or intimidation. They would have the immediate advantage of having well defined objects assigned to them, powerful means at their disposal, and clear rules for their guidance; and they would soon have the aid of varied and extensive experience; and it appears to us, that the best means of preventing their negligent or improper use of the discretion with which it appears to be necessary to invest them will be, not to restrict that discretion, but to render their interest coincident with their duty, and to let them be removable at Your Majesty's pleasure.

We entertain, however, no hope, that the complicated evils with which we have to contend, will all be eradicated by the measures which we now propose. The mischiefs which have arisen during a legislation of more than 300 years, must require the legislation of more than one Session for their correction. In order to secure the progressive improvement from which alone we hope for an ultimate cure; and in order to bring the proceedings of the Commissioners more constantly and completely within the super-intendence of the executive and the legislature, we propose that the Com-missioners should be charged with the duty, similar to that which we now endeavour to perform, of periodically reporting their proceedings, and sug-gesting any further legislation which may appear to them to be desirable.

WE RECOMMEND, THEREFORE, THAT THE BOARD BE REQUIRED TO SUB-MIT A REPORT ANNUALLY, TO ONE OF YOUR MAJESTY'S PRINCIPAL SECRE-TARIES OF STATE, CONTAINING—1. AN ACCOUNT OF THEIR PROCEEDINGS; 2. ANY FURTHER AMENDMENTS WHICH THEY MAY THINK IT ADVISABLE TO SUGGEST; 3. THE EVIDENCE ON WHICH THE SUGGESTIONS ARE FOUNDED; 4. BILLS CARRYING THOSE AMENDMENTS (IF ANY) INTO EFFECT, WHICH BILLS THE BOARD SHALL BE EMPOWERED TO PREPARE WITH PROFES-SIONAL ASSISTANCE.

We consider that three Commissioners might transact the business of the Central Board. The number of the Commissioners should be small, as they should habitually act with promptitude, as responsibility for efficiency should not be weakened by discredit being divided amongst a larger number, and as the Board, whenever the labour pressed too severe-ly, might avail themselves of the aid of their Assistants. The Central Board would probably require eight or ten Assistant Commissioners, to examine the administration of relief in different districts, and aid the preparations for local changes. As the Central Board would be responsible for the per-formance of the duties imposed upon them by the legislature,

WE RECOMMEND THAT THE CENTRAL BOARD BE EMPOWERED TO AP-POINT AND REMOVE THEIR ASSISTANTS AND ALL THEIR SUBORDINATE OFFICERS.

* * *

The abolition of partial relief will remove the main discouragement to emigration, while it will ascertain the extent to which emigration may be useful; it will increase the disposition to emigrate on the part of those whose emigration is to be desired. We believe, therefore, that in proportion as our other remedies are applied, there will be an increased disposition on the part of parishes to supply the means to paupers desirous of emigrat-ing, if they be enabled by law so to do.

WE RECOMMEND, THEREFORE, THAT THE VESTRY OF EACH PARISH BE EMPOWERED TO ORDER THE PAYMENT, OUT OF THE RATES RAISED FOR THE

RELIEF OF THE POOR, OF THE EXPENSES OF THE EMIGRATION OF ANY PER-
SONS HAVING SETTLEMENTS WITHIN SUCH PARISH, WHO MAY BE WILLING
TO EMIGRATE; PROVIDED, THAT THE EXPENSE OF EACH EMIGRATION BE
RAISED AND PAID, WITHIN A PERIOD TO BE MENTIONED IN THE ACT.

We think it also would be expedient to adopt the measures for facilitat-
ing and regulating emigration contained in the Bill introduced into the
House of Commons in 1831, and to be found (as amended by a Committee) in the Parliamentary Papers of that Session (No. 358).

It has occasionally happened that emigrants have returned to burthen
the parishes at the expense of which they have been removed; and to
remedy this evil it has been proposed that every person who should with
his own consent be removed to the Colonies at the expense of his parish,
should lose his settlement. But we do not think it expedient that this proposal should be adopted. We do not believe the instances of the return of
emigrants are now frequent enough to affect the profit to a parish of an
emigration judiciously conducted, and we believe that the instances would
be still more rare if it were known that the emigrant on his return would
not be entitled to relief otherwise than in a well-managed workhouse. But
the chief objection is, that to deprive the emigrant of his settlement—while
it might operate to prevent the pauper from emigrating by the threat of an
imaginary forfeiture—would only enable returned emigrants to be relieved as casual poor in any places, not excluding their own parishes, where
they might be pleased to fix themselves.

We should propose rather, that the expenses which any parish shall have
defrayed, or contracted to pay for the removal of any voluntary emigrant
shall, upon the return to England of the emigrant, become a debt due to the
overseers for the time being, and shall be recovered by an attachment of
any wages to which the debtor may become entitled, as we have before
recommended in the case of other expenses incurred on account of a
pauper or his family.

* * *

Closely connected with the relief provided by the Poor Laws is the
relief provided by charitable foundations. As to the administration and
effect of those charities which are distributed among the classes who are
also receivers of the poor's rate, much evidence is scattered throughout our
Appendix, and it has forced on us the conviction that, as now administered,
such charities are often wasted, and often mischievous. In many instances

being distributed on the same principle as the rates of the worst managed parishes, they are only less pernicious than the abuse in the application of the poor rates, because they are visibly limited in amount. In some cases they have a quality of evil peculiar to themselves. The majority of them are distributed among the poor inhabitants of particular parishes or towns. The places intended to be favoured by large charities attract, therefore, an undue proportion of the poorer classes, who, in the hope of trifling benefits to be obtained without labour, often linger on in spots most un-favourable to the exercise of their industry. Poverty is thus not only col-lected, but created, in the very neighbourhood whence the benevolent founders have manifestly expected to make it disappear.

These charities, in the districts where they abound, may interfere with the efficacy of the measures we have recommended, and on this ground, though aware that we should not be justified in offering any specific recom-mendation with respect to them, we beg to suggest that they call for the attention of the Legislature.

WE have now recommended to YOUR MAJESTY the Measures by which we hope that the enormous evils resulting from the present mal-administra-tion of the Poor Laws, may be gradually remedied. It will be observed, that the Measures which we have suggested are intended to produce rather negative than positive effects; rather to remove the debasing influences to which a large portion of the Labouring Population is now subject, than to afford new means of prosperity and virtue. We are perfectly aware, that for the general diffusion of right principles and habits we are to look, not so much to any economic arrangements and regulations as to the influence of a moral and religious education; and important evidence on the subject will be found throughout our appendix. But one great advantage of any measure which shall remove or diminish the evils of the present system, is, that it will in the same degree remove the obstacles which now impede the progress of instruction, and intercept its results; and will afford a freer scope to the operation of every instrument which may be employed, for elevating the intellectual and moral condition of the poorer classes. We believe, that if the funds now destined to the purposes of education, many of which are applied in a manner unsuited to the present wants of society, were wisely and economically employed, they would be sufficient to give all the assistance which can be prudently afforded by the State. As the subject is not within our Commission, we will not dwell on it further, and we have ventured on these few remarks only for the purpose of recording our conviction, that as soon as a good administration of the Poor Laws shall have rendered further improvement possible, the most important duty of the Legislature is to take measures to promote the religious and moral education of the labouring classes.

All which We humbly Certify to YOUR MAJESTY.

C. J. LONDON	(L. S.)
J. B. CHESTER	(L. S.)
W. STURGES BOURNE	(L. S.)
NASSAU W. SENIOR	(L. S.)
HENRY BISHOP	(L. S.)
HENRY GAWLER	(L. S.)
W. COULSON	(L. S.)
JAMES TRAILL	(L. S.)
EDWIN CHADWICK	(L. S.)

Whitehall Yard,
20 February 1834.

Report of the Royal Commission on the Poor Laws and Relief of Distress

Majority Report (1909)

Review of Existing Conditions and Proposed Changes

In this Part we propose to give a general review of the existing conditions of Poor Law administration, and to enumerate the chief recommendations we propose to make.

(1). LEADING DEFECTS OF THE POOR LAW SYSTEM

1. The preceding pages of this Report, and the voluminous evidence we have collected, will have laid bare the main defects in our present system of Poor Law administration. They may be briefly summarised under the following heads:

(i) The inadequacy of existing Poor Law areas to meet the growing needs of administration.

(ii) The excessive size of many Boards of Guardians.

(iii) The absence of any general interest in Poor Law work and Poor Law elections, due in great part to the fact that Poor Law work stands in no organic relation to the rest of local government.

(iv) The lack of intelligent uniformity in the application of principles and in general administration.

(v) The want of proper investigation and discrimination in dealing with applicants.

(vi) The tendency in many Boards of Guardians to give outdoor relief without plan or purpose.

(vii) The unsuitability of the general workhouse as a test or deterrent for the able-bodied; the aggregation in it of all classes without sufficient classification; and the absence of any system of friendly and restorative help.

(viii) The lack of co-operation between Poor Law and charity.

(ix) The tendency of candidates to make lavish promises of out-relief and of Guardians to favour their constituents in its distribution.

(x) General failure to attract capable social workers and leading citizens.

(xi) The general rise in expenditure, not always accompanied by an increase of efficiency in administration.

(xii) The want of sufficient control and continuity of policy on the part of the Central Authority.

2. These defects have produced, notably in urban districts, a want of confidence in the local administration of the Poor Law. They have also been mainly the cause of the introduction of other forms of relief from public funds which are unaccompanied by such conditions as are imperatively necessary as safeguards.

Any reform to be effective must be thorough. We will now state what portion of the old system we propose to sweep away, what to retain, and the conditions necessary in order to create for the future a trustworthy and elastic administrative system of Public Assistance.

(2). PUBLIC ASSISTANCE

3. It has been impressed upon us in the course of our enquiry that the name "Poor Law" has gathered about it associations of harshness, and still more of hopelessness, which we fear might seriously obstruct the reforms which we desire to see initiated. We are aware that a mere change of name will not prevent the old associations from recurring, if it does not represent an essential change in the spirit of the work. But in our criticism and recommendations we hope to show the way to a system of help which will be better expressed by the title of Public Assistance than by that of Poor Law.

We therefore recommend that the new Local Authority shall be known as the Public Assistance Authority, and that the Committees which will carry on its work locally shall be known as the Public Assistance Committees. The name is not intended to disguise the fact that those who come within the scope of the operations of the new authority are receiving help at the public expense; but it is intended to emphasise the importance of making that help of real assistance. We hope also that the change may make it easier for those directly engaged in administrating relief to build up new traditions, and to carry on their work with a higher aim before them.

(3). Description of those qualified for Public Assistance

4. The principles dominating the spirit of the existing English Poor Law, so far as they determine the definition of those qualified for relief, seem to us both sound and humane. They contain a positive and a negative element; to relieve those who are qualified for public relief, and to discourage those who do not legitimately come within this category from becoming a public burden. The conditions under which relief is given ought to be prescribed, not by the applicant, but by the authority that relieves the applicant. We do not recommend any alteration of the law which would extend the qualification for relief to individuals not now entitled to it, or which would bring within the operation of assistance from public funds classes not now legally within its operation. The term "destitute" is now in use to describe those entitled to claim relief. Mr. Adrian, Legal Adviser to the Local Government Board, thus defined those who, in his judgment, come under the term "destitute":

Destitution, when used to describe the condition of a person as a subject for relief, implies that he is, for the time being, without material resources (i.) directly available and (ii.) appropriate for satisfying his physical needs— (a) whether actually existing or (b) likely to arise immediately. By physical needs in this definition are meant such needs as must be satisfied (i.) in order to maintain life or (ii.) in order to obviate, mitigate, or remove causes endangering life, or likely to endanger life or impair health or bodily fitness for self-support.

We prefer the term "necessitous," for we believe that it more accurately describes those who are at present held to be qualified for relief. We recommend, therefore, that the term "necessitous" take the place of "destitute."

Those, however, who are now qualified for relief by coming within the definition of destitution, fall into many classes, and the treatment of each class, and of each individual within that class, should be governed by the conditions surrounding the class or the individual. Help, prevention, cure and instruction, should each find its place within the processes at the disposal of the new authorities. Too much importance cannot be attached to the organisation to which the selection of the appropriate treatment is to be entrusted.

(4). AREA OF THE PUBLIC ASSISTANCE AUTHORITY

5. As a preliminary to any scheme of public assistance it was necessary to form areas for administrative purposes. In doing so we have been guided by the experience of the past and by the needs of the present, and both, in our judgment, point to great changes.

We are fully conscious of the difficulties involved. In the matter of areas, public opinion is tenaciously conservative. The sentiment, based on associations and traditions, which unites those within an area and detaches them from those without it, is a force in local government which cannot be ignored. Consequently, it is wiser to take, if possible, areas well defined and familiar, and to attach to them new administrative functions, rather than to create a fresh area for each successive development.

The Royal Commissioners of 1832 found that the parish was almost universally the unit for Poor Law purposes. They were impressed with its inadequacy. They found in the great majority of cases no guarantee that a supply would be forthcoming of persons qualified for the difficult and delicate duties of administering relief. Even were such persons forth-coming, there was a complete lack of any healthy public opinion to support them. Continuity and uniformity, whether of policy or practice, were hardly to be hoped for; a proper classification was impossible.

True, this inadequacy of the parish had been realised by the statesmen of the eighteenth century, and they had fallen back on the magistracy to correct its shortcomings. In a sense, therefore, they endeavoured to make the county the area for administration, inasmuch as its government was vested in quarter sessions. The attempt proved a failure, partly because joint action on the part of magistrates was uncommon, at least in Poor Law matters, and individual magistrates were unequal to the strain put upon them; partly because the statesmen themselves had no real grasp of the problems involved.

The Commissioners in their Report recommended that a new area should be formed, half way between the parish and the county, viz., the union. It is now our duty to report that in our judgment, the union, as an area, is open to many of the same objections as attached to the parish at the date of the Report.

I. We think that the number of areas is in itself a source of weakness in administration. There are 643 unions in England and Wales. They vary in size from Welwyn, with a population of 2,200, to West Ham, with a population of 580,000. Such variations are inconsistent with uniformity of administration. The difference again in the number of members of Boards of Guardians, as representing a varying number of parishes, is a disturbing factor. A reduction in the number of areas by their enlargement is essential to any reform.

II. It was objected to the parish, as an area, that, in the great majority of cases, it was not large enough to guarantee a supply of persons qualified for the work of administration. The Royal Commissioners were sanguine that with a larger area this defect would be remedied, and experience has to some extent justified them. But the evidence we have received goes to show that often the policy of a Board of Guardians and its successful application have been due to the influence of an individual. Sometimes it has been a chairman, who set before himself a clear line of discrimination and decision and explained it so as to win the suffrages even of those who might on other grounds have been opposed to his views. Sometimes a similar deference has been paid to a clerk who, remaining in office while the *personnel* of the board was constantly changing, acquired authority and used it with good effect. Sometimes, again, a relieving officer who was devoted to his duty, and had experience of the people among whom he worked, was able, without presumption, to make acceptable suggestions in individual cases and in the general conduct of the business of relief. On such men as these and on the grouping of members round them in carrying out different branches of inspection and supervision, the goodness of the administration has depended. But of late years two important changes have taken place. First, the Act of 1894 has made it necessary for all those who are desirous of entering upon this form of public service to go through the "storm and stress" of public election. There is evidence to show that there is a growing reluctance to face this ordeal. And, second, the migration from the country districts is not confined to any one class, and it is increasingly difficult to find men who, by local associations or a sense of public duty, are qualified for the office of Guardian. With an enlarged area, the chances of securing men with the requisite insight and sympathy will be greater than now. Again, the scale of the work being larger and the work itself more important, it will be more attractive to capable men. We rely on these causes to bring about a rise in the standard of administration.

III. The history of Poor Law administration since 1834 shows that the hopes of the Commissioners have not been realised. Boards of Guardians have wavered and vacillated in their application of principles. This failure to secure continuity has inflicted great hardship on the poor. Within certain limits the inhabitants of a union will adapt themselves to the policy of a board. But uncertainty as to that policy, and a doubt whether it will be consistently followed, year by year, or even week by week, is fatal to the formation of habits of foresight and thrift. We hope and believe that, with the larger area which we propose, this uncertainty will be very greatly reduced.

IV. Another complaint against the present area is that it makes uniformity of treatment difficult to obtain. The complaint, indeed, is often made without regard to the special characteristics of poor relief. Of mechanical uniformity there is more than enough in Poor Law administration. The repetition of routine decisions, *e.g.*, the indiscriminate application of a scale of outdoor relief to case after case, without regard to individual differences, is the bane of administration. But true uniformity lies rather in the general acceptance of certain definite principles and their consistent application. Such principles are thorough enquiry, the consideration of each case in all its bearings with a view to ascertaining how it can best be treated, the granting of assistance at once appropriate and adequate, the securing of co-operation between all the various agencies of public assistance. We believe that one supervising authority acting over a large area will produce a uniformity of this kind.

V. Again, we need but repeat in this connection what we have before urged, namely, that only with an enlarged area is it possible to secure that classification of institutions which is so necessary to-day. In the great majority of unions there is but one workhouse; and it is the practice of those unions to keep within that workhouse and its curtilage all those, with the exception of children, to whom institutional relief is given. They are kept there because there is no other available building or institution at the disposal of the Guardians. The Royal Commission of 1832, as has been stated more than once, attached great importance to classification; the old Poor Law unit, *i.e.*, the parish, was in their opinion too small and too poor for the purpose of classification; and one of the reasons for the extension of area which they advocated was the belief that it would facilitate classification. But the Commission also pointed out that, even in large workhouses, a proper classification was difficult and could be much better obtained in separate buildings than under one roof. It may safely be asserted that the universal experience of the last eighty years endorses this opinion. A proper or thorough system of classification is very difficult, if not impossible in a workhouse through whose doors all classes of paupers pass. We advocate a change in this method of administration. Until the present areas are enlarged, no proper classification on uniform lines throughout the country can take place, but the substitution of a large area, within whose limits are several institutions, will at once place at the disposal of the new authority much of the necessary accommodation for carrying through and developing this most urgent reform.

VI. With an enlarged area we believe that it will be possible to improve the position and the prospects of the officials engaged in administration. Division of labour can be carried further, promotion can be made more common, the scale of salaries and pensions can be brought into accord with the scale of the work. We welcome the opportunity which this change will give for adequate recognition of a class of men whose services to the community have not always been valued, as our experience leads us to think that they deserve.

6. We have set out at some length our reasons for proposing an enlarged area, because we feel that, cogent as is each individual reason, the cumulative effect of the whole is irresistible.

We propose that in future the unit of administration shall be the County and the County Borough. In view of the strength of sentiment as regards areas, we have thought it better to adopt an existing area. We are well aware that objections may be made to it, but the fact that it is already recognised and familiar has had great weight with us.

7. The main objection urged against any enlargement of area, and the association under one authority of institutions distant from one another, is that some of the recipients of institutional relief may be so far away from their friends and relatives as to make visits to them difficult. We believe that any such inconvenience is greatly exaggerated. Communica-

tion has been so far facilitated and cheapened that the several parts of a county are now, for practical purposes, no more distant from one another than were the individual parishes of a union in 1834. Moreover, analysis of the inmates of a country workhouse shows that the greater proportion of the adults so relieved are infirm or old persons. We have recommended that the old shall in future be cared for in small homes, and these would be available in different parts of the county. For those needing special care, we think that the superior treatment offered in a county institution would far outweigh any inconvenience to relatives and friends. In pursuance of our proposals we would therefore lay down the following principles as governing the readjustment of areas:

a) That the area of the Public Assistance Authority shall be coterminous with the area of the county or county borough, and that no exception from this principle shall be permissible unless the Local Government Board is satisfied that such exception would, in each particular case, be in the best interests of administration.

b) Any union area, which at present overlaps a county or county borough, shall be divided up so that each part of it will be attached for Public Assistance purposes to the county or county borough within the boundaries of which such part is at present situated.

c) Any injustice or anomaly arising from this arrangement may be remedied subsequently by the ordinary procedure for altering county or county borough boundaries, supplemented, if necessary, by further powers to the Local Government Board.

d) Financial adjustments necessitated by the partition of a union area shall be determined by agreement between the authorities concerned, and, failing agreement, by arbitration as under Section 62 of the Local Government Act, 1888.

8. It remains to determine the area of charge. The Royal Commissioners of 1832 found that under the 43rd Eliz. the area of charge was the parish. The changes which they proposed necessitated its enlargement, and by successive Acts of Parliament, the Union was gradually substituted for the parish. In view of the fresh changes which we suggest, we have been led to the conclusion that the area must be once more enlarged. If the classification of institutions which we propose is adopted, it will logically follow that the area of charge should coincide with the area of administration. It may well be that some new institutions will be required, and that some of the old can be dispensed with. But however that may be, it would clearly

be difficult or impossible for the new Authority to enforce a common standard of efficiency in the institutions in their area, unless the cost of maintaining such institutions was a charge common to the whole area. And with regard to out-relief, or, as we shall call it, home assistance, the same holds good. We anticipate that the Public Assistance Authority of the future will supervise the work of its Committees. If this supervision is to be thorough and effective, the Committees must be dependent upon the Authority for the necessary funds. We propose therefore that the cost of Public Assistance, so far as its incidence remains local, shall be borne by a County or County Borough rate.

(5). Division of Existing Poor Law Work

9. The enlargement of the area will in itself be an administrative benefit in many ways; but it is only one item in the list of improvements we suggest in the existing machinery of the Poor Law. By increasing the size of each administrative unit, classification and specialised treatment, so far as institutional relief is concerned, will be facilitated. But a proper and discriminating classification can be successfully carried out only by a careful inquiry into the case of every applicant for relief, and this inquiry must be common to all applicants whether they receive ultimately outdoor or institutional relief or whether their claim is rejected. The treatment of all who apply should be individualised; that is to say, special inquiries should be made into the circumstances connected with the individual case; and the treatment should be governed by consistent principles. The construction of the machinery for this investigation requires close and careful consideration. The decisions arrived at upon individual cases, even although those who do this work may form but a fraction of the Board, initiate and govern the practice of the whole Board. This work is in one sense the most difficult and invidious that falls to the lot of the Guardians. A knowledge of the principles which should govern the distribution of public money—kindliness, firmness, impartiality, an aptitude for discerning truth—are required, and in addition the administrator should be familiar with the locality and with the needs and characteristics of its inhabitants.

10. Under a system of enlarged areas the work of Public Assistance would seem naturally to divide itself between:

1) A Local Authority for the central administration and control of Public Assistance within the enlarged area.

2) Local committees for dealing with applications and for the investigation and supervision of cases and such other duties as may be delegated by the Local Authority.

Those who are best qualified to discharge the one service not infrequently have less aptitude for the other, and the two kinds of work are so different that both would be better done if thus distributed.

11. Devolution rather than division is the term which should be associated with the distribution of work which we propose. Where a public service affecting the whole community is placed under local supervision, it is generally found to be necessary, if good and uniform administration is to be secured, to combine unduly small areas until they attain a considerable and convenient size as an administrative unit. This has been done in connection with various services, and recently with education, but this process of enlargement, if it is to be really successful in combining effective supervision with a knowledge of local wants and peculiarities, should carry with it another change—the association of unpaid nominated persons of local experience and knowledge with the paid officials of the enlarged local authority. To these non-elected persons duties can be entrusted of investigation, inspection, and report, which should give the authority at headquarters of the enlarged area, the local information it requires, the trend of opinion in outlying districts, and an accurate measure of the wants and efficiency of the services locally rendered. As we have before shown, the principles dominating our system of poor relief, whether we regard the laws themselves or the orders and regulations issued in their explanation, are humane and sensible in their intention. The difficulty for centuries past of giving intelligent expression to this intention has been the want of an efficient and suitable local machinery. Instruments of high finish and fine temper are required, and under our present system of popular election in small areas these are not easily found. Enlarged areas for relief purposes, if they are to confer real benefits in the shape of improved administration, carry with them as a necessary concomitant the recognition and utilisation of non-elected and nominated members for purely local and district work.

(6). Breaking up of the Poor Law

12. There was a scheme brought to our notice known as the "Breaking up of the Poor Law." Its ideas appear to be the foundation of the alternative proposals recommended by certain of our colleagues who dissent from our Report. Under this scheme the whole existing machinery of Poor Law

administration would disappear with the abolition of the Guardians, and the work previously performed by them would be broken up into sections and transferred to existing Committees of County and County Borough Councils.

13. Though we have had the scheme fully before us, we do not propose to criticise it in detail. It seems clear to us that the idea upon which it is founded is faulty and unworkable. The question at issue is, whether the work of maintaining those members of the community who have lost their economic independence can be safely entrusted to authorities whose primary duty is something quite distinct—such as that of Education or Sanitation—or whether it is essential that there should be an authority devoting itself entirely to the work. We consider that the many and subtle problems associated with Public Assistance, especially when it is a family rather than an individual that requires rehabilitation, cannot be solved by the simple process of sending off each unit to a separate authority for maintenance and treatment. What is needed is a disinterested authority, practised in looking at all sides of a question, and able to call in skilled assistance. The specialist is too apt to see only what interests him in the first instance and to disregard wider issues.

Moreover, the existing educational and sanitary authorities ought not, in our judgment, to be converted into agencies for the distribution of relief; and the less their functions are associated with the idea of relief, the better will they perform the public work for which they were specially called into existence. To thrust upon these Authorities, while their work is still incomplete, the far more difficult and delicate duties of dealing with families which have already broken down, would be to court failure in both directions—that of prevention and that of cure.

14. There are further difficulties which would inevitably arise from this multiplication of agencies authorised to grant public relief. Whilst a combination of incompatible duties is imposed upon the Education and the Health Committees by the scheme, its operation in another direction is to dislocate and separate work which cannot be effectively discharged unless it is combined and under the control of one authority or committee. The functions of granting relief, and of the recovery of the cost either from the recipients or those legally liable for them, should be in the hands of one body and not divided between two or more organisations with separate staffs, and methods of investigation. Such a separation must result in a multiplication of inquiries and visitations, causing annoyance and waste

of time and money. The same criticism applies to domiciliary and institutional relief. Being the two recognised methods of Public Assistance they should be utilised together as one system under one supervision. Their disconnection by being placed under two tribunals must lead to administrative inefficiency and confusion. Whilst a multiplication of authorities and organisations for the discharge of local duties is to be deprecated as tending to delay and friction, care must be taken not to run to the other extreme by the abolition of organisations specially qualified for a certain class of work and the transfer of such work to existing bodies who are not specially qualified for its discharge.

(7). COMPARISON OF FOREIGN AND BRITISH METHODS OF ADMINISTRATION

15. Before coming to any conclusion as to the form which the organisation of Public Assistance should take, we were careful to make inquiry into the experience of other countries. We invited evidence from those best qualified to give it, and some of our members visited the Continent and reported to us on the working of different systems. We are greatly indebted to both these sources of information.

16. We found at the outset a sharp contrast between this country and others in the constitution of the bodies administering Public Assistance. Nowhere, save in our own country, is this duty placed in the hands of a body of men directly elected for the purpose. In most cases it is entrusted to a Committee appointed by the general administrative authority of the town, district, or place. It is thus regarded and treated as a branch of municipal government. Moreover, there is no special rate in aid of the poor, but grants are made for the purpose by the Municipal Authority on an annual estimate. By this means the relations between the department of Public Assistance and the other branches of the public service are made much closer than in this country. All form part of one great organisation, and all are maintained out of the same general fund.

17. Still more in contrast with our methods is the place and power of the official element. In many cases a paid and trained official presides over the local administrative body. In Paris, the Director is a member of a consultative committee of supervision. In Hamburg, he sits and votes on the Committee as Assessor to the President.

18. In the Colonies the work is mainly carried on by paid official holding permanent office. These officials, both in Europe and in the

Colonies, may be credited with expert knowledge upon the subject of relief. Many of them have been thoroughly trained and have risen to their position after having given proof of capacity. An expert knowledge may, therefore, be said in foreign systems to be at the head of local administration. In this country the reverse method largely prevails. The unpaid and elected element dominates the paid, or expert element. We do not in any way wish to decry the splendid service which has been, and is still being rendered to the public by the elected and unpaid members of local administration. When a man of ability, probity, and leisure can be found willing to give his continuous services gratuitously to the public to promote good government in his locality, his freedom from remuneration or official ties not infrequently gives him an authority and an influence in excess of that which any official could exercise. But a system of voluntary unpaid workers has its limits, and there are certain forms of work which are apt to strain the capacity of all but the ablest and most conscientious. The work of investigating and deciding upon the relative claims of applicants for public relief is of this character. The expert or official element ought in this class of work to have great weight. We would strongly recommend that, whenever an Assistance Committee sits and adjudicates upon claims, the official associated with that Committee should be in a position of greater authority and influence than the clerk or the relieving officer is now supposed to possess. What his authority and influence will be in any particular case must always depend in great measure on his personal qualities. We propose that definite guarantees of his efficiency shall be forthcoming, and that he shall be a man who by capacity and training is qualified to share and even to guide the deliberations of the body to which he is attached. We propose further to safeguard his independence by making him irremovable, save by or with the assent of the Central Authority, and to improve his position by throwing open to him a wider prospect of promotion.

19. There should be associated with each Public Assistance Committee, both in London and the provinces, an official of experience whose position towards such committee should, as regards decisions upon the claims of applicants for assistance, resemble that of an Inspector of the Poor in Scotland . . . . He should be designated the Superintendent of Public Assistance, and he would be responsible for all the Relieving Officers, or, as we propose to call them, Assistance Officers working within the area of the Committee. He should be a whole-time officer and

the Assistance Officers referred to should stand to him in the position of assistants. He should attend all meetings of the Committee.

Similarly the Clerk to the new County or County Borough Authority, whom we propose to call the Director of Public Assistance, will have greater responsibilities than the average clerk to the Guardians of the present day. We have also made elsewhere in our Report a number of important recommendations which should go far to maintain and increase the efficiency of Officers generally. There will thus be a Public Assistance Service of trained and competent officials to assist the new local authorities in their work.

Taking then the division of that work as above defined, we would designate the Local Authority entrusted with the central supervision and control in each new area as "the Public Assistance Authority" and the body discharging the local duties of hearing and deciding individual cases, as "the Public Assistance Committee."

(8). DUTIES AND POWERS OF THE PUBLIC ASSISTANCE AUTHORITY

20. We now propose to define more carefully the duties each of the two bodies should be asked to undertake, their respective composition and the relative positions of the one to the other so far as finance, area, and authority are concerned.

We have separated the duties now performed by Boards of Guardians into two categories, and we propose to call into existence two bodies for the discharge of the two sets of functions, viz., Public Assistance Authorities and Public Assistance Committees. The powers and duties of the Public Assistance Authorities would, subject to the regulations and general control of the Local Government Board, be as follows:

a) To set up and supervise the Public Assistance Committees for investigating and deciding applications for Assistance, and for dealing with applicants in accordance with the regulations of the Local Government Board.

b) To make rules and standing-orders for the guidance of the Public Assistance Committees.

c) To dissolve any Public Assistance Committee subject to the assent of the Local Government Board.

d) To organise, provide, and maintain the institutions necessary for the supply of sufficient and suitable Assistance within their area, or to combine with other Public Assistance Authorities for that purpose, and to be responsible for all contracts and stocktaking.

e) To provide for the cost of the administration of Public Assistance within their area, and, generally, to undertake financial responsibility for such administration.

f) To appoint and allocate to the Public Assistance Committees such officers as are necessary for their work.

The expenditure which each Public Assistance Authority determines to be required for the administration of public assistance within its area, should, in the case of a County, be paid out of the County fund in the same way as the expenditure of a Standing Joint Committee is payable under Section 30 of the Local Government Act, 1888, and it should be the duty of the County Council to provide for such payment accordingly.

Similarly in the case of a County Borough, the expenditure should be made payable by the Town Council out of the Borough fund.

Any loan required would be raised by the Council of the County or County Borough as the case may be.

(9). CONSTITUTION OF THE PUBLIC ASSISTANCE AUTHORITY

21. We now approach the most difficult part of our proposed reconstruction, namely, the constitution of the Public Assistance Authority. The simplest method would be that of direct election by the existing County Council and Borough Council electorates. But direct election for Poor Law purposes, as our evidence over and over again shows, has brought in its wake, whether the elected body be the old Vestry or the more modern Board of Guardians, unmistakable evils which in our judgment ought not to be perpetuated. We cannot recommend this method of selection. Going to the other extreme, namely, that of direct appointment, it has been suggested to us that a local authority, composed of a limited number of Commissioners appointed by the county council and the Government in the ratio of three to one for a fixed period, would, for all purposes of administration, best discharge the duties we propose to assign to the Public Assistance Authority. We are not prepared to contest this assertion. A body so constituted, if composed of capable men would, being free from outside pressure, in all probability discharge the work of Public Assistance better than any elected body. But we hesitate to put this suggestion forward as an authoritative proposal. The difficulties of selection, and of fixing

the tenure constitute together obstacles of a most serious character to the realisation of such an idea, and it is difficult to believe that local authorities would consent to power being given to a body of this kind to spend funds derived from local rates.

22. Rejecting these two proposals, there remains the creation of a Statutory Committee of the County Council and County Borough Council, to whom the existing work of the Guardians might be given. We are well acquainted with the objections to this proposal. It is alleged that the County Councils are overworked; that they have no aptitude or inclination for this kind of work; that all power would ultimately slip into the hands of the permanent officials in their employ. But if the alternative is a second elected body with power to rate the whole county, the finance and credit of the county would be prejudicially affected by this duplicated spending power. In proposing the creation of a Statutory Committee of the County Councils and County Borough Councils, it is very desirable that the change should not break continuity of administration, and we hope that Guardians of ability and experience will not be dissociated from future participation in the work with which they are already well acquainted. Accordingly we recommend that one half of the members of the new Statutory Committee shall consist of persons of experience in Public Assistance and cognate work.

23. As regards the constitution of the Public Assistance Authority then, we propose:

a) That the Public Assistance Authority shall be a Statutory Committee of the County or County Borough Council constituted as follows

(i) One-half of the members to be appointed by the council of the County or County Borough, and the persons so appointed may be persons who are members of the council.

(ii) The other half of the members to be appointed by the council from outside their number, and to consist of persons experienced in the local administration of public assistance or other cognate work

(iii) The actual number of members of the Public Assistance Authority, in each case and from time to time, to be determined by the Local Government Board, after consideration of a scheme submitted on the first occasion by the council of the County or County Borough, and on subsequent occasions by the Public Assistance Authority.

(iv) Women to be eligible for appointment under either head (i) or (ii).

b) That one-third of the members of the Public Assistance Authority shall retire each year, but shall be eligible for reappointment if duly qualified. A member ceasing to be a member of County Council or County Borough Council shall *ipso facto* cease to be a member of the Public Assistance Authority, but shall be eligible for reappointment if otherwise qualified.

(10). AREA OF THE PUBLIC ASSISTANCE COMMITTEE

24. The area of the Public Assistance Authority being determined, we now define within those limits the area of the Public Assistance Committee:

a) In the first instance the areas of the Public Assistance Committees shall be the union areas.

b) Ultimately, the areas of the Public Assistance Committees shall be such as the Public Assistance Authority, with the consent of the Local Government Board, shall prescribe, and those areas shall as far as possible be coterminous with one or more rural or urban districts.

c) Every union overlapping the boundaries of a County or County Borough shall be dealt with so that each part of such union entirely within a County or County Borough shall be either provisionally constituted a separate Public Assistance Committee area, or else provisionally attached to another Public Assistance Committee area within the County or County Borough in which such part is situated, and the Local Government Board shall issue Orders accordingly.

(11). DUTIES OF THE PUBLIC ASSISTANCE COMMITTEE

25. The following will be the duties of the Public Assistance Committee, under rules laid down by the Public Assistance Authority:

a) To make careful inquiry into the circumstances and condition of all persons applying for Assistance within their area with a view to ascertaining the cause and nature of their distress.

b) To review periodically the circumstances and condition of persons in receipt of Assistance.

c) To investigate the means of persons liable for maintenance and to take the measures necessary for the recovery of the cost of the Assistance given.

d) To sub-divide their area when desirable for the purposes of local Assistance, subject to the assent of the Public Assistance Authority.

e) To determine in the case of each person applying for or receiving Public Assistance whether such person is by law entitled to such Assistance.

f) To decide upon the best method of assisting applicants with a view to removing the cause of distress.

g) To co-operate with the Voluntary Aid Committee with a view to the assistance of cases of distress.

h) To co-operate with other public and voluntary agencies.

i) To inspect, supervise, and administer the Public Assistance Authority's institutions within their area and such other institutions as the Public Assistance Authority shall direct.

j) To secure periodical visitation of all cases in receipt of Home Assistance.

k) To make half yearly an estimate of their expenditure and requirements, and submit it to the Public Assistance Authority who shall from time to time remit such sum or sums as may be necessary.

l) To control and supervise the officers assigned to them by the Public Assistance Authority.

m) To furnish the Public Assistance Authority from time to time with such information concerning the proceedings and work of the Committee as the Authority may require.

n) To discharge such other duties as the Public Assistance Authority may, from time to time, call upon them to undertake.

(12). CONSTITUTION OF THE PUBLIC ASSISTANCE COMMITTEE

26. For each area constituted as in paragraph 24, the Public Assistance Authority shall appoint a Public Assistance Committee, which shall include a certain proportion of persons nominated by the Urban and Rural District Councils, and, where a Voluntary Aid Committee has been established, a certain proportion nominated by that Committee. The persons so nominated shall be experienced in the local administration of Public Assistance or other cognate work and shall include a proportion of women, in our judgment not ordinarily less than one-third. One-third of the members shall retire each year, but shall be eligible for re-appointment.

(13). Poor Law Authority for London

27. Whilst the general principles we have laid down as to the future administration and distribution of relief work apply with equal force to London as to other parts of England, the area to be included in the London district and the administrative machinery to be established within that area require special attention. The case for the abolition of Boards of Guardians has been more conclusively demonstrated in London than in any other part of the kingdom. Quite independently of inquiries proving corruption and malversation in certain unions, we found that there was an almost universal opinion amongst those acquainted with Poor Law work in the Metropolis that the present system, based on popular election in a multiplicity of separate districts, does not, under the conditions surrounding it, produce the right class of Poor Law administrator, or secure generally economical and efficient administration. That there are many capable hard-working Guardians in London at this moment, and that there are unions in London well-worked and managed, is not disputed. But London unions, as separate and distinct organisations, have not been able to adapt themselves to the needs of the Metropolis, and the legislation of the last half-century for the improvement of poor relief in London is based on a recognition of this fact. The characteristic of almost every statute effecting changes in London has been in the direction of throwing fresh charges upon a common fund. The variations of rateable value, as compared with needs and population, make it very difficult to establish a common standard of treatment without an equalisation of expenditure. An examination into the policy, practice, scale of relief, and cost of institutions shows a wide divergence between the different unions and sometimes between unions immediately adjacent to one another. These differences exist whether the unions in contrast are rich or poor, in the south, the east, or the west. Neither locality, nor wealth, nor poverty seems to have been the main contributing cause of this variation of treatment and of policy. An inquiry into the amount of public interest shown in the elections or in the subsequent policy of the Guardians, gives little hope that outside pressure is likely to revive such interest, so long as the present system prevails. The first reform necessary in our judgment is the total abolition of the present Boards of Guardians, and the establishment of a unified London for all purposes of Public Assistance. The financial effect of such a change would

be comparatively small, as under the present system by far the largest proportion of Poor Law expenditure is not a union charge. The charges upon the Common Poor Fund, the disbursements made by the County Council to the separate Boards of Guardians, and the expenses of the Metropolitan Asylums Board, in the aggregate, amount to about 70 per cent. of the whole Poor Law expenditure in London, and they are directly or indirectly levied upon the whole rateable area of London. The transfer of the remaining 30 per cent. to a common fund would, we believe, be economical to London as a whole.

28. There are, outside the boundaries of the London County Council area, a number of urban communities, such as West Ham, Edmonton, Hornsey, and Kilburn, rapidly growing in population, and with a very low valuation per head of the population. These areas are, practically, a continuation of London. The poor rate in some of them is high and will probably rise. Although these districts possibly might, for administrative purposes, be advantageously included in the London of the future, we cannot on the knowledge before us make this recommendation. The question involves many considerations relating to other local branches of expenditure and administration which are outside our purview. We therefore suggest that a series of local inquiries should be undertaken by the Local Government Board in these districts, to ascertain what are the opinions of the localities themselves as to incorporation with London.

29. The area for the new Public Assistance Authority which we would recommend would be that of the London County Council. The areas of the Public Assistance Committees would generally be the areas of existing unions, though in certain cases some re-adjustment would be necessary.

30. The County of London with its central body in the shape of the London County Council, and with its borough councils within that area, some of which have control over populations exceeding 300,000 persons, presents a different problem from that of the ordinary county. The abolition of Boards of Guardians is necessitated by the impossibility of establishing a good general system of Public Assistance, so long as London is divided into sections,—each having an independent and separate authority of its own. There must be one central body for the control of the administration. If this reasoning be sound, it is equally effective against any proposal to put the Metropolitan Borough Councils in the place of the deposed Boards of Guardians.

31. This was the plan officially placed before us by the London County Council. The scheme, as well as the examination of those recommending it, will be found in Vol. IX, Qs. 97473 to 98066. They suggested a committee of the London County Council as a central administrative body, and the substitution of the Borough Councils for the Guardians, each borough council to discharge locally the work of their predecessors, subject to certain restrictions, and supervision by the London County Council as a central authority. These restrictions and supervision were not clearly defined. The division of charges between those falling on local rates and those met out of a fund common to the whole Metropolis were to be much the same as before, with this one exception. The responsibility for maintaining children, either those in institutions or those whose parents were in receipt of poor relief, was to be transferred to the Education Committee of the London County Council, and the cost was to be defrayed as an item of expenditure separate from that relating to education. We fail, however, to understand how, or by what machinery, this was to be done, unless the relief of the child was to be dissociated from the relief given to the parent.

32. From an administrative point of view, this scheme has little, if any, advantage over the system now in force. It might be summed up as a practical continuance of the present plan of separate and independent Poor Law administration in London, Borough Councils being substituted for Boards of Guardians, accompanied by a transfer to the London County Council of some of the powers of supervision now exercised by the Local Government Board. It gives little hope of better classification or of improved or uniform general treatment; the control proposed to be given to the London County Council over the Borough Councils would not, in our opinion, be administratively effective.

33. We are not inclined to favour this scheme, as it does not seem to conform with the main principles we had laid down as the foundation of a reformed administration.

There remain, then, the following alternatives viz.:

First—Direct election.

Second—Nominated Commissioners.

Third—A transformed Metropolitan Asylums Board.

Fourth— A Statutory Committee of the London County Council.

34. We have already given our opinion upon the evils resulting from a direct system of election for Poor Law purposes, and we are not disposed

to perpetuate a system by which Poor Law administration in London would be disturbed by the oscillatory results of triennial political contests concentrated upon the one subject of eleemosynary relief.

35. Some of us are of opinion that, looking to the enormous size of London, to the constant shifting of its population, and to the lack of cohesion between, and the different character and wants of, individual districts, the nomination of Commissioners as a central and controlling authority would be the best form of administration for it; such a body to be small in numbers, partly appointed by the London County Council and the Local Government Board, and assisted by local committees. We think that such a scheme would well suit the case of London and would give the best results both as regards efficiency and economy. It would, however, be an innovation certain to be strongly opposed and it may be that the political difficulties attendant upon it would be more than any Government would care to encounter.

36. The Metropolitan Asylums Board, whose duties and composition have been described in evidence, have efficiently discharged as a central body for London the task entrusted to them. The Board, as was shown by the statements and examination of Mr. Helby, the Chairman, and Mr. Duncombe Mann, the clerk, believe in their ability to undertake other duties. In fact, Mr. Helby was confident that they could discharge as the central controlling and supervising body, in addition to their existing work, all the duties now performed by the Guardians.

We have, in a previous portion of our recommendations, expressed a strong opinion that the work now performed by the Guardians, especially if areas of administration be enlarged, should be divided into two branches:

Firstly—That of administration and control to be discharged by a central body.

Secondly—That of dealing with individual cases to be discharged by local bodies.

37. The division of labour would hold good whatever the character and composition of the Public Assistance Authority for London. Assuming, then, that satisfactory Public Assistance Committees can be established, each in an area corresponding to an existing union, it remains to consider whether the constitution of the Authority should follow the lines of the Metropolitan Asylums Board. It would then be in part representative, in part nominated, and independent of the political issues of the day. It would in many respects resemble the Conseil de Surveillance in Paris.

Two methods have been suggested for supplying the representative element, viz.:

1) Direct election in each borough.

2) Direct selection or nomination by each borough council.

It is not suggested that the whole of the Public Assistance Authority should be elected by the ratepayers in the various boroughs, but that a part only—say two-fifths—should be so elected. By this means the Authority would be kept in touch with the several districts, each of which would contribute a representative.

38. Though some of our colleagues favour the first of the two methods suggested above, the evils of direct election for Poor Law purposes seem to the majority of us too patent to permit of their continuance in London. If the representative area of the future is to be the Metropolitan borough, its magnitude, and the fact that there are within each borough political organisations actively employed in promoting the candidature of their nominees for Parliament, county councils, and municipal work, would inevitably draw the administration of relief into the vortex of local politics. A direct election for Poor Law purposes has this danger; if the poll be small, it is in the power of a small fraction of the electorate to reverse the whole existing policy of relief; if the poll be large, then the question of how relief was, or was not, to be locally dispensed would be a burning question in the locality with corresponding discontent and unsettlement. The Public Assistance Committee in the locality where the election took place might, under the instructions of the Public Assistance Authority, be conducting investigations and granting relief on principles which a majority of those polling in the district condemned, and friction would at once arise.

39. There remains the selection and nomination by the borough councils, and, assuming that it was considered that these bodies generally were, in *personnel* and standing greatly superior to the Boards of Guardians, they might be entrusted with the selection of nominees to the Public Assistance Authority. But we have no reason to believe that direct nomination by the Borough Councils of representatives to serve upon the Public Assistance Authority would result in securing the services of those best qualified for the work.

40. The main objections to the fourth suggestion are two. The London County Council is already heavily worked, and would with difficulty, therefore, it is said, find the *personnel* for yet another committee, whose work would be responsible and exacting. Again, the county councillors are,

to a greater extent than in the country, mainly elected on political grounds, and the echoes of the platform are not unfrequently heard in the council chamber. These drawbacks must be admitted, even though the first of them may be minimised by providing that the new committee shall consist, to a great extent, of persons who are not members of the council. On the other hand, if there be an advantage in including the relief of the poor within the purview of a municipal authority—and this assumption has prompted our proposed reconstitution of the Public Assistance Authority throughout England—it does not seem reasonable to exclude London from participating in this advantage. Nowhere are problems of poverty, under-employment, and public assistance more acute and more difficult, and nowhere do they require a more sympathetic and firm handling than in London.

41. After a full consideration of the advantages and disadvantages of the various schemes we have considered in connection with the establishment of a Public Assistance Authority for London, we recommend a Statutory Committee of the London County Council with statutory duties as being most in harmony with modern developments of local government.

42. In fact, we apply to London the scheme drawn up for Counties and County Boroughs with the following modifications:

a) One-half of the members of the Statutory Committee to be nominated by the London County Council either from their own number or from outside;

b) One-quarter of the members of the Statutory Committee to be appointed by the London County Council from outside their own number and to consist of persons of skill and experience in the administration of Public Assistance or other cognate work;

c) One-quarter of the members of the Statutory Committee to be nominated by the Local Government Board so as to secure representation on the Committee of such interests as the medical and legal professions, employers and working men, hospital administration, charitable organisations, etc.

d) We propose that a scheme on these lines should be drawn up by the London County Council and submitted to the Local Government Board for approval. The scheme should secure a considerable number (such as fifty or sixty) of members on the Committee and the inclusion of a certain proportion of women.

43. The Statutory Committee of the London County Council thus

constituted we would call the Public Assistance Authority for London, and to it we would transfer the Poor Law work of the Metropolis.

44. As in the country, so in London, we propose that the work of hearing and deciding applications for Assistance shall devolve on Public Assistance Committees to be constituted in London as follows:

a) Each Public Assistance Committee shall be appointed by the Public Assistance Authority, care being taken that, amongst those so appointed, there shall be included a certain proportion of persons nominated by the Metropolitan Borough councils, and, where a Voluntary Aid Committee has been established in a district, a certain proportion nominated by that Committee. The persons so nominated shall be experienced in the local administration of Public Assistance or other cognate work and shall include a certain proportion of women, which proportion in our judgment should not ordinarily be less than one-third.

b) One-third of the members shall retire each year, but shall be eligible for re-appointment.

c) The number of members on the Public Assistance Committees should be largely regulated by the area and population of the districts in which they will act, and should be fixed by schemes submitted by the Public Assistance Authority to the Local Government Board for approval. As a large area will require a considerable body of members, such schemes should provide, if necessary, for sub-divisions of the Committee, it being understood that each sub-committee will act in a smaller area as a section of the Committee.

45. We also propose that Poor Law expenditure in London be a uniform charge over the whole area according to rateable value.

(14). THE CENTRAL AUTHORITY

46. Having laid down the area, constitution, and functions of the future local authority to be established for the purpose of public assistance, we will now consider what should be the *status* and powers of the Central Authority, and its relations to, and control over the local authority.

47. We have given a full account in a preceding chapter of the origin and growth of the Local Government Board so far as Poor Law control was concerned. We have shown that out of the Poor Law Commissioners appointed in 1834 grew the Poor Law Board with its Parliamentary representatives, and how that Board was merged later in the Local Government Board. This Board has now to perform many duties relating to the local

administration of the country in addition to those connected with Poor Law. To a large extent it discharges the duties of a Ministry of the Interior. Its *status* does not seem to us to be adequate, considering the importance, authority, and character of the multifarious work it discharges. We are in full accord with the proposal to raise the salary and *status* of the head of the Department to that of a Secretary of State.

48. Although our reference brought us into contact chiefly with the Poor Law side of the Local Government Board, yet this was sufficient to convince us that the Department is greatly over-worked. The enormous mass of administrative questions brought within its cognisance, upon subjects which do not brook of delay, gives to the higher officials insufficient time for the study of new and perplexing problems as they arise and come up before them. The volume and importance of such questions are on the increase. We feel it, therefore, of great importance that the staff of the Office should be adequately increased so as to relieve the Permanent Secretary and the higher officials of the undue strain which the present conditions often impose upon them. These considerations are of special weight at a time when it is proposed to reorganise the whole service of Public Assistance.

49. There are five "Divisions" of work in the Local Government Board, of which Poor Law is one; and this is again divided into two branches—the Poor Law Administration Department and the Poor Law Officers' Department. There are incidental and general questions connected with the Poor Law, such as questions of law, the issue of orders and statistics, questions of audit and accounts which are referred to and dealt with by the Order and Audit Departments of the Board. The aggregate powers and control exercised by this combination of departments over the local Poor Law administration and expenditure have already been fully explained. But we think it would be an advantage if the public generally could recognise that there is a separate "Division" of the Local Government Board, devoting its whole attention to Poor Law work. To this end we recommend that greater prominence should be given to the fact that there is a separate Division of the Local Government Board, under a separate Assistant Secretary, which will deal with the work of Public Assistance. We also recommend that in future the annual Report of the Public Assistance Division should be printed and presented to Parliament in a volume separate from the rest of the Report of the Local Government Board.

50. We recommend that there should be closer co-operation between the Public Assistance Division, and the Statistical and Audit Divisions of the Local Government Board. Similarly, the Public Assistance Division of the Local Government Board should be in close touch with other Government offices in work in which they are commonly interested. One other large department which fulfils similar duties is the Home Office: and we think that there should be the closest co-operation between the Home Office and the Local Government Board. In the hands of the Local Government Board and the Public Assistance Authorities of the future will be the management of Public Assistance. In the hands of the Home Office is the provision made for persons who have been convicted and are placed in detention. These cases and the cases of persons who, amongst others, should be detained as inebriates, "ins-and-outs," or vagrants can be rightly treated only by measures which fall within the province of the Home Office, and we recommend that they should all be placed under the control of that office. It is only by the recognition of this division of labour and by its observance by the Local Authorities and the Central Government Departments that the task of either can be properly accomplished.

51. The eyes and ears of the Local Government Board are the General Inspectors and, in Part IV, Chapter 1 of our Report, we have made a number of recommendations in regard to them. Appointments should in the future be given only to those who have special qualifications, and these qualifications should, as a general rule, be tested by service for a probationary period as an Assistant Inspector.

The number of Assistant Inspectors should be increased. This would relieve the Inspectors of their routine and less important duties, and enable them to strengthen their grasp of the administration of Public Assistance in their districts. We have already described the existing duties of Inspectors. We think that, for the future, these duties should be extended, and that the Inspectors should be authorised to attend, not only the meetings of the Public Assistance Authority, but also those of the Public Assistance Committees and sub-committees, as well as to visit institutions. They should be ready to advise the Public Assistance Committee in regard to the general principles and methods of Public Assistance; they should, in conjunction with the Assistance Officers and otherwise, visit individual cases, so as to ascertain whether the Assistance is given under suitable conditions.

Upon appointment, Inspectors should receive written or printed instructions as to their duties, and such instructions should be periodically revised. Conferences should take place between the Inspectors, at least annually, to enable them to exchange views and experiences, and thus to carry out methodically the policy of the Department.

52. With regard to the Auditors of the Local Government Board, we recommend that appointments should be made from the ranks of Assistant Auditors; that qualifications for Assistant Auditors should be defined and tested by examination; and that there should be an increase of the auditing staff.

53. We consider that the increase in the number and efficiency of the inspectors and auditors which we propose is no more than is essential for the normal control and supervision of the administration of Public Assistance. But, in addition, we recommend that adequate funds should be placed at the disposal of the Local Government Board, to enable it from time to time to undertake inquiries, or to obtain expert assistance, upon particular subjects. The Central Authority responsible for the administration of Public Assistance should be abreast of expert knowledge, both at home and abroad, in regard to the constantly changing problems with which it has to deal.

54. We will now consider the relations of the Central Authority to the new Local Authorities. We see every reason to anticipate that, under the new *régime*, it will be possible for the Local Government Board to keep more closely in touch with the Public Assistance Authorities than it has been in the past with the Guardians.

Under the existing law, while the poor relief administration is in the hands of 643 different Boards of Guardians, meeting as a rule weekly or fortnightly, it is obviously out of the question for the Local Government Board to follow very closely the various methods and proceedings of each and all of them. The Board is not responsible for the due and effectual relief of the poor in the direct sense that the law has made the Irish Local Government Board responsible. For both these reasons the periodic survey by the Board at Whitehall of the Guardians' work, by means of Inspectors' and auditors' reports and statistical returns, must be a review of the past rather than of the current questions of administration, although the Board is frequently consulted by Boards of Guardians on questions of importance and as regards many current matters as to which some action on its part is required.

55. The change which will be effected by concentrating everything but the routine work of these 643 bodies in the hands of 133 County and County Borough Authorities, gives an opportunity for a great advance in the way of a closer linking up of the central and local authorities in regard to important matters of current administration, and we suggest that this object might perhaps be achieved by the transmission of the minutes of Public Assistance Authorities to the Local Government Board immediately after each meeting.

56. The minutes might set forth not only the proceedings and orders of the Public Assistance Authority upon all reports and correspondence received, but also the financial position of the Authority and its subordinate Committees at the end of each month, as well as the statistics of admissions and discharges and other relief afforded during the same period. In Ireland this practice is adopted, and it is found that the minutes form a convenient means of communication between the Local Government Board and the Authorities; and when any matter comes up for consideration upon which the sanction, approval, or advice of the Local Government Board is desired, the clerk indicates the fact by a marginal note on the minute in question, thereby obviating the necessity for a separate letter on the subject. We suggest whether this practice might not be found suitable for adoption in England.

57. If such a system were adopted, the whole policy of each Public Assistance Authority would, as it were, be passed in review before the eyes of the Local Government Board and its Inspectors. The difficulties of the Authorities would be seen, their successes and failures would be followed and understood, and the Inspectors would be enabled to judge when their attendance at the meetings of the Authorities would be most likely to be helpful. Whether this system would be necessary or expedient as a permanent arrangement, time alone can show, but at all events, when these new county Authorities are first started and the reins of the new administration are thrust into their hands, it seems desirable that, if the new *régime* is to be carried out wisely and with uniformity throughout the country, with due regard to the principles laid down by Parliament and the orders of the Local Government Board, there should be some such intercommunication in the progress of business, between the Central and the County and County Borough Authorities.

58. To assist the new local authorities to understand the spirit of their duties and the intention of the legislature, the codification and consolida-

tion of existing Poor Law statutes should at once be undertaken as well as of the orders and circulars issued under the authority of those statutes. To expedite this work, we would suggest the appointment of a small committee of Poor Law and legal experts to sit continuously until the task is completed.

59. We think also that it would be useful for the Central Authority to issue, or cause to be issued, a small manual of instructions for the guidance of the local authorities. The manual should contain a clear exposition of the main features of the law relating to Public Assistance, and of the policy of the Central Authority as laid down in their orders and circulars. The manual should be periodically revised and brought up to date.

60. We will next briefly review the changes which we propose in the powers and functions of the Central Authority.

We have not attempted to draw up a detailed list of those minor functions of the Local Government Board which might be handed over to the new Public Assistance Authorities, but we trust that the constitution of these bodies will enable the Local Government Board to devolve upon them the power to give assent to many individual cases of relief, such as emigration cases, children sent to homes, etc. The devolution of such powers would lighten the work of the Local Government Board considerably and advantageously.

We have recommended that, subject to more precise qualifications being laid down for higher officers, the local authorities should have full discretion to appoint such officers so long as the prescribed qualifications are fulfilled.

We have also recommended that the power of the Local Government Board to sanction prospective expenditure under the Local Authorities Expenses Act should be abolished.

With these exceptions we do not propose any diminution in the powers of the Local Government Board. On the contrary, we think it of importance that its powers should be increased in the following directions.

61. The Local Government Board at present cannot order a new workhouse to be built unless a majority of the Guardians of the union or of the owners and ratepayers consent. It is desirable that this limitation should cease, and that the Board should have power to compel the local authority to provide adequate buildings and adequate classification.

The Local Government Board should have power to direct that a particular class or classes of paupers for whom there is no suitable accommodation in the area of a Public Assistance Authority should be removed to and treated in any available and suitable institution of another Public Assistance Authority.

62. We feel that a stronger check should be exercised than heretofore over the cost of buildings erected by loan. To prevent extravagance, they should be built more in accord with some accepted plan, and care should be taken that the buildings are actually erected in accordance with the approved plans.

The Local Government Board should have power to authorise the Public Assistance Authority to purchase land compulsorily for the provision or enlargement of institutions.

63. Previous to 1894 the Central Authority were able through the *ex officio* Guardians to carry on the business if the elected Guardians refused to act. Though we do not contemplate the likelihood of any such hitch occurring as that the new authority would decline to act, it would be well, in the legislation which will be necessary to give effect to our recommendations, that the Local Government Board should be given authority in such a contingency to empower persons to exercise temporarily all or any of the powers which they may consider necessary for the object in view.

64. We recommend further that the Local Government Board should be empowered to compel Public Assistance Authorities to combine to provide for certain classes of cases, when sufficient and suitable accommodation is not otherwise available, and failing agreement between the authorities concerned.

(15). Grants in Aid of Local Taxation

65. The control to be exercised over Government grants to local authorities for Poor Law purposes is a more complicated question. At present the Guardians do not receive any grant direct from the Government, except that in respect of agricultural rates, which is given to make good part of the deficiency caused by an alteration in the law of rating. The other grants are given to the Guardians through the County and County Borough Councils, and are paid to them by such Councils in connection with certain specified services and payments. When the County and County Borough Councils become the Poor Law authority, they will retain the money they previously passed on to the Guardians, and, if the poor

rate be a county and county borough rate, the Government grants will simply be an annual sum in reduction of the county and county borough rates, which would otherwise have to be raised.

66. The principle upon which for the future these grants should be calculated and paid over to the various localities has been a subject of much controversy, and the Royal Commission on Local Taxation were divided upon it.

The majority of the Commission were in favour of grants being made in respect of selected items of expenditure, but the minority, including Lord Balfour of Burleigh, Sir Edward Hamilton, and Sir George Murray, believed that the sounder principle would be to base the amount on calculations made from the assessable value, the population and the expenditure in each locality. Tersely expressed, their argument was that the grant should be measured by necessity and ability, necessity being represented by the population and expenditure, ability by the assessable value.

67. When, after years of special investigation, authorities, so high as those quoted above, differ upon a question of such intricacy, it is difficult for us, who have not been able to give any exceptional attention to the subject, to express a decided opinion one way or the other. What we feel strongly is that these grants should be conditional; that is to say, that there should be a power to refuse any or all of such grants to a local authority, if the services or work towards which they are a contribution is not up to a proper standard. The plea upon which such grants are given from the Imperial Exchequer is that the services towards which they go are national in their character; if they be of that character the nation, through its recognized authorities, has a right to see that the services are efficiently rendered.

We are, therefore, of opinion that such grants, or portions of such grants, should be withheld from any County or County Borough authority, in cases where the Local Government Board reports that the administration, or branches of administration, of Public Assistance are not efficient, in the same way as the police grant may be forfeited if the Secretary of State withholds his certificate as to efficiency in discipline. We should be disposed to favour that system of calculation which makes the withholding of such grants under the conditions contemplated the most effective weapon for enforcing efficiency, and it would seem to us, as at present advised, that the block grant system would be the most suitable in this respect.

68. As regards the amount of the grant, we note that both Reports of the

Local Taxation Commission recommended an increase. We concur in that view, and recommend that it be raised to the sum of £5,000,000 per annum, the amount suggested by the minority.

(16). OFFICERS OF THE LOCAL AUTHORITIES

69. We have recognised that the efficiency of the officers of the local authority entrusted with Public Assistance is a matter of the utmost importance and we have made a number of detailed recommendations (Part IV, Chapter 3) as regards their qualifications, appointment, terms of service and superannuation with a view of establishing and maintaining a high standard of efficiency. We repeat verbatim here for purposes of convenience these recommendations:

1) When a Local Authority and the Local Government Board concur in the opinion that the retention of any officer is, on general grounds, detrimental to the administration, the Local Authority should have power to terminate that officer's appointment after proper notice.

2) No person should be appointed as Clerk who has not some knowledge and experience of the Poor Law, no person as superintendent of an institution who has not had some experience in dealing with the classes which the institution contains, and no person as a relieving officer who has not had some previous training as an assistant relieving officer or has not passed an examination and obtained a certificate of an examining authority recognised by the Local Government Board.

3) There should be qualifying examinations for the higher officers. Once qualifications for each office are laid down, and the Local Government Board satisfied that they are fulfilled, the entire responsibility for the appointment of all officers might be left to the new Local Authorities.

4) The Local Government Board might sanction a scale of officers' salaries for each Local Authority, and so long as the salaries, or increases of salaries, were in accordance with that scale, it should not be necessary for the Local Authority to require the sanction of the Local Government Board to individual salaries.

5) A Central Superannuation Fund should be established for the whole service, and in the case of teachers transferring themselves from public elementary schools to the Poor Law service and *vice versa*, arrangements should be made by which any sacrifice of pension is avoided.

6) The Clerk of the future or any officer performing analogous duties to any Local Authority shall not, save under very exceptional circumstances, and subject to the consent of the Local Government Board, be a part-time officer.

7) If the General Workhouse is abolished, each of the specialised institutions which takes its place, will require a superintendent, qualified by knowledge and experience, for its management. The salary offered must be sufficient to attract men not merely of organising power, but having the moral qualities necessary to develop the capacities of those under their charge.

8) Highly trained officers will be required in what are now regarded as less important posts, as *e.g.*, that of labour master.

9) Provision should be made for inmates of all denominations receiving religious administration and instruction from the clergy of their respective churches.

10) The indoor staff should be allowed to live out, where circumstances permit, and so far as is consistent with discipline and the proper discharge of their duties.

11) Where adequate relief is offered and refused, the responsibility for the consequences arising from such refusal should not rest with the relieving officer.

12) The relieving officer must not be burdened with too large a number of cases. In any scheme or regulations for the administration of relief in local areas, the proportion of cases to officers should be carefully and periodically revised.

13) Pay stations should be abolished.

14) In some places an officer might be appointed who, like the Inspector of Poor in Scotland, might fill the position both of Clerk and relieving officer with such assistance as is necessary.

15) A Local Authority should not be allowed to appoint an ex-member as a paid officer, unless he or she has ceased to be a member of the Local Authority for a period of, say, twelve months before appointment.

16) Women visitors might be employed for certain classes of out-relief cases.

17) A graded Public Assistance Service should be set up which should include all officers concerned with the supervision, control, and disciplinary treatment of the poor, including relieving officers, both male and

female, masters, matrons and superintendents of institutions of every grade, labour masters and mistresses. In this service there should be more opportunity of promotion from the lower to the higher ranks, and no question of superannuation should hinder the transfer of efficient and promising officers from one Local Authority to another.

70. We have also recommended, in this Part of our Report, that the officer referred to in recommendation No. 14 above, who will be the chief officer of the Public Assistance Committee, shall be called the Superintendent of Public Assistance, and that the relieving officers working under him shall be called Assistance Officers. The Clerk of the Public Assistance Authority we propose to call the Director of Public Assistance.

(17). Main Principles of a Reformed Poor Law

71. We have now completed the description of the new machinery we propose to set up in the place of the Boards of Guardians and their officers, and we turn to the principles which we hope this new organisation will keep before it in its exercise of its powers. These principles may be thus epitomised:

1) That the treatment of the poor who apply for Public Assistance should be adapted to the needs of the individual, and, if institutional, should be governed by classification.

2) That the public administration established for the assistance of the poor should work in co-operation with the local and private charities of the district.

3) That the system of Public Assistance thus established should include processes of help which would be preventive, creative and restorative.

4) That every effort should be made to foster the instincts of independence and self-maintenance amongst those assisted.

72. Any treatment adapted to the needs of cases, especially if applied on a large scale, requires not only many helpers but also such a distribution of cases amongst officials and workers as will allow time and attention to be given to each individual case. Our scheme of organisation permits of this sub-division, for it will always be competent for the Public Assistance Authority to increase the number of Public Assistance Committees in any district, or to divide the district.

73. We now pass on to the methods of Public Assistance, and the treatment to be applied to the different classes who seek it.

(18). "INDOOR" OR INSTITUTIONAL RELIEF

74. The Royal Commission of 1832 intended that the workhouse should be a place in which the able-bodied could be set to work, and that for other recipients of indoor relief provision should be made in separate and appropriate institutions. We have found that this intention has been only partially realised. In the great majority of Unions the workhouse contains several distinct classes of inmates. As the outcome of this system we have found that:

(i) Proper classification is impossible.

(ii) There is a great want of uniformity in the various workhouses.

(iii) Indoor relief is deterrent to some and attractive to others.

(iv) The cost of erection, equipment, and indoor maintenance all tend to rise.

(v) A class of "ins and outs" has come into existence.

(vi) Residence in a workhouse has a demoralising effect.

75. We recommend that in the future:

(i) General workhouses should be abolished.

(ii) Indoor relief should be given in separate institutions appropriate to the following classes of applicants, viz.:

Children

Aged and Infirm

Sick

Able-bodied men

Able-bodied women

Vagrants

Feeble-minded and epileptics

(iii) All indoor cases should be revised from time to time.

(iv) Powers of removal to and detention in institutions should be given, with proper safeguards, to the Public Assistance Authority.

(v) The treatment of inmates should be made as far as possible curative and restorative.

(vi) The Central Authority should exercise a more strict control over expenditure on buildings and equipment.

(vii) In every institution for the aged and for the able-bodied a system of classification should be adopted on the basis of conduct before and after admission.

(19). Outdoor Relief or "Home Assistance"

76. We have dealt at some length with the history of outdoor relief and the problems which are bound up with it. We have seen that the Royal Commission of 1832 proposed the abolition of outdoor relief in the case of the able-bodied, and that Parliament accepted that principle. We have described the various orders issued from time to time by the Poor Law Commissioners, the Poor Law Board and the Local Government Board for its prohibition or regulation. We have also traced the fluctuations of public opinion which have greatly influenced its administration in those cases in which it is permitted.

77. The results of our investigations into its history, of our own observation in visiting Boards of Guardians in different parts of the country, and of the evidence given before us, may be summarised as follows:

We have found a total want of principle and of uniformity in its administration, due, as we think, in part at least, to a lack of sufficient supervision. This want of uniformity does not necessarily arise from a difference in the circumstances of unions, but is generally the result of careless administration. We have been impressed by the inadequacy which often characterises it, particularly in the case of widows with families, and by the absence of thorough knowledge of applicants on the part of Boards of Guardians, and sometimes even of their officers. We have had to record cases in which it was distributed with a complete disregard of sound policy, and, though rarely, on grounds, so far as we could judge, inconsistent with any high standard of administrative honesty. We have found that in few cases is any care or thought given to the conditions under which those who receive it are living. We do not recommend its abolition, partly because we hope that, if our proposals are adopted, the need for it will gradually disappear, and, in any case, its mischiefs will be reduced to a minimum, and partly because we feel that time is needed for the development of a curative system of treatment, and that the abolition of out-relief might cause hardship. We also feel that it may be, if used wisely, a means of restoring to independence those to whom it is given, and that the strict supervision which we recommend of the housing, surroundings and habits of the recipients may do much to raise the level of a neighborhood.

78. We think that the work done by out-relief, so far as it is useful, might be better done by voluntary agencies, and we hope that in the future

it will be so, and that a clear line will be drawn between the "necessitous," who are properly relieved by the community, and the "poor" who are the proper objects of voluntary aid.

79. Our chief recommendations are:

1) That Out-relief, or as we shall call it, Home Assistance, should be given only after thorough inquiry, except in cases of sudden and urgent necessity.

2) That it should be adequate to meet the needs of those to whom it is given.

3) That persons so assisted should be subject to supervision.

4) That, with a view to inquiry and supervision, the case-paper system should be everywhere adopted.

5) That such supervision should include in its purview the conditions, moral and sanitary, under which the recipient is living.

6) That voluntary agencies should be utilised as far as possible for the personal care of individual cases.

7) That there should be one uniform Order governing Outdoor Relief or "Home Assistance."

(20). CHILDREN

80. Prior to 1834, of all classes that came under the authority of the Poor Law, children were, perhaps, the most neglected. According to the evidence then given, the majority of the Poor Law children in workhouses outside London were merely trained in ignorance, idleness and vice, and not one-third of them found any respectable employment. The majority dropped almost mechanically into the ranks of pauperism and crime.

81. It is gratifying to us to be able to give a very different account of the present condition of the children. The evidence was almost unanimous as to the good results obtained under the various systems of education and training in force, and this evidence was confirmed by our own experience when visiting and inspecting the various educational institutions and domiciles. Few such children in after life fall back into pauperism, and it is probable that the children in some, at least, of the present Poor Law schools are being better fitted for earning their living than those educated outside. This substantial improvement must be put to the credit of the existing Poor Law administrators. We consider that they have, through the educational methods now in force, weakened if not stopped an old and copious source of pauperism.

82. We may briefly summarise our opinion upon the different systems of dealing with Poor Law children now in force.

83. First of all, we are strongly of opinion that effective steps should be taken to secure that the maintenance of children in the workhouse be no longer recognised as a legitimate way of dealing with them. We put this in the forefront of our recommendations.

84. As to the other systems in force, viz.: District Schools, Grouped Cottage Homes, Scattered Homes, Boarding-out, we consider that each system has its merits and its drawbacks, and that more depends upon the administrators than upon the system.

85. The District Schools, established first in 1844, give an excellent education, and those trained therein do well in after life. We do not endorse the wholesale condemnation of these institutions by the Committee on the Care of Poor Law Children in 1896. All large schools have inherent evils connected with the aggregation of children of various ages, and the District Schools are not free from such defects. We would not, however, in any case, recommend the multiplication of large institutional schools, as we think that there are other methods of education and training, particularly for girls, which are more adaptable and produce even better results.

86. Grouped Cottage Homes, introduced in 1867, give an excellent education and training, but there are grave objections to their elaborate construction and equipment, and the growing cost of maintenance in them.

87. The Scattered Homes, which have the great advantage of involving very little capital expenditure and of securing a kind of home life particularly valuable for girls, have been increasingly adopted by other unions since they were started in Sheffield. Such Homes, when closely supervised and under competent foster-mothers, promise good results.

88. Boarding-out is another method of training children which might and should be greatly extended. Here the expense is comparatively small and involves no capital outlay whatever, and where the system is well managed a real home life is secured for the children, and they enter upon industrial life on the same terms as the children of the independent working classes. In Scotland, it is the general system for the upbringing of Poor Law children, and there it works exceedingly well; but a most careful and constant supervision over all such children is indispensable, and where such a system of inspection cannot be had, boarding-out ought not to be attempted. So far as our evidence and special investigations go, the system

of boarding-out within the Union has been liable to be very unsatisfactory owing to lack of proper supervision.

We have recommended that the work of supervision of boarding-out within the Union by the Public Assistance Committee should be placed in the hands of competent women officers, and that special care should be taken when the boarding-out is with relatives.

89. We think that the power to adopt children of vicious parents should be more frequently exercised and accompanied by a stricter dealing with the parent, and that the Public Assistance Authorities should, in future, retain supervision of adopted children up to the age of twenty-one.

90. We think also that, in all cases, there should be systematic records of the after life of children leaving the care of the Public Assistance Authorities.

91. The condition of the out-relief children—that is, children whose parents are in receipt of out-relief—is much less satisfactory. The Guardians have not in the past assumed the same responsibility, or, in fact, in some cases, any responsibility for these children. The condition of many of them is far from what it should be.

It should be a direction to the Public Assistance Authority that when Home Assistance is given for the maintenance of children, it should see that the assistance is adequate in amount; that the children are being properly nourished; that the housing conditions are satisfactory; and, particularly that no children are maintained in immoral surroundings. Otherwise the children should be sent to an institution or industrial school.

92. As regards the difficult question of the employment of widows in receipt of Public Assistance, we have recommended that the mother, when a widow and respectable woman, should not be separated from her children, and that the Assistance should be such as to enable her to give the time necessary for taking care of her children. If the children are more numerous than she can manage, they or some of them should be sent as day boarders to a school where they can be fed during school hours. In populous districts these schools might be started much on the lines of the day industrial schools, but care must be taken to give to them such a designation and surrounding as will altogether dissociate them from crime or misconduct. When the children are too young to go to school, the mother should not go to work unless a sufficient substitute for her can be provided.

93. As regards the emigration of children, we are of opinion that its

advantages on the whole outweigh its dangers, particularly where the parents are neglectful and unworthy. Boards of Guardians are well advised in taking advantage of this mode of treatment.

94. Since 1834, a large number of specialised charitable institutions dealing with special classes of children have grown up. These, when certified and put under inspection, have been largely utilised for Poor Law children, and we see in this a beginning of co-operation between Poor Law and voluntary charities which might form the basis of a much wider scheme. As regards other large charitable institutions for dealing with poor children generally which are not certified, it is a question whether they should not be registered as proposed in Part VII and subject to some supervision.

95. Whilst we recommend special co-operation between the Poor Law and the Education Authorities, we are not in favour of transferring the education of Poor Law children wholly to the local Education Authorities, but we would recommend a scheme by which teachers in either service should have the same status and be interchangeable.

(21). THE AGED

96. The question of the aged poor, as is shown in the chapter relating to that class, has in recent years received much attention; their diet and institutional accommodation have been improved, and the scale of outdoor relief has been raised. Of all the adult classes receiving relief, there is none whose condition appeals more strongly to public sympathy, and whose treatment requires more discrimination and greater variety.

97. The respectable aged regard a good character as their most precious possession; those who have sunk low in the scale of respectability consider good or bad character as a matter of indifference. By associating the respectable and the disreputable in institutions without classification, a sense of wrong is aroused in the minds of those of good character. They feel that a public authority, by forcing them to associate with the depraved, has stained and tarnished their most valued treasure. This feeling is recognised by many Boards of Guardians, who have classified the aged by character as far as the accommodation of a single institution permitted.

98. The health and strength of the individual which, in any case, must be on the wane, is a factor which obviously must be carefully taken into account in the treatment and classification of the aged. But there is another human element which, under our present system, is not called into

action—that is, the capacity and willingness of the old person to help himself. When the institution is on a large scale he may become a mere *numero*; the aged person is, day by day, fed, clothed, and accommodated mechanically as one unit amongst many. His everyday life is deprived of all opportunity for exertion, thought and independence, and this has its inevitable effect upon the *morale* of even the active and the willing. The physical comfort of such a life may be enhanced, but that again is purchased by the loss of much that makes existence pleasant and cheerful even to the aged.

99. By the reforms we propose, the Public Assistance Authority will have at their disposal all the institutions within a county, and will, therefore, have facilities for classifying the necessitous poor by institutions. We recommend that one or more of those institutions, according to the requirements of each county area, should be set aside for the necessitous aged, and that their classification should be determined by their physical condition, the record of their lives previous to their admission into the institution, and their behaviour after admission.

100. We have greatly admired the small homes which some Boards of Guardians have erected, purchased, or rented for the accommodation of a limited number of respectable aged persons, who are there helped and looked after by a matron. The cost per head, including maintenance, rent, or repayment of building loan, is not greater than the cost in the workhouse, but the tone, and vivacity of the individual and his willingness to help himself is incomparably greater. In each room are the little treasures of the inmates—sometimes furniture, sometimes china, sometimes a keepsake—intrinsically worth little, but the very sight of them, and the daily task they suggest, make the life of their owner very different from the colourless and dreary routine of workhouse existence. Whenever additional accommodation for the respectable aged is required, we recommend that the system of small homes should be adopted; but, with its adoption, visitation and supervision must at the same time be organised.

101. As regards outdoor relief or Home Assistance given to the aged, we recommend that greater care be taken to ensure its adequacy; and that the recipients be periodically visited by the officers of the Public Assistance Committee and by voluntary visitors. In rare cases in which the old person is hopeless, has no friends, and is neglected, there should be power for compulsory removal to an institution to secure the comfort and even the safety of the person concerned.

(22). MEDICAL RELIEF AND ITS PROPOSED REORGANISATION

102. In a previous part of our Report we have dealt at some length with the development of the present system of Poor Law medical relief. We have enumerated its main defects. We have described the working of the various agencies, public and private, which provide medical assistance to poor persons outside the Poor Law. We have shown the evils which arise from the present want of co-operation, and the consequent overlapping between these agencies and the Poor Law. We have also stated our objections to proposals which were submitted to us for making medical assistance gratuitous for all who cared to apply for it, and for transferring to the Sanitary Authorities the work of the Guardians in connection with medical relief.

103. We have drawn up a scheme with the object of co-ordinating and systematising the work of the various agencies now administering medical assistance to poor persons in sickness. Among other advantages we are hopeful that it will do much to bring the voluntary hospitals into closer co-operation with the rate-supported hospitals. So urgent and difficult is this question that it has been suggested to us that a special Royal Commission should forthwith be appointed for the purpose of endeavouring to secure a *modus vivendi* on reasonable and advantageous terms between all those agencies. Such a Commission may ultimately be necessary, but in the first instance we are inclined to await the results of the efforts at co-operation which will be initiated all over the country if the organisation which we propose to set up be adopted.

104. The organisation we propose will not only fit into and utilise existing medical agencies and institutions, but, by inducing the wage-earning population to provide medical assistance to themselves on a contributory basis, it will, we hope, encourage qualities of providence and independence. Our main proposals for medical assistance are as follows:

1) That, the Public Assistance Authority, to assist them in carrying out their functions in connection with medical assistance, shall appoint a committee from among their number, to which shall be added representatives of the Health Committee of the County Council or of the County Borough Council, and of the local branch or branches of the British Medical Association. This committee shall be called the County or County Borough Medical Assistance Committee, as the case may be, and shall have power to co-opt representatives of local hospitals, county

or county borough nursing associations, dispensaries, and registered friendly societies.

2) That where necessary a local committee on similar lines shall be appointed by each Public Assistance Committee for the purposes of the local administration of medical assistance. This committee shall be termed the Local Medical Assistance Committee.

3) That all or any of the functions of the Public Assistance Authority in regard to medical assistance may be referred to the County or County Borough Medical Assistance Committee.

4) That, in all matters affecting medical assistance, there should be systematic co-operation between the Public Assistance Authorities, the Public Health Authorities, the Education Authorities, and the Voluntary Medical Institutions, based on a clear definition of their respective functions.

5) That the medical and nursing needs of each area, whether institutional or otherwise, should be reviewed, and, if necessary, supplemented, regard being had to the available provision made by Poor Law, Sanitary, or Voluntary Authorities.

6) That Medical Assistance should be organised on a provident basis.

7) That a general system of provident dispensaries should be established, of which existing voluntary outdoor medical organisations be invited to form an integral part, and that every inducement should be offered to the working classes below a certain wage limit to become, or to continue to be, members of a provident dispensary. To this end the subscription to the provident dispensary should cover the following advantages to its members:

a) Power to choose their own doctor from the doctors upon the list of the dispensary.

b) The provision of adequate medical assistance at a rate or fee within the reach of those subscribing to the Provident Dispensary.

c) Institutional treatment upon a recommendation from the dispensary doctor.

8) That medical treatment should be more readily accessible to all who are in need of it; that, in cases of illness in which immediate treatment is necessary, the physical condition of the patient should be the first consideration; that in such cases medical aid should be obtainable

in the first instance by application to any medical officer in the service of the Provident Dispensary.

9) That, except as regards the cases requiring immediate attention above referred to, all necessitous persons shall receive medical assistance through the Public Assistance Committee.

10) That certain cases in receipt of public assistance, such as the aged and widows with young children, might be made members of the Provident Dispensary on payment of the necessary fees by the Public Assistance Committee.

11) That domiciliary medical assistance at the public cost should be conditional upon the maintenance of a healthy domicile and good habits.

12) That no disfranchisement should be attached to any form of medical assistance.

(23). THE VOLUNTARY AID ORGANISATION

105. We have said so much in preceding parts of our Report as to the reorganisation of charity, that we need not here do more than indicate generally what the functions of charity should be, and the position it should occupy towards Public Assistance. The Public Assistance Authority can help only those who are destitute or, as we prefer to call it, necessitous, it cannot help many others who are, from various causes, steadily slipping downwards in the social scale. To stop this downward progress is the special duty of charity which, if properly organised, should be an effective agent combating the incipient development of destitution and distress.

But, in addition to this, charity has a still larger task of effective co-operation with the Poor Law, and Mr. Goschen's Minute of 1869 sent to Metropolitan Boards of Guardians laid down admirable principles as a foundation for such co-operation. We believe that it is mainly due to the want of general and systematic organisation that the principles there enunciated have not been extensively applied and made an operative force in our national system of relief.

106. We have endeavoured to create out of existing voluntary and charitable agencies an organisation, established by statute, to form a recognised link between Public Assistance and charity. We have therefore proposed that in every County and County Borough there shall be a

Council of Voluntary Aid, and in every district a Voluntary Aid Committee, which shall carry on and develop the functions of charity by methods which we have detailed in Part VII.

107. The functions of Public Assistance and Voluntary Aid, as we have sketched them, are so closely allied that it may be asked whether the applicants for help can be divided out between them, and, if so, on what principle. The materials for an answer are supplied partly by the evidence tendered to us, and partly by our own personal observation. In addition to those of the able-bodied whom we have referred to in Part VI as suitable for Voluntary Aid, there is a class of case which is in constant danger of falling into pauperism, viz., the mother of a family who is suddenly left a widow. To such cases Boards of Guardians make a grant of money and do little more. But money is the least of a widow's many needs. If her independence is to be preserved and her family to be well started in the world, she must have encouragement to persevere, opportunities for self-help, and openings for her children. Such a case should clearly be dealt with by Voluntary Aid; for Voluntary Aid is more sympathetic and more elastic than official assistance can be. Old people, again, who have done their best to make provision for themselves, and perhaps through the dishonesty of others have been disappointed, may be appropriately helped by Voluntary Aid. Even where a pension has been provided under the Old-Age Pensions Act, additions to the comforts may very fairly be made by charity. But we go further than this and express the hope that, when our proposed reforms are in full working order, the great majority of cases will pass, as it were, through the sieve of Voluntary Aid before they reach Public Assistance.

108. The special return of persons relieved during the year ended 30th September, 1907, suggests that many cases of temporary distress might be dealt with by voluntary agencies instead of by the Poor Law. Thirty per cent. of the applications to the Poor Law were cases of persons whose aggregate period of relief during the year did not exceed one month, and who were not relieved on more than two occasions during the year.

109. Our recommendations in regard to the Voluntary Aid Organisation are as follows:

(A) Establishment of the Voluntary Aid Councils and Committees

(1.) That in the area of each Public Assistance Authority, that is in each County or County Borough, there be formed a Voluntary Aid

Council, consisting in part of Trustees of endowed charities, of members of registered voluntary charities, as defined below, of some members of the Public Assistance Authority, and of such persons as members of friendly societies and trade associations, of clergy and ministers, and of other persons being co-opted members, as may be settled in schemes approved by the Charities Commission.

(2.) That a statutory obligation be imposed upon the Lord Lieutenants, the Chairmen of County Councils, the Lord Mayors, and Mayors of County Boroughs to take steps, within a given period, and after consultation with the managers of charitable societies, Trustees of Endowed Charities and members of the Public Assistance Authority, for drawing up schemes in accordance with the preceding recommendation, which schemes must be submitted to the Charities Commission for approval.

(3.) That the Voluntary Aid Council submit to the Charities Commission proposals for the formation of Voluntary Aid Committees to be drawn up in the form of schemes to be approved by the Commission, and that the Voluntary Aid Council under such schemes appoint as members of the Voluntary Aid Committees persons such as those mentioned in Recommendation I.

(4.) That Voluntary Societies or Charities as defined in Recommendation 17, be entitled to register at the Charities Commission on lines similar to those of the registration of Friendly Societies under the Friendly Societies' Act.

(5.) That a registered voluntary society be entitled to nominate members of its own body for appointment to the Voluntary Aid Council and to the Voluntary Aid Committee of the district in which either its institution or any branch of its institution has an office.

(6.) That it is desirable that the Voluntary Aid Committee have its offices in the same building as the Committee of Public Assistance.

(B) Functions of the Voluntary Aid Council

(7.) The duties of the Voluntary Aid Councils would be for the most part not executive but supervisory. The executive work would be assigned to the Voluntary Aid Committees. The Voluntary Aid Council would supervise the operations of these Committees generally and would, as far as possible, maintain the same principles of help and relief throughout County or County Borough. They would collect funds for distribution to Voluntary Aid Committees, and they would allocate funds to poor districts. The County is already the accepted area for many benevolent and philanthropic purposes. The local infirmary or hospital is frequently a County institution. There are County nursing associations, and the County is the recognised centre in connection with various naval and military charitable associations. We propose that the Voluntary Aid Council acting for the County should promote any voluntary institutions, associations, or societies for which the County, as a whole, has need. Its duties would thus be important and distinctive.

(C) Functions of the Voluntary Aid Committee

(8.) That the Voluntary Aid Committee aid (1) persons in distress whose cases do not appear to be suitable for treatment by the Public Assistance Committee, and (2) applicants for Public Assistance whose cases have been referred to the Committee by the Public Assistance Committee.

(9.) That, with a view to the thorough treatment of individual cases, the Voluntary Aid Committee make such arrangements for the investigation of the applications made to them as the Charities Commission may deem necessary and sufficient.

(10.) That in dealing with persons in distress for whom it is desired to provide aid by way of monetary relief, it shall be the duty of the Voluntary Aid Committee to obtain such sums as may be possible from relations of the applicant, from friends, and from charitable sources generally for the aid of individual cases.

(11.) That with the administration of aid on the part of the Voluntary Aid Committee there should be associated such a system of voluntary visitation as the Committee may deem advisable in view of the responsibilities of their work in providing effectual aid, and in view of the physical needs and the habits of those whom they decide to assist.

(12.) That the Voluntary Aid Committee be empowered to appoint such Local Committees as it may deem necessary, subject to the approval of the Voluntary Aid Council.

(13.) That a Voluntary Aid Committee shall, as far as possible, register the cases dealt with by the Public Assistance Committee and by the Charitable societies and institutions in the district.

(14.) That Voluntary Aid Committees receive the support of the Public Assistance Committee, and of the Inspectors of the Local Government Board, with a view to systematising the relations between the Public

Assistance and Voluntary Aid Committees and promoting co-operation between them.

(15.) That Voluntary Aid Councils or Committees be eligible for subscriptions from the Public Assistance Authority, on the lines of 42 and 43 Vict., c. 54, Section 10.

(D) The Charities Commission

(16.) That the Charity Commission be attached to the Local Government Board, and that the Commissioners and Assistant Commissioners, permanent or temporary, be appointed by the Local Government Board, whose President should represent it in the House of Commons.

(17.) That the Charity Commission be enlarged, and that there be assigned to it two departments of work, the supervision of endowed charities on the lines of the Charitable Trusts Acts, and the registration of Voluntary charities or Societies which hold any property in land or houses by purchase, or by leasehold, or are the tenants of any property under yearly or other agreements.

(18.) That the name of the Charity Commission be the Charities Commission.

(19.) That the staff of the Commission be strengthened so as to fulfill all the various additional duties that may devolve upon them:

1. As a centre for the registration of voluntary charities.

2. In assisting in the preparation of schemes for the establishment of Voluntary Aid Councils and for registering such schemes.

3. In assisting in the preparation of schemes for the establishment of Voluntary Aid Committees and for registering and supervising their administration.

4. In the scrutiny of accounts and statements relating to Voluntary Aid Councils and Committees.

5. In the supervision of other schemes; and

6. In the scrutiny of the accounts of endowed and registered charities.

(20.) That Section 30 of the Endowed Schools Act, 1869, by which certain charities founded for purposes of relief may be applied to purposes of education, be repealed.

(21.) That it be provided in a Statute amending the Charitable Trusts Acts that, by order of the Charities Commission, any charities, as defined in Section 30 of the Endowed Schools Acts, 1869, exclusive of Loan Charities, Apprenticeship Charities, and Charities for Advancement in

Life, may be used for the relief of distress, subject to such conditions respecting enquiry and other matters as the Commissioners may determine under a general order.

[To prevent misunderstanding, it should, perhaps, be mentioned that we are not concerned with educational charities, whether ecclesiastical or not ecclesiastical, but with eleemosynary charities; and further, neither here nor elsewhere do we intend to include in our recommendations the endowed or the voluntary charities of churches or congregations granted for religious purposes, nor the voluntary charities of churches or congregations provided for eleemosynary purposes.]

(24). INVALIDITY INSURANCE

110. On the very difficult and complex question of Invalidity Insurance, we arrived at certain tentative conclusions which we stated concisely in Part VIII of our Report. To further compress these views might lead to ambiquity or misunderstanding. We therefore here repeat the opinions we have already expressed.

111. We have shown in another Chapter the great changes that have taken place in the organisation of industry during the last eighty years. The more intimate and inter-dependent relations that often used to exist between employers and employed have been superseded by a system which, in appearance and also largely in fact, divides the interests of the employers from those of the workmen. This in turn tends to efface duties which might have been urged on the one side or on the other as a kind of moral obligation.

112. The evidence shows that, with very few exceptions, what working-men desire is the "cash nexus"—the bare wage contract uninfluenced by any but purely economic considerations—and the employing classes generally have accepted the situation and consider their obligations fulfilled when they pay the wage. Over the great trades, wages are determined by collective bargaining between Trade Unions on the one side, and large employers and associations of employers on the other. The issue of the system is, for those who find employment, a maximum wage during the prime of life, and no wage at all when the prime is passed.

113. The theory of industry which used to prevail was that the worker should maintain himself throughout life by his own exertions, providing for contingencies and for old age by thrift, or that, if he could not do so and his relatives were unable to help, he should receive poor relief. But

of late years the "cash nexus" has been supplemented and modified in two different ways—the Employers' Liability and the Workmen's Compensation Acts and the Old Age Pensions Act—the one insuring the operative against the accidents more incidental to work than heretofore, the other providing for a time when he is no longer able to work for his own support.

But it has become evident that these two methods do not meet all the exigencies which have arisen under this system. Accidents are not the only checks to wage-earning during active life, and wage-earning itself, as we have seen, generally ceases long before the pension age of seventy.

114. From the Chapter on "Social and Industrial Developments since 1834," it seems clear that the present organisation of industry, with its excessive specialisation and universal application of machinery, has raised the standard of work required from the ordinary operative. From such an organisation, many, we fear, owing to want of original capacity and want of early training, must always be excluded and fall into intermittent and ill-paid occupations. Trade Union regulations have worked in the same direction. The "standard wage" is based on the assumption that the worker employed is worth that wage to his employer; if the employer does not consider him so, the man is dismissed. The same tendency seems to have been strengthened by the working out of the Employers' Liability Act and the Workmen's Compensation Acts. Whatever be the cause, the fact remains that, since the passing of these Acts, the number of injuries registered has constantly increased. Against the undue extension of this liability, the insuring bodies, whether employers themselves or outside companies, must protect themselves, and the system necessarily excludes many who cannot fulfill the insurance standard whatever it may be. Those presumably more liable to accident, though still more or less efficient, are excluded, and a new standard of ability is created which reacts on industry generally. A large class grows up of partially efficient unemployed men. They accept the situation, with complaint, indeed, but with submission, and thus assume a new position which imposes on society many new anxieties and difficulties.

115. We have, again, evidence to show that industrial demand, as it now exists, draws many younger unskilled men into a kind of employment, in its earlier stages remunerated by a wage which will not increase at any later period of their lives but will rather diminish. Such a demand in effect puts a premium on want of skill; if it be inevitable, it suggests that

measures should be taken by way of insurance to prevent in part the evil results which must follow.

116. The years between the withdrawal from wage-earning and the pension age present a more serious problem than ever before. Trade Union regulations make it difficult for men skilled in the great trades to work on at their trades and accept a lower wage, and partial employment is more difficult to get. If, as frequently happens, there is not enough put by to cover this period, insufficiency of means or the acceptance of relief seems inevitable. In such cases the fact of other men getting a State pension at the age of seventy, on the ground that they are unable to earn a wage, may create a feeling of injustice on the part of those who have not attained the age and are yet as effectually barred from wage-earning.

Unless, therefore, some system of wages graduated according to age can be adopted, it is clear that workmen above a certain period of life will for the future find it more difficult to keep themselves in continuous employment. We do not forget that, for the solution of these and other industrial problems, we may look with growing confidence to methods of remuneration such as co-operation and co-partnership. Of their importance and promise we are convinced; but we have felt that to deal with them fully would take us far beyond the terms of our reference.

117. We seem almost driven to the conclusion that a new form of insurance is required, which, for want of a better name, we may call Invalidity Insurance. The early superannuation of the best workmen is so well recognised that it will, in all probability, give rise to demands for lowering the pension age, and will, at some point or other, entail a financial burden beyond the power of the national resources to bear.

118. We have made strong recommendations as regards insurance against temporary unemployment, but this does not meet the case of such persons when entirely incapacitated from wage-earning. It would, at any rate, be more agreeable to them, and more consonant with the feeling of the community, that they should fall back on an insurance fund to which they had at least contributed a part, than that they should be forced to have recourse to the Public Assistance Authorities. Such a scheme of Invalidity Insurance strongly appeals to us as calculated to meet many of the evils which we have been discussing. One thing, however, must be borne in mind. Whatever be the risk insured against, whether it be sickness, accident, old age, or unemployment, the possibility of such

insurance depends on the existence of savings, whether these savings be in private or collective hands, or be put in the hands of the State by taxes which represent the savings, or what otherwise might be the savings, of its citizens. Insurance, in short, is only a method for the utilisation of those savings. Whatever may be said, in order to insure, some people must have saved individually or collectively.

119. As the necessity for such insurance seems to arise from the very organisation of industry which the nation has adopted, such a fund, it seems to us, might appropriately be supported partly by contributions from employers, partly by contributions from employees, and partly by a subsidy from the State. But in considering the amount of any subsidies to be granted by the State, we think that full weight should be given to the fact that a very heavy charge has recently been imposed upon the revenue of the country by the Statute granting gratuitous old age pensions to all persons above 70 years of age who comply with certain conditions.

120. We have consulted three eminent actuaries as to the weekly premiums for which a man, aged twenty-one, in good health, and employed in a healthy occupation, could ensure the receipt of 10s. 6d. a week during the first twenty-six weeks of illness, and 7s. 6d. a week during the remainder of illness up to age sixty-five. Mr. T. G. Ackland, F.I.A., taking a 3 per cent. basis, places the amount at 3·9d.; Mr. George King, F.I.A., assuming 2½ per cent. as the rate of interest, estimates the amount at 3·74d., and Mr. F. G. P. Neison, F.I.A., at 3·62d. These sums are little in excess of the average weekly fee payable per child at school up to 1891, and remitted by the Act of that year.

121. Though we have obtained a good deal of information from the Board of Trade concerning systems of insurance, both at home and abroad, and also from a number of witnesses representing the provident and benefit societies of this country, the information is not sufficient to enable us to make specific recommendations . . . . It will be seen that none of them exactly meets the case, and, moreover, generally the schemes have not been long enough in operation to enable us to judge as to their measure of success. The foundations of any future legislation ought to be very closely scrutinised. They should be broad, solid, and capable of continuous extension, and the organisations resting upon them should be so constructed as to expand automatically according to need. The great trade and benefit organisations in existence in this country ought to be

very freely consulted before any proposals are made in Parliament. If time had permitted, we might have been able to make definite recommendations under this head, but in view of the urgent necessity of laying our more important proposals before Your Majesty, all we feel justified in doing is to state our opinion that the information at our disposal requires to be supplemented before legislation can be attempted.

(25). The Able-bodied and Unemployment

122. In the sections of the Report dealing with distress from unemployment, we gave a consecutive narrative of the social and industrial developments since 1834. Such a recital was necessary to establish the groundwork of our subsequent conclusions. A review of existing conditions has led us to two definite conclusions:

1) We have an increased aggregation of unskilled labour at our great ports and in certain populous districts.

2) This aggregation of low-grade labour is so much in excess of the normal local needs as to promote and perpetuate under-employment.

123. We went on to consider the conditions connected with skilled and high-grade labour, in order to ascertain if they were such as tended towards the aggravation of under-employment in the unskilled labour market. Though the survey of this part of our industrial system was far more satisfactory, yet there were causes in operation even here, which tended from time to time to add to the number of those seeking casual or intermittent employment. The growth and continuous expansion of our trade places cyclical fluctuations more and more beyond the control of any one single industrial district. The high pressure of competition raises the standard and shortens the period of efficiency of the worker, whilst changes both in fashion and in methods of production are becoming not only more sudden but also more uncertain in their duration. Employment once lost by the middle-aged and less efficient is regained with greater difficulty than heretofore. When to these ordinary conditions are added the cyclical depressions in trade, a serious state of affairs is created, and we came to our third conclusion that—

3) This normal condition of under-employment, when aggravated by periodic contraction of trade or by the inevitable changes in methods of production, assumes such dimensions as to require special machinery and organisation for its relief and treatment.

124. We then carefully scrutinised the constitution and operations of the various relief organisations, both public and private, normal and abnormal, that are now in existence. We looked at their work from various points of view and asked ourselves, firstly: was the relief given in times of distress adequate and suitable? and secondly: were the after consequences of such relief beneficial or prejudicial to the community affected—did it, in a word, strengthen or weaken the original causes of the distress?

125. We regret to state that our investigations point to the conclusion that the relief given was frequently unsuitable and inadequate, and that its effects were often pernicious.

Poor Law relief, if deterrent, is at times deterrent to the wrong people and restorative treatment plays a very small part in its methods.

Charity, when organised and working in co-operation with the Poor Law and other relief agencies, is always helpful, but, in the absence of these conditions, charitable effort too frequently takes the form of doles to the unworthy and results in demoralisation.

The relief works carried on by Municipal Authorities, and by Distress Committees under the Unemployed Workmen Act, have in certain instances been successful in reaching the class for whom they were intended. In the vast majority of cases, however, they have perpetuated a system of able-bodied relief reproducing some of the bad features of the methods in force before 1834, which the Commission of that date so vigorously condemned.

It is impossible to contend that the relief measures and organisations now at work in any degree come within the category of "special machinery or organisation for the relief or treatment of distress" caused by underemployment.

126. But, during the Cotton Famine, there was a period of distress, historic both by reason of its duration and of the number of skilled workers affected by it, and in its latter phases we there found charitable and Poor Law organisations working in co-operation with marked smoothness and success. Charity and the Poor Law were supplemented not by relief works but by public works of utility managed on commercial principles, and not only was this combination most effective in times of distress but, when the distress was over, it left the community with a minimum of demoralisation. We propose to refer to these methods—which contrast so favourably with recent failures—together with certain other suggestions, which, while

preventive in their character, are designed to elicit co-operation and self-support from those whom they assist. We will deal with preventive measures first.

(A) Education

127. In previous parts of our Report we have shown how serious and widespread is the tendency for children to slip into occupations and callings which lead first to casuality and then to unemployment. Unless we can arrest at its source this increasing stream of casuality and under-employment our subsequent remedial measures may be futile. We therefore regard with favour the proposals of our Special Investigator Mr. Cyril Jackson:

1) That boys should be kept at school until the age of 15.

2) That exemption below this age should be granted only for boys leaving to learn a skilled trade.

3) That there should be school supervision till 16, and replacement in school of boys not properly employed.

We also believe that there is urgent need of improved facilities for technical education being offered to young people after the present age for leaving school. We consider that to prevent the deterioration of physique it is necessary that physical drill should be more prolonged and thorough than it has hitherto been. Although we are not unanimous upon this point, some of us believe that the most effective and thorough method of infusing into boys approaching adolescence a sense of discipline and self-restraint, both physical and moral, and of improving their physique for subsequent industrial occupations, would be a universal system of a short period of military training.

128. Before we leave the subject of education we must refer to one criticism that has been made with almost absolute unanimity. There seems to be outside the circle of the teaching profession a very strong general feeling that the education of our children in elementary schools is not of the kind which is helpful to them in after life. Education is the accepted antidote to unemployment and pauperism. The cost of elementary education in this country in 1905-6 was twenty million sterling. This is an almost entirely new national charge since 1870. It should have steadily reduced unemployment and diminished pauperism. If it has failed in this, its accepted mission, it cannot be said that the failure is due to lack of funds.

The desire of the young to raise themselves in the social scale and improve their position should ever be encouraged, but this desire seems to us too frequently to take the shape of trying to avoid handicraft and manual labour by recourse to other occupations which, though associated with a black coat, are less remunerative and less progressive than skilled handiwork. Clerical labour is a glut upon the market; high-class artisans are, according to our evidence, at times obtained with difficulty. We doubt if the atmosphere of our school life is altogether congenial to a career of manual labour. We would suggest to the Board of Education the advisability of meeting these criticisms by a thorough reconsideration of the time table and curriculum in our elementary schools as well as of the aims and ideals of elementary education. Though employers of labour may perhaps be apt to look at questions too much from their own standpoint, still, the unanimity of opinion that our school curriculum does not supply the right class of instruction and training for industrial purposes, cannot lightly be put on one side.

(B) Labour Exchanges

129. In the forefront of our proposals we place labor exchanges. We propose their establishment under the control and direction of the Board of Trade. We look to them to achieve two distinct objects:

1) An increase in the mobility of labour. To do this it is essential that they should be used freely by employers and employed, and that their management should be associated with a joint committee of these two classes. We think that Local Authorities and Government Departments should be encouraged to make use of them when engaging either skilled or unskilled labour. Their usefulness will be greatly increased if they are linked up all over the United Kingdom.

2) The collection and distribution of information. The most obvious form of this would be the dissemination of information as to demand and supply of labour in the country, and as to public works and other large contracts. But their area of usefulness should extend much further. The Board of Trade should receive weekly from the labour exchanges accurate and detailed information as to the amount of unemployment and also as to the demand for employment throughout the whole country. Owing to our vast international trade and our dependence upon external sources for the supply of the raw material we require, industrial

depression in this country is not unfrequently due to causes far away from the districts affected. We see no reason why the Board of Trade, availing itself of the information obtainable from our Consuls and other officials stationed abroad, might not in course of time become a kind of trade meteorologist, and by publishing the information received, which gradually will become greater and more exact, indicate the causes likely to affect our home industries. With this information from abroad and the returns of the labour exchanges at home, trade storm signals might be hoisted in time to prepare the districts likely to be afterwards affected.

Such a scheme would require time, money, and trouble to be expended upon it before it became a trustworthy source of advice and guidance; but in our judgment the experiment is well worth attempting.

Associated with the labour exchange there should be, in connection with every public elementary school, an intelligence bureau which would advise parents and teachers as to the branches of employment likely to give the best opening for children leaving school. By this means we hope to divert boys from the "blind-alley occupations" which so many enter at present, into occupations which will lead to permanent employment.

If this be accomplished we hope to cut off at its source one of the most fruitful supplies of casual labour.

(C) Casual Labor

130. We have dwelt in several parts of our Report on the phenomena of casual labour and its far-reaching evils, both as regards the character of the man and the disastrous effect on his family life, and we have ventured on the statement that a system so dangerous to the social life of the whole community cannot be regarded solely from the standpoint of the employer and the employee.

The remedies, however, are not very obvious, as they must be undertaken in face of a dead weight of apathy on the part of the public, and perhaps an active opposition on the part of the various interests.

131. So far as casual labour is encouraged and fostered by mere thoughtlessness on the part of those who employ it, the remedy lies in an awakening of the public conscience, and we hope that some good may be done by the mere exposure of the evils entailed. We are convinced that Government Departments and municipal bodies might do more than they do to regularise the work of those they employ.

But in its most prominent form, dock labour, the more serious problem is that, at the great ports of the kingdom, many thousands of men are engaged in an occupation which seems almost of necessity casual, and moreover, the occupation is one which seems as attractive to the docker himself as it is advantageous to his employer. Here the formidable objection is that if decasualisation on something like the lines adopted by the London and India Dock Company is attempted, a certain proportion of persons at present under-employed will be thrown out of employment altogether until re-absorbed in other industries.

With full consciousness of the gravity of this issue, we venture to think that such an effort must be made, and we have recommended that the Board of Trade should send to our large ports and industrial centres, officers who might confer with masters and workmen, with a view to reducing casual and intermittent employment to the smallest dimensions.

(D) Insurance Against Unemployment

132. Whatever the methods adopted to promote regularity of employment, the old-fashioned virtue of thrift must still occupy a central place in preventing distress. Since 1834 the opportunities of husbanding small savings and making insurance against sickness, accident, old age, and death have very greatly increased. But there seems room and necessity for a great extension of insurance against Unemployment, and in this case we have not hesitated to recommend the encouragement of a State subsidy.

The difficulty here is that the classes who are not insured against unemployment are the classes most liable to unemployment, and that the uncertainty and intermittence of their occupation makes it very difficult for them to raise by combination the necessary aggregate amount for individual insurance.

We have examined the many experiments now being tried in other countries in this direction. None of them have been quite effective in reaching these classes. But by encouraging and promoting unemployment insurance amongst the labouring classes above the rank of casuality, we hope to foster the downward growth of a desire for it.

133. Our review of unemployment insurance enabled us to arrive at the following conclusions:

First, that the establishment and promotion of Unemployment Insurance, especially amongst unskilled and unorganised labour, is of paramount importance in averting the distress arising from unemployment.

Second, that the attainment of this object is of such national importance as to justify, under specified conditions, contributions from public funds towards its furtherance.

Third, that this form of insurance can best be promoted by utilising the agency of existing trade organisations or of organisations of a similar character which may be brought into existence by a hope of participation in public contributions.

Fourth, that no scheme either foreign or British which has been brought before us is so free from objections as to justify us in specifically recommending it for general adoption.

134. Accordingly, we have recommended that a small Commission or Inter-Departmental Committee of experts and representatives of existing trade benefit organisations be appointed, with an instruction to frame a scheme or schemes for consideration.

135. Before leaving the question of insurance against unemployment, there is one point in connection with it to which we would draw attention. We have referred to the excellent work done by trade unionists in insuring against unemployment, and thus protecting themselves against one of the most formidable risks of a workman's life. But the attention of trade unions seems to us too much concentrated upon the amount of wage, too little upon the duration and regularity of the work. Irregular work, even if paid per hour at a high rate, is the workman's bane; regular and continuous work, even if the rate per hour be somewhat low, is his salvation. Whilst we admit that both considerations should be taken into account, we think that the first ought not to entirely override the second.

(E) Voluntary Aid and Unemployment

136. We have already indicated our general proposals for establishing a Voluntary Aid Organisation. At a time of general unemployment there is usually a widespread desire to render voluntary assistance of some kind. This, as we have shown, can be done in many ways (*see* Part VI and Part VII), by help given to the man and his family, or to some member of his family. Voluntary Aid Committees, working in close co-operation with Public Assistance Committees, may prevent distress due to want of work at its earlier stages, and often a little aid for a comparatively short time will prove effectual in making other and more elaborate measures

for the provision of unemployment relief unnecessary. Assistance should by this means be forthcoming to an unemployed workman who has a prospect of work in any quarter. Men and women who have acquired some experience of the personal administration of relief become then most serviceable. Indeed, we look forward to the provision by means of Voluntary Aid Committees of an outlet for the countless forms of personal service which now, owing to lack of insight and co-operation, run to waste. We hope to find here, even more than in carefully administered money help, the prevention and cure of much of the poverty and suffering which form so sad a picture at the present day.

(F) *Public Assistance and Unemployment*

137. Behind the organisation of Voluntary Aid will be the new Public Assistance Authority, which, freshly constituted and with increased powers, will be a far more potent agency in dealing with distress amongst the able-bodied than the bodies which it will supersede.

138. The methods at its disposal for dealing with the able-bodied out of employment will be many and graded. They have been described in much detail in Part VI of our Report and include:

1) Home Assistance, on condition of daily work, which will be available for men of good character requiring only temporary employment.

2) Industrial and Agricultural Institutions and Labour Colonies, with classification for those whose industrial antecedents perhaps are not so good, or who require more prolonged treatment.

3) Detention Colonies under the Home Office to which the "ins-and-outs," the work-shy, and the loafer will be committed for periods of detention and training.

139. If the powers thus given to the new authority are exercised with discrimination, firmness and kindness, and if the treatment of all those of inferior efficiency and character applying for Assistance is governed by the idea of industrial and moral restoration, a change for the better should soon be effected in the management of that heterogeneous mass of persons now known as the Unemployed. At the root of the new system lies the principle of classification. Classification will in future be aided by the system of case-papers and by the records of workmen registered at the Labour Exchange.

(G) Transitional Measures as to Distress from Unemployment

140. The changes which we have proposed will take some time before they can fully mature themselves. When they have separately and in combination attained a reasonable standard of working efficiency, we believe that they will be adequate to deal with local distress. But, pending their development, we consider it necessary to formulate a supplemental scheme, so safeguarded as to be put into operation only under a number of specified conditions, to meet any exceptional and protracted distress. Under this scheme, the Local Government Board may after consultation with the Board of Trade authorise the Public Works Loan Board to grant special financial facilities to Local Authorities for the prosecution of public works. Before any such authorisation is given, the two first-mentioned Departments must be convinced, by ascertained and verified facts, that local distress due to severe and prolonged industrial depression is overtaxing the resources of the newly-established Public Assistance Authorities. The works must, moreover, be of public utility in the locality, and the plans and estimates in respect of them be approved beforehand by the Local Government Board.

141. We lay great stress on the condition attaching to such works, that they should be promoted and managed on ordinary commercial lines, and that those employed should be taken on not as paupers, nor as persons to whom work will be found because they are in distress, but as workmen capable of giving an adequate return for the wage paid. Fitness for the work will in fact be the governing consideration in the engagement and retention of such workmen as may be required.

142. We are well aware that this doctrine is very unpopular in certain quarters, where it is held that the mere existence of distress is sufficient to entitle everyone affected by the distress to have work provided for him at standard wages. We contest this proposition, not from lack of humanity, but because we know that such a theory is absolutely subversive of self-respect, self-exertion, and independence, and is detrimental to the industrial efficiency of the community.

(H) General Principles Governing Public Assistance to the Able-bodied

143. Efficiency and inefficiency cannot work side by side at the same rate of pay without the certainty of inefficiency in the course of time lowering the standard of efficiency and determining the rate of pay and of

progress. In all our proposals for dealing with poverty, distress, destitution, loafing, and laziness we have relied upon being able, under the treatment we suggest, to appeal to the better and worthier instincts of the individual. These may sometimes seem to be dead, and in certain cases even may be so, but in the vast majority of cases, by working for the moral regeneration of the individual, we may hope to restore him to independence and respectability. Such a process must often be slow, and in its earlier stages inflict personal discomfort. But in no case ought it to be possible to reverse this process and to allow the malingerer or the loafer to obtain a better payment than the diligent and well-conducted.

144. It has been pointed out that the increased comfort of our workhouses has made them attractive to a class of able-bodied to whose comfort it is not desirable to add. The elaborate proposals we now make will be nugatory unless for the future it is possible to segregate and deal separately with this class. It is not easy to formulate the principles of classification; but as, in the great majority of cases, it is curative treatment which is needed, we think that the determining factor should be the hopefulness of the case in the light of the present position and past life of the applicant. In some cases, no doubt, it will be found that a certain amount of preliminary discipline is indispensable before an applicant can be trusted to make a proper use of the opportunity and assistance given to him.

(26). POLITICAL DISQUALIFICATIONS ON ACCOUNT OF PUBLIC ASSISTANCE

145. The question how far relief from the Public Assistance Authority should disfranchise its recipient is more closely connected with the relief of the able-bodied than with that of any other class of recipients of public assistance. We hold generally to the principle that those who, either from misfortune or otherwise, have failed to manage their own affairs successfully ought not by law to have power to interfere in the management of the affairs of others. But public assistance often assumes a transient form, and we are not disposed to disfranchise wholesale and unconditionally all who receive it. We therefore recommend that only those persons be disfranchised on account of public assistance who have received assistance other than medical relief for three months or more in the aggregate in the qualifying year.

As we have already stated, we do not think that medical assistance in any form should entail disfranchisement.

(27). RECOVERY OF COST OF PUBLIC ASSISTANCE

146. In our review of the working of the present law as regards the recovery of the cost of relief from the persons relieved and from their relatives, we point out that, even under the present uneven and irregular application of the law, a considerable sum is annually obtained. We in no sense wish to diminish this help to the ratepayer. On the contrary we think that the present procedure requires strengthening in various details, and we make the following recommendations:

(A) Loan Relief

(1.) Procedure for recovery should be simplified.

(B) Recovery from Relatives

(1.) Relatives who are liable should be required to contribute, and this policy should be pursued uniformly and with firmness and discretion.

(2.) Poor persons should have power to proceed directly against liable relatives, and the Public Assistance Authorities should have power to proceed against liable relatives before the applicant becomes actually chargeable.

(3.) Simplification of procedure applicable to recovery of relief from relatives.

(4.) The cost of relief given should be recoverable from relatives after the person has ceased to be chargeable.

(5.) A man should be liable to contribute to the support of his grandparents.

(6.) Non-liable relatives should also be induced to contribute where they are able to do so.

(28). BASTARDY

147. Representations have been made to us that the procedure as to the recovery of maintenance under Bastardy Orders is difficult and uncertain, and that the power of the Guardians to obtain such orders is too limited. These representations appear to us to be generally well founded. We have, therefore, made a number of detailed recommendations which will operate to the advantage of the Pubic Assistance Authorities and of the mothers. One recommendation which we make in the interests of morality is that the money paid by a putative father to the mother of an

illegitimate child under a Bastardy Order should be paid through the agency of a third person.

148. As to the treatment of unmarried mothers, regarding which we have received a great deal of evidence, we make the following recommendations:

a) *Single Lapse Cases*—These should be dealt with in institutions apart from the workhouse, preferably in charitable institutions, but if these are not available the Public Assistance Authorities should institute homes of their own. Charitable workers to watch over the girls on their first return to the world.

b) *Depraved, Immoral Women*—Detention and reformative treatment on lines similar to those adopted for "in-and-out" cases should be organised.

c) *Feeble-minded Unmarried Mothers*—These should be dealt with in accordance with the recommendations of the Royal Commission on the Feeble-minded. Meantime the Public Assistance Authorities should have power to detain such mothers.

d) For the purpose of advising in regard to all maternity cases, a Women's Committee should be appointed in connection with every Public Assistance Committee, consisting of members of that Committee and of voluntary workers.

(29). THE DETENTION OR CONTINUOUS TREATMENT OF CERTAIN CLASSES OF PERSONS RECEIVING OR APPLYING FOR PUBLIC ASSISTANCE

149. It will have been observed that from time to time in our Report, we have recommended "detention" for certain classes of cases. We now propose to summarise our various proposals in this respect and explain very shortly our reasons for recommending this form of treatment.

150. The term "detention" is perhaps, however, infelicitous. It is generally associated with the idea of punishment by imprisonment. Our primary object in proposing detention is neither punishment nor imprisonment. We aim at obtaining opportunities for applying ameliorative treatment to particular individuals over a continuous period. We desire to substitute, for the present system of incontinuous and inefficacious relief, a continuity of care and treatment which shall benefit both the recipient and the community. To secure this continuity of treatment, some powers of control are necessary, but these powers of control are intended in the vast majority of cases to be curative and stimulative rather than punitive,

nor need they necessarily be always exercised in an institution, as we shall see when we go into particulars of the various classes of cases.

Sometimes the continuity of treatment which we propose, is required primarily in the interests of the individual, sometimes primarily in the interests of the community, and sometimes indistinguishably in the interests of both the community and the individual. But all these cases have this common characteristic, viz., that the absence of power of continuous treatment constitutes a danger either to the individual or the State.

(A) Classes of Cases requiring Continuous Treatment

151. We may classify the cases according as the Continuous Treatment is necessitated by:

I. Extreme Age or Extreme Youth.

II. Illness or Disease of Mind or Body.

III. Persistent Indulgence in Vice or Pernicious Habits.

We will now describe more particularly the cases coming within these categories, and the conditions and safeguards under which we think that Continuous Treatment should be applied to them.

Class I. Those Requiring Continuous Care and Treatment on Account of Extreme Age or Extreme Youth

This will be subdivided into: (a) The Aged, and (b) Children.

a) *The Aged.* There are certain helpless, friendless, old people receiving or needing relief, and living in a state of neglect which is very harmful. Such, for instance, would be frail old persons who might fall into the fire or otherwise injure themselves, who cannot clean or feed themselves properly, or, again, who are suffering from some ailment which, though slight in itself, is yet crippling to advanced age. It does not seem right that such old people should be maintained by public money in conditions so distressing and so dangerous. They should clearly be dealt with either in almhouses or, if necessary, in infirmaries, where their wants and ailments could be properly attended to. But these cases require very considerate treatment, and it is only in the event of their being friendless, or, of the inability of their friends or relatives to look after them in their own homes, that we think that, in their own interests, what we shall call an Order for Continuous Treatment should be obtained in regard to them. The conditions under which such an Order should be obtainable are as follows:

1) A medical certificate that continuous care and treatment are essential in the interests of the health or safety of the person concerned.

2) Sufficient proof that neither such person, nor his or her friends or relatives are able and willing to provide the continuous care and treatment.

b) *Children*. The children to whom we think "Continuous Treatment" should be applied are children of "ins-and-outs" and of parents whose mode of life is so harmful to the children, that in the interests, both of the children and of the State whose future citizens they will be, the children should be separated from parental control. Under existing Acts, the Guardians already have the power to take over the rights of the parents of children until the age of eighteen, where they are of opinion that a parent of a child, by reason of mental deficiency or of vicious habits or mode of life, is unfit to have control of it. We consider that the principle of these Acts should be applied to the class of children we have specified, and that the control should continue until the age of twenty-one. More especially the Acts should automatically apply in all cases where parents have rendered themselves liable to detention through indulgence in vice or pernicious habits as explained in Class III below.

Class II. Those requiring Continuous Care and Treatment owing to Illness or Disease of Mind or Body

a) *Feeble-minded*. Under this heading come those persons who, though not certified as insane, are yet not in such sufficient possession of their faculties as to be capable of properly looking after themselves. With regard to this class, their case is fully dealt with in the report of the Royal Commission on the Care and Control of the Feeble-minded. If, as we hope, the recommendations of that Commission are carried into effect, a system of control over the feeble-minded will be initiated which will free the Poor Law administrator from one of his greatest difficulties. Meanwhile, we think that as a provisional measure, the Poor Law Authorities should be given power to detain feeble-minded persons who come under their care.

b) *Persons Suffering from Serious (Non-infectious) Illness*. Such cases would be, for instance, persons bedridden with rheumatism, or suffering from some malignant disease which could not properly be treated in their own homes. The conditions under which such persons should become liable for Continuous Treatment should be those which we have specified for the "Aged" above, viz.:

1) A medical certificate that Continuous Care and Treatment is essential in the interests of the health or safety of the person concerned.

2) Sufficient proof that neither such person, nor his or her friends or relatives are able and willing to provide the Continuous Care and Treatment.

c) *Persons Suffering from Certain Infectious or Contagious Diseases.* These may be divided into three classes:

1) *Phthisis in an Advanced Stage*—We have dealt in Par. 155, Part V, with the difficulties surrounding this class of case, and with the difference of opinion in the medical profession as to when the development of this disease does become so infectious as to be a danger to those with whom the afflicted one may come in contact. We would, therefore, only advocate a compulsory Order for Continuous Treatment in advanced cases where a medical certificate is produced, certifying that the patient is likely to infect others, or where the home conditions of the patient are such as to lead, with practical certainty, to the spread of the disease.

2) *Children Suffering from Ophthalmia or some other Infectious Complaint*—As regards ophthalmic children of "in-and-out" parents, we have recommended that they should be "detained," and the same recommendation should be applied to all children suffering from infectious complaints of such a character as to be a source of danger to other children. In their case an Order for Continuous Treatment should be obtainable upon the production of a medical certificate to the effect that the diseased child is either in a state dangerous to others, or else is likely to communicate the disease to others, and that such danger or likelihood is not being obviated by the treatment provided by the parents, guardians, relatives, or friends.

3) *Venereal Diseases*—Those affected by these diseases come under a different category. In the vast majority of cases, they have contracted this ailment by their own misconduct. We have received evidence to the effect that these diseases work terrible havoc with the physique and stamina of the community, and that much of the infant mortality and bad health of children is due to their after consequence. If the object be the arrest and stamping out of these poisonous ailments, caution must be exercised in not prescribing treatment so drastic as to lead to

their concealment. We are, however, clearly of opinion that whenever sufficient proof is produced that an individual is in such a condition as to be a danger to the community amongst whom he or she may be living, an Order for Detention or Continuous Treatment should be obtainable.

Class III. Those Requiring Continuous Care and Treatment Owing to Indulgence in Vice or Pernicious Habits

a) Unmarried Mothers. We have recommended that "first" cases should be dealt with in charitable institutions, and where the mothers are feeble-minded, they will be dealt with under that head. We have, however, to consider the case of the more depraved women who habitually make a convenience of the workhouse for the purpose of being confined with illegitimate children, who in their turn become a permanent charge upon the rates. We recognise the difficulty of dealing with these cases; on the one hand, they may not resort to the workhouse sufficiently frequently within the year to come within the ordinary category of "ins-and-outs"; on the other hand, whilst it is right to check, if possible, their career of vice, it must at the same time be recognised that the not always accessible putative father is largely to blame. We think that women of this class should be liable to an Order by Justices for a period of Continuous Treatment, and that after recovery from confinement they should be sent to some suitable institutions for a fixed period and placed under reformatory influence.

We commend this course in the interest of the woman herself. Unfortunate women, when they have fallen thus low, have often no means of subsistence except through a resumption of their vicious mode of life. The treatment we suggest may afford them some chance of regaining a respectable existence.

b) Adults Repeatedly Becoming Chargeable through Wilful Neglect or Misconduct. The last class of cases which we have to consider are those in which there appears to be no hope of applying beneficial continuous treatment, except under conditions of discipline and deterrence, such as could more efficiently and more suitably be exercised by an authority other than the Public Assistance Authority.

We have accordingly recommended that persons should be committed to a "Detention Colony" under the Home Office, for any period between six months and three years, who have been guilty of wilful and persistent repetition within a given period of any of the following offences:

1) Wilful refusal or neglect of persons to maintain themselves or their families (although such persons are wholly or in part able to do so), the result of such refusal or neglect being that the persons or their families have become chargeable to the Public Assistance Authority.

2) Wilful refusal on the part of a person receiving assistance, to perform the work or to observe the regulations duly prescribed in regard to such assistance.

3) Wilful refusal to comply with the conditions, laid down by the Public Assistance Authority, upon which assistance can be obtained, with the result that a person's family thereby becomes chargeable.

4) Giving way to gambling, drink, or idleness, with the result that a person or his or her family thereby becomes chargeable.

The results of this provision will be, we hope, that the loafer, the "in-and-out," the person who neglects his family, or who makes them chargeable owing to habits of gambling, drink, or idleness, etc., etc., will be submitted to a course of severe discipline and training, which, even if it does not restore the man to a comparative state of industrial efficiency, will at the least for a certain period prevent him from further demoralisation, and will to some extent deter both himself and others from indulging in the vice or habit responsible for his downfall.

(B) Procedure for Obtaining Order for Continuous Treatment for Classes I and II and Class III, a

152. We will now consider the procedure by which an Order for Continuous Treatment should be obtained, and also what the effects of that Order should be.

It has been suggested that in certain cases an Order for Detention or Continuous Treatment should be an administrative matter in the hands of the Public Assistance Authority, just as the Guardians now have power to detain certain paupers for short periods in the Workhouse. It must be remembered, however, that the Continuous Treatment which we now propose would extend in some cases to three years. We feel, therefore, that a proposal to commit a person to compulsory control for such a period on a mere Order of the Public Assistance Authority might meet with great opposition, and would not, in the present state of public opinion, be accepted. We therefore propose that in all these cases an Order for Continuous Treatment should only be obtainable after an application on behalf of the Public Assistance Authority to Justices of the Peace and upon such Justices being satisfied that the conditions which we have specified as rendering persons liable to continuous treatment have been fulfilled. In making these suggestions we have in mind the existing procedure under the Public Health Act, 1875 (Sect. 124), and the Infectious Disease Prevention Act, 1890 (Sect. 12), under which persons suffering from certain diseases can be removed to or detained in infectious hospitals on a Justice's order. We do not think that the application for an Order for Continuous Treatment need be made in open court; but we would allow an appeal to Quarter Sessions. Such appeal, however, should not be allowed to interfere with the temporary validity of the Order.

We have suggested that cases of inebriety should be dealt with as far as possible in their earlier stages, on the ground that the inebriate is reducing himself and his family to such straits that he will have to apply to the Public Assistance Authorities for maintenance. We have already drawn attention to the recent report of the Departmental Committee on the subject generally, with which we are in substantial agreement.

(C) Effect of an Order for Continuous Treatment

153. Persons against whom an Order for Continuous Treatment had been obtained would be under continuous control for the period named in the Order, or for a lesser period, if the Public Assistance Authority were satisfied that the conditions which had given rise to the order had ceased to exist.

It would not always be necessary that the control of the Public Assistance or other Authority should be exercised for the whole, or in some cases, for any part of the period in an institution. For instance, it would be within our view of what was right that an able-bodied man in a Detention Colony might be let out from such colony before the expiry of his Order for Continuous Treatment, on condition of reporting himself periodically to the Public Assistance Authority, in order to test the progress he had made in overcoming the habit which had led to his detention. If necessary, however, the issue of an Order for Continuous Treatment would empower the Public Assistance Authority to remove the cases to which the Order applied to an institution and to detain them in such institution for the whole period of the Order.

154. Our survey of the evils and futilities of the present system con-

vinces us that it is not possible to deal humanely, adequately, and restoratively with the cases we are considering unless there is power to give them continuous treatment under conditions which can be enforced.

(30). SETTLEMENT AND REMOVAL

155. Theoretically, there is much to be said in favour of the proposal to abolish the Law of Settlement and Removal. From a practical point of view, however, there is much to be said against its entire abolition, and, accordingly, until experience has been gained of the work of our new organisation of Public Assistance, we think it better to retain the law, but in a modified and simplified form. The specific recommendations we make are:

a) That the County or County Borough shall be the area for all purposes of settlement and removal.

b) That the forms of settlement be reduced to four, viz.: Birth, Parentage, Marriage, Residence.

c) That a settlement be acquired by one year's residence in a County or County Borough.

d) That the Local Government Board determine all cases of disputed settlement unless the Board consider that a particular case should be decided in a Court of Law.

e) That there be reciprocity of removal as between England, Scotland and Ireland.

If these changes be given effect to, the labour of inquiry, the cost of litigation, and the hardship of removal under the existing law will be very greatly diminished. We would thus hope that most of the objections to the law would be met. But, if experience showed that total abolition of the law was preferable, that course might be adopted later.

(31). VACCINATION AND REGISTRATION OF BIRTHS, ETC.

156. If the Boards of Guardians are abolished, and their Poor Law functions are transferred to a Statutory Committee of the County and County Borough Councils, their duties in connection with vaccination and registration of births, etc., which are altogether extraneous to the work of public assistance, should be handed over to the committees of these councils dealing with kindred matters. The Registrar-General considers that a closer relation between the Sanitary and Registration Districts is

highly desirable, and has furnished us with a Memorandum containing a proposal having this object in view.

(32). COMPOUNDING FOR RATES

157. A survey of the evidence upon the subject of Compounding for Rates submitted to the Local Taxation Commission as well as to ourselves has convinced us of the desirability of the direct payment of rates by those who elect Local Authorities; and although we are well aware of the difficulties which would prevent a sudden abolition of the compounding system, we are fully persuaded that it should be reduced to the lowest possible limit. This would involve more careful and detailed arrangements for the direct collection of rates; but in the long run the community would benefit not only from less extravagent administration, but from a more active and intelligent interest in local self-government on the part of the electorate. If this policy were pursued, it might also be found desirable to modify the provisions of the Poor Rate Assessment and Collection Act of 1869, in the direction of reducing the limit of rateable value for compounding purposes.

(33). THE COMPILATION OF THE STATISTICS OF PUBLIC ASSISTANCE

158. The marshalling and interpretation of the mass of statistical evidence on the subject of our inquiry has been a matter of some difficulty. Notwithstanding the many Poor Law statistical returns issued periodically we found it essential to call for further statistical information. Reference is made elsewhere to the various statistics we obtained, and to which we attach considerable value. Most important, perhaps, was the Return of the persons relieved during the twelve months ended September 30th, 1907, and of the periods and recurrence of their relief. The results of this Return have thrown a flood of light upon the character of the pauper population, and they reveal in a striking manner the varying problems which confront the Poor Law Authorities. One the one hand there are cases in which relief has been obtained on four or five different occasions during the year whilst not extending to a period of one week in the total, and on the other hand there are the many cases chargeable uninterruptedly throughout the year. Between those extremes all manner of cases are to be found, cases of the merest touch with the Poor Law, persistently recurring cases, and cases of protracted, though not permanent relief. So important

do we consider this information that we recommend the collection at regular intervals of statistics upon the same lines.

We also recommend the regular compilation of medical and age statistics, an amendment in the principle of classification according to physical ability and special Returns as to the cost of various classes of persons relieved and of various methods of relief.

(34). CONSTRUCTIVE RELIEF IN THE CASE OF THE AFFLICTED

159. We suggest an extension of the exceptions to the rule of constructive pauperism. Under the existing law a man or a widow whose dependents receive relief is considered to be constructively relieved and may be disfranchised. If, however, the dependent be blind, or deaf and dumb, this rule does not apply, and we think that similar exceptions should be made in the case of the mentally defective, epileptic, lame, deformed, and crippled, provided that the assistance rendered from public funds to or on account of the afflicted wife or child is occasioned by such infirmity. It will be seen that this extension has an important bearing on the question of disfranchisement on account of relief.

(35). TEMPORARY COMMISSION, ETC.

160. If our proposals are accepted and passed into law, we recommend that a small Temporary Commission working under the Local Government Board be appointed composed of persons of administrative experience, who should place themselves in direct communication with the Local Authorities with a view to securing the early and effective development of the new system. The appointment of such a Commission and a definition of their powers and objects should, in our judgment, be made part of the Act reforming the present Poor Law system.

We do not feel called upon to set out in much detail the transitional arrangements which may be necessary to carry the reforms we suggest into operation, and we believe that it would not even be possible to do so in an Act of Parliament.

We assume that the Local Government Board will be given the widest possible discretion to make all orders and regulations which may be necessary, and to take any steps which, in their opinion and upon the advice of the Temporary Commission, may be required to remove any difficulties arising in the establishment of the new authorities and the organisation of their work. There are one or two points, however, which we must notice.

We believe that the appointed day upon which the new bodies will be constituted and the expenses will become chargeable upon the new areas, cannot be earlier than the commencement of the financial year next ensuing after the passing of the Act. But we see no necessity for any similar postponement in the formation of the Labour Exchanges, and the appointment of the Central organisation to control them. In our opinion, this part of our proposal might be embodied in a separate Bill which should be passed at the earliest possible date. It will, of course, be understood that the new Public Assistance Authority and their Committees will, on the appointed day, take over the existing Poor Law institutions and officers, and will carry on the work of relief.

(36). Our Proposals in Relation to Scotland

161. The case of Scotland will be dealt with in a separate report which is being prepared, and will be issued as soon as possible. The Poor Law system of Scotland is in many respects essentially different from those of England and Ireland. For example:

1. The area of Poor Law administration in Scotland is the parish. The parish is also the area for educational purposes.

2. The Parochial Boards established under the Poor Law Act, 1845, for administering the Poor Laws were superseded as recently as 1894 by Parish Councils—the present authority—and these Councils discharge other functions besides those connected with the relief of the poor.

3. An able-bodied person is not legally entitled to poor relief.

4. The form of relief granted (although not to the same extent in the large burghal parishes) is mainly outdoor relief.

It is thus apparent that, while the principles of the scheme of Public Assistance which we have recommended for England may be applied to Scotland, modifications will be required. It should perhaps also be observed that, so recently as 1904, a Departmental Committee of the Local Government Board for Scotland took evidence and reported on the system of Poor Law Medical Relief and on the Rules and Regulations for the management of Poorhouses in Scotland.

162. It is thus apparent that, while the principles of the scheme of Public Assistance which we have recommended for England may be applied to Scotland, considerable modifications will in any case be required. It is also to be observed that, so recently as 1904, a Departmental Committee

of the Local Government Board for Scotland took evidence and reported on the system of Poor Law Medical Relief and on the Rules and Regulations for the management of Poorhouses in Scotland. Further, the administration of medical relief in Scotland is not on all-fours with the practice of England. For instance, in Scotland, there is an obligation resting on the Sanitary Authority to deal with and control Pulmonary Phthisis as an infectious disease in terms of the Public Health Statutes. It would be inadvisable to alter that law which is now in operation, and there may therefore be, in this and other respects, deviation as regards Scotland from the principles and scheme which we have proposed for England.

163. The Unemployed Workmen Act of 1905 applies to Scotland as well as to England, and although we are aware that the conditions and the methods of administration are not wholly identical in the two countries, we think that, in the main, our recommendations as regards the unemployed and relief of distress are applicable equally to Scotland and England. The sections of our Report describing the preventive measures which we propose, such as the decasualisation of labour, the establishment of a national system of labour exchanges, and the institution of a system of insurance against unemployment are of general application, and could be put in operation simultaneously in England and Scotland.

(37). Our Proposals in Relation to Ireland

164. We also deal in a separate volume with Poor Law administration in Ireland. The Poor Laws of England and Ireland have much in common, on many points they are identical. Thus we have often found that the experience of one country suggests a reform in the other, and it may be convenient to state here that we intend that our recommendations in regard to the extension of areas, the constitution of the new authorities, and the classification of institutions should apply equally to both. At the outset of our inquiry we found that a Vice-Regal Commission had lately reported on several points in connection with Poor Law administration in Ireland, and had formulated certain proposals for reform. The Commissioners were men of great experience and wide local knowledge, and their recommendations appear to have received general support throughout the country. We are greatly indebted to their Report, so much that we have not thought it necessary to take any further evidence on matters with which they had dealt exhaustively. But we visited Ireland in order to make ourselves acquainted with the existing state of things, and some reports on the institutions, etc., in different parts of the country will be found in the

Appendix. Our scheme, it will be seen, in the main falls in with the views of the Vice-Regal Commission, and although, in recommending the abolition of Boards of Guardians and the substitution of Statutory Committees, we have carried the reform a step further than the Vice-Regal Commissioners have gone, still we believe this will be found on the whole to be an advantage, as it will secure that the authority which provides the funds for the relief of the poor will also be responsible for their administration.

It is true that the suggestion of the Irish Commissioners to revert to the old District Electoral Division as the area of rating for outdoor relief would not harmonise with the general principle of central county administration we have outlined. But now that the Old-Age Pensions Act has so greatly restricted the sphere of out-relief, this will become a minor consideration. Moreover we believe that in practice the experiment of collecting separate rates over different areas for indoor and outdoor relief might be found difficult of application.

165. Save as regards their proposals affecting outdoor relief, and the retention of the old Boards of Guardians to administer the county rates for the relief of the poor, we find ourselves generally in accord with the recommendations summed up in the concluding chapters of the Vice-Regal Commissioners' Report, and it appears clear that the statutory enactment required to give effect to our scheme of Poor Law reform would, if extended to Ireland, be found to give legislative authority for carrying out the almost identical reforms in Ireland which were recommended by the Commissioners in 1906.

166. We do not suggest that our transitional arrangements for the relief of temporary exceptional distress should be applied to Ireland. The Local Government (Ireland) Act of 1898 has already made provision for any temporary emergencies which may arise, by a system which is no doubt better suited to the requirements of an agricultural country like Ireland than that which we propose for the relief of distress in centres of industrial population in England.

Our separate Report in regard to Ireland will fully describe the differences between the English and the Irish Poor Law systems, and will explain in detail the application of the suggested reforms to Ireland.

(38). CONCLUSION

167. The proposals we make cover a large field of administration, will conflict with many old traditions, and will take time before they can come into really effective operation. But the evils we have had to describe are so

widespread and deep-rooted, and form so integral a part of the social life of the country, that no remedies less in scope or in force would in our judgment be sufficient.

168. But great as are the administrative changes which we propose, and costly as some of the new establishments may be, we feel strongly that the pauperism and distress we have described can never be successfully combated by administration and expenditure. The causes of distress are not only economic and industrial; in their origin and character they are largely moral. Government by itself cannot correct or remove such influences. Something more is required. The co-operation, spontaneous and whole-hearted, of the community at large, and especially of those sections of it which are well-to-do and free from the pressure of poverty, is indispensable. There is evidence from many quarters to show that the weak part of our system is not want of public spirit or benevolence, or lack of funds or of social workers, or of the material out of which these can be made. Its weakness is lack of organisation, of method, and of confidence in those who administer the system. We have so framed the new system as to invite and bring into positions of authority the best talent and experience that the locality can provide. In addition to those vested with such authority we have left a place in the new system for all capable and willing social workers; but they must work in accord, under guidance, and in the sphere allotted to them.

169. Great Britain is the home of voluntary effort, and its triumphs and successes constitute in themselves much of the history of the country. But voluntary effort when attacking a common and ubiquitous evil must be disciplined and led. We have here to learn a lesson from foreign countries whose charitable and social organisations, notably in France, Germany, Belgium and Holland, work under official guidance with efficacy, promptitude, and success. Looking at the voluntary resources and societies at our disposal there is every reason to believe that we can vie with and surpass any results obtained abroad. To this end it is organisation we need, and this organisation we now suggest.

170. There are other forms of assistance and prevention which we hope this Report may evoke from certain sections of society whose attitude hitherto has not been helpful. "Example is the school of mankind," and this aphorism was never truer than in these days of publicity. In every community the mode of life, the habits and the expenditure of the rich and ostentatious, reflect and reproduce themselves in the lower grades of

society. Witness after witness has noted the extravagance in dress, the restless craving for amusement, the increasing time spent in watching sports or games—in a word, the subordination of the more serious duties of life to the frivolity and amusements of the moment. These are habits which cannot exist side by side with thrift, self-restraint, and self-improvement. In the judgment of these witnesses these habits are largely responsible for much of modern pauperism and distress. A reform in these respects is required. May it not be fairly urged that to be effective and rapid the lead and example should be given from above?

171. But over and above these we must notice two other causes which exercise a subtle but important influence—we mean irregularity of demand and the confusion which exists in the minds of many consumers between cheapness and low price:

1) It is perhaps Utopian to imagine that men and women will ever free themselves from the bondage of fashion, and indeed its power seems to be greater now than ever. But fashion with its incessant changes exercises a powerful influence on production. The lace-trade at Nottingham may be cited as a typical case. The popular use or disuse of lace determines to a large extent, the amount of unemployment in Nottingham, which is thus dependent on a demand of which it can only be said with certainty that it is irregular.

2) It was laid down by Adam Smith that the consumer is the best judge of the quality of a product, and the dictum had an important bearing on legislation. But experience shows that many people, and the working classes themselves at least as much as any other, prefer commodities which are not durable, and which have the apparent advantage of being low priced. It is in the production of such commodities that much of the worst paid labour is employed. Furniture and clothing are prominent examples, but the list might be greatly enlarged. If consumers could be induced to spend their money thoughtfully on articles of permanent value, and of real use, many of the labour problems of the day would be in a fair way towards solution.

172. In our analysis of the modern development of industry we have drawn attention to the inherent evils of casual and intermittent employment upon those so engaged. We are convinced that the reason why the bulk of those employing this kind of labour have made no serious or combined effort to mitigate its evils is that they are unaware of their magnitude. We hope to remove from all sections of society this uncon-

sciousness of and unconcern in the wants, the failings and the sufferings of those outside their immediate circle, and to replace them by knowledge sympathy and co-operation.

173. "Land of Hope and Glory" is a popular and patriotic lyric sung each year with rapture by thousands of voices. The enthusiasm is partly evoked by the beauty of the idea itself, but more by the belief that Great Britain does, above other countries, merit this eulogium, and that the conditions in existence here are such that the fulfilment of hope and the achievement of glory are more open to the individual than in other and less favoured lands. To certain classes of the community into whose moral and material condition it has been our duty to enquire, these words are a mockery and a falsehood. To many of them, possibly from their own failure and faults, there is in this life but little hope, and to many more "glory" or its realisation is an unknown ideal. Our investigations prove the existence in our midst of a class whose condition and environment are a discredit, and a peril to the whole community. Each and every section of society has a common duty to perform in combating this evil and contracting its area, a duty which can only be performed by united and untiring effort to convert useless and costly inefficients into self-sustaining and respectable members of the community. No country, however rich can permanently hold its own in the race of international competition if hampered by an increasing load of this dead weight; or can successfully perform the role of sovereignty beyond the seas, if a portion of its own folk at home are sinking below the civilization and aspirations of its subject races abroad.

We have from the outset worked under the knowledge that it was necessary to report upon the questions referred to us in time to guide impending legislation. The pressure thus imposed compelled us to accelerate our proceedings and in consequence we have not been able to give to all the subjects brought under our cognisance the time and investigation we desire. Even so it would have been quite impossible for us to have compressed our work into a period of three years, but for the exceptional assistance we have received from the staff placed at our disposal. This staff, though small for the burden of work imposed upon it, was admirably organized and skilfully handled. The arranging, distribution, annotation and correction of the vast masses of evidence and the papers brought before us was daily performed with unfailing punctuality and precision.

Our Secretary, Mr. Duff, of the Local Government Board, displayed great organising power, a clear judgment, and a complete grasp of the problems involved. His tact, energy, and enthusiasm have gone far to smooth the way and lighten the work of the Commission.

Of our Assistant Secretaries, Mr. Jeffrey, of the Scottish Local Government Board, over and above the invaluable assistance which he gave to us in all matters relating to Scotland, has throughout been fertile in suggestions, as well as clear and accurate in his handling of detail.

Mr. Craven, of the Statistical Department of the Customs, to whose conversance with statistical methods we are specially indebted, has shown conspicuous ability in dealing with these and with all the other matters that have come under his charge.

We desire to bring to the notice of the heads of their respective Departments our strong sense of the value of the services which these gentlemen have rendered to the Commission.

All which We Humbly Submit for Your Majesty's Gracious Consideration.

(Signed)   GEORGE HAMILTON
             DENIS KELLY
             H. A. ROBINSON
             S. B. PROVIS
             F. H. BENTHAM
             ARTHUR DOWNES
             THORY GAGE GARDINER
             CHARLES S. LOCH
             J. PATTEN MACDOUGALL
             THOMAS HANCOCK NUNN
             L. R. PHELPS
             W. SMART
             HELEN BOSANQUET
             OCTAVIA HILL

R. G. DUFF, *Secretary*
JOHN JEFFREY, *Assistant Secretary*
EDWARD J. E. CRAVEN, *Assistant Secretary*
    4th February, 1909

Report of the
Royal Commission on the Poor Laws and Relief of Distress

———————◆•◆•◆———————

Minority Report (1909)

Introduction to Part 1
by Sidney and Beatrice Webb

THE Poor Law Commission of 1905-9 can hardly fail to be epoch-making in the history of the English Poor Law. For what we believe is the first time since 1834, a public inquiry into the Poor Law has ended without paying even lip-homage to the "principles of 1834." A Royal Commission of eighteen members, including half-a-dozen members of the Charity Organisation Society, half-a-dozen Guardians or ex-Guardians, and four official representatives of the Local Government Boards of England, Scotland and Ireland, has *unanimously* recommended "a clean sweep" of the English Poor Law and Poor Law organisation, together with all its most characteristic principles. Although the Majority Report is flanked by half-a-dozen dissents—of which the longest is here republished—the members of the Commission are remarkable in the extent of their revolutionary unanimity. All the Commissioners, without exception, agree that drastic changes in the Poor Law and its administration are urgently required; all agree that the "principles of 1834," whatever they once were, are now hopelessly antiquated and inapplicable to the present state of things;[1] all agree even in discarding the very terminology of the Poor Law, to which administrators and paupers alike have grown accustomed, in order to mark the completeness of the break from the past; all agree that the Boards of Guardians in town and country alike must imperatively and immediately be replaced by some other Authority; all agree in condemning, and in recommending for abolition, the General Mixed Workhouse, which has been, for seventy-five years, the characteristic feature of English Poor Law administration; all agree that the treatment of the children, the sick and the aged needs to be greatly improved. Similarly, all but two out of the eighteen agree that the Union area, which has dominated English administrative geography for more than half a century, must disappear from the map; that the future unit of local administration must be the County Borough and the County; and that the County Borough Councils and County Councils must add to their other functions those hitherto discharged by the Boards of Guardians. There has, we think, never been a representative Royal Commission, constituted of members of such diverse opinions, dealing with a subject of so great an extent, and of such far-reaching importance, which has, after three years' investigation, found itself agreeing with so much unanimity to conclusions of such sweeping character.[2]

There is one point, amid all this unanimity, to which we wish to call attention. The Minority of the Commissioners protest—as we think, rightly—against the terms in which the majority have thought fit to speak of the Poor Law Guardians of England and Wales. In passage after passage of the Majority Report, the blame for the failure of the present Poor Law is laid on their shoulders. They are condemned by implication,

[1] "The administrators of the Poor Law," we are told in the Majority Report, "are, in fact, endeavouring to apply the rigid system of 1834 to a condition of affairs which it was never intended to meet. What is wanted is not to abolish the Poor Law, but to widen, strengthen and humanise the Poor Law" (par. 337 of Chapter I of Part IV of Majority Report).

[2] The Commission consisted of Lord George Hamilton (Chairman); Sir Samuel Provis, Sir Henry Robinson, Mr. J. Patten-MacDougall, and Dr. Arthur Downes, of the Local Government Boards for England, Ireland and Scotland; Mr. F. H. Bentham, Mr. F. Chandler, and Mr. George Lansbury, sometime Chairmen of the Boards of Guardians for Bradford, Chorlton and Poplar respectively; Mr. C. S. Loch, Secretary of the Charity Organisation Society; the Bishop of Ross, Rev. Thory Gardiner, Mr. T. Hancock Nunn, Rev. L. R. Phelps, Professor W. Smart, Rev. Russell Wakefield, Chairman of the Central (Unemployed) Body for London; Miss Octavia Hill, Mrs. Bosanquet and Mrs. Sidney Webb. The O'Conor Don was a member until his death; and Mr. Charles Booth until his resignation on account of ill-health.

not only of incompetence, but of worse. "The work," we are told, "is tending more and more to fall into the hands of persons who, caring more for their own interests than for those of the community, direct their administration more towards the attainment of popularity than towards a solution of the real problems of pauperism." We see no warrant for such a description of the 646 Boards of Guardians in England and Wales, or of their 24,000 members. What we have personally witnessed, all over the country, in the ten years that we have been specially studying English local administration, is an enormous amount of devoted, patient, disinterested service of the community, by men and women who have spent large parts of their lives in an onerous and disagreeable duty, for which they receive neither recognition nor thanks. We regret that the work thus done for three-quarters of a century by the Guardians of the Poor has not been better appreciated. We believe it to be true that, from first to last in English Poor Law history, no public honour of any kind has been awarded for even the longest, the most faithful, and the most eminent service as a Poor Law Guardian. Yet we make bold to say that the work which Boards of Guardians have done has been just as important to the community, and just as onerous and disinterested, as that of the Town Councils, and that there has been as large a proportion of honest men on the one body as on the other.

What the Royal Commission of 1905-9 was confronted with was, not any special delinquency on the part of the 24,000 Guardians of the Poor, but an astonishing amount of overlapping, confusion and waste resulting from a gradual process of supersession of the Poor Law by other public activities. Broadly speaking, the Boards of Guardians make a failure of their job, put what zeal and devotion into it they may, not because of the personal shortcomings of their members, but because their work is nowadays cut into on all sides by other public Authorities, which are better equipped than the Boards of Guardians for their specialist functions. This point the Majority of the Commissioners have either missed or ignored.

In 1834 the Poor Law Commissioners were faced with the difficulty that there existed, up and down the kingdom, no public authority to which they could entrust the administration of the public provision for any of the classes of persons whom they had to deal with. There was in 1834 no Health Authority in existence responsible for the prevention and treatment of disease, and having its own hospitals and medical staff. There was no service of sanitary inspectors and health visitors, charged to search out disease as a public nuisance. There was in 1834 no Education Authority, taking in hand the schooling of the children, and having its own elaborate network of schools and staff of teachers. There was no service of school attendance officers, visiting systematically the homes to discover whether the children are receiving efficient education. There was in 1834 (outside the Metropolis) no force of salaried police, whose duty it is to prevent the public nuisance of vagrancy. There was, we may add, in 1834 even no systematic prison organisation, such gaols as existed being mere dungeons dispersed among entirely autonomous Lords of Manors, Close Corporations and the County Justices. There was, of course, no idea of curative or reformatory treatment of the persons compulsorily detained. There was in 1834 no general public provision for lunatics, outside one or two progressive counties. There was no public provision at all for idiots, defectives or epileptics. There was in 1834 no public authority dealing, as the Distress Committee of the Borough or Urban District Council now assumes to do, with Unemployment. There was in 1834 no idea of a national service of pensions, providing superannuation for all over 70 who need it. The Poor Law Commissioners of 1834 were therefore compelled to recommend that a new authority should be established to deal with all the classes for which public provision had then to be made; and this provision, however diverse in character it needed to be, was governed by the only factor then common to all the classes, namely, that of being in need of public aid. This was called destitution.

The problem before the Poor Law Commissioners of 1905-9 was very different. It is no longer possible to unite, under one authority elected for the purpose of relieving destitution, all the provision made by the State for those in receipt of public assistance. Quite apart from the question of relieving destitution, there have grown up, in the course of the seventy-five years, extensive systems of public provision, out of the rates and taxes, for particular classes of persons, costing, in the aggregate, much more than the whole Poor Law expenditure. For the children of the whole country, irrespective of the affluence of their parents, the State now provides— usually gratuitously and in the other cases far under cost price—the whole service of education, from the kindergarten to the University. For various sections of these young people—more extensively than is commonly realised—the State provision of education is accompanied by partial or complete maintenance. We do not here allude to the tens of thousands of children in endowed and publicly-aided secondary boarding-schools. But leaving these out of account, it is interesting to note that the State provision of maintenance with education outside the Poor Law now extends to more than a hundred thousand children, some of them because they are the best (scholarships which cover maintenance), some of them because they are the worst (reformatory schools), and some for indiscriminate reasons, including the undesirable character of the parents, the children's truancy, or the children's physical or mental shortcomings (industrial schools, residential schools for the blind, crippled, etc.). In not a few cases the Local Authorities actually run their own boarding-schools—at a lower cost per head, be it noted, than the new Cottage Homes of the Boards of Guardians. All this public assistance to the children is without the stigma of pauperism, whether the parents are bad, good or indifferent.

With regard to the sick, there has grown up a Public Health service, ubiquitous in scope and becoming ever larger in volume, for the prevention of all diseases, irrespective of the wealth or conduct of the persons concerned; and for the cure (including maintenance in hospital and domiciliary treatment) of those deemed specially injurious to the community. More than 700 Municipal Hospitals are now maintained by the Local Health Authorities. Every year this notion of the protection of the community is advancing on the idea of merely relieving the individual. In 1906 it was made the duty of the Education Authority to provide repeated medical examination of all the millions of children in the public elementary schools; whilst food and medical treatment were to be provided where absolutely required. All this is without the stigma of pauperism; and the question of which of the services should be rendered quite gratuitously, and which of them should be made the subject of a nominal and quite inadequate fee, has ceased to be a matter of general principle, and is now one of mere administrative expediency in each case.

With regard to the great army of the mentally defective of all grades, whether lunatics or idiots, epileptics or chronic inebriates, or merely feeble-minded, it has just been authoritatively declared by a powerful Royal Commission that, henceforth, these are all to be treated by the community in respect not of their poverty, but of their defect; and that the whole of them should be removed, once for all, from the sphere of pauperism and of the Boards of Guardians.

With regard to the persons over 70, there is now, in every County and County Borough, a Local Pension Committee, awarding Old Age Pensions at the expense of the Exchequer, entirely unconnected with the Poor Law.

With regard to the able-bodied in need of assistance, there has latterly grown up an extensive network of Distress Committees under the Unemployed Workmen Act of 1905. But this did not begin with Mr. Gerald Balfour's Act or Mr. Long's Joint Committees. We see it initiated by the Local Government Board itself in 1886, in the celebrated circular calling on the Municipal Authorities to take the treatment of the Unemployed out of the Poor Law. The whole purpose and intention of this municipal organisation has been to provide something other than the Poor Relief for the whole class of workmen unemployed through no fault of their own, irrespective of whether or not they were technically destitute.

At the other end of the able-bodied class, we have the recommendations of the 1906 Departmental Committee on Vagrancy that the vagrant should henceforth be dealt with not by the Poor Law Authority but by the police, and the incorrigible wastrel by a penal settlement—in both cases irrespective of whether or not they apply for relief, or are technically destitute. There is, in fact, no section of the great pauper host, which the Poor Law Commissioners of 1834 indiscriminately placed under the care of the Boards of Guardians, of which, in 1909, they are left in undisturbed possession. The costly provision made by the Poor Law Authorities of the United Kingdom—who will, this year, be spending nearly twenty millions sterling on Poor Relief—is thus overlapped at all points. What the Poor Law Authorities are doing for the infants, the children, the sick, the mentally defective, the aged and infirm, and the unemployed able-bodied man or woman respectively, already forms (or is on the point of forming) only a fractional part of the public provision made from the rates and taxes for each of those very classes; and a part that cannot be marked off from the rest by any significant characteristic—not even by the 1834 attribute of "being in a state of destitution."

The majority of the Commissioners have chosen to ignore the silent upgrowths of the past half a century which have, on the one hand, produced so costly and wasteful an overlapping, and on the other, have left behind them the Boards of Guardians and the Poor Law Division of the Local Government Board, without any fault of the persons concerned, in a state of antiquated inefficiency. The Majority Report, implying that the cause of the failure of the Poor Law is to be found in the personal shortcomings of the 24,000 Poor Law Guardians, proposes the setting up again what is practically the same system of Poor Relief, with new members and under another name! The proposed constitution is significant. Though the County and County Borough Councils are to find the whole of the money, they are to exercise absolutely no control. A complicated hierarchy of partly nominated and non-elective committees, controlled by all sorts of outside agencies and not responsible to the electorate, are to have an uncontrolled power of deciding the new Poor Law policy, and of spending the County Rate. The whole proposal seems inspired by the determination, at all hazards, to free the new "Public Assistance Authority," into whose hands not only the pauper but also the Unemployed workman and the child found hungry at school are to be thrust, from any electoral control. But this is not all. The non-elected Public Assistance Committees are themselves to be virtually controlled by statutory "Voluntary Aid Committees," to be constituted on the lines of the Charity Organisation Society, and to be eligible for grants from the Public Assistance Authority out of the rates. To these committees, we are told, applicants are to go in the first instance. If they are refused assistance by the Voluntary Aid Committees, they may, of course, apply to the new Poor Law Authority. But that Authority is to make it a principle that the assistance it affords is to be "in some way less agreeable" than that which the Voluntary Aid Committee would have given. Thus, the new Charity Organisation Committee is to have the power of setting the standard of what the Poor Relief is to be. We do not think the case is mended by the bewildering change of names. What is proposed by the Majority, in substitution for the relief afforded by the Distress Committees to the Unemployed, and for the meals supplied to the hungry children by the Education Authorities, as well as for the work of the Boards of Guardians, is, for all the novel terminology, essentially the present Poor Law under non-elective administration. *Plus ça change, plus c'est la même chose!*

With Majority proposals of this character, the dissentient Minority[3] felt compelled to present an alternative Report covering the whole ground; bringing out the essential fact of the overlapping and duplication of ser-

[3] Mr. F. Chandler, General Secretary of the Amalgamated Society of Carpenters and Joiners, and member of the Parliamentary Committee of the Trade Union Congress, Chairman of the Chorlton Board of Guardians; Mr. G. Lansbury, member of the Central (Unemployed) Body for London, and of the Poplar Board of Guardians; Prebendary Russell Wakefield, Chairman of the Central (Unemployed) Body for London, Rector of St. Marylebone; Mrs. Sidney Webb.

vices, and concluding with an Alternative Scheme of Reform. Their Report is divided into two independent parts, the one dealing with the various sections of the non-able-bodied, and the other with the able-bodied or unemployed. Each of these parts is, for convenience, now reprinted *verbatim* in a separate volume.[4] In the Blue-Book version the student will see every statement of fact, every figure, every piece of evidence, and every quotation authenticated by exact references to sources and authorities, to be found either among the Proceedings of the Commission itself or in other Parliamentary papers; in the official Proceedings of Local Authorities, or in published works; and supported, moreover, by innumerable footnotes. But all this apparatus of verification—amounting in bulk to about one-third of the text—indispensable as it is in the official document, merely makes the Report hard reading for the public. The whole of these references have therefore been cut away from this popular edition, in which the text alone is given in pleasant typographical form.

It remains only to be said that the numerous references to "our Investigators" are to the valuable Reports of the various ladies and gentlemen whom the Commission, with the sanction of the Lords Commissioners of the Treasury, appointed to investigate particular subjects. Among the most interesting of these Reports (which will, in due course, be published by the Commission) are those by Mr. A. D. Steel-Maitland and Miss Rose Squire (Industrial and Sanitary Conditions); Mr. Cyril Jackson and Rev. J. C. Pringle (Relief Works); Mr. Cyril Jackson (Boy Labour); Mr. Thomas Jones and Miss Constance Williams (Outdoor Relief); Dr. J. C. MacVail (Medical Relief); Dr. Ethel Williams, Miss M. Longman and Miss M. Phillips (Condition of the Children); Miss Harlock (Cases refused Outdoor Relief); Dr. Parsons (Able-bodied in Scottish Poorhouses); Mr. Kaye and Mr. Toynbee (Charities), etc.

---

[4] Part II is published under the title of *The Public Organisation of the Labour Market* (Longmans, 1909).

Minority Report (1909)

Part 1:

The Destitution of the Non-Able-Bodied

The Scheme of Reform

The state of anarchy and confusion, into which has fallen the whole realm of relief and assistance to the poor and to persons in distress, is so generally recognised that many plans of reform have been submitted to us, each representing a section of public opinion. In fact, throughout the three years of our investigations we have been living under a continuous pressure for a remodelling of the Poor Laws and the Unemployed Workmen Act, in one direction or another. We do not regret this peremptory and insistent demand for reform. The present position is, in our opinion, as grave as that of 1834, though in its own way. We have, on the one hand, in England and Wales, Scotland and Ireland alike, the well-established Destitution Authorities, under ineffective central control, each pursuing its own policy in its own way; sometimes rigidly restricting its relief to persons actually destitute, and giving it in the most deterrent and humiliating forms; sometimes launching out into an indiscriminate and unconditional subsidising of mere poverty; sometimes developing costly and palatial institutions for the treatment, either gratuitously or for partial payment, of practically any applicant of the wage-earning or of the lower middle class. On the other hand, we see existing, equally ubiquitous with the Destitution Authorities, the newer specialised organs of Local Government—the Local Education Authority, the Local Health Authority, the Local Lunacy Authority, the Local Unemployment Authority, the Local Pension Authority—all attempting to provide for the needs of the poor, *according to the cause or character of their distress.* Every Parliamentary session adds to the powers of these specialised Local Authorities. Every Royal Commission or Departmental Committee recommends some fresh development of their activities. Thus, even while our Commission has been at work, a Departmental Committee has reported in favour of handing over the Vagrants and what used to be called the "Houseless Poor," to the Local Police Authority, as being interested in "Vagrancy as a whole," apart from the accident of a Vagrant being destitute. The Royal Commission on the Care and Control of the Feeble-minded has recommended that all mentally defective persons now maintained by the Poor Law should be handed over to the Local Authority specially concerned with mental deficiency, whether in a destitute, or in a non-destitute person. The increasing activities of these specialised Local Authorities, being only half-consciously sanctioned by public opinion, and only imperfectly authorized by statute, are spasmodic and uneven. Whilst, for instance, the Local Education Authorities and the Local Health Authorities are providing, in some places, gratuitous maintenance and medical treatment, for one set of persons after another, similar Authorities elsewhere are rigidly confining themselves to a bare fulfilment of their statutory obligations of schooling and sanitation. Athwart the overlapping and rivalry of these half a dozen Local Authorities that may be all at work in a single district, we watch the growing stream of private charity and voluntary agencies—almshouses and pensions for the aged; hospitals and dispensaries, convalescent homes and "medical missions" for the sick; free dinners and free boots, country holidays and "happy evenings" for the children; free shelters and soup kitchens, "way tickets" and charitable jobs for the able-bodied, together with uncounted indiscriminate doles of every description—without systematic organisation and without any co-ordination with the multifarious forms of public activity. What the nation is confronted with to-day is, as it was in 1834, an ever-growing expenditure from public and private funds, which results, on the one hand, in a minimum of prevention and cure, and on the other in far-reaching demoralisation of character and the continuance of no small amount of unrelieved destitution.

(A) Schemes That We Have Rejected

We may distinguish, amid the various proposals for reform that have been brought before us, three main policies to be carried out by new legislation in England and Wales, Scotland and Ireland alike. These all contemplate the continuance, under one constitution or another, of an Authority specifically charged with the relief of destitute persons, and of destitute persons only. As each of these policies has received substantial support, we think it expedient to state briefly what they involve, and our reasons for not adopting them.

(i) *The Continuance of a Denuded Destitution Authority alongside of other Local Authorities Providing for the Poor*

The easiest policy to pursue, by way of bringing the chaos into some sort of order, would be to restrict the Destitution Authorities to a "deterrent" and "less eligible" relief of actual destitution, whilst giving free play to the other Local Authorities to develop assistance out of the rates and taxes on their own specialised lines of prevention and treatment. This policy has not been explicitly recommended to us as a definite scheme of reform. But it is implied in many of the fragmentary proposals that have been laid before us; as, indeed, it is in much of the legislation of the last few years. It was this policy which seems to have inspired the momentous Circular of 1886, by which Mr. Chamberlain, when President of the Local Government Board, inaugurated the Municipal Relief Works for the Unemployed, and the same policy is plainly embodied in the Unemployed Workmen Act of 1905. "Any relaxation," said Mr. Chamberlain, of the ordinary deterrent tests in Poor Law Relief, "would be most disastrous." But another form of public assistance of men who would otherwise have been relieved by the Poor Law was to be provided by another Local Authority. Similarly, as an explanation of the Unemployed Workmen Act of 1905, we were informed by Mr. Walter Long, that, in his view, "the object of the Poor Law," in respect of the able-bodied, was "to check" the manufacture of paupers "by imposing upon those who are thriftless, idle or intemperate the strictest possible regulations," in which he desired no relaxation whatsoever. But for "strong, healthy, industrious men," who are "by force of circumstances" in distress "some fresh powers and new machinery are required." The same idea lay at the root of the persistent advocacy, by Mr. Charles Booth, of a national scheme of pensions for the aged. A wise system of non-contributory pensions for the aged, together with municipal hospitals for the sick, would, he held, enable the Poor Law to be made wholly deterrent. The same idea has been embodied in nearly all the legislation on these problems of the last few years; and it has inspired the recommendations of nearly all the Royal Commissions and Committees of Inquiry, in favour of providing, outside the Poor Law, milk depots and school dinners for the infants and children, municipal hospitals for all sorts of diseases, "custodial homes" for the feeble-minded, and pensions for the aged.

This policy offers to-day the attraction of requiring no reversal of recent legislation, and no discouragement of municipal efforts to raise the standard of life. It involves, however, the denudation of the English Boards of Guardians and the Scottish Parish Councils of all the forms of specialised provision for the children, the sick and the aged that we have described; and the rigid curtailment of the activities of these Destitution Authorities to the maintenance of a deterrent Workhouse. This means, in England and Wales, the abrogation of nearly all the Orders and Circulars of the Local Government Board since the date of the General Consolidated Order of 1847 and the Outdoor Relief Prohibitory Order of 1844. It would, by depriving the elected members and the officials of all the interest of managing educational, curative and philanthropic institutions, take the heart out of Poor Law administration; and make it more difficult than ever to induce men and women of zeal and integrity to devote themselves to what would be nothing but a hateful service. Moreover, experience with regard to vagrants and the "Ins-and-Outs" has shown that the most deterrent Workhouse does not prove continuously deterrent, unless its administrators can apply powers of compulsory detention. To grant such powers would be to make the Destitution Authorities very nearly akin to the Prison Authorities. It was on such grounds that the Departmental Committee on Vagrancy was constrained to recommend that the Vagrants should be taken out of the Poor Law, and entrusted to the Police Authorities, and that a penal colony for their detention should be provided by the Prison Department under the Home Office. Indeed, it is difficult to discover what class of destitute persons would, under this scheme, be found, in practice, to remain under the jurisdiction of the denuded Destitution Authority, after all those who required curative treatment, all those for whom honourable maintenance ought to be provided, and all those subjected to penal detention had been withdrawn. Meanwhile, the other Local Authorities, specialising on particular services, would be free to go ahead in their several ways, increasing the municipal debt in all directions, and relieving whole classes of persons and whole forms of destitution, without any check against overlapping, without any insistence on charge or recovery, without inquiry into economic circumstances before the grant of food or money in the home, and without, in fact, any safeguards against developing afresh all the evils of an unregulated Poor Law. On the other hand, as rigid deterrence is found to leave much destitution unrelieved, and as the other Local Authorities would have no responsibility for preventing starvation, we should have, in some districts, practically the evil of there being no relief of distress; whilst nowhere would the Local Authorities be under any obligation to make whatever provision they chose to develop, in any one service, adequate to the needs of the poor.

(ii) The Monopoly of Public Assistance by a Deterrent Destitution Authority

The idea of limiting all assistance out of rates and taxes to the operations of a Deterrent Poor Law was unreservedly advocated, with regard to the Able-bodied, by the Royal Commission of 1834, and put into practice by the Poor Law Commissioners of 1834–1847. Some students of the 1834 Report consider that this policy was also intended to be applied to the non-able-bodied. But the application of this policy to the "Disabled" was reserved for the talented Inspectorate of 1869–86. It was then argued that just as under the Act of 1834 the introduction of a Deterrent Poor Law had "obliged the Able-bodied to assume responsibility for the able-bodied period of life, an application of the principle to the other responsibilities would produce equally advantageous results." To ensure the maximum of deterrence, it was suggested that the "Workhouse Test" should be universally applied, so that the only relief offered to any class, "the Disabled" as well as the Able-bodied, should be bare subsistence in a disciplinary Workhouse, combined with the humiliation and disgrace that— so it was argued—should be attached to "living upon funds that have been raised by compulsion." This policy, it was fervently believed by its advocates, would, by reason of its very harshness to the aged, to the sick and to the children, so stimulate private charity and voluntary agencies, and so encourage parental and filial, brotherly and cousinly feeling, that every aged person, every sick person and every child, who was at all "deserving," and many even of those who were not deserving, would be maintained without "pauperism," and without cost to public funds.

The uniform enforcement of this policy throughout the country has been advocated by many of our witnesses, including some having great experience of the actual administration of the Poor Law. The official representatives of the Poor Law Officers' Association, for instance, presented this policy to us as embodying "the fundamental principles of the English Poor Law." They laid it down that the principles upon which we ought to insist, with regard to all assistance from public funds, were that "the condition of the person relieved should not in any respect be better than that of the lowest class of independent labourer; and the next, that it is essential to associate with the receipt of relief such drawbacks as will induce the poor, so far as lies in their power, to make provision for the future."

We find some difficulty in estimating the exact changes that would be required for universal adoption of this policy, owing to the fact that its advocates are not clear whether they really desire it to be applied to all classes of paupers. Mr. Crowder, for instance, whose long and devoted service as a Poor Law Guardian in St. George's-in-the-East is so well known, emphatically declared to us that all relief of distress from public funds should be through the Poor Law, and that all such relief should be "less eligible," should be "deterrent," and should be subject to "the stigma of pauperism." But it subsequently appeared that Mr. Crowder was unprepared to apply this policy to the not inconsiderable section of the paupers who are children, nor yet (except "to some extent") to the still larger number who are sick. Some witnesses, however, were more consistent. Mr. T. Mackay, for instance, would have us boldly apply this historic policy to the aged and to the sick, as well as to the Able-bodied. One important witness, the Rev. Canon Bury, who was so long mainly responsible for the Poor Law administration of Brixworth, frankly advocated the application of the same principles even to the children, for whom he recommended residence in the General Mixed Workhouse, as the only way of making their condition less eligible than that of the children of the lowest grade of independent labourer. "I think," said Canon Bury, "the child must bear, as it were, the sins of the father . . . and I should not like Poor Law relief to interfere with that." Thus, we have maintenance in the Workhouse advocated as the sole form of public assistance to be afforded to any class. The only alternative appears to such reformers to be a grant of Outdoor Relief which cannot be made either adequate or conditional. For "it is evident," remarks one of the Inspectors, "that if out-relief were granted in sufficient amount to afford adequate relief (which may be defined as relief which would place the recipient in reasonable comfort) it would raise the pauper class to a better condition than the independent persons in a similar position of life (miserable as that position may be in the estimate of more favoured sections of society) and would offer a premium to dependence upon the rates. Besides, no out-relief can teach cleanliness and decency (again, according to a higher standard), or can prevent persons in great poverty from parting with any article they can turn into money."

The adoption of this policy would involve the repeal of the various Acts of recent years enabling the Local Education Authorities to feed necessitous children, and to provide medical treatment for those who need it. It would involve, not only the abandonment of all this activity by Local Education Authorities, but also their closing their residential schools for defective children, and their day industrial schools. The Local Health Authorities would have either to close their 700 hospitals, or else—what indeed, the Legislature seems originally to have intended—make such a substantial charge for admission to them as would automatically throw back on the Poor Law every destitute person stricken with fever. Similarly the most progressive of the Local Health Authorities would have either to close their Municipal Milk Depots, and dismiss their Health Visitors; or else make such charges for these services as would render them self-supporting, and, at the same time, leave to the Destitution Authority the monopoly of public assistance in the poorest districts. We should have to ignore the recommendations in favour of specialised provision for particular classes, which have emanated from every Royal Commission, every Select Committee of the House of Commons, and every Departmental Committee which has, during the last twenty years, been set to consider any one of these problems. We should, in particular, have to neglect the recommendations of the Departmental Committee on Vagrancy and those of the Royal Commission on the Care and Control of the Feeble-minded. Finally, we should have to repeal the Unemployed Workmen Act of 1905 and the Old-Age Pensions Act of 1908. The Destitution Authorities themselves would have to be revolutionised. The Poor Law Division of the Local Government Board would have to revert to the policy and the Poor Law technique of the Inspectorate of 1869–86; and this would involve the reversal of nearly all the official Orders and Circulars of the last sixty years with regard to the children; of all those of the last forty years with regard to the sick; and of all those of the last twenty years with regard to the aged. The Boards of Guardians of England and Wales would have to give up their Cottage Homes and Scattered Homes, their Infirmaries and Sanatoria. The Parish Councils of Scotland would have to give up their Parochial Homes and pensions for the aged, and their roll of widows with children on exceptional home aliment, far above what is enjoyed by the wives of the lowest class of independent labourers. We do not think that any such revolution is possible or desirable.

What, indeed, has become apparent is that the condition of the lowest grade of independent labourers is unfortunately one of such inadequacy of food and clothing and such absence of other necessaries of life that it has been found, in practice, impossible to make the conditions of Poor Law relief "less eligible" without making them such as are demoralising to the children, physically injurious to the sick, and brutalising to the aged and infirm. Nor do private charity and Voluntary Agencies suffice as a substitute or as an alternative for the public provision for the destitute. It is not merely that private charity has a least as many evils of its own, and at least as many dangers, as the public provision has. What has been abundantly demonstrated is that, without State action, private charity and Voluntary Agencies nowhere fit the need—they are in most places and for most purposes lamentably insufficient, and in some places and for some purposes demoralisingly superabundant. Finally, they never rise above the individual hard case. With such problems as the excessive infantile mortality of a whole district, the wide prevalence of tuberculosis, or the preventable illnesses of school children, it never occurs to them to attempt to cope.

(iii) *The Extension of Public Assistance by a Disguised and Swollen Poor Law*

We pass now to the recommendations of the majority of our colleagues in respect of the functions and constitution of the bodies which they suggest should take the place of the Boards of Guardians in England and Wales. We confess to some difficulty in discovering or understanding what it is that they propose. They sweep away all existing Poor Law Authorities—doing, as it seems to us, grave injustice in the terms they apply to the existing Guardians—but they recommend the creation of a new Poor Law Authority under another name. They are emphatic in laying down the principle that "the responsibility for due and effective relief of all necessitous persons at the public expense should be in the hands of one and only one Authority." Moreover, they declare that they "do not recommend any alteration of the law which would extend the qualification for relief to individuals not now entitled to it, or which would bring within the operation of assistance from public funds classes not now legally within its operation." So far we might be dealing with the plan of "a Monopoly of Public Assistance by a Deterrent Destitution Authority" that we have just described. But our colleagues reject that plan. They carefully avoid any recommendation in favour of a return to the "principles of 1834." These principles, hitherto acclaimed as the basis of any sound policy, are left aside as antiquated and inapplicable. "The administrators of the present Poor Law," we are told, "are, in fact, endeavouring to apply the rigid system of 1834 to a condition of affairs which it was never intended to meet. What is wanted is not to abolish the Poor Law, but to widen, strengthen and humanise the Poor Law." The new Poor Law Authority is, therefore, no longer to be confined to dealing with "the destitute"; it is to provide for the much larger class of "the necessitous." Its work is no longer to be "relief," but to be concentrated mainly on curative and restorative treatment of the most varied kind. This policy, it will be perceived, involves not only the continuance of the array of specialised institutions which a few Boards of Guardians in England have latterly established, but their multiplication in every district, and the development of new varieties. Besides the Poor Law residential Schools (or Cottage Homes, or Scattered Homes), there is to be established in every populous district a Poor Law day school, providing meals for the children of widows on Outdoor Relief, as well as an improved form of education, better adapted than that given in the Public Elementary Schools for the preparation of pauper children for industrial careers. There are to be also Poor Law almshouses or Cottage Homes for the deserving aged, and Poor Law Rescue Homes for destitute young women of immoral life.

What puzzles us is how the new Poor Law Authority can provide all these things for "the necessitous," without enormously increasing its present costly overlapping and rivalry with the Local Education Authority and the Local Health Authority. For it is very far from being true that, under the plan to which our colleagues have committed themselves, there would be "one and only one Authority" administering public assistance.

Some classes which have lately been withdrawn from the Poor Law are, it is true to be thrust back. The respectable mechanic temporarily out of a job, who is now obtaining "Employment Relief" from the Distress Committees under the Unemployed Workmen Act, is again to come under the jurisdiction of the Poor Law Authority. The necessitous child now being fed at school, or medically treated under the newly constituted organisation of the Education Authority, is once again to depend on the Poor Law Authority, and on the Poor Law Authority alone. We gather that in England the phthisical patients who are now being treated in Municipal Hospitals are to be transferred to the Infirmaries of the Poor Law Authority. These changes will involve the repeal of the Unemployed Workmen Act, 1905, the Education (Provision of Meals) Act, 1906, and the Education (Administrative Provisions) Act, 1906. On the other hand our colleagues concur with the recommendations of the Royal Commission on the Care and Control of the Feeble-minded in advocating that all mentally defective persons, however destitute, shall cease to be paupers and be transferred to the Local Lunacy Authority. They also repeat (though whether or not with approval we are unable to ascertain) the recommendations of the Departmental Committee on Vagrancy in favour of divorcing the whole provision for this section of the Able-bodied from the Destitution Authority, and of entrusting it to the Watch Committees of Borough Councils and (outside the Metropolitan area) to the Standing Joint Committees of County Councils. With regard to these not inconsiderable portions of the destitute—amounting to at least one-fifth of the entire pauper host—our colleagues are proposing, to use their own condemnatory words, to break up into sections "the work previously performed" by the Boards of Guardians, and to transfer it to "existing committees of County and County Borough Councils." We fail to understand the reasonableness of a change, involving great expense and disturbance, which withdraws the Vagrant, the Lunatic, the Epileptic, and the Feeble-minded person from the Poor Law and throws back into the hands of the Poor Law Authority the respectable artisan in want of work, the child found hungry at school, and the phthisical patient requiring isolation, who are now being dealt with by other Authorities. Nor do the recommendations of our colleagues even approach, still less attain, their own ideal of there being "one and only one Authority," dispensing Public Assistance. We should still have the overlapping between the hospital provision made by the 700 institutions of the Local Health Authorities in all diseases other than phthisis, and the sick wards and infirmaries of the Poor Law Authorities; between the residential schools, day feeding schools, and "boarding out" of the Local Education Authorities and the exactly similar schools and boarding out of the Poor Law Authorities.

But it is with regard to the Able-bodied that our colleagues depart most widely from their principle of having "one and only one Authority." Besides the vaguely suggested Local Police Authority, for relieving such of the Able-bodied as are vagrant, and the new Poor Law Authority for such of them as are stationary, there are to be, in every district, a Labour exchange managed by the Board of Trade, providing Migration Relief in the form of railway tickets at the expense of the Treasury for such of the Able-bodied as are Unemployed; a Local Insurance Organisation, of uncertain constitution, dispensing Treasury subsidies as Unemployment Relief to insured workmen; and a Detention Colony giving "Continuous Treatment" at the expense of the Home Office to those "who will not work, or whose recent character and conduct are an insuperable bar to their re-entering industrial life." The situation is to be further complicated by the existence of a semi-statutory Voluntary Aid Committee, which is evidently intended to direct the operations of all the other authorities; for, we are told, "a first application for assistance will naturally be made to the Voluntary Aid Committee," to be dealt with at its discretion. If it decides to refuse its own aid, it is to be a principle that the Poor Relief afforded "shall be in some way less agreeable than" what the Voluntary Aid Committee would have given. Thus, the Voluntary Aid Committee is to set the standard which the new Poor Law Authority is never to exceed. "In course of time," we are told, "the practice of the committees would be so well-known in the district that the applicants for assistance themselves would know to which of the two committees they ought to apply." But, so far as we have been able to follow the maze of Authorities to be set up, there will be, not two, but six different Authorities more or less supporting the Able-bodied of any one district. We fear that we must agree with our colleagues when, in another part of their Report, they say that "it is difficult to conceive any system in which different public Authorities have power simultaneously to administer relief to much the same class of applicant in the same locality which will not result in overlapping, confusion and divergence of treatment and practice."

Our colleagues seem to us to be even less successful in carrying out, in their detailed recommendations, their axiom that they do not desire "to bring within the operation of assistance from public funds classes not now within its operation." We have already alluded to the proposed substitution for the classic, narrow category of "the destitute," of the far wider category of "the necessitous." The same desire, as they express it, "to widen, strengthen and humanise the Poor Law," is shown, we think, in an almost morbid wish to alter the names of things, in order to give a flavour of generosity, if not of laxness, to the new Poor Law. Their new Poor Law Authority is to be euphemistically designated the "Public Assistance Authority"; its Relief Committees are to be "Public Assistance Committees"; the Able-bodied Test Workhouse is to be known in future as the "Industrial Institution"; the Outdoor Labour Test is described under "Outdoor Relief"; and simple Outdoor Relief, far from being abolished, obtains consecration in the official phraseology of the future as "Home Assistance." The good old-fashioned term "detention" is deemed "infelicitous," and whenever the new Poor Law Authority wishes to detain a pauper against his will, the instrument will be disguised as an "Order for Continuous Treatment." But passing from these innocent devices of "illusory nomenclature," we find, in some of the proposals— not, as the "principles" would lead us to expect, a restriction of the area of pauperism, but actually an extension of its area, and an increase in its amenities. With regard to the sick in particular, the new Poor Law axiom is to be, "Investigation should follow upon Treatment." Whether the medical treatment is to be peremptorily terminated whenever the enquiry discloses pecuniary resources, is not stated. But being necessitous is not always to be the condition of eligibility under the new Poor Law. It is expressly recommended that institutional treatment, including mainte- nance, should be provided by the Poor Law Authorities *without charge and without disfranchisement,* for all persons who are members of Provi- dent Dispensaries and are recommended by their own doctors for such treatment, apparently in rivalry with the Local Health Authorities, and equally whether or not the patients have sufficient means to obtain such institutional treatment for themselves. This extension of entirely gratuitous treatment to persons who are not necessarily destitute, and from whom the cost of this treatment is not to be recovered, involves a serious exten- sion of the area of Public Relief, and of the work of the new Poor Law Authority, and no inconsiderable increase of expenditure. What seems to us even more extraordinary is the proposal to grant to every destitute sick person the privilege of a free choice among the doctors of the town, exactly as if such sick persons had belonged all their lives to a well-organised Provident Dispensary. If it is desired to make relief less desirable than maintenance by individual exertion and foresight, we should have thought that "free choice of doctors" was exactly the privilege to be withheld from the person coming on the rates for treatment. The proposal seems to us all the more dangerous as it is plain that the poor patient will tend to choose the doctor who interferes least with his habits, and whom he finds most sympathetic in ordering "medical extras"; from which, it must be remembered, food and even alcoholic stimulants are not excluded. We cannot but agree with our colleague, Dr. Downes, who states in his Dissent that "the scheme . . . appears . . . to offer what amounts to a large measure of free medical relief without adequate safeguard either to the medical profession generally, or to the ratepayer."

The promoters of this scheme seem not unnaturally to feel that the present Boards of Guardians in England and Ireland, and the present Parish Councils in Scotland, would not be equal to the administration of so multifarious an array of services, each having its own technique. The failure of the present Destitution Authorities to cope with the difficulties presented by the existing mixture of classes with which they have to deal makes it clear, in fact, that to administer the new congeries of functions would demand instruments of "high finish and fine temper," which cannot, it is contended, be ensured by popular election. Thus the new Poor Law Authority, though in form a Committee of the County or County Borough Council, is to have its own autonomy, even as to the rate to be levied or the capital outlay to be made; and is not to be subject to the control of the Council. Though Councillors will sit upon it, it is to consist largely of co-opted and nominated members, who are to be drawn from amongst men and women of greater experience, wisdom and local knowledge than popular election can supply. The powers and duties of the new Poor Law are not even entrusted to this packed Poor Law Committee disguised under a new name, but are to be distributed among a whole series of "Public Assistance Committees" and "Medical Committees," the bulk of the work devolving upon these nominated local committees, each with its own dilution of non-elected members—the Medical Committees largely composed of the doctors who are going to be selected by their pauper patients, and paid their fees out of the rates; and the Public Assistance Committees made up to a great extent of persons nominated by voluntary charitable agencies. But this is not all. What might seem the generous laxness of the whole terminology of the proposed new Poor Law, if not also of some of its provisions, is to be counteracted by statutory "Voluntary Aid Committees"; constituted on the lines of the Charity Organisation Society; eligible to receive grants from the Public Assistance Authority out of the County Rate; but in no way under public control. *To these irresponsible Committees of benevolent amateurs all applicants will apply in the first instance*; and in case of refusal of aid, the Public Assistance Committee is to be bound to assist the applicant, if at all, "in some way less agreeable" than the Voluntary Aid Committee would have done! We have found some difficulty in unravelling the complicated details of the constitution recommended in this scheme for the administration of an annual expenditure from the rates and taxes of, in England and Wales alone, at least £15,000,000 sterling. What is clear is that the unconcealed purpose of constructing this elaborate and mysterious framework,

> With centric and eccentric scribbled o'er,
> Cycle and epicycle, orb in orb,

is to withdraw the whole relief of distress from popular control.

But apart from this undemocratic constitution, which, in our judgment, makes the scheme politically impracticable, we consider the whole conception of a Swollen Poor Law, under whatever name disguised, unsound in principle. The experience of the past, as shown by the analysis contained in the preceding chapters of this Report, demonstrates, we think, beyond possibility of doubt that when a Destitution Authority departs from the simple function of providing bare maintenance under deterrent conditions, *it finds it quite impossible to mark off or delimit its services from those which are required by, and provided for, the population at large.* The function of preventing and treating disease among destitute persons cannot, in practice, be distinguished from the prevention and treatment of disease in other persons. The rearing of infants and the education of children whose parents are destitute does not differ from the rearing of infants and the education of children whose parents are not destitute. The liability of persons to be compulsorily removed from their homes, because they have become a public nuisance or a source of danger, must surely be the same whether or not they are technically "destitute." The exercise of the power of compulsorily adopting the children of parents who are leading a vicious life, or who are cruelly treating them, has no reference to the "destitution" of such parents. In short, if we are going to provide preventive and curative treatment—if the treatment of each class, and of each individual within that class, is to be governed not by the fact of their destitution but by the conditions surrounding the particular class and the particular individual of the class—the category of the destitute becomes an irrelevancy. *What is demanded by the conditions is not a division according to the presence or absence of destitution, but a division according to the services to be provided.* Each public service requires its own "machinery of approach" of the population at large, its own technical methods of treatment of the class entrusted to it, its own specialised staff, and its own supervising committee, bent upon the performance of the particular service. Those from whom the cost of their treatment ought to be recovered, can be effectively made to pay without vainly trying to separate the treatment of the destitute from the treatment of the poor. To seek to withdraw, from the elaborate specialised public services, already in existence for the population at large, the 5 or 10 per cent. of each class who are technically "destitute," and to set up duplicate services for their separate treatment under the Poor Law, even if disguised under the name of Public Assistance, would be both injurious to themselves and unnecessarily costly to the public.

(b) The Scheme we Recommend

We have now to present the scheme of reform to which we ourselves have been driven by the facts of the situation. The dominant exigencies of which we have to take account are:

(i) The overlapping, confusion and waste that result from the provision for each separate class being undertaken, in one and the same district, by two, three, and sometimes even by four separate Local Authorities, as well as by voluntary agencies.

(ii) The demoralisation of character and the slackening of personal effort that result from the unnecessary spreading of indiscriminate, unconditional and gratuitous provision, through this unco-ordinated rivalry.

(iii) The paramount importance of subordinating mere relief to the specialised treatment of each separate class, with the object of preventing or curing its distress.

(iv) The expediency of intimately associating this specialised treatment of each class with the standing machinery for enforcing, both before and after the period of distress, the fulfilment of personal and family obligations.

We have seen that it is not practicable to oust the various specialised

Local Authorities that have grown up since the Boards of Guardians were established. There remains only the alternative—to which, indeed, the conclusions of each of our chapters seem to us to point—of completing the process of breaking up the Poor Law, which has been going on for the last three decades. The scheme of reform that we recommend involves:

(i) The final supersession of the Poor Law Authority by the newer specialised Authorities already at work.

(ii) The appropriate distribution of the remaining functions of the Poor Law among those existing Authorities.

(iii) The establishment of suitable machinery for registering and co-ordinating all the assistance afforded to any given person or family; and

(iv) The more systematic enforcement, by means of this co-ordinating machinery, of the obligation of able-bodied persons to support themselves and their families.

(i) *The Supersession of the Destitution Authority*

We think that the time has arrived for the abolition of the Boards of Guardians in England, Wales and Ireland; and, so far as any Poor Law duties are concerned, of the Parish Councils in Scotland. We come to this conclusion not from any lack of appreciation of the devoted public service gratuitously rendered on these Boards of Guardians and Parish Councils by tens of thousands of men and women of humanity, ability, and integrity, which, we feel, has never received adequate recognition. But it has become increasingly plain to us in the course of our inquiry—it is, in fact, recognised by many of the members of these bodies themselves—that the character of the functions entrusted to the Poor Law Authorities is such as to render their task, at best, nugatory; and, at worst, seriously mischievous. The mere keeping of people from starving—which is essentially what the Poor Law sets out to do—may have been useful as averting social revolution: it cannot, in the twentieth century, be regarded as any adequate fulfilment of social duty. The very conception of relieving destitution starts the whole service on a demoralising tack. An Authority having for its function merely the provision of maintenance for those who are starving is necessarily limited in its dealings to the brief periods in each person's life in which he is actually destitute; and has, therefore, even if it could go beyond the demoralising dole—too bad for the good, and too good for the bad—no opportunity of influencing that person's life, both before he becomes destitute, and after he has ceased to be destitute, in such a way as to stimulate personal effort, to strengthen character and capacity, to ward off dangers, and generally to keep the individual on his feet. As regards the effect on individual character and the result in enforcing personal and family responsibilities, of the activities of the Destitution Authority on the one hand, and those of the Local Education Authority and the Local Health Authority on the other—even where these latter give food as well as treatment—there is, as all our evidence shows, no possible doubt on which side the advantage lies. Yet if a Poor Law Authority attempts to do more than provide bare subsistence for those who are actually destitute, for the period in which they are destitute; if it sets itself to give the necessary specialised treatment required for birth and infancy; if it provides education for children, medical treatment for the sick, satisfactory provision for the aged, and specialised compulsion for the able-bodied, it ceases to be an "*ad hoc*" Authority, with a single tradition and a single purpose, and becomes a "mixed" Authority, without either the diversified professional staff, the variety of technical experience, or even a sufficiency and continuity of work in any one branch to enable it to cope with its multifarious problems. Moreover, as has been abundantly demonstrated by experience, every increase in the advantageousness of the "relief" afforded by the Destitution Authority, and every enlargement of its powers of compulsory removal and detention, brings it into new rivalry with the other Local Authorities, and drags into the net of pauperism those who might otherwise have been dealt with as self-supporting citizens. If, as it seems to us, it has become imperative to put an end to the present wasteful and demoralising overlapping between Local Authorities, it is plain that it is the Destitution Authority—already denuded of several of its functions—that must give way to its younger rivals.

Besides this paramount consideration, there are two incidental reasons which support our recommendation for the abolition of the Boards of Guardians in England, Wales and Ireland, and, so far at any rate as their Poor Law work is concerned, of the Parish Councils in Scotland. These are:

a) The grave economic and administrative inconveniences of the existing Poor Law areas; and

b) The unnecessary multiplication of elected Local Authorities.

In the great majority of cases the population dealt with by the Destitution Authority is too small to permit either of economical administration or of proper provision being made in separate institutions for all the various classes of paupers. Out of the 1,679 districts into which the United Kingdom is divided for Poor Law purposes, four-fifths have populations which do not amount to 20,000 families each. Even in England and Wales more than two-thirds of the Unions include fewer than 10,000 families; and 81 of these Unions actually have populations of fewer than 2,000 families each. In Ireland, out of the 130 Unions, there are only 9 having as many as 10,000 families; and there are 12 having fewer than 2,000 families. In Scotland where this *morcellement* is carried to an absurd extent, a population smaller than that of London is dealt with by 874 separate Poor Law Authorities, nearly three-eighths of which rule over fewer than 200 families each. Any proper provision of specialised institutions for such small groups of people is absolutely impossible. In short, even apart from any other considerations, there are not more than about 100, out of all the 1,679 Poor Law districts of the United Kingdom, in which it would be possible to make decent provision for the many separate classes which have to be differentially dealt with. We have received a large amount of evidence demonstrating conclusively that, if any new area is adopted for administration and rating it cannot, on all sorts of grounds, practically be any other than that of the County and County Borough. On this point, which we think needs no further argument, we are glad to find ourselves in agreement with the majority of our colleagues.

If the new area adopted be that of the County and County Borough, the Local Authority to be entrusted with the work cannot, we are assured by those best acquainted with local administration, be any other than the County Council and County Borough Council acting through its several committees. "You could not have two Authorities in the County area," declared to us a practical County administrator, "we should always be clashing." "It would have to be done by the County Council," Mr. Walter Long informed us. "Would you contemplate," he was asked, "setting up a new *ad hoc* Authority in the county area for any purpose whatsoever?" To this he replied emphatically "None." The same testimony was given by Lord Fitzmaurice, who has so long worked in County government, and who declared himself opposed to any new County Authority for Poor Law purposes only. The setting up in London or in the County Boroughs, of any separately elected body, for the same area, and levying rates on the same occupiers, appears equally impracticable. We therefore come inevitably to the proposal to transfer the duties of the Boards of Guardians to the Councils of the Counties and County Boroughs.

In favour of this course there are many different arguments. We think that it will be generally recognised that the mere reduction in the number of separate Local Authorities, having separate powers of expenditure of the rates, and making separate demands on the time and service of the citizens willing to stand for election, is an advantage in itself. It fortunately happens that, at any rate in the County Boroughs of England and Wales, which comprise one-third of all the population of that country, the various rivals to the Poor Law—the Local Education Authority, the Local Health Authority, the Local Pension Authority, the Local Unemployment Authority, the Local Police Authority and the Local Authority for the Mentally Defective—have one and all become committees of the Town Council. In the Metropolis, and in the counties, the several Committees of the County Council already deal with the same services, though they may share their administration, so far as local duties are concerned, with corresponding committees of minor local authorities. The abolition of the Boards of Guardians, and the adoption of the area of the County and County Borough would, in England and Wales at any rate—with appropriate arrangements to meet the cases of the Metropolitan Boroughs in London and of the non-County Boroughs and Urban and Rural District Councils in the other Counties—enable a very desirable unification of Local Government to be carried out. In this proposal to make the County and County Borough Councils financially responsible for all the duties at present performed by the Boards of Guardians, we are glad to find ourselves in agreement with a majority of our colleagues. We differ from them in this matter in the extent to which they seek to withdraw the new services from the control of the County or County Borough Council itself, and in the way in which they attempt to determine by what machinery of committees and sub-committees the Councils shall carry out the work entrusted to them. We cannot help thinking that these are matters which, in practice, the Councils will decide for themselves. We doubt whether any provision of Parliament will prevent a Town or County Council exercising whatever measure of control it chooses over a service entrusted to one of its committees for which it has to find the money. And we cannot help thinking that in adopting as their own the proposal that the unit of area should henceforth be the County and County Borough, and that the supreme authority should be the County Council and County Borough Council, the majority of our colleagues have rendered inevitable the adoption of the principle of distributing the Poor Law services among the committees already concerned in those very services. We cannot imagine, for instance, the Education Committee of the Manchester Town Council handing over to the tender mercies of any new statutory Poor Law Committee, the residential schools for defective children, the Day Industrial Schools, or the provision of dinners for hungry children, in which the Councillors take so much pride; or the Health Committee handing over to the new Poor Law Committee the exact contingent of the patients in its Isolation Hospitals and Phthisis Wards who are declared to be destitute. If the responsibility for the administration of the various services of the Poor Law is imposed on the Manchester Town Council at all—if it has to levy the Poor Rate to support the Poor Law Schools at Swinton and the Poor Law Infirmary at New Bridge Street—it may confidently be predicted that it will make its own Education Committee and its Director of Education answerable for the one, and its own Health Committee and Medical Officer of Health answerable for the other.

(ii) *The Distribution of the Services of the Destitution Authority*

We have satisfied ourselves that, in England and Wales at any rate, and we think also in Scotland—Ireland presenting a somewhat different problem—there would be no serious difficulty in all the various functions of the Poor Law being undertaken by the several committees of the existing Local Authorities. We prefer to reserve for subsequent examination, in Part II. of this Report, the whole class of the Able-bodied, whether Vagrants, Paupers or the Unemployed, for whom we shall propose a national organisation. If, however, it were decided to leave this class also to Local Authorities there would be no difficulty in entrusting this branch of the work to its own appropriate Committee of the County or County Borough Council, in which the existing Distress Committee under the Unemployed Workmen Act would be merged.

(a) The Duties to be Transferred to the Local Education Authorities

With regard to the children of school age at present dealt with under the Poor Law, the course is easy. We believe that public opinion is wholly in favour of the transfer, in England and Wales, of the entire care of the pauper children of school age to the Local Education Authorities, under the supervision of the Board of Education. We need not recapitulate the manifold advantages of dissociating, once for all, the whole care of the children from any connection with pauperism. Up and down the country

the Local Education Authorities, as we have seen, are already providing
not only schooling but also maintenance for many thousands of children;
they have actually, in some cases, their own residential schools and their
own arrangements for "boarding-out"; they have their own machinery for
searching out cases where the children are being neglected, and for the
systematic medical supervision of practically the whole child population.
Already, throughout Great Britain, there has been transferred to the Local
Education Authorities the whole schooling of nine-tenths of the children
under the control of the Destitution Authorities, and to the Board of
Education for England and Wales the inspection of the remaining Poor
Law schools, etc., in that country. The Local Education Authorities
already deal with so many children that the addition to their work involved
by this transfer is proportionately small. The Education Committee of the
Gloucestershire County Council, for instance, has about 50,000 children
under instruction. The dozen or so of Boards of Guardians in the corresponding area of the County have among them all scarcely 1,000 children
of school age in their charge, and of these only between one and two
hundred receive institutional care. The thirty-one Boards of Guardians of
the Metropolis have in their charge perhaps as many as 25,000 children of
school age, of whom some 15,000 receive institutional treatment. The
supervision of this number would make no great difference to the work
of the Education Committee of the London County Council, which deals
already with nearly 1,000,000 children. Where educational administration
is shared between the County Education Committee and a Minor Authority—as, for instance, where the Council of a Non-County Borough or of
an Urban District administers its own elementary day schools—the responsibility for the custody and care of the children at present under the
Board of Guardians would naturally pass to the County Education Authority, which might use the day schools of the Minor Authority just as
the Board of Guardians does.

(b) The Duties to be Transferred to the Local Health Authorities

The duties to be transferred from the Board of Guardians to the Local
Health Authorities—the provision for birth and infancy, the treatment of
the sick and the incapacitated, and the institutional provision for the aged
—cannot be disposed of so simply as those relating to children of school
age. Let us begin with the case of the County Boroughs, which now
include one-third of the whole population of England and Wales. Here

there is already a Health Committee of the Town Council, which has its own Medical Officer of Health, its own staff of doctors and sanitary inspectors, often also of Health Visitors and nurses. It usually has its own hospital or hospitals, and sometimes its own sanatorium. If it were made responsible for all the treatment of the sick, domiciliary as well as institutional, the addition of the Poor Law Medical Officers to its staff, and of the care of the pauper sick to its work, would involve practically no difficulties. Similarly the provision for birth and infancy and for the institutional treatment of the aged could easily be added to the existing duties of the Health Committee.

Outside the County Boroughs the functions of the Local Health Authority are at present everywhere shared between the County Council, with its County Medical Officer, and a Minor Health Authority, which may be (in the Metropolis) a Metropolitan Borough Council or the Corporation of the City of London; or (in other Counties) the Council of a Non-County Borough, or that of an Urban Sanitary District, or that of a Rural Sanitary District. We have received much evidence in favour of the abolition of the smaller Minor Health Authorities, and of the extension of the Public Health functions of the County Council. But assuming the existing organisation in this respect to remain undisturbed, at any rate so far as the larger Local Health Authorities are concerned, it would, we think, not be difficult to divide the duties now performed by the Boards of Guardians in respect of Birth and Infancy, the treatment of the sick and incapacitated, and the institutional treatment of the aged, appropriately between the County Health Authority and the Minor Health Authority. To the former would fall, along with the general supervision of the Public Health of the County as a whole, the administration of all the institutions transferred from the Boards of Guardians, or established in order to provide for the classes of patients hitherto dealt with by the Poor Law Authorities. The advantages of a unified and properly graded institutional organisation for the County as a whole, together with the financial saving of such an organisation to every part of the County, appear to us so great that this unified County service should, at all hazards, be insisted on. In the Non-County Boroughs having over 10,000 population, and in the Urban Districts having over 20,000 population, we should be inclined, with regard to the Outdoor Medical Service of the Poor Law, to follow the precedent set by the Education Act of 1902 with regard to elementary day schools, and to allow these Minor Health Authorities, if they so

desired, to take over the present District Medical Officers, and to undertake, under the general supervision of the County Medical Officer, the
domiciliary medical service for their respective districts—provided always
that they were prepared to organise, out of these officers and the present
Public Health staff, a unified medical service under the direction of an
adequately salaried, qualified Medical Officer devoting his whole time to
the work. With regard to the Non-County Boroughs of less than 10,000
population, the Urban Districts of less than 20,000 population, and the
Rural Sanitary Districts, whatever their size, we are satisfied that these
Authorities have neither the means nor the official staff that are requisite
for the performance of the duties already assumed by them under the
Public Health Acts. For them to bring their sanitary services, and especially their drinking-water supply and their drainage systems, even up to
the National Minimum, would involve, in many cases, a local rate of
crushing weight. To expect them to equip their little districts adequately
with hospital accommodation for scarlet fever, let alone for tuberculosis,
is, for the most part, hopeless. We cannot recommend the transfer to such
Authorities of any part of the work now done by the Boards of Guardians
in this department. This work should, in respect of their districts, be
wholly assumed by the Health Committee of the County Council, under the
direction of the County Medical Officer. The small Non-County Boroughs
and Urban Sanitary Districts should be encouraged (as the former have
been in the matter of their autonomous police forces) to cede even their
present Public Health services, in whole or in part, to the County Council,
in order that they may be merged in the unified establishment under the
County Medical Officer. They should, for instance, receive no part of
the proposed new Grant-in-Aid of the expenditure of the Local Health
Authorities, payable as this would be in order to enable the larger Health
Authorities to undertake new services which will not devolve upon these
smaller Health Authorities. The same lines should be followed with regard
to the Rural District Councils; unless, indeed, these can be, on their
ceasing to be also the Boards of Guardians, altogether abolished, and
their duties with regard to road maintenance, sanitation, etc., shared
between the County Council and the Parish Councils. In the Metropolis,
pending a more complete re-organisation of Local Government, the
transfer should proceed on analogous lines, all the Poor Law institutions,
including the hospitals and special schools of the Metropolitan Asylums
Board, passing to the Health Committee of the County Council; whilst the

District Medical Officers in each Metropolitan Borough would become part of a unified medical service for street and house sanitation and domiciliary treatment, directly under a qualified Borough Medical Officer, and subject to the general supervision of the County Medical Officer.

(c) The Duties to be Transferred to the Local Pension Committee

Even whilst we were considering the matter there has been established, by every County and County Borough Council under the Old-Age Pensions Act of 1908, a Local Pension Committee, charged with the confirmation of the pensions to be granted to more than half the poor persons over seventy years of age. We propose that this Committee should deal also with those aged, who are for one reason or another not entitled to National Pensions, but for whom Local Pensions are recommended. The practical convenience of there being one and the same Committee to deal with both classes of aged—those whose pensions will be payable from the National Exchequer and those whose pensions will be payable from Local Funds—is so obvious that we do not think the point needs further discussion.

(d) The Duties to be Transferred to the Local Committee for the Mentally Defective

The Report of the Royal Commission on the Care and Control of the Feeble-minded makes it clear, we think, that there should be transferred to a new Local Committee for the Mentally Defective—virtually the existing Asylums Committee of the County or County Borough Council—the care of all persons legally certified to be of unsound mind, whatever their age or physical condition, whether these be lunatics, idiots, imbeciles, or epileptics; whether they be certified under the Inebriates Act; or whether they be registered as feeble-minded, or as morally defective, under the proposed extended classification. This conclusion, which we entirely accept, involves the transfer, to an enlarged Asylums Committee of the County or County Borough Council, of the institutions established by one or two such Councils under the Inebriates Act, of the special institutions here and there established for epileptics, of the special schools for mentally defective children, and of those inmates of Poor Law institutions —estimated, for England and Wales alone, at 43,000 in number—who may in due course be certified as feeble-minded. It involves also, in London, the transfer of the asylums for imbeciles, etc., of the Metropolitan

Asylums Board to the new Mentally-Defectives Committee of the London County Council, in which its present Asylums Committee would be merged.

(iii) *New Machinery for the Co-ordination of Public Assistance*

At the present time, whilst much distress goes wholly untreated, some families are in receipt, at one and the same time, for one or other of their members, of regular Outdoor Relief from the Board of Guardians, school meals for the children from the Education Committee, milk below cost price, medical advice gratis, and maintenance in hospital from the Health Committee, and, in some towns, even gratuitous clothes from the police—besides a flow of doles from religious and charitable agencies. Whether or not any of the public assistance given to one family by the various agencies will be charged for, and whether or not the charge will be enforced, is, as we have seen, almost a matter of chance. One family may be getting everything free, even free of inquiry. Another family, in receipt of relief on account of its destitution, may find its head suddenly removed to gaol for not refunding the cost of the maintenance of his child in an industrial school. To abolish the Board of Guardians, and merge its duties in those Committees of the County or County Borough Council who are already dispensing their own forms of public assistance, will diminish the present overlapping but will not, of itself, end it. Some systematic co-ordination, within each local area, of all forms of public assistance and, if possible, of all assistance dispensed by Voluntary Agencies, is essential, if we are to put an end to the present demoralisation.

(a) The Registrar of Public Assistance

The first condition of co-ordination is a centre of information about all the public assistance that is being dispensed in a given locality. We, therefore, recommend the appointment, by the County or County Borough Council, of one or more responsible officers, each having jurisdiction in a district of suitable area and population. For the less populous County Boroughs and the smaller Counties, one such officer, sitting on successive days in different parts of the district, would probably suffice. For the most extensive Counties, as for the Metropolis, there might have to be half a dozen, sitting weekly in as many as thirty different localities. We propose that these officers, who might be designated Registrars of Public Assistance, should have a threefold duty. They should be responsible for keeping a register, with "case papers" of the most approved pattern, of all persons receiving any form of public assistance within their districts, including treatment in any public institution. They should have the duty of assessing, in accordance with whatever may be the law, the charge to be made on individuals liable to pay any part of the cost of the service rendered to them or their dependents or other relations according to their means, and of recovering the amount thus due. Finally, we propose that these officers should have submitted to them any proposals by the several Committees of the Council for the payment of what is now called Outdoor Relief, but what should in future be termed Home Aliment, in connection with the domiciliary treatment of cases in which such treatment was deemed preferable to institutional treatment. The Registrar should also determine, in case of need, to which Committee of the Local Authority any neglected or "marginal" cases belonged for treatment.

(b) The Public Register

To the first of these duties, the keeping of one common Register of all the various forms of assistance given in the locality, we attach great importance. This registration should be automatic and continuous, without regard to status or means, or the kind of treatment given. All public Authorities should be required to forward, daily or weekly, full particulars of every case in any way dealt with, whether it were that of a rich man admitted as a paying patient to the County Lunatic Asylum, or that of a poor man whose child was being fed at school, or whose wife was receiving milk at a nominal charge; whether it were a County Bursary to Oxford or compulsory admission to an industrial school. We should earnestly invite all voluntary hospitals, dispensaries, and other institutions regularly to send in similar information. In course of time, we should hope to get recorded in this Register the persons assisted by every public or private agency within its district. The Registrar would thus be able to see, at once, whether different members of the same family were receiving assistance without this being known, or whether different Authorities, in ignorance of each other's doings, were simultaneously aiding the same person. In this branch of his duty, he would confine himself to communicating the information to the various Local Authorities, to the Registrars of other districts where necessary, and to such voluntary organisations as had affiliated themselves.

(c) Charge and Recovery

The second function of the Registrar would be to put on a systematic and impartial basis the recovery of the cost of the public assistance rendered, where any legal liability existed for its repayment, and where the recipients or other persons liable were really able to pay. We have already described the unutterable confusion that at present exists in this respect— a confusion in which the Local Health Authority and the Local Education Authority have their shares, no less than the Destitution Authority. We do not here discuss the question as to which public services should be charged for, to what extent relations of different degrees of kinship should be made to pay for those to whom they are akin, and what amount of earnings or income should be held to constitute ability to pay. These points must be determined by Parliament, in a consistent code. But, as we have seen, clearness and consistency of the law will not bring about impartiality and consistency in the practice, so long as the matter is left to the haphazard decisions of irresponsible committees of shifting membership. It is, we think, essential that the charge to be made in each case should be assessed, according to the exact terms of the law and the definite evidence as to means, after systematic inquiry, by a single officer dealing with the cases judicially. His decisions might, of course, be made subject to appeal.

We regard it as a special advantage of this proposal that, under it, the question of chargeability and recovery of cost is altogether removed from the consideration of the officers and Committees who are responsible for the decision of whether or not a case is in need of treatment, and of what kind of treatment. At present, some Local Authorities refuse to treat a person, who is admittedly in need of treatment, because they choose to think that he or his relations could pay for what he needs. The result is that, to the grave injury of the community, many cases remain untreated. Other Local Authorities go on the plan of treating all who need treatment, on the assumption that anyone found to be in actual need of treatment has not the pecuniary resources to enable him to get it at his own expense. The result is that many persons who might fairly pay something escape all contribution. If we desire that all those should be treated whom it is important, in the public interest, not to leave untreated, and that, in the interest of public economy and personal independence, all those should pay who can afford to do so, we must separate the two processes. If it is thought right to segregate all the different grades of the mentally defective, to leave no child uneducated, to prevent disease and restore as quickly as possible the sick to health, and to provide decent maintenance for the aged, we ought not to allow the Local Authorities responsible for the treatment to be hampered in their work by considerations as to whether or not the individual, or any of his relations, ought, according to the law of the land, to pay for what is required to be done; and whether or not he or they are of sufficient ability to do so. On the other hand, if we wish to put a check to the practice of getting gratuitously from the public what the individual is quite well able to pay for, and to restrict to the really necessitous cases the spread of gratuitous treatment by the Local Authority, we ought not to let those who are charged with the recovery of contributions be hampered by considerations of whether it will not be dangerous to let the case remain untreated, or by the natural desire of the managers of institutions to make them as widely useful as possible.

The Registrar of Public Assistance, having nothing to do with the treatment of the cases, would deal with them exclusively from the standpoint of legal liability to pay, and economic ability to do so. In whatever branches of public service Parliament decided that charge should be made—for instance, maintenance in the County Lunatic Asylum—the Registrar would automatically investigate all cases reported to him; and would assess the charges on the patients' estates, or on their legally liable relations, exclusively according to the law and to the evidence of means, exactly as the Inland Revenue officers deal at present with the assessed taxes. For this purpose, the Registrar would be provided by the County or County Borough Council with a suitable staff of Enquiry and Recovery Officers, dealing impartially and on like principles with rich and poor. We feel no doubt that the additional revenue which would thus be obtained, from patients and from the relations legally liable for their maintenance—even after exempting all those who were not of sufficient ability to contribute—would be very large, and would more than cover the entire expense of the Registrar and his establishment.

The existence of such an officer would, if it were desired, enable effective measures to be taken to stop what is called "hospital abuse." It is complained that, among the crowds of patients of the voluntary hospitals and dispensaries of the Metropolis, and of some other large towns, there are many persons well able to pay the whole or part of the cost of the treatment or maintenance that they are obtaining from the benefactions of the charitable. The hospitals, absorbed in the desire to treat cases, especially those that are instructive or interesting, and without any effective machinery for ascertaining the resources of their patients, have hitherto failed to cope with this problem. If the hospitals and dispensaries chose to make it a rule that the names and addresses of all persons whom they were benefiting should be forwarded daily to the Registrar of Public Assistance, he would be able, by means of his staff of Enquiry and Recovery Officers, to discover their economic circumstances. He might even, at the request of the hospital, be authorised to present a bill for the whole or part of the cost of the treatment, to such persons as might be found to be able to pay. Payment of this bill, under the present state of the law, would be optional; but we have been informed by trustworthy witnesses that in many cases such patients would willingly discharge their debt, if a bill were sent in. It might be a matter for further consideration by Parliament, whether the practice of charge and recovery for treatment in voluntary hospitals and dispensaries might not, with advantage, be put on the same legal footing as treatment in the hospitals and dispensaries of the Local Authority.

(d) Sanction of Home Aliment

So far as institutional treatment is concerned, there would be no harm in letting all the various Authorities—for instance, the Health Committee, the Education Committee, and the Asylums (or Mentally-Defectives) Committee—admit, to the several institutions in their charge, all the persons whom they deemed in need of the particular treatment of these institutions, without any other co-ordinating machinery than that of the Public Register and the automatic recovery of the cost when legal liability and sufficient ability were found to exist. But in the great majority of cases —at present three out of every four—it is not necessary or desirable to incur the great expense of institutional treatment, especially as, in many instances, the cases can actually be more efficiently treated in their own homes. To permit the same freedom in the granting of Home Aliment to all the various committees of the County or County Borough Council, each one merely considering the needs of the particular member of the family—the child, the mother and infant, the sick father, the aged grandmother—might easily result, *as it frequently does at present,* in one family obtaining more than the current income of a respectable artisan. Nor will the establishment of a common register do more than mitigate this evil. What is required is that, before any (beyond temporary) public assistance is given in the home, there should be due consideration, not merely of the need, in respect of treatment, of any individual, but of the circumstances of the family as a whole. We cannot afford to have the Education Committee granting Home Aliment for the children of an admirable widow, who is living in an altogether insanitary home; or the Committee for the Mentally-Defectives deciding, for the sake of economy, to pay for the retention at home of a feeble-minded girl without regard to the consequences to the young children in that home. And it would never do to let all the several Committees be granting Home Aliment without a common standard of economic necessities, and due regard for the possible effect in subsidising wages. The only way to ensure that the family shall always be regarded as a unit, and that all the circumstances—educational, moral, sanitary, and economic—shall be taken in due proportion into account, is to make each Committee submit its proposals as to Home Aliment to an authority external to them all. For this purpose, the Registrar of Public Assistance, himself an officer of the County or County Borough Council, necessarily in constant communication with every department through his Public Register and his proceedings for charge and recovery, equipped with his own staff of income assessors, and able to hear evidence from the educational and sanitary officials of the various treating Committees, seems the ideal arbiter. We propose, therefore, that (apart from the provision for "sudden or urgent necessity") it should be necessary for any Committee thinking the domiciliary treatment of a case desirable, and proposing to grant Home Aliment, to submit the case for sanction to the Registrar of Public Assistance, who would be charged to satisfy himself that the circumstances of the family as a whole warranted the grant, and that the amount proposed was neither inadequate nor excessive. If the grant was sanctioned, we propose that the case should come up automatically before the Registrar for revision every three months, or even every month, whichever may be thought preferable. If sanction were withheld, it would still be open to the Committee to admit the patient to the appropriate institution; and where the need was urgent, it would be their duty to do so. But there should be an opportunity of appeal, *by the Committee responsible for treatment*, against the decision of the Registrar; an appeal which, in view of the importance of securing uniformity of practice throughout the Kingdom with regard to Home Aliment, we think should lie, following the successful precedent of the present appeal to the Local Government Board for Scotland, to a Central Department; which (in order to keep it apart from Education, Public Health, etc.) might conveniently be that supervising Local Finance.

An incidental advantage of the distribution, among the various committees of the County and County Borough Council, of the different services now aggregated together under the Destitution Authorities, would be that it would thus enable us to bring uniformity and judicial impartiality into the grant of what is now called Outdoor Relief. As we have seen, it is impossible to expect to get either uniformity or impartiality in decisions on successive cases, if these decisions are arrived at, without automatic check or guidance, by such a many-headed tribunal, of such mutable membership, as is presented by a representative committee. There is no reason to think that the several committees of the County or County Borough Councils, subject as they would be, though possibly to a lesser extent, to the same influences, would, if they had to perform exactly the same duties as a Board of Guardians, be able to arrive at much greater uniformity or impartiality between case and case, than the members of the Destitution Authority. Merely to transfer the work of the Board of Guardians to a single Poor Law Committee of the Town Council would, therefore, in this respect, produce no sufficient reform. Nor could the Outdoor Relief be withdrawn from their jurisdiction. So long as it can be assumed that all the members of the same family—the infant, the child of school age, the sick adult, and the helpless aged person—will all be treated by one and the same Committee, it will never be practicable to withdraw from that Committee the duty of considering all the economic and other circumstances of the family as a whole, and the right to decide according to its own view of what is desirable, how much Outdoor Relief should be granted. But when the services are divided among several committees the case is obviously altered. The Education Committee will admit that it is impossible to allow the Health Committee, the Mentally Defective Committee and the Pension Committee—not to mention the possible Local Committee for Unemployment—all to be giving Home Aliment to the different members of one and the same family, without the proposals being made subject to some co-ordinating control. Thus, for the first time it will become possible, whilst leaving to representative committees, directly responsible to the ratepayers, the whole treatment of the cases, whether in the institutions or in the home, and even the full responsibility for proposing the grant of Home Aliment, to secure the advantage of a judicial consideration, case by case, of the economic and other circumstances involved.

(e) The Registrar's Receiving House for Omitted Cases

Under the scheme we propose, each treating Committee would have its own arrangement (as, indeed, exists at present wherever the service is well-organised) of Receiving Homes, or Observation or Probation Wards, into which it would take its patients, on their way to one or other of its institutions. But there are "mixed" cases, in which several Committees may be concerned; there are the cases of persons without known abode, who have not been discovered by the searching officers; there are the cases of persons found "on the road" by the police, or reported by neighbours to be in distress without the nature of the distress being ascertained; there may even be cases in which treatment has been refused, and is alleged to have been wrongfully refused, by one or other of the Local Authorities. Moreover, if we are to distribute the various forms of public assistance among three or four specialised Committees, it will be necessary that there should be, in each district, one well-known public office where immediate relief can be obtained, in cases of sudden or urgent necessity, or when it is not known to which Department application for treatment should properly be made. We propose, therefore, that there should be in each district, under the immediate direction of the Registrar, a small and strictly temporary Receiving House, which might often be combined with some other public office, and which should be always open.

The number and extent of such Receiving Houses would naturally differ from county to county. It should be rigidly insisted on that no person should be allowed to stay in them for more than the few days required for the adjudication of his case. In London and other populous places each Receiving House would have to be sufficient to accommodate all the cases coming in during, say, one week. In rural counties the number would be governed more by geographical considerations. But with a complete use of telegraph and telephone and a motor ambulance, it is suggested that very few Receiving Houses would be needed. With every police-station, every medical practitioner, and every county officer in telephonic communication—presently, we may assume, with every village post office on the telegraph, if not even on the telephone—and with a motor ambulance at call that would take a person 20 miles in an hour—the area that might be effectively served by a centrally-placed Receiving House in a rural district might be (even assuming only a 30 miles radius) as much as 2,800 square miles, which is much larger than most counties. With the general specialising of institutions, it would be possible to set aside some of the smaller Workhouses as Receiving Houses.

It would be part of the function of the Registrar, on his daily or weekly visit to each part of his district, to "deliver" the local Receiving House of all the persons who had drifted in there since his last visit; allocating them, and directing their conveyance, to the Receiving Departments of the institutions appropriate to their state. It would be obligatory that the Registrar's instructions in this respect should be obeyed; but the Committees concerned would be free to bring the cases before him at a subsequent sitting and to show cause why they should be transferred to the care of some other Committee, or placed on Home Aliment, or summarily discharged as not needing treatment.

(f) The Registrar as National Pension Officer

We think that the Registrar of Public Assistance—associated as he would be with all forms of public service, those enjoyed by persons in easy circumstances as well as those taken advantage of only by the poor—would be an ideal officer to adjudicate, on behalf of the National Government, on applications for Old-Age Pensions. He would have at his command his own permanent staff of Inquiry and Recovery Officers, who would possess an unrivalled knowledge of the economic circumstances of the great majority of the families of the district. After the first award of pensions has been made in 1909, the number of applications to be dealt with annually will be only about one-tenth of the numbers of that year; and, spread as they will be over the whole twelve months, will be insufficient to occupy the whole time of even one officer in each locality. Nevertheless, it would be very inconvenient to all concerned not to have Pension Officers available in each locality. We cannot help suggesting that there would be positive advantages in making the Registrar of Public Assistance act also as National Pension Officer; and in placing the Local Pension Committee—at any rate in respect of the Local Pensions which we propose that it should grant—in the same sort of relation to him as the Local Education Committee and the Local Health Committee will be when they propose to grant Home Aliment as an adjunct of their domiciliary treatment.

(g) The Status of the Registrar

We propose that the Registrar of Public Assistance should be an officer of high *status* and practical permanence of tenure. We would leave the appointment freely in the hands of the County and County Borough Councils, relying on their choosing officers of tried experience in administration (especially in connection with the Poor Law), and preferably of some kind of legal training. As it is essential that the Registrar should be entirely independent of the committees concerned with the grant of Home Aliment, we propose that he and his staff, and his Receiving House, should be placed under the General Purposes Committee of the County or County Borough Council. If the Registrar were made use of, as we suggest, by the National Government, as the adjudicator of claims to Old-Age Pensions, this would have the great advantage of enabling the Treasury to contribute a portion of the salary and expenses of his office; an arrangement which, whilst affording some financial relief to the County and County Borough Councils, would, of course, entail the concurrence of the Treasury in the appointment and dismissal, and thus secure, in the least invidious manner, that practical security of tenure which seems desirable.

(c) Conditions of Eligibility for Public Assistance

In describing the overlapping and confusion of spheres between the Destitution Authority on the one hand, and the Local Health Authority, the Local Lunacy Authority, the Local Education Authority, the Local Police Authority, the Local Pension Authority, and the Local Unemployment Authority on the other, we found the position obscured by two rival and inconsistent conceptions—not explicitly stated or clearly realised —of what exactly constituted "destitution," or the condition in respect of which the public assistance was rendered. Under the Poor Law, whether in England or Wales, Scotland or Ireland, no one, it is asserted, can be relieved who is not in a state of destitution, and this term has a technical meaning. "Destitution," as we were authoritatively informed, "when used to describe the condition of a person as a subject for relief, implies that he is for the time being *without material resources* (1) directly available and

(2) appropriate for satisfying his physical needs, (*a*) whether actually existing or (*b*) likely to arise immediately. By physical needs in this definition are meant such needs as must be satisfied (1) in order to maintain life or (2) in order to obviate, mitigate or remove causes endangering life, or likely to endanger life, or impair health, or bodily fitness for self-support." It will be seen that, to the Destitution Authority, it is not the actual mental or physical condition of the patient, but the absence of material resources, that is the governing consideration. Thus, if a child is, in fact, suffering in health, or is even in danger of death, from lack of food, clothing or medical attendance, or from a total absence of home care, but the responsible parent, being present, has himself £2 a week coming in, and food actually in the house, the Destitution Authority cannot legally relieve the child. There is no lack of the necessary "material resources," and therefore in the Poor Law sense, the child is not destitute. Similarly, the Destitution Authorities are advised that they can take no action in cases of disease, so long as the disease has not as yet interfered with a man's earning his livelihood, and so long, in fact, as he has money in the house. It is even doubtful whether a Board of Guardians can lawfully intervene when a miserly and half-imbecile old woman is lying alone in her cottage, in a state of filth, disease and neglect likely to lead to early death, and yet, to the knowledge of the Relieving Officer, has a bag of gold under her bed, and bread in the house. There is no absence of material resources, and therefore, in the Poor Law sense, no destitution. And, as our analysis of the By-laws and practice of the Boards of Guardians shows, it is held not to be necessary that these economic resources should belong to the applicant, if he has, in fact, access to them. "Destitution," states the Clerk of Dudley Union, "is always a question of fact, and the Guardians are bound to take into consideration *all* sources of income or assistance which affect the applicant."

There are two remarkable statutory exceptions, which, by their very existence, confirm this accepted interpretation of "destitution" under the Poor Law. In the case of the lunatic, the Relieving Officer intervenes whether or not there are material resources. But this action of the Poor Law Authorities required special legislation. Similarly, when it was thought expedient to give Poor Relief to members of Friendly Societies, in spite of the fact that they possessed definite incomes, it required an Act of Parliament. Thus, in the absence of special legislation, the view taken is that Poor Relief is only for those who are *pecuniarily* destitute. This view it is, whether or not legally correct, which has dominated the Destitution Authorities, and coloured all their activities.

Very different is the standpoint of the other Authorities. Under the various statutes which the Local Education Authority, the Local Health Authority, and even the Local Unemployment Authority carry out, the condition which sets them in motion is not destitution in the sense of the absence of *material* resources, but the existence in the person dealt with of conditions which, without the intervention of the public Authority, would produce consequences inimical to the common weal. This we must designate, for lack of a better term, "personal destitution" or "physiological destitution." The necessary conditions may or may not co-exist with the presence of material resources—a consideration which may affect the pecuniary charge to be made in return for the services of the public Authority, but not the rendering of the services themselves. Thus, in the case of a child found destitute of education, of a person suffering from smallpox destitute of proper treatment and facilities for isolation, of a boy running wild in low company, destitute of proper parental control, *the presence or absence of material resources is wholly irrelevant to the rendering of the appropriate service.* Moreover, these specialised Local Authorities are not required to wait, and do not, in practice, wait until the injury to the community has actually begun. Thus, the School Attendance Officer registers the child long before it actually attains school age, and advises the mother which school it should presently attend, so that there may never be any "personal destitution" in respect of this service. The Health Visitor counsels the mother, and even tenders municipal milk, before the infant is ill, deliberately in order that it may not become ill. The Medical Officer isolates "contacts," though they are not ill, and though there is no known contagion, merely out of precaution. But Boards of Guardians in England, Ireland and Wales, and Parish Councils in Scotland, take the view that they have no power to intervene until the state of destitution—however broadly they may choose to interpret this term— *has been actually entered upon.* "It is certainly not the duty of the Guardians to anticipate it."

This contradiction between the two versions of the conditions of eligibility for Public Assistance has a large share in producing the confusion and overlapping that we have described. Moreover, a lack of appreciation of the exact contrast has, we think, on both sides, stood in the way of a proper exercise of the powers of Charge and Recovery. We think it important that this confusion of thought should be cleared up. It is essential for the attainment of the very objects for which the several "treating" Authorities are constituted, that they should continue to adopt, so far as their treatment is concerned, the definition that we have designated "personal" or "physiological" destitution. These Authorities must, in order to prevent injury to the community, take action whether or not there are material resources. We propose that they shall act on the same principles in the enlarged sphere that we assign to them. We consider that it is the maintenance of the contrary view by the Destitution Authorities—the insistence on pecuniary destitution—which has excluded them from the whole domain of preventive work, and has given to their operations, humane and philanthropic though they are, their characteristic barrenness. On the other hand, *after the appropriate service has been rendered to the person in need of it*, the question may quite properly be raised whether a Special Assessment ought not to be made upon him in repayment of the cost. At this point what is relevant is not whether he needs the service ("personal" or "physiological" destitution); but whether he or any one responsible for him has sufficient means to warrant a charge being made upon him. In our chapter on "Charge and Recovery" we have described the chaos into which this realm has fallen. It is one of the adventures of the Scheme of Reform that we advocate that, under it, the "treating" Authority—acting on what we have called "personal" or "physiological" destitution—is entirely divorced from the official machinery for Charge and Recovery, the Registrar of Public Assistance acting according to "pecuniary destitution," at whatever level of means Parliament may decide.

We pass now to the question of the degree of need—that is, of "personal" or "physiological" destitution—which should set the several "treating" Authorities in motion. The Legal Adviser of the Local Government Board informed us that a person was entitled to have satisfied, at the expense of the Poor Rate, if he was without the means of satisfying them, "such needs as must be satisfied (i.) in order to maintain life or (ii.) in order to obviate, mitigate or remove causes endangering life or likely to endanger life or impair health or bodily fitness for self-support." This would seem to entitle an artisan or small shopkeeper, able to maintain himself and his family, but needing, to save his life, an expensive surgical operation, not merely to have this performed at the expense of the Poor Law, but even to have provided for him whatever was necessary—

expensive treatment, mechanical appliances, and maintenance in convalescence—to restore his "bodily fitness for self-support." It is clear that the Local Government Board's definition would involve a great increase in Poor Law expenditure in respect of specialised hospitals, convalescent homes and "medical extras." We are disinclined to go as far in the provision of Public Assistance as is involved in Mr. Adrian's words. We accept as a better working definition of the conditions under which Public Assistance should be granted that given by the Royal Commissioners on the Aged Poor, when they said that "Destitution might be taken in practice to mean a want of the reasonable necessaries of life, such as food, lodging, warmth, clothing, and medical attendance according to the normal standard of the times." The "normal standard of the times" implies a changing standard, increasing with the customary expenditure of the ordinary man. This is a less alarming proposition, and one well within our means. As a matter of fact, we do not find that the expenditure on sanitation, education, etc., even keeps pace with the rise in personal incomes; still less does the total of all forms of Public Assistance keep pace with the growth of the public revenue of the country. Our whole expenditure on the poor, great as it is, bears a much smaller proportion to the aggregate revenue of the nation than it did a century ago.

(d) Disfranchisement

It is, we think, one of the advantages of our Scheme of Reform that, with the break-up of the Poor Law and the abolition of Poor Relief, the whole apparatus of electoral disfranchisement of persons who have the residential qualifications for the franchise, will fall to the ground. We can see no practical advantage in disfranchising a person because he has received the treatment which Parliament has provided for his case. The evidence goes to show that, so far as disfranchisement has any effect at all, it is a "Test" of the very worst kind; deterring the good and self-respecting, and in no way influencing the willing parasite. Moreover, the present position is so illogical that it could not, in our opinion, anyhow, have been maintained. There is no disfranchisement for the person convicted of crime, even of the most shameful kind. There is even, contrary to the common opinion, nothing to prevent a pauper voting if he is on the electoral register; and many of them actually do vote. Moreover, although the Statute does forbid paupers in England and Wales to vote at an election of Guardians, no means are usually taken to prevent those paupers who happen to be on the electoral register from exercising their franchise at an election of Guardians; and there is nothing on the face of the register to hinder their votes being received. What does happen is that, once a year, when the register is being revised, those persons (usually men only) whom the Clerk to the Guardians reports as having received Poor Relief (other than Medical Relief) at any time during the preceding twelve months are struck off, whatever may have been the cause or occasion, or the momentary character of the destitution to which they were reduced. This does not prevent them from voting, although they are paupers, during the two or three months that the old register remains in force; and it does prevent them from voting, even if they have long since ceased to be paupers, during the ensuing twelve months that the new register will be in force. In strict law the disqualification is absolute, even if the whole cost of the relief be immediately repaid; and even if the pauperism be actually forced on the elector by law, as when a dependent is, by magistrate's orders, compulsorily removed to the County Lunatic Asylum. On the other hand, Medical Relief only does not disqualify, and Revising Barristers differ from place to place, how far treatment and maintenance in the sick ward of the Workhouse, or the Poor Law Infirmary, is merely Medical Relief. Where the patient is sent by the Board of Guardians to the Municipal Hospital, or to a voluntary institution, he may or may not find his name struck off the register according to the *form* in which the Board of Guardians takes the cost of his treatment out of the Poor Rate. If he is paid for at so much per case per week, he will lose his vote, because this is (by Local Government Board instructions) entered as Outdoor Relief! If (as is more usual) he is paid for in a lump sum, he will not lose his vote. Nor will he be disqualified (even for voting for the Home Secretary who has let him out of gaol!) if he has been maintained in prison at His Majesty's expense; and if he is a freeholder or a University graduate, he will not even lose his qualification for next year's register by his enforced residence in prison. Nor will he be disqualified (even for voting for the Town Council which provides his relief) if he is admitted to the Municipal Hospital by the Medical Officer of Health, or given relief under the Unemployed Workmen Act; or if his eldest son is maintained in a Reformatory School, his younger son in an Industrial School, and his feeble-minded daughter in a Custodial Home, or if his infant gets milk at the Municipal Milk Dispensary, or if his other children are medically treated and provided with spectacles out of the Education Rate; or even if they are regularly fed at school. The absurdities of the present position are, indeed, so gross that no Minister of the Crown would think of proposing, and no House of Commons would dream of entertaining their explicit re-enactment.

(E) THE SPHERE OF VOLUNTARY AGENCIES

It is one of the advantages of the proposed distribution of the various services at present aggregated together under the name of Poor Law that it affords the opportunity for initiating a really systematic use of voluntary agencies and personal service, to give to the public assistance that touch of friendly sympathy which may be more helpful than mere maintenance at the public expense, and to deal with cases in which voluntary administration may result in more effective treatment than can be given by public authorities exclusively. It is a drawback of the Destitution Authority, which increases with its hypertrophy, that it is constantly becoming the rival of these voluntary agencies. Relief Committees have never known how to use volunteer helpers, and they seem even to look upon philanthropic institutions as interlopers, because they are not managed by the Board of Guardians itself.

We think that it should be a cardinal principle of public administration that the utmost use should, under proper conditions, be made of voluntary agencies and of the personal service of both men and women of good will. But it is, in our opinion, essential that the proper sphere of this voluntary effort should be clearly understood. In the delimitation of this sphere, a great distinction is to be drawn between the use of voluntary agencies in the visitation of the homes of the poor, and the use of these agencies in the establishment and management of institutions. In the one case there should be absolutely no finding of money. In the other case, the more private money the better.

With regard to the whole range of charitable work in connection with the home life of the poor, there is, in our judgment, nothing more disastrous, alike to the character of the poor and to the efficiency of the service of public assistance which is at their disposal, than the alms dispensed by well-meaning persons in the mere relief of distress. This distribution of indiscriminate, unconstitutional and inadequate doles is none the less harmful when it is an adjunct of quite kindly meant "district visiting," the official ministrations of religion or the treatment meted out by a "medical mission." Even when such gifts are discreetly dispensed by the most careful visitor, they have the drawback of being given without knowledge of what the other resources of the family may be, without communication to other agencies which may be simultaneously at work, and without power to insist on proper conditions. We are definitely of opinion that no encouragement whatever should be given to any distribution of money, food or clothing, in the homes of the poor by any private persons or charitable societies whatsoever. The only exception to this rule should be a regular pension to a particular person; and this ought, in all cases, to be notified to the Registrar of Public Assistance. It is not that we undervalue the utility of the personal visits of sympathetic and helpful men or women. On the contrary, we wish to see much more use made of this devoted service, which could, we think, be greatly augmented, if it were called for by public authorities. But this service of visitation, to be effective, must be definitely organised, under skilled direction, in association with a special branch of public administration. Such specialisation of home visitation is the only means of keeping at bay the mere irresponsible amateur, and of ensuring that the volunteer has been sufficiently in earnest to undergo some sort of technical training. The utility of such a service of specialised visitation has already been demonstrated in many directions. Thus, there are now a thousand or two of unpaid Health Visitors, acting under the direction of the Medical Officers of Health. Another example is afforded by the members of the Children's Care Committees, established in connection with the public elementary schools, and the analogous committees of the special schools of the London County Council. We see no reason why some such voluntary assistance should not be organised in connection with the Local Health Authority and the Local Education Authority in every district. We think, too, that similar voluntary assistance could be usefully employed in connection with the work of the Local Pension Authority and the Local Authority for the Mentally Defective. Such a band of volunteer helpers, acting within the frame-work of a specific municipal service, forms, in the densely populated districts of the great towns, an almost indispensable supplement to official activity. Such volunteers, able to devote to each case as much time as it requires, and bringing to bear a wider experience of everyday life than the specially trained and hard-worked official can do, may not only "search out" those who need public assistance, but may keep them constantly under observation before and after the treatment afforded at the cost of the rates, and may ensure that nothing is overlooked by which they may effectively be helped, and that, when restored to self-support, no relapse occurs without its being noted. It is, however, we repeat, essential that such domiciliary visitors should not have the distribution of money or relief in the homes, whether this be from public or private funds, their own or other people's.

On the other hand, there is still enormous scope for beneficent gifts of money, to be administered under voluntary management. There are many kinds of institutional treatment which the various public Authorities are not likely themselves to initiate; and there are others that they are almost debarred from conducting. There is room for many pioneer experiments in the treatment of every type of distressed person. The whole tendency of modern applied science is to subdivision and the breaking-up of old categories into newer specialisations. We cannot expect our County and County Borough Councillors to launch out into experiments of this kind. Such private experiments in Industrial and Reformatory Schools, Technical Institutes, Farm Colonies, Inebriate Retreats, Rescue Homes, and what not, have already greatly advanced the technique of these services. In this field of initiating and developing new institutional treatment—whether it be the provision of perfect almshouses for the aged, or the establishment of vacation schools or open-air schools for the children; whether it be the enveloping of the morally infirm, or of those who have fallen, in a regenerating atmosphere of religion and love, or some subtle combination of physical regimen and mental stimulus for the town-bred "hooligan"—very large sums of money can be advantageously used, and are, in fact, urgently needed. And not the financing alone, but also the management of such institutions affords a sphere for unofficial work. Just as no public Authority can hazard the ratepayers' money in these experimental institutions, so no public Authority can assume responsibility for the desirable unconventionality of their daily administration. We should wish to see the several Committees of the County and County Borough Councils make full use of these voluntary institutions, entrusting to their care the special types of cases for which they afford appropriate treatment. But in this use there should be invariably two conditions. Any voluntary institution receiving patients from the Local Authority must place itself under the regular inspection both of that Local Authority and of the National Department having the supervision of the particular service. And if payment for the treatment is required, even without other subsidy, the Local Authority must be given the opportunity of placing its own representatives on the actual governing body of the institution.

(F) The Practical Application of the Scheme

It is, of course, more easy to devise a scheme of reform on paper, than to be sure that it can be applied in practice. We have, therefore, individually taken means, not only by special investigation, but also by specific personal inquiry of Poor Law Guardians and County and County Borough Councillors, of still more experienced Clerks to Boards of Guardians, Masters of Workhouses, and Relieving Officers, and of various officers of County and County Borough Councils, to satisfy ourselves that what we are proposing could actually be put into operation, without serious difficulty. Those practically concerned in the working of the existing machine, whom we have consulted on this point, have given us very favourable opinions. We are accordingly convinced that what we are proposing is practicable as well as desirable. It is, in fact, a great advantage of the scheme that it does not involve the creation of any novel area, or the establishment of any new Authority. In fact, in all the County Boroughs it amounts only to the transfer of the powers of the Boards of Guardians to the Town Council; though, instead of handing them over *en bloc*, it provides for their distribution among the Education, Health, Asylums, Pension and General Purposes Committees of that body, thereby greatly lightening the additional burden of work to be imposed on the Councillors, whose numbers might, of course, be increased if desired. As with the duties of education and lunacy at present, we propose that all business relating to the several duties should automatically "stand referred" to the appropriate Committees for consideration and report, the Councils being left free to give to their Committees as much or as little delegated authority as they choose (except as to actually levying the rate or raising money on loan), and subject to such conditions as they think fit. The troublesome re-adjustment of areas, too, would be reduced to a minimum. The merging in the County or County Borough, of all the Unions wholly within each of them, would involve the minimum of readjustment of property and liabilities. The only alterations of area required would be in those cases in which Unions at present cut County or County Borough boundaries. These, which in England and Wales are 197 in number, would be required in any adoption of the County as the new area.

Moreover, the scheme involves the minimum of expense for compensation of dispossessed officers. It would, of course, be necessary to give to all officers whose posts were abolished, the usual generous treatment that Parliament in such cases accords. But many of the Clerks to Boards of Guardians would make admirable Registrars of Public Assistance, and could be offered these appointments. The best of the Masters of Workhouses could be found places in the various specialised institutions (including the Receiving Houses). Most of the Relieving Officers would become the Enquiry and Recovery Officers of the Registrars of Public Assistance. The District Medical Officers would be simply made part of the unified Medical Service under the Local Health Committee, at their existing emoluments, etc. The existing Workhouses, Casual Wards, Poor Law schools, etc., would, of course, be utilised for the various specialised institutions that would be required, being divided up among the various committees as might be found most convenient.

The scheme could be applied gradually. England and Wales, Scotland and Ireland could be separately dealt with. There would be no great difficulty in the transfer of the administration from the Boards of Guardians to the County and County Borough Councils taking place in one locality after another, on "appointed days" to be fixed as the arrangements made by the Executive Commission (which would in any case have to be appointed) were completed for the particular localities. We can even imagine the scheme being applied to one service after another; the functions of the Boards of Guardians with regard to the children or the sick or the mentally defective being successively dealt with, and the final abolition of the Destitution Authority being deferred until the last remnant of its duties could be handed over.

(i) The Rural Counties

In the application of the scheme to the counties of England and Wales, the only serious difficulty appears to be the division of the medical service between the County Council and the existing minor sanitary authorities (the Councils of Non-County Boroughs, Urban Districts and Rural Districts); and for this we have offered specific suggestions. The establishment of the Registrar of Public Assistance, visiting once a week or so every part of the County—which should, we suggest, be divided into districts at least as small as the present Unions—would go far to relieve the members of the County Council of the most burdensome part of the work. There could, of course, be local visiting committees of volunteers chosen from among the local residents attached to the several institutions.

(ii) *The Metropolis*

In the application of the scheme to London, a similar division of the medical service would be necessary between the Health Committee of the London County Council and the Health Committees of the Corporation of the City of London and the Metropolitan Boroughs. The asylums for imbeciles and idiots of the Metropolitan Asylums Board would naturally pass to the new Committee for the Mentally Defective (virtually the present Asylums Committee of the London County Council) and the isolation hospitals to the Health Committee of that body. If there were appointed, say, half a dozen Registrars of Public Assistance for the whole of the Administrative County, they would be able to sit for an entire day in each week in districts somewhat smaller than the present thirty-one Unions. But an even prompter "delivery" of the Receiving Houses could easily be arranged if required. In London, too, there could easily be special local visiting committees for the several institutions. The scheme is not dependent on any general reform of London Local Government, or on any enlargement of the Administrative County, though it would fit in easily with either of these proposals.

(iii) *Scotland*

In the application of the scheme to Scotland, we speak with less assurance. We do not feel that our knowledge of Scottish Local Government warrants us in doing more than suggest that, so far as we can learn, the same principles of reform are applicable. The enlargement of the unit of area is—with 874 separate Parish Councils distributing relief—even more urgently necessary than in England. The new area can hardly be any other than that of the County and perhaps those of the larger Burghs. There are the same advantages to be gained by the distribution, among the existing specialised committees, of the various services now aggregated together in the Poor Law. With regard to the provision for all grades of persons of unsound mind, we can accept the recommendations of the Royal Commission on the Care and Control of the Feeble-minded, which adopt and continue the existing Lunacy Authorities; or, on the other hand, these might be simply re-constituted as Committees of County and Burgh Councils. In the one-third of Scotland which is in the large towns, the care of the children would naturally pass to the School Boards. We assume that the other services would pass to the County and principal

Town Councils, with a division of the medical service between the District (Health) Committee of the County Council and the Health Committees of the smaller Burghs within the County similar to that suggested for the English Counties. This District (Health) Committee, or perhaps the County Committee of a District constituted under the Education Act of 1908 might take over the care of the children. Whether it would be desirable to continue in existence the Parish Council in Scotland, any more than the Rural District Council in England and Wales, once all the Poor Law functions had been assumed by other Authorities, we do not venture to decide.

(iv) *Ireland*

In the application of the scheme to Ireland, we wish to speak even more tentatively than with regard to Scotland. Yet Ireland has already progressed further in the direction of breaking up the Poor Law, and distributing its services among the other Authorities than either England or Scotland. The whole provision for persons of unsound mind, for instance, even for those who are destitute, is already entirely outside the Poor Law, and in the hands of the County Councils. The medical service of the public dispensaries, too, is not deemed to be Poor Law relief, and could apparently easily be re-organised as a County Medical Service on Public Health lines. The provision of a complete system of hospitals by the County Councils, admitting all patients requiring hospital treatment, whatever their diseases, is one of the recommendations of the recent Vice-Regal Commission on Poor Law Reform in Ireland. And, though that Commission did not recommend the abolition of the Boards of Guardians, we feel that our own scheme proceeds almost entirely on the same lines as their proposals, and that the establishment of the Registrar of Public Assistance would probably make it easy to adopt our recommendations almost in their entirety. The one exception lies in the case of the children. Ireland has, at present, no Local Education Authority to which the care of the children could be transferred. We agree with the Vice-Regal Commission in recommending that the children for whom the community has to find maintenance should, wherever possible, attend the existing day schools under the National Elementary Education Board. We suggest that their further care should be entrusted to new "Boarding-Out Committees" of the County and County Borough Councils, on which women members should be co-opted, charged to find suitable homes for these children, either in the duly inspected cottages of foster-parents, or in institutions under voluntary management, properly certified by the Local Government Board for Ireland. The two existing Poor Law schools could probably be most advantageously utilised as schools for some special kinds of children who cannot be suitably dealt with by boarding-out.

(v) *The Departments of the National Government*

Whilst the scheme relates mainly to local administration, no reform of the Poor Law can be effected without, in England and Wales at any rate, considerable changes in the central departments. We have already described how important it is, for efficiency and economy alike, that the Local Authorities should have the assistance, in each of the various services they undertake, of the supervision of a Department of the National Government *charged solely with that service.* We feel that the confusion and inefficiency into which so much of Local Government has fallen is to be ascribed in some degree to the absence of this specialised central supervision and control. Incredible as it seems, forty years after the Report of the Royal Commission on Sanitation in 1869, there is to-day no Department, and no Division of a Department, charged solely with Public Health as such. Even the Education Departments of England and Wales, Scotland and Ireland, find, at present, a great deal of the public provision for children of school age outside their control. With the abolition of the Destitution Authorities, the existing "Poor Law Division" of the Local Government Board would, of course, come to an end; and a redistribution of functions and officers would be necessary. We do not presume to make any recommendations as to how the duties of the several Departments should be allocated among the Ministers who would be responsible to Parliament for their policy and administration. Nor need we consider which of the Divisions (each being self-contained and complete in itself) can conveniently be grouped together, under the name of the Local Government Board or otherwise, with the Permanent Heads of the Divisions (as in Scotland and Ireland) sitting at a Board or Council under the presidency of the responsible Minister. We are, however, convinced that it is of the highest importance that there should be separately organised and completely self-contained Departments—each having the supervision and control of all the local services falling within its subject-matter—not only for Education, but also for Public Health (including all the services entrusted to the Local Health Authorities); for all the provision for the Mentally Defective (including the feeble-minded and the inebriates, as well as the lunatics and idiots); for the National Pensions for the Aged; and (as we may here add) for the whole provision for the Able-bodied, the Vagrants, and the Unemployed. Each of these five separate Departments or Divisions of Departments should issue its own regulative orders, and have the administration of all the Grants-in-Aid that may be made in respect of the services with the supervision of which it is charged; and all such Grants-in-Aid should be conditional on proper efficiency in local administration, and proportionate partly to the local expenditure and partly to the local poverty, according to some such scale as we have suggested. Each such Department or Division of a Department would, of course, have its own specialist Inspectors, who should be chosen, in the first instance, from the technically qualified members of the present staffs. The existing General Inspectors of the Local Government Board would, we suggest, form a suitable nucleus for the new Inspectorate that will be required by any Department dealing with the Able-bodied Unemployed —a service in which no *technique* has yet been worked out, and in which the General Inspectors would start with greater knowledge than anyone else possesses. Alongside these five separate Departments or Divisions of Departments, there must, we think, be another, distinct and apart from them all, charged with the supervision of the audit, the sanctioning of loans, and local finance generally, and to this might be entrusted also the supervision of the Home Aliment sanctioned by the Registrars of Public Assistance.

In Scotland and Ireland, whilst the same principles are applicable, the local circumstances will require some modifications of these proposals. Where England and Wales need separate Departments, Scotland and Ireland may be able to do with separate Divisions of one Department, especially if, as we think advisable, the Permanent Heads of the several Divisions sit in a Board or Council under the presidency of the responsible Minister.

It may, in conclusion, be noted that any scheme of reform will involve the appointment of an Executive Commission to adjust areas and boundaries, and assets and liabilities, and to allocate buildings and officers according to the new organisation.

(G) Some Theoretical Objections Answered

We have, of course, not failed to weigh carefully the various objections that have been made to our proposals. These objections, it need hardly be said, are theoretical. There is the objection that the breaking up of the Poor Law involves the breaking up of the family. There is the objection that the proposed scheme would lead to the harassing of the poor in their homes by a multiplicity of officers, each bent on enforcing his own conditions. There is the objection that the transfer to specialised committees of the Local Authority of the obligation to relieve the destitute may lead to an extravagant extension of gratuitous treatment at the cost of the rates. Finally, there is the objection, in exact contradiction to this fear of increased collective provision, that the abolition of the Destitution Authority may, somehow or other, abrogate the existing statutory right to relief.

(i) *The Integrity of the Family*

There are conditions under which the transfer of the functions of the Board of Guardians to the County or County Borough Council will undoubtedly cause more separation of the members of families than prevails at present. In our chapter on "The General Mixed Workhouse of To-day" we have described how all the members of a destitute family are now usually admitted simultaneously, by one gate, into one institution. These "mixed" institutions have undoubtedly the advantage—if it be an advantage—of keeping all the members of a family under the same roof, and even of permitting, especially in the smaller and less rigidly administered Unions, continued intercourse between husband and wife, and parent and child. In visiting some of the Workhouses in the wilds of Ireland, we have been struck by the homeliness of the arrangement, by which a whole family, rendered destitute by an eviction, will be found crouching round the peat fire of the one common day-room; the able-bodied father smoking his pipe, the mother suckling her infant, the children playing around, and an aged grandparent dosing in the one armchair. When this domestic interior is supervised by a group of kindly nuns, visited by the parish priest, and illuminated by the dignity of agrarian martyrdom, the public assistance afforded has doubtless a charm of its own; though we may question, not only its deterrent, but also its curative and restorative effects. But in the well-regulated English Workhouse—still more, in the mammoth Poor Law establishments which now characterise the great towns of England, Scotland and Ireland—the inclusion under one roof, or within one curtilage, of a whole family—the able-bodied man, the ailing woman and infant, the children of school age, the feeble-minded girl and the aged grandparent—means a promiscuous intercourse, not between the members of that family alone, but between all ages and different sexes, which is anything but edifying. It certainly does not conduce to the integrity of family relationships. And when the Destitution Authority, responding at last to the constant pressure of the Local Government Board, consents so far to "break up the family" as to treat the different members of it in different institutions—as the 1834 Report so strongly advised—it often nullifies the very improvement at which the reform has aimed. In a desire, we suppose, to treat the family as a unit, at any rate at the moment of admission and the moment of discharge, the Guardians at present summon the wife and her infant from the Infirmary, the children from the Cottage Homes in the country, and the feeble-minded daughter from the laundry, to meet, at the lodge of the Able-bodied Workhouse, the husband and father who has claimed his discharge because he is tired of test work. It is this insistence on dealing with the family as a unit which gives the gravest aspect to the terrible problem of the "Ins-and-Outs." Let the man determine to take his discharge—however evil his character, however notoriously vicious his habit of life, however homeless he may be—all his dependents are at present summoned, from the specialised institutions at which they are being treated at great expense, as if to his death-bed! The children are brought in by an officer from the country boarding school, clean and even smart in their neat clothes and handed over to him at the Workhouse lodge, with the almost certain prospect that "the family," after unspeakable experiences, will be readmitted within a few days, in a state of filth and demoralisation.

In common with every experienced Poor Law administrator we accept the responsibility of so far "breaking up the family" as to insist (with the authors of the Report of 1834) that, if there is to be institutional treatment at all, it shall be treatment of the different members of a family, according to age, sex and physical state, *in separate specialised institutions under distinct management and supervision.* We do not see any reason for imagining any greater dissolution of the family when these institutions are administered by different committees of a Town Council than when they are administered by different committees of a Board of Guardians. But we go further. In common with, we think, the majority of experienced Poor Law administrators, we recommend that no sick dependent should be discharged from the Infirmary, and that no child should be brought back from the school to be handed over to its father, unless and until some reasonable assurance can be given that there is a home for them to go to, offering, at any rate, minimum conditions of decency and safety. It is one of the advantages of our scheme that the Education Committee and the Health Committee, under the advice of their own officers, will certainly wish to satisfy themselves on this point before they forcibly eject any child or sick person committed to their charge. In our proposal of a Registrar of Public Assistance specially charged with the duty of proceeding against defaulting heads of families, we provide a far more effective means of enforcing parental responsibility than the present remarkable practice of casting out the wife and child whenever the man chooses to leave.

A curious question has, in this connection, been asked of us. How, it is said, are the various members of a family, once sorted out into different institutions, under different committees of the Town Council, ever to get together again? What seems to puzzle some naïve objectors is the vision of the Health Committee's ambulance carrying off to its hospital the mother with puerperal fever, the Education Committee's officer conducting the children found wandering in the streets to the Industrial Schools, the Asylums Committee taking charge of the imbecile girl, the Unemployment Authority giving the man his railway ticket to the Farm Colony, whilst the police "run in" the hooligan son for commitment to a Reformatory School. The answer to this enquiry is that this very process is taking place daily under our eyes in any large city, without the difficulty arising. The existence of a Destitution Authority over and above all the existing specialised committees does nothing to bring these scattered members of the family together. In practice, they find each other without difficulty when they emerge from their several institutions, just as they would if they had gone at their own cost to school, to search for work, or to get medical treatment. But in so far as any difficulty may arise—as, for instance, with the feeble-minded or with truant children, or with parents wishing to evade their responsibilities—our scheme provides, for the first time, effective machinery for "re-uniting" the family, either voluntarily or compulsorily. The Registrar of Public Assistance, advised daily of all admissions and discharges in every public institution, with an office at the Local Receiving House always open to applicants, and with his Inquiry and Recovery Officers instantly in pursuit of husbands and fathers who have run away from their responsibilities, will, in fact, make it very difficult for families not to re-unite.

There is, however, a far more insidious "breaking up of the family" constantly going on to-day, than any that could possibly be caused, whenever institutional treatment becomes necessary, by there being separate institutions for each sex, age-period and physical condition. Owing to the unfortunate limitation of the action of the Board of Guardians to the period of actual destitution, thousands of families are disintegrating to-day under our eyes, from lack of the timely strengthening which might have prevented their becoming destitute. But when the cost and trouble of providing for the several members of the family when destitute fall upon committees which have, as part of their ordinary duty and machinery, the periodical visitation of the home, irrespective of destitution, these committees will have the families continuously under observation. Is the child unfed at school? A member of the Children's Care Committee calls to ascertain the cause. At every birth, at every death, at every occurrence of notifiable disease, the officer of the Health Committee becomes acquainted with the circumstances of the household. Thus, the several Committees of the Town Council, as a mere measure of economy, so as not eventually to incur the cost of institutional treatment, with its concomitant of "breaking up the family," will be perpetually doing whatever may be necessary to maintain the family intact, to encourage those members of it who are striving to keep the home together, and forcibly to restrain any member whose conduct is threatening it with ruin.

(ii) *The Withdrawal of the Destitution Officer*

The suggestion that the great expense to the ratepayer, and the "break up of the family," involved in the institutional treatment of the present Poor Law, can, in many cases, be obviated by friendly supervision and well-informed advice before and after the crisis of destitution, rouses another set of theoretical objections. Under the scheme of reform now proposed, it is objected that there would be a great increase in the number of salaried officials, all "harassing" poor families with inquisitorial enquiries and officious advice. This, however, is an error. As a matter of fact there would, under the reform proposed, be actually fewer officials on the salary list, and each of them would ask fewer questions than is at present the case in any well-administered district. An efficient Town Council has already its staff of Sanitary Inspectors and Health Visitors, of School Attendance Officers and School Managers or members of Children's Care Committees. These domiciliary agents at present investigate, not only questions of sanitation and the hygienic condition of the family, school attendance and the care of the children, but also—now that school meals, medical treatment, milk for the infant and so on, are being provided—find themselves compelled to inquire, however imperfectly, into the economic circumstances of the household. Meanwhile, the family, in many cases, is obtaining, or asking for, Poor Law Relief. The well-administered Board of Guardians accordingly sends to the house, one after another, in order to make successive enquiries, the Relieving Officer, the Cross Visitor, the Collector and Removal Officer, and, if the case presents any difficulty, also the Superintendent Relieving Officer. All the latter Destitution Officers inquire into exactly the same facts as have been inquired into by the officers of the Local Health Authority and the Local Education Authority. It is true that their primary investigation is into the pecuniary resources of the family, but the Guardians expect them to report also on the sanitary state of the home, the health of all the members of the family, the attendance of the children at school, and even whether the mother can or will suckle her infant. On these points the Destitution Officers, whether one, two, three or four in number, are unqualified to judge—a fact which does not make their inquiries less annoying. Incredible as it may seem to those unacquainted with the working of the conflict in Local Government to-day, this curious multiplicity of domiciliary visitors, all going, one after another to the same house, unaware of each other's visits, and all inquiring indifferently into subjects in which they may be assumed to possess some professional competence, and into those about which they frankly know nothing, is actually the present practice of town after town. It may be seen, for instance, in Edinburgh or Paddington, Glasgow or Bradford.

With the remodelling of the Poor Law that we are recommending, this overlapping and confusion will cease. The Sanitary Inspector or Health Visitor, the School Attendance Officer or the member of the Children's Care Committee, will still be found visiting the homes; but their hygienic or educational inquiries and advice, like their information as to the available public assistance appropriate to the case, will no longer be hampered by vague questioning as to the total earnings coming into the home, or about the existence of relatives able to contribute. The three or four Destitution Officers, with their unsavoury hotch-potch of inquiries into all sorts of subjects, will be replaced, in each locality, by the one Inquiry and Recovery Officer of the Registrar of Public Assistance. His business will be limited strictly to the ascertainment of the pecuniary resources of the family—not with any view of *preventing* the requisite treatment being afforded, for that will already have begun—but in order to ascertain what charge, if any, should be made for it, and upon whom it should be made. He, having no concern with the health or morals of the family, will have no more right than the agent of an insurance company or the Assessor of Income-Tax to do what in the Relieving Officer excites such resentment, namely, pry into the bedroom, cross-examine the woman as to her relation with the male lodger, or comment on the cough and expectoration of the delicate daughter—all in order to find a reason for refusing Outdoor Relief and offering the Workhouse instead. Finally, this agent of the Registrar of Public Assistance will be in no sense a Destitution Officer. His visits will imply no pauperism. They will be paid alike to the family requiring Home Aliment for its bread-winner, and to the family regularly paying the full charge for the maintenance of a member in the Tuberculosis Sanitorium; to the old woman claiming a National Pension, and to the household which has distinguished itself by the gaining of a County Scholarship; to the husband of the woman using the Maternity Hospital, as well as to the propertied lady who is paying for her husband's detention in the most luxurious villa of the County Lunatic Asylum. In fact, therefore, the proposed "sorting-out" of the present multiplicity of officers, and the restriction of each to his own sphere, will positively diminish both their number and the multifariousness of their questions. And with the final abolition of the Destitution Officer, and his hateful combination of functions, any prejudice that the poor may have against domiciliary visitation as such will, we anticipate, disappear.

(iii) *The Economy of Efficient Administration*

We pass now to what appears to us the most genuine of the objections made to our proposals, namely, that they will involve:

   a) A large increase of expense to the ratepayers; and

   b) An unnecessary multiplication of those for whom gratuitous service is provided

Our answer is that whilst our proposals involve increased expense in some directions, they bring great saving in others. What is even more important is that the increases in expenditure will tend to be temporary only, whilst the saving is calculated to be permanent and cumulative.

To begin with the 234,000 infants and children on Outdoor Relief, we accept the responsibility (in common, we think, with a majority of Poor Law administrators) of proposing increased expenditure on those among them who—to use the words of our own Children's Investigator—are now suffering, definitely, and seriously, from the circumstances of their lives. We do not think that it is possible, under any scheme, to continue to pretend to maintain children on a shilling or eighteenpence a week each. The chronic under-feeding, stunted growth, and premature death, to which we are at present condemning many tens of thousands of Outdoor Relief children—children for whom the community has, by enrolling them in the register of paupers, definitely assumed responsibility—is surely the most wasteful and extravagant arrangement that could be devised. We admit that when the responsibility for these children passes into the hands of the Local Health Authority and the Local Education Authority, the reports from the Health Visitors and the Medical Officers, the mere sight of their condition in the school, and the reports as to their home circumstances by the members of the Children's Care Committees, will compel the proposal to the Registrar of Public Assistance, where the mothers are to be trusted, of Home Aliment much more adequate than a shilling a week, the provision of day industrial schools for many thousands more, and the adoption, and removal from their parents, of those found to be living in actually vicious homes. On the other hand we may anticipate that the enormous capital outlay, and the high charge for maintenance, now incurred by some Boards of Guardians, for every child in their Cottage Homes, owing to their inexperience of the real requirements of efficient school buildings, will not continue under Local Authorities who are perpetually erecting such buildings for children at large, on more economical principles. We may, however, frankly admit that the net result of a transfer of destitute children from the present Poor Law to the Local Education Authorities—in common, we think, with all serious proposals for reform in this department—will be, during the next few years, an increase in the total spent on the children. But as it is exactly these children, brought up on insufficient food or in undesirable homes, who presently recruit the great army of pauperism, we think that it will be agreed that the expenditure is a good investment. Meanwhile, the Registrar of Public Assistance will be at work, enforcing payment from parents whose ill-treatment of their children proceeds not from lack of income, but from self-indulgence in drink, etc., or from mere inhumanity. It may well prove that whilst there will be more spent on the children who are really destitute, the number of claimants for school dinners or spasmodic relief, or of those who shovel their children into costly Poor Law schools, will, under the steady and impartial pressure of the new system of Charge and Recovery, actually be diminished.

Much the same argument applies to the sick. We accept the responsibility of recommending the adoption of the Public Health principle of searching out disease in its incipient stages, in place of the Poor Law attitude of waiting until the disease has gone so far as, on the one hand, to produce destitution, and, on the other, to render the belated but costly treatment of no avail. This will mean, in the first years, an increased expenditure on domiciliary treatment, and, where really required, on the provision of hospitals. But seeing that no less than half of the present pauperism—that is to say, £9,000,000 a year out of the present Poor Law expenditure of £18,000,000—is directly caused by the diseases of early or adult life, and that most of these are known to be "preventable," we regard this expenditure also as a good investment. Let us assume, for a moment, that the United Kingdom and all its inhabitants formed the property of a great slave-owning company, much as whole districts in Russia used to belong to a great proprietor. With the modern knowledge of preventive medicine, it is clear that it would "pay" the slave-owner, not only to provide for his "hands" or his "souls" good sanitation and a supply of pure water, but also to train them in hygienic habits of life, and to take care that no incipient disease among them, more especially contagious or infectious disease, remained untreated. It is surely the worst of all forms of national waste to allow the ravages of preventable sickness to progress unchecked; and this not merely because it kills off thousands of producers prematurely (burdening us, by the way, with the widow and the orphan), but because sickness levies a toll on the living, and leaves even those who survive crippled, debilitated, and less efficient than they would otherwise have been. There is even, by the taking of timely measures, an eventual decrease in the expenditure required to cope with a disease. To put up an Isolation Hospital is at first costly; but when (as has been repeatedly found to be the case with smallpox) the disease has been stamped out, the hospital stands empty, and is available for other public use. And the treatment need not be gratuitous. As we have seen, there is at present great diversity of practice as to which diseases shall be treated gratuitously, and which shall be charged for. The tendency, under the present system, is to increase the range of gratuitous treatment; and it is significant that even whilst we were enquiring into the matter, the responsibility for the gratuitous treatment of phthisis (including maintenance in hospital when required) has been formally and explicitly assumed by the Local Health Authorities of Scotland, under the authority of Parliament and the Local Government Board. The whole question of the pecuniary basis of the public treatment of disease seems to us to need further consideration, with the object of securing the maximum result from whatever expenditure the nation decides to afford. But when charges are decided on by Parliament they ought to be impartially enforced; and for this no adequate provision at present exists or has been included in any other proposals. We rely for this purpose on the establishment in every district of a Registrar of Public Assistance, unconnected with the medical service and bent on really enforcing whatever charges may be legally imposed on those for whom hospital maintenance is provided. This may well lead to an actual decrease in the area of gratuitous treatment, which, under the present system, is shovelled out, with the very minimum of inquiry, to all who ask for it.

(iv) *The Right to Relief*

It is curious to notice that our insistence on treatment rather than relief, and the importance that we attach to enforcing payment from those who are legally liable and of sufficient ability to pay for what they receive, has raised an objection quite the opposite of that with which we have just dealt. It is feared by some that in the supersession of the Destitution Authority by the more specialised organs of Local Government the poor will lose their present statutory right to relief. Our answer is that whilst we recommend the repeal of the Poor Law Amendment Act of 1834, which created the Boards of Guardians, we do not advocate the repeal of the Statute of the 43rd of Elizabeth. We propose that there should be no less legal obligation on the Local Authority, than there is at present, to provide the necessities of life to all those who are without them. Just as the Local Education Authority is under statutory obligation to provide schooling for all children within its district who are without schooling, so we propose that it should assume the statutory obligation (now imposed upon the Board of Guardians) of providing, for those children who are destitute, whatever other things are required. Just as the Local Health Authority is under statutory obligation to make certain sanitary provisions for its district, so we propose that it should assume the statutory obligation (now imposed upon the Board of Guardians) of providing, for those of the sick who are destitute, whatever their necessities require. And similarly for the other sections of the present pauper host. The obligations which the Poor Relief Act of 43 Elizabeth, c. 2, embodied in our Statute law can be simply transferred from the Board of Guardians to the County or County Borough Council.

There remains to be noticed what may be considered the present safeguard of the poor in the liability of the Relieving Officers to criminal prosecution, even for manslaughter, if any person is injured owing to their failure to afford relief when relief is required. This liability has the special characteristic of not being affected by any orders of the Destitution Authority under whom the Relieving Officer has been placed. Moreover, if a destitute person refuses the particular form of relief offered, the Relieving Officer still continues liable in case of any harm occurring, and is compelled therefore to provide relief in some other form. The majority of our colleagues propose to abolish all this criminal liability of the Relieving Officer. We do not think that this is either necessary or desirable. There is, we think, an advantage, in so important a matter as preserving human life, in there being, in each district, an officer who is definitely responsible, whatever other Authorities may be prescribing, for preventing deaths from starvation or neglect. We recommend that the present responsibility of the Relieving Officer should be transferred to the Registrar of Public Assistance and the keeper of the local Receiving House, together with some person in each parish or other convenient area whom the Registrar may appoint for this purpose and for the giving of relief in kind in cases of sudden or urgent necessity. Every such case would be automatically reported to the Registrar, who would place the case in charge of the officers of one or other of the committees concerned, or arrange for removal to the Local Receiving House pending his decision. If the relief was refused, we recommend that the Local Health Authority should be empowered, in any case in which, through inanition or neglect, life might be endangered, or a public nuisance caused, to obtain a magistrate's order (to be granted only under careful safeguards) for the compulsory removal of the person concerned to the appropriate institution. We think that, in cases of urgency, the Registrar of Public Assistance might be given power to make a similar order. In short, what our scheme of reform ensures is that, whilst the Right to Relief is fully maintained, the obligation to accept relief in its most appropriate form is, under penalty of compulsory removal in extreme cases, practically insisted on.

Minority Report (1909)

Introduction to Part 2
by Sidney and Beatrice Webb

WE have explained in the Introduction to a companion volume[1] to the present how it was that a Minority of the Royal Commission on the Poor Laws and the Unemployed felt compelled to dissent from the conclusions of the Majority with regard to the Poor Law; and to present an alternative report covering the whole ground, and concluding with an alternative Scheme of Reform. With regard to the Unemployed, this Minority considered the Majority Report as even more inadequate and reactionary than with regard to the Poor Law. To undo the work of the Unemployed Workmen Act of 1905, and to thrust back the necessitous workmen into the sphere of a resuscitated Poor Law Authority under a new name, seemed no solution of the grave economic and social problem of Unemployment.

The Minority Report (Part II), which is here reproduced, accordingly surveys in detail what is actually the provision now made for all sections of the able-bodied men or women in distress; whether by the Boards of Guardians in England, Wales and Ireland, and the Parish Councils in

[1] *The Break-up of the Poor Law* (Longmans, 1909).

Scotland, under the Poor Law; by the various philanthropic and religious agencies under voluntary management; or by the Distress Committees under the Unemployed Workmen Act. This survey leads naturally to an analysis of the nature and extent of the distress from Unemployment as it actually exists to-day—a survey which is impressive in its revelation of the magnitude, the permanence, and the grave social consequences of the evil. It is for this evil that the Commission was required to find a remedy.

To find a remedy, it will be clear, is no light task. One thing at once emerges—the remedy will be neither simple nor obvious. Indeed, he who sets himself to devise a remedy for Unemployment must, of all things, beware of "hammering on the bulge." We must take to heart Herbert Spencer's pregnant apologue of the iron plate that bulged.

You see that this wrought-iron plate is not quite flat: it sticks up a little here towards the left—"cockles," as we say. How shall we flatten it? Obviously, you reply, by hitting down on the part that is prominent. Well, here is a hammer, and I give the plate a blow as you advise. Harder, you say. Still no effect. Another stroke? Well, there is one, and another, and another. The prominence remains, you see: the evil is as great as ever—greater, indeed. But this is not all. Look at the warp which the plate has got near the opposite edge. Where it was flat before it is now curved. A pretty bungle we have made of it. Instead of curing the original defect, we have produced a second. Had we asked an artisan practised in "planishing," as it is called, he would have told us that no good was to be done, but only mischief, by hitting down on the projecting part. He would have taught us how to give variously-directed and specially-adjusted blows with a hammer elsewhere; so attacking the evil not by direct, but by indirect actions. The required process is less simple than you thought.

For a whole century, whenever the distress from Unemployment has risen temporarily into the consciousness of the governing class, we have been, in our desire to do something promptly for those in need, merely "hammering on the bulge." It is time to take a lesson from the skilled artisan; to set ourselves really to understand the conditions of the problem; and to adopt, deliberately, patiently and persistently, exactly those measures, *and all those measures*, that are necessary to remedy the evil. What, in the light of the most accurate information and the best science available, those measures are is explained in the last chapter of this volume.

It is, indeed, urgently necessary, whatever may be the nature of the social organisation to which we aspire, that we should take in hand the "cleaning up the base of society," of which one principal part is here set forth. At present, it is not too much to say that the morass of Under-Employment and Sweating in which the bottom stratum of the population is condemned to live is draining away the vitality and seriously impairing the vigour of the community as a whole. The continued existence and, we fear, the spreading of this morass does not infect alone those unfortunates whom it engulfs, and the rest of the wage-earning class who are always slipping into it. By the heavy charges that it imposes on us for Poor Relief, hospitals, police and prisons, it lays an unnecessary burden on those who are better off. By the diseases which it engenders and spreads—for a hundred hidden threads of communication connect the slum and the square—it levies a needless toll of death on the families even of the richest. By the deterioration in character and skill of the manual workers whom it degenerates, it insidiously nibbles away at the profits of capital, and puts the enterprises even of the ablest captains of industry increasingly at the mercy of Foreign Competition. Nothing will avail to save a nation whose workers have decayed. From the standpoint of the strictest believer in Private Enterprise, of the staunchest defender of the beneficent administration of the world by the propertied class, it is essential, on the narrowest calculation of profit and loss, to "clean up the base of society."

To those who look to the substitution of a deliberately ordered Co-operative Commonwealth for the present industrial anarchy, it will be obvious that no such Collectivist community could stand for a year, if it did not drain the morass. What is not always realised is that, even under a completely organised Socialist State, with all industries administered by Municipalities and Government Departments, much the same national organisation for remedying Unemployment would be needed as is here proposed. For the Socialist State would still have to meet the cyclical fluctuations of demand, whether these were caused by periodical famines in China or failures of crops elsewhere. It would still have to meet the seasonal fluctuations in the volume of employment in particular industries; so that the electricity works, the railways and pleasure places, the hop-picking and the harvesting might have the extra workers that they temporarily required. It would still have to face the necessity of providing for workers displaced by local or industrial changes, and for training them in the new occupations for which they might be best fitted. It is clear that, unless there was, in the Socialist State, something equivalent to a National Labour Exchange, to which all the thousands of Government Departments and Local Authorities resorted, we should have, over again, the keeping of separate reserves of men, the Stagnant Pools of Labour which Mr.

Beveridge has so well described,[2] and, in short, all the evils of Under-Employment. The Public Organisation of the Labour Market is, in fact, a requisite for the social health of any industrial community, whether its industry be run on Individualist or on Collectivist lines.

[2] W. H. Beveridge, *Unemployment: A Problem of Industry* (Longmans, 1909).

Minority Report (1909)

Part 2:

The Destitution of the Able-Bodied

Proposals for Reform

We have now to state the Proposals for Reform to which our consideration of the problem presented by the Distress from Unemployment and the Destitution of the Able-bodied has led us. We put forward these proposals, far-reaching in character as some of them are, with a deep sense of responsibility. We have done our best to investigate the actual facts and conditions of the problem, and to weigh carefully all the considerations that have to be taken into account in grappling with it. We have tested our proposals, so far as this is possible, by individually and privately consulting, with regard to each of them, the men of practical experience, both official and commercial, whom we thought best qualified to judge as to what could, and what could not, be successfully put into operation. We must however point out that, with regard to this Part of our Report, the conditions do not permit the presentation of the same sort of detailed and finished Scheme of Reform as that with which we were able to conclude Part I. In respect of all the classes of the Non-Able-bodied, what we had to recommend lay rather in the domain of administrative policy and organisation, than in the *technique* of the several services. When we were considering the appropriate treatment of Children, the Sick or the Insane, we could take for granted the existence of an elaborate body of knowledge, worked out by specialised Local Authorities, as to how to run a school, a main drainage system, an isolation hospital or an asylum. All that we had to do was to show cause and devise means for transferring from an antiquated system of Destitution Authorities such of the members of these classes as had fallen into the hands of those Authorities; and for the assumption of the necessary responsibilities by the several specialised Local Authorities already dealing with similar services. But in the prevention and treatment of Able-bodied Destitution and Distress from Unemployment, we are, at the beginning of the twentieth century, in a position somewhat similar to that in which the prevention and treatment of sickness stood at the opening of the nineteenth century. We have still to work out by actual practice the appropriate *technique*.

For this reason among others, we wish to make it clear that the adoption of the Scheme of Reform, with which we have concluded Part I of this Report, is in no way dependent upon an adoption of our present Proposals for Reform with regard to Distress from Want of Employment. We are, for instance, compelled to propose that the Local Authorities, to whom would be entrusted the whole administration of the Children, the Sick, the Mentally Defective, and the Aged, should have nothing to do with the provision for the Unemployed. In our view the task of dealing with the Able-bodied person in destitution or distress transcends, by its very nature, the capacity of even the best Local Authorities, and must, if success is to be attained, be undertaken in its entirety by the National Government, on new principles, and with the help of new administrative machinery. If, however, organisation on a national basis is deemed inadvisable, or premature, the addition, to our Scheme of Reform, of a Committee for the Unemployed, dealing with all Able-bodied persons in distress, would even give to that Scheme administrative symmetry and logical completeness. In that case, there would need only to be a distinctive committee of the County or County Borough Council, dealing with all sections of the Able-bodied and with the Able-bodied exclusively. In this committee (which might be called the Committee for the Unemployed) the existing Distress Committee would be merged. It would have at its disposal all or any of the devices of the Poor Law and the Unemployed

Workmen Act; the Able-bodied Test Workhouse, the Outdoor Labour Test, the Casual Ward, the Municipal Relief Works and the Farm Colony, the Labour Exchange and Emigration. To have one Local Authority, and one only, dealing with Able-bodied men, whether Paupers, Vagrants or Unemployed, would be, in itself, a vast improvement on the present conflict and confusion caused by the existence of two rival Local Authorities simultaneously relieving the same class of men. To have this Statutory Committee for the Unemployed, entirely distinct from the Statutory Committees for Children, for the Sick, for the Mentally Defective and for the Aged—administering its own separate institutions, by its own staff of officials, and working out its own specialised *technique*—would be an enormous advance on any general Destitution Authority, with its inevitable "mixed" policy, its "mixed" officials, and its "mixed" institutions, always crumbling back into the General Mixed Workhouse.

The dominant exigencies that must govern all proposals for reform in this field are, as we have described in the preceding chapter:

a) The existence, practically at all times, of honest and respectable workmen in distress from Unemployment; either because they have fallen out of permanent situations, of because the interval between jobs is unusually prolonged.

b) The chronic state of Under-employment in which hundreds of thousands of workers, especially at the seaports, and in all the great towns, habitually exist, owing to the casual and intermittent nature of their engagements.

c) The vague and aimless wandering in search of work, either within a large town, or from town to town, which leads to demoralisation and vagrancy.

d) The lack of any systematic provision for the training in new means of livelihood, whether in industry or in land settlement, of men displaced by new processes, machinery or other industrial changes.

e) The intermixture among the Unemployed, the Under-employed and the Vagrants, of all sorts of "unemployables"—the debilitated and the demoralised, loafers and wastrels, beggars and criminals, who, whilst in one way or another maintaining a degenerate existence at the public expense, are always ready to appropriate and pervert any provision made for the more deserving sections.

Our Proposals for Reform are designed to meet all these exigencies.

(A) The National Labour Exchange

The first requisite is the organisation throughout the whole of the United Kingdom of a complete system of public Labour Exchanges on a national basis. This National Labour Exchange, though in itself no adequate remedy, is the foundation of all our proposals. It is, in our view, an indispensable condition of any real reform.

We are impressed by the need, throughout nearly the whole field of industrial life, of some better means than at present exist by which those seeking employment can discover, *quickly, gratuitously and with certainty*, exactly what places are vacant, and where these are situated; by which employers seeking assistance can have before them those persons who happen to be disengaged; and (what in our view is no less important) by which it may be conclusively ascertained that no opportunities of employment exist for particular kinds of labour at particular times. Some such organisation of information has clearly become necessary in practically all trades, if not to employers, at any rate to all sections of the Unemployed. It was easy, in the village, or even in the small town, with scant variety of occupation, for employers and wage-earners to be aware of all vacancies and of all available men. But in the huge wildernesses of London and other great cities, with the bewildering multiplication of occupations and specialisation of employments, a deliberate organisation of means of communication between employers and employed is as indispensable, if time is not to be wasted in endless runnings to and fro as the central sorting room of the Post Office or the Telephone Exchange.

(i) *The Experience of Germany*

But the utility of the Labour Exchange has been abundantly demonstrated. In nearly all the large towns of Germany such an institution has now been established; and we have available, in some cases, the testimony of ten, and even of twenty years' experience. Over 700 Labour Exchanges of one kind or another are now regularly reporting to the Imperial Statistical Office at Berlin. They are filling about *two millions of situations annually*. These Labour Exchanges are of various sorts, but the most interesting to us are the Public General Exchanges, established by the municipal authorities in practically every town of 50,000 inhabitants. Perhaps the most remarkable example is that of Stuttgart, a town standing in population between Leicester and Newcastle-on-Tyne, where the Public Labour Exchange, which has been in operation since 1895, finds situations for *more than a thousand male and female workers every week in the year.* Here the Labour Exchange has the hearty support of both employers and workmen. All the large Trade Unions (with one exception) have voluntarily given up their own registers of unemployed members, preferring such members to utilise the Public Exchange. Many Trade Unions (including those of the wood-workers, metal-workers, bookbinders, saddlers, millers and brewers' operatives) compel their unemployed members to report themselves daily at the Public Exchange as a condition of receiving their out of work pay. Turning to another German city, we may note that the Labour Exchange at Munich, which has a salaried staff of eighteen clerks, etc., and fills *over* 200 *situations a day*, "is situated on an island over which passes the principal bridge connecting the two halves of the city. The accommodation consists in essence of a number of waiting-rooms opening off a central corridor, and each communicating directly with the office of the superintendent in charge of the particular section. There are, for instance, three sections for men—unskilled, skilled workers in iron and wood, and all other skilled workers—each with its own waiting-room and superintendent; one for apprentices and two for women (industrial workers and domestic servants). Applicants for employment come to the appropriate waiting-room and fill up there a short form, indicating name, address, age, whether married, single, or widowed, occupation and work desired, last employer, and one or two other details. Applications for work-people are received in the corresponding office by personal call on the part of the employer or his representative, by post, or most commonly by telephone. As they are received they are announced by the superintendent in the waiting room, and the number required picked out from the men presenting themselves. From the forms already filled in by the men the superintendent enters the essential points in a current register, and sends the men off to the employer with a card of indentification. The employer receiving the card is requested to note on it which, if any, of the men he has engaged, and to return it through the post—it is already stamped and addressed—to the Labour Office. Where the employer has called in person or sent an agent, this is, of course, not necessary; the hiring is concluded there and then at an interview in the superintendent's office. In the unskilled section men may stay in the waiting-room all day. In the skilled sections there are fixed hours—generally one in the morning and one in the afternoon for each trade. It should be added that any situation not at once filled is notified on a blackboard in the waiting-room, so that any man coming in later and desiring to apply for one of them may at once present himself to the superintendent. Twice a week, moreover, lists of situations unfilled are drawn up and exhibited in public places. They are also inserted in the Press and sent round to all the neighbouring Labour Exchanges.

"The Labour Office appears to concern itself very little with inquiries as to the character of applicants for employment. They are not even always asked to produce their infirmity insurance cards. Efforts are, of course, made to send the sort of man asked for by the employer, but, in the unskilled section at least, the attitude is taken that it is ultimately the employer's business to satisfy himself as to the capacity of the men he engages. The Labour Office is essentially a means of communication. It does, no doubt, in the long run, give the employer a better workman than he would get by chance from the street; the superintendent has almost always a certain choice in the waiting-room, and can pick the abler or the better-known man. This, however, is only an indirect service. The direct utility of the Labour Office—as it presents itself unmistakably to anyone spending a morning in any one of its rooms—is to prevent economic waste by reducing to a minimum the period during which employers are seeking for men or men for employers. *In the unskilled section, with men always in the waiting-room and applications from employers arriving in an almost continuous stream, business has to be conducted at lightning speed.*"

(ii) *The Experience of London*

Nor are we without experience of the working of a Public Labour Exchange in this country. As we have mentioned, the Central (Unemployed) Body began, in 1906, the organisation of a system of Labour Exchanges for London as a whole. In spite of many difficulties, which are gradually being overcome, this score of Metropolitan Labour Exchanges, at last covering all London, are now, each year, regularly receiving from employers information as to about thirty to forty thousand permanent situations that are vacant; and are actually filling, from among the work-people who gratuitously register themselves as desiring places, no fewer than 25,000 situations a year. What is interesting is to find that, although there are many applicants for employment for whom situations are not found, *there are also many vacancies notified by employers, for workers of particular experience, which cannot be filled.* Still more numerous are the situations notified to any one Exchange which that Exchange, for all its long list of waiting applicants, is unable to fill. A steadily increasing use is accordingly being made of the Exchanges in other parts of London, and the central office. An employer sends to the local Exchange for a workman of such and such a kind. The Superintendent of the local Exchange finds that he has none on his "live register." He telephones to the central office, and the inquiry is sent to every one of the London Exchanges. It is significant of the proved value of the organisation that no fewer than *a hundred situations per week are filled from applicants in other districts*. The working of the Metropolitan Exchanges shows, in fact, that, whatever the state of trade, the wider the area covered by the Labour Exchange organisation, the larger is the proportion of situations filled, the fewer the employers whose wants remain unsatisfied and the smaller the remnants of applicants for employment for whom places cannot be found. But the Metropolitan Exchanges are working under great difficulties. They find their operations confined by the boundary of the Administrative County of London, whilst industry has spread out into West Ham and Tottenham, Willesden and Ealing, Wimbledon and Croydon. With such industrial "overflows" from London as the rapidly-growing factories of Luton and Reading, Chelmsford and Erith, and all the intervening country, the London Exchanges are practically unable to get into easy and regular communication. From places further afield they are wholly cut off. It is, in fact, a grave misfortune that, as we have seen, the "network of Labour Bureaux" covering the whole country, which the Unemployed Workmen Act ordered to be established, has not yet come into existence.

(iii) *The Experience of the Seamen's Labour Exchange*

What is in some respects an even more interesting experiment in Labour Exchanges is that, confined to a single industry, but extending to the whole of the United Kingdom, which the Board of Trade has conducted for nearly half a century under the Merchant Shipping Acts. Under certain sections of these Acts, which were designed to suppress the evils of "crimping," every engagement of a seaman, a fireman, a cook, a cabin-boy, or other person in the mercantile marine is required to be entered into at the public office maintained by the Government for that purpose. There are nearly 150 Mercantile Marine Offices in as many different seaports, at which places alone seamen can be hired. Thirty-seven of these are nothing but Labour Exchanges, whilst the others are adjuncts of the local Customs offices. There is a waiting room where Jack can sit and smoke; a register where he can inscribe his temporary address; even a small staff of "runners"—in the Civil Service Estimates euphemistically entered as messengers—whose business it is to know Jack's haunts, so as to find him promptly when he is required. "We undertake practically to find a crew for every ship," said one enthusiastic Superintendent. The master mariner comes to the waiting-room; questions the men; picks out those whom he thinks will best suit his ship; and enters into contract with them then and there, in the presence of the Superintendent, who sees that the conditions of the contract include such as the law makes obligatory, but has otherwise no authority in the matter. These offices are situated where most convenient to the shipping trade, and they are open for the most suitable hours—even, as at Grimsby, where fishing boats need to catch the tide, in the middle of the night. If no suitable man can be found in the port—say, for a boatswain's place—the Superintendent may, at the master's expense, telegraph to the Mercantile Marine Office at the next port and have, as a favour, a suitable man advanced his railway fare and sent along. These 150 Mercantile Marine Offices fill more than half a million situations a year; 492,133 in 1906 in the 37 principal offices alone. No seaman is ever at a loss where to apply for whatever situations in his calling may be vacant. It is an interesting reflection upon this experiment that in all our investigations into the tens of thousands of Unemployed whom the Distress Committees have had on their hands, *we have seldom found a seaman*—practically none from the Royal Navy, and very few from the Mercantile Marine.

(iv) *The Functions of the National Labour Exchange*

We propose that the institution of the Labour Exchange, using the experience of Germany and the Metropolis, should be adapted to the needs of each of our four classes of the Unemployed.

(a) The Labour Exchange and the Men from Permanent Situations

The Men from Permanent Situations—our Class I—would discover at once what situations were vacant, and in what towns; would learn promptly if there was nowhere any opening for them; would ascertain whether the particular services for which they had been trained were being superseded by industrial changes; and, if so, to what occupations they could best turn. Where Trade Unions existed, they could, if desired, use the public offices of the Labour Exchange for keeping their "Vacant Books," and even for their branch meetings. For the Men from Permanent Situations, indeed, the National Labour Exchange would, as we shall presently describe, become the axis of a system of subsidised Trade Insurance against Unemployment. But for the whole of this class, and for their employers, and therefore for the majority of the persons engaged in the industry of the nation, the use of the Labour Exchange might, we suggest, be left entirely optional.

(b) The Labour Exchange and the Men of Discontinuous Employment

For the second class, the Men of Discontinuous Employment, the Labour Exchange has to fulfil a more important function. The need for bringing together employer and workman, in our Class I only an occasional requirement, is, in our Class II, a perpetually recurring need. By its rapid and continuous collection of information, the Labour Exchange would be able to obviate the present futile drifting about in search of work and the incessant "leakages" of time between jobs by which so many men are ruined. The operatives in the building trades and the navvies might ascertain, even before the actual expiration of one job, what other jobs were beginning. In each large urban aggregation, whether the 300 square miles of the Metropolitan business area, or the 50 to 100 square miles of the other great centres, it would be possible, by a free use of the telegraph and telephone, to make known, hour by hour, exactly what openings there were, for each class of labour, in each part of the town. Every morning it could be published all over the Kingdom, in which towns, if any, there was an unsatisfied demand for labour, and for what kind of labour. No less important would it be to make known in which trades, and in which towns, there was an ascertained surplus of workers for whom no places could be found. The navvies, for instance, instead of wandering hither and thither on mere rumours of public works, could be directed straight to the places in which they were needed, in exactly the numbers required. We think that it will probably be found desirable—and, indeed, for the common convenience of employers and employed—that, as in the case of the seamen, it should be made compulsory, at any rate, in certain scheduled trades, for all engagements to be made, not necessarily on the premises of the Labour Exchange, but at least through its organisation, and registered in its books.

(c) The Labour Exchange and the Seasonal Trades

A special type of Discontinuous Employment is presented by those trades which have fairly regular fluctuations in the volume of work according to the season of the year. Here the workers find themselves busy during certain months, and habitually short of work during others. As workers in these "seasonal" trades supply a considerable proportion of the Unemployed, we were glad to be furnished by the Board of Trade with statistical returns of their fluctuations during the decade, 1897-1906.

These Returns show, in the first place, a good many spring and summer trades. Of these building . . . is the most obvious. During spring, employment improves rapidly, and receives a fresh impetus in July; from the end of August it falls off quite steadily, till the end of the year. Furnishing follows the same general course with a busy time more concentrated in the spring, and coach-building with one in June and July. In coopering, the season comes somewhat later, and is carried on with only slightly diminished briskness till the end of the year. Brush-making and hat-making have each a second season in the autumn. In clothing, the worst time is in October and November; every subsequent month shows improvement till the late spring. Leather-workers and mill-sawyers, though also busiest in spring and summer, and slacking off to the winter, have not such well-marked seasons. . . .

The Returns show, in the second place, certain trades whose general tendency is directly the contrary of that outlined above. They may be regarded as winter trades. Steel-smelting, while somewhat irregular, has undoubtedly its slackest times in June and July.

In the third place, certain trades have . . . very characteristic fluctuations, which are apparently more dependent on social habits than on climatic conditions. Printers are always busiest at the end of November, grow slack as soon as Christmas is past, grow busy in February and March, and slack again from April to June, always recover a little in July, and then fall into a dead season during the summer holidays. Paper-makers, as might be expected, follow the same course, though not so regularly. Tobacco-workers also are busiest in November, and stand idle in July and August. Book-binders . . . agree with printers in being busiest in November, but have a slack season more or less throughout the late spring and summer.

It will be seen that there is, in coal-mining, a definite seasonal fluctuation. December is busiest; employment falls off in January to recover in February and March; after which it falls off in April, and though recovering in May, becomes slack again throughout June, July and August. With September, there is, in all cases, a recovery. . . . Iron-mining shows definite though limited seasonal fluctuations. The last four months of the year, and May, are busy times; January, April and June to August are times of comparative slackness. For iron and steel works . . . the three months June to August, and January, are marked out as periods of comparative slackness. The tin-plate industry . . . has apparently a similar fluctuation.

It thus appears that there is no such marked predominance of briskness in the spring and slackness in the winter as is commonly supposed. On the contrary, many industries are at their busiest in the winter months. There is, indeed, no month in the year in which some trades are not usually at their busiest; and no month in the year in which some trades are not usually at their slackest. Thus, January is the busiest of all months at the docks of London and most other ports and one of the busiest for coal-miners; February in paper-making; March in steel-smelting and textile manufacture; April in brush-making and the furnishing trades; May in engineering and ship-building, coach-making, hat-making and leather work; May, June, and July in all the ramifications of the clothing trades, as well as among mill-sawyers; July and August for the railway service and all occupations in holiday resorts, as well as for carpenters and coopers; August and September for all forms of agricultural harvesting; September for plumbers and iron-miners; October in iron and steel works; November for printing and book-binding, for the tobacco trade, the tin-plate manu-facture and the metal trades generally; whilst in December coal-mining, the very extensive theatrical industry, the Post Office service and the gas and electricity works are all at their greatest volume of employment. On the other hand, January shows iron-mining and the furnishing trades to be at their slackest; in February (contrary to popular belief), the plumbers have the most Unemployment of any time of the year; in March and April the coopers; in May and June the London dock labourers and the coal-miners; in July the iron and steel and tin-plate workers; in August the paper-makers, printers, book-binders and tobacco workers; in Septem-ber the textile operatives and various metal-workers; in October all the clothing trades are at their slackest; in November ship-building is, on the average, at its minimum; whilst December is the worst month for carpen-ters and engineers, mill-sawyers and coach-builders, leather-workers and brushmakers.

The inference is irresistible that, if we had accurate statistics of the daily volume of employment in all industries, it might well be that we should find the aggregate for all trades, in all parts of the country, to be approxi-mately uniform throughout the year. And this, when we come to think of it, is suggested by the character of the consumers' demand. The income of any highly differentiated industrial community accrues to it from day to day, and becomes available for personal expenditure from week to week, in approximately equal instalments throughout the year. Though each family varies its consumption of different services and commodities at different seasons—now buying winter clothes, now summer clothes, now using more coal, now taking holidays—the total amount of the weekly outlay of the typical household does not exhibit any great variation throughout the year. It is clear, at least, that the variation from season to season, when we take the aggregate for all industries and for the nation as a whole, must be very much smaller than the seasonal slackness which, at present, in trade after trade, annually brings tens of thousands of families into the desolation of prolonged Under-employment.

The Discontinuous Employment due to seasonal slackness is, in fact, so far as the labourers and all unspecialized workers are concerned, strictly analogous to the Under-employment of the dock and wharf-labourer. Just as each employer of this kind of labour tends to keep his own reserve, or "Stagnant Pool," which he drains only on his busiest day, so each seasonal trade attracts to itself, not merely enough workers to do its daily average of business throughout the year, but enough for its busiest season, with the result that each trade in turn, as its own particular slack season comes round, has a large proportion of its workers under-employed.

This, however, overstates the case. In some cases the seasonal industries avoid variations of staff by working more continuously in the busy season and "short time" in the slack months. This, in various forms, is the practice of the coal-miners, the textile operatives, the iron and steel and tin-plate workers, and many kinds of factory operatives. It is also to a great extent the practice in agriculture and many minor industries. Where wage-earners enjoy practical continuity of employment under the same employer (but only in those cases), this variation of the length and assiduity of the working time is no doubt the most convenient way of meeting the variation of the demand, especially for the men of any specialized skill.

In other seasonal trades there is a certain amount of unorganised "dove-tailing." The hop-gardens get their harvesting done by 20,000 workers drawn each September and October from other occupations. About 25,000 Irish labourers still come from Connaught to help to reap the potatoes, and do other harvesting work from Perthshire to the Fen Country. Some of the Thames riverside workers supply the increased staff still required in the winter (though to a lesser extent than before so much machinery was employed) in the London gas-works. And everywhere in all sorts of industries a certain amount of individual and almost casual "dove-tailing" goes on, by which workers, in their own slack season, contrive to earn a little irregular income at other occupations.

With a National Labour Exchange in effective operation this "dove-tailing" of one seasonal trade into another could be enormously increased, at any rate among the labourers who follow each trade, the women workers, the less specialised of the skilled workers, and the "handy men" and nondescripts whom every industry employs. Thus, to take dock labour and three other large industries only, employing a large proportion of general labourers and only slightly specialized men, we have been furnished by the Board of Trade with figures showing the average number of men employed daily in each month of the year, during 1906, at the London docks and wharves, and in the gas-works, at the waterworks, and on the tramways of the whole country. Each of these industries, by itself, shows a variation between its busiest month and its slackest month of between 9 and 22 per cent., the fluctuations affecting some 10,000 men, and that repeatedly. Adding them together, the variation between the total employed at the extremes of high pressure and slackness is only 7 per cent.; the most extreme fluctuation affecting only some 5,000 men, *and the busiest months being those of November, December and January,* when the building trades and brick-making are at their slackest. It is probable that the inclusion of the unskilled men in these two further industries would reduce the aggregate seasonal variation to a vanishing point. This it would be the business of the National Labour Exchange to accomplish. In this way, a much greater continuity of employment throughout the year could be secured for those persons who were employed at all; at the cost (which accompanies every stage in the Suppression of Under-employment) of squeezing out altogether, once and for all, some of those not really required for the work to be done, who now pick up, owing to the absence of organisation, half a subsistence in chronic Under-employment. For these, of course, as a condition of the reform, suitable provision would have to be made.

(d) The Labour Exchange and the Under-employed

The Men from Permanent Situations, the Men of Discontinuous Employment, and especially those among them whose industries are subject to considerable seasonal fluctuations, are, as we have shown, in the preceding chapter, constantly dropping into our Third Class—the men who are, year in and year out, chronically Under-employed. It is with regard to this class that the Labour Exchange reaches its highest utility. It presents us, with what, in our opinion, is the indispensable instrument for dealing with Under-employment. We must postulate, to begin with, the great desirability, from the standpoint of the community, of putting an end at all this "casual" or irregularly intermittent wage-labour, if we could do so, because of its social effects. No housekeeping can stand a demoralising uncertainty as to whether the week's income will be five shillings or five and twenty. We cannot, however, hope to abolish the irregularity of demand which lies at the root of Under-employment. At every port the loading and unloading of ships necessarily depends on their arrival and departure. Whether we have to do with the private enterprise of unloading ships or harvesting crops, or with the public service of the Post Office or the tramways, we cannot expect ever to prevent incessant fluctuations from day to day in the number of men required. But although we cannot prevent, and may not even be able appreciably to lessen, the fluctuations of employment, by each separate firm, and in each separate industry, it is not necessary that these fluctuations should work themselves out, in the world of labour, into *an army of hundreds of thousands of men who are chronically Under-employed*. What a National Labour Exchange could remedy would be the habit of each employer of keeping around him his own reserve of labour. By substituting one common reservoir, at any rate for the unspecialized labourers, we could drain the Stagnant Pools of Labour which this habit produces and perpetuates.

For this purpose, an element of compulsion is indispensable. The evils of the present way of engaging Casual Labour are so manifest, and its direct results in Pauperism and demoralisation have been so clearly ascertained, that our Investigators were led to propose, with regard to dock labour at any rate, that it should be prohibited by law.

There seems to be no right [they report] to claim that such a state of things should continue. We believe that the voluntary establishment of a weekly wage for the great majority of the labourers employed, if not for all of them, is possible, and that if this is done, an employment of such a nature, which requires its extra hands in the winter, might prove a boon to the unskilled workers in other trades, whose busy time is in the summer. Lastly, if no system of weekly engagements is voluntarily established (and we believe it would be an advantage to employers as well as employed), we would be prepared to go further, and suggest *that such a minimum period of engagement be made a legal obligation.*

To some such legal prohibition of a method of hiring labour that is demonstrably quite as injurious to the community as was the Truck System, we must inevitably come, if no other remedy can be found. Stopping short, however, of the legal prohibition of casual hirings, we may reasonably ask those employers who continue to adopt this mode of engaging labour to submit to some slight regulations calculated to reduce the social evil that they undoubtedly cause. We propose that it should be made legally compulsory on employers (being persons carrying on industrial or commercial operations for profit), in all those cases in which it is not convenient to them to guarantee a minimum period of employment, which might be put at a month (subject, or course, to the power of dismissal of any particular individual for misconduct, and even of arbitrary replacement of one man by another if desired), to hire such labour as they want, whether for a job, a day, or a week, exactly as is done without complaint in the mercantile marine, *exclusively through the National Labour Exchange.*

We recommend that the National Labour Exchange should make a point of accommodating itself to the needs of every kind of fluctuating industry; that it should be assisted in each locality by an advisory committee of employers and employed; having offices opened exactly where most convenient to employers (for instance, actually inside the dock gates, or at the principal wharves, or at any other places where sudden demands for labour occur); keeping whatever office hours were required (ready, for instance, to supply labourers at five in the morning); and, of course, telephonically interconnected, and organised up to the maximum efficiency. As there would be no other opportunity of getting casual employment at all (with the possible exception of the odd jobs offered by private persons, not engaged in business; and even these we may hope to diminish), it would not be necessary to make it legally compulsory on the labourers to enrol themselves at the Labour Exchange, except under the circumstances that we have described. Nor would it be necessary legally to prohibit the existence of other agencies for filling situations. As employers would not be able to use them for casual labour, such agencies, dealing, as they do, almost entirely with certain specialised kinds of employment, such as domestic servants, hotel employés and secondary school teachers, would scarcely compete with the National Labour Exchange, and would have, perforce, to confine themselves, as they practically do now, to filling situations of at least a month's duration.

This plan, it will be seen, reduces to a minimum the proposed restriction on the employer, or the interference with his business. It would cause him absolutely no increase of expense. In so far as he can offer regular employment of a month's duration, he is not affected at all. Even for casual labour, he remains as free as before to hire it by the job or by the day only, for as short a period as he chooses. He will have at his disposal all the men in the whole town who are not already engaged. He is able, in fact, to draw from a common reservoir instead of from his own Stagnant Pool. He may have his own choice of men (assuming that they are momentarily disengaged). He may ask for this man or that; he may keep his own list of "preference men"; he may send for ten or a hundred men in order of his preference, or send merely for so many men without naming them. He may even bargain privately with the man of his choice, and virtually secure him beforehand; provided that he lets the formal hiring take place through the Labour Exchange.

The result to the labourer living by casual employment will be that he will find effectively open to him, not merely the particular demand for labour of this or that wharf, or this or that foreman, on which he has been in the habit of waiting, but the whole aggregate demand of the town. One employer needs men to-day only, but another needs men to-morrow; one trade is busy this month, another next month. The policy of the National Labour Exchange would be, subject to any preferences expressed by employers, so to distribute the available men, and so to "dovetail" the engagements offered to each of them, as to secure to each man who was employed at all five or six days' work in every week. In so far as this was achieved, we should have done for Casual Labour what has been done compulsorily for every person employed in the mercantile marine, and voluntarily for skilled nurses in most large towns by the various nurses' institutes, etc., and for the members of the Corps of Commissionaires in London, namely, combined freedom to the employer to hire only for a job, with practical continuity of work to the person employed. To quote the words of an able student of this problem, "decasualisation will reconstruct the whole conditions of life in the lowest ranks of industry, sifting out for remedial treatment a certain number of 'unemployables' and forcing up the level of all the rest. It will replace the casual class—always on the verge of distress, always without reserves for an emergency—by a class for whom the words foresight, organisation, and thrift may represent not a mockery but a reality."

The question may present itself, why, if the chronic Under-employment of the labourers can be thus prevented, has it not already been prevented? The answer is to be found, as has been demonstrated at Liverpool and elsewhere, partly in the difficulty that each individual employer experiences in attempting to reorganise the habits of a trade; partly in the difficulty of even a whole trade by itself affecting a change; but very largely also in the very real opposition which the labourers themselves have offered to the introduction of regular employment. There is, indeed, a difficulty which has to be faced. If, by means of an effective Labour Exchange at Liverpool, the whole work of the docks could be done by 8,000 men continuously employed, with a thousand or two more retained for exceptional times of pressure, instead (as at present) being spread over 15,000 men who are chronically Under-employed, the social gain to Liverpool would be great, but there would be 5,000 men squeezed out altogether. Every dock labourer in Liverpool fears that he would be among the excluded. It is, in fact, not possible to abolish Under-employment, except at the cost of depriving some of the Under-employed men even of the employment that they have. Hence the task cannot be undertaken except by a public Authority, and by one prepared at the same time to provide, adequately and honourably, for the men displaced by the improvement. We deal with this in our sections on the Absorption of the Surplus and the Provision for the Unemployed.

(e) The Labour Exchange and the Suppression of Vagrancy

The National Labour Exchange presents what, in our opinion, is the only effectual way of suppressing Vagrancy. As is recited in the Report of the recent Departmental Committee, every variety of treatment of the Vagrant, from the most penal severity to the most generous laxity, has been tried in vain. So long as the only method of finding work is for the workman simply to go and seek it, there is no possibility of preventing the Unemployed from wandering from town to town. So long as the workman in search of a job has to wander, it is impossible to distinguish between him and the Professional Vagrant. So long as the "public works men" are left to stream helplessly from one job to another on mere rumour, without any kind of adjustment between the numbers attracted and the numbers required, it is impracticable to stop the swarm of "cadgers," who prey on the generosity of the navvy and contaminate the locality in which the contractor is at work. "The knowledge of men of this class which I have gained," sums up Captain Eardley-Wilmot, "in my experience as governor of both convict and local prisons, and more recently as an Inspector, has convinced me that no alteration in treatment, within the limits that would be allowed in this country, could affect their number. Causes for increase must be looked for in the social and economic conditions of the period under discussion. I may add that this is the opinion of every thoughtful and experienced prison official with whom I have discussed the question."

With the National Labour Exchange organised in all towns it will become possible for the unemployed workman in any part of the Kingdom to inform himself, with precision, whether or not he is required in any other place. There will cease to be any excuse for wandering in search of work. We propose that, if it appears, on telegraphic or telephonic communication, that there is reason to believe that a workman can obtain employment in another town, and if he wishes to go there for that purpose, but has not money, a special non-transferable railway-ticket should be supplied to him, upon an obligation to report himself the same day at the Labour Exchange of the town to which he is sent, and to repay the cost of the ticket by weekly instalments from his wages. Arrangements could be made, whenever thought desirable, for the man to be met on arrival, and conducted to the Labour Exchange. If this were done, it would be possible to prohibit all wandering without means of subsistence and to abolish the Casual Ward. But we do not propose that the man found destitute "on the road" should be sent to prison. His duty would be to report himself to the nearest branch of the National Labour Exchange, where he would find, without fail, either opportunity of working, or else the suitable provision that we shall describe. If this were done it would be possible to make all the minor offences of Vagrancy—such as begging, "sleeping out," hawking or peddling without a licence, wandering without means of subsistence, wandering with children in such a way as to subject them to hardship or deprive them of the means of education, etc.—occasions for *instant and invariable commitment* by the Justices, not for short sentences to the ordinary prison, which experience shows to be useless, but to one or other of the reformatory Detention Colonies which must form an integral part of the system of provision, and which will be described in our section on the Provision for the Unemployed.

(f) The Labour Exchange as a Method of Enforcing Personal Responsibility

A large part of what is erroneously classed with Vagrancy is, as we have seen, merely a failure of a section of the residents of the great cities to get work sufficient even to provide themselves with a night's lodging. At present there is, indeed, no practical method of enforcing upon able-bodied men the obligation of working. Every large town has its class of "houseless poor" who, with the aid of Free Shelters and philanthropic distributions of food, and occasional resorts to the Casual Ward and to "sleeping out," manage to exist with the very minimum of work. This deteriorating and contaminating class cannot at present be suppressed, because (in the absence of any proof that they could get work for the asking) public opinion does not permit of any real punishment of their offence, and persists, in fact, in relieving their physical wants. An analogous difficulty stands at present in the way of any real enforcement on negligent or drunken parents of their parental obligations. The Local Education Authorities, who find children hungry at school, and the Local Health Authorities, who are driven to supply milk to starving infants, find it practically impossible to prosecute even the most criminally negligent parents, because there is no proof that they could get work if they chose. We have seen, moreover, in our chapter on Charge and Recovery, how difficult it is for the Poor Law Authorities, even where men could earn substantial wages, to bring sufficient proof to convince County Court Judges and Magistrates that they are in a position to pay what is due from them. In all these directions the existence of the National Labour Exchange, where any man may be ensured either the opportunity of working, or else the provision that we shall presently describe, will enable personal responsibility to be far more effectually enforced than is now possible. Whilst no man who is fulfilling all his obligations need be compelled to report himself to the Labour Exchange, even if he is Unemployed, such attendance and report would, of course, be an imperative requirement and condition of any form of Public Assistance. If a child is found hungry at school, or without boots, the first question will be why is the parent not at the Labour Exchange, where either work or adequate provision is available for him.

When this is understood, it will be found possible to take much more drastic action against those who, out of idleness, selfishness or negligence, or through drunkenness, refuse to provide themselves with lodging, or deprive their wives and children of the necessary food and clothing, or fail to make any payments that are due from them.

(B) THE ABSORPTION OF THE SURPLUS

Some enthusiastic advocates of the Labour Exchange think so highly of the improvement that it would introduce in the organization of the nation's industry that they believe it would be possible to give continuous employment to those at present unemployed, and at the same time, through the constant growth of the nation's industry, obtain other places for the section of the Under-employed who would thereby be squeezed out. We do not take this view. We think that the "Decasualisation of the Casual Labourer" and the Suppression of Under-employment cannot be undertaken, and ought not to be undertaken, without simultaneously providing, in some way or other, for the men who would be thrown out. We have shown that there exists in the United Kingdom to-day no inconsiderable surplus of labour—not, indeed, of workmen who could not, with an improved organization of industry, be productively employed; but of workmen who are, as a matter of fact, now chronically Under-employed, and of whose potential working time a large part is, to their own mental and physical hurt, and to our great loss, at present wholly wasted. By the working of a National Labour Exchange such as we have proposed, and by the deliberate draining of the Stagnant Pools of Labour into a common reservoir, we contemplate that a rapidly increasing number of these Under-employed men will find themselves employed with practical continuity, whilst there will be a corresponding section left without any employment at all. For the surplus of labour power which already exists in the partial idleness of huge reserves of Under-employed men, and which will then for the first time stand revealed and identified in the complete idleness of a smaller number of wholly displaced individuals, we want to ensure that the National Labour Exchange shall be able to find appropriate employment at wages. It so happens that there are three social reforms of great importance which would promote this object, and which, accordingly, we recommend for adoption concurrently with any attempt to drain the morass of Under-employment.

(i) *The Halving of Boy and Girl Labour*

We have seen that one of the most prolific sources of Casual Labour, with its evil of chronic Under-employment, is the employment of boys in occupations which afford them no industrial training; and which, whilst providing them with relatively high wages during youth, leave them stranded when they reach manhood. The extensive and, as we fear, the growing use of boy-labour in this uneducational way produces a four-fold social detriment:

There is, first of all, the evil, through the multiplication of van-boys, errand boys, messenger boys, etc., of recruiting a chronically excessive army of unskilled, casually employed, merely brute labour. There is, further, the illegitimate use, by employers, of successive relays of boys, not as persons to whom a skilled trade has to be taught, but, by ignoring that responsibility, as cheap substitutes for adult workers, who are thereby deprived of employment. There is, as the other aspect of this, the failure to provide for the healthy physical development of the town boy, whose long hours of monotonous and uneducational work leave him a "weedy," narrow-chested, stunted weakling, whom even the recruiting sergeant rejects, and who succumbs prematurely to disease. Finally, there is the creation of the "hooligan"—the undisciplined youth, precocious in evil, earning at seventeen or eighteen more wages than suffice to keep him, independent of home control, and yet unsteadied by a man's responsibilities.

It may be said that it is the duty of the parents to take care that their sons are placed out in situations where they will receive proper industrial training. Unfortunately, as is only too clear, the great majority of parents, even when they give sufficient thought to the matter, find it impossible to give their sons a proper start in life.

What stares in the face the exceptionally careful parent of the poorer class who tries to start his son well is, in London, the difficulty of discovering any situation in which his boy can become a skilled worker of any kind, or even enter the service of an employer who can offer him advancement. We have, on the one hand, a great development of employment for boys of a thoroughly bad type, yielding high wages and no training. We have, on the other hand, a positive shrinkage—almost a disappearance—of places for boys in which they are trained to become competent men. London employers not only refuse to teach apprentices, even for premiums—they often refuse to have boys on those parts of their establishments in which anything can be learnt.

Exactly the same difficulty is found, in fact, by the Poor Law Authorities in placing out the pauper children for whom they are responsible. We are not satisfied that, as regards the boys in particular, these do not, to a considerable extent, eventually recruit the ranks of the Under-employed; so that the Boards of Guardians in England, Wales and Ireland, and the Parish Councils in Scotland, may be, to no small degree, creating their own future difficulties. Out of the 300,000 boys and girls maintained out of the Poor Rate, for whose upbringing the Poor Law Authorities are definitely responsible, something like 20,000 have annually to be started in employment. With regard to some 15,000 of these, whom the Boards of Guardians and Parish Councils have elected to maintain on Outdoor Relief, we cannot discover that any care is taken that they should be either apprenticed or brought up to a trade at which they can get regular employment. There is, in fact, only too much reason to fear that practically the whole of these 15,000 "Children of the State" pass into ill-paid occupations, in which they can eventually earn no regular livelihood, and that (as regards the boys at any rate) they almost wholly recruit one or other sections of the Under-employed. With regard to the remaining 5,000 who have been in Poor Law Schools, or Cottage or Scattered Homes, or "boarded-out," more care is taken by the Poor Law Authorities; and practically all the girls go into domestic service. For the boys, too, in many places, as much as possible is done, but the dearth of openings for indoor apprentices in skilled trades compels a very large proportion to enter the Army as bandsmen; and it is hoped that on the expiration of their military service they find remunerative occupation as musicians. We think that there should be more alternatives open.

There is, unhappily, no little evidence to show that the difficulty that parents and Poor Law Authorities alike experience in placing out boys in occupations affording them regular work and a constant livelihood is not confined to the Metropolis. There is the same difficulty in Glasgow and Liverpool, Manchester and Hull. The evil is not that boys are employed, or that they suffer from Unemployment; but that they are employed all day at non-educational occupations. In Dundee a large majority of the boys have to find employment in places in which they learn no trade by which they can subsequently earn a livelihood. In the cotton-spinning mills of Lancashire three-fourths of the piecers necessarily fail to become spinners; and have eventually to change their occupations. Even the Postmaster-General, the largest individual employer of labour, employs far more boys in his service than he can use as men; and has accordingly annually to dismiss, about 16, several thousand boys to whom he has taught no trade by which they can earn their bread.

Such a state of things in which an enormous number of boys obtain no useful industrial training before attaining manhood, calls obviously for remedy. We cannot restore the old apprenticeship system, even if that had anything like its commonly-supposed advantages. At no time did it provide trade teaching for more than a small minority of the population, and then by a method which Adam Smith denounced as extravagantly costly to the community. There is now no method by which, over the greater part of the industrial field, the great mass of boys can be technically educated—whether we mean by this the teaching of manual crafts or merely a wider education of hand, eye, and brain into all-round industrial capacity—other than that of Trade Schools. We see no other way of turning the boy into a trained and fully developed man than that of providing the necessary training between fifteen and eighteen *by the community itself*. The parent demonstrably cannot do it. The employer will not and (under the present industrial conditions) is really often not in a position to do so. We have had before us various proposals for increasing the facilities for evening instruction, and for rendering attendance at evening continuation classes compulsory. It is, however, clear that, useful as evening continuation classes may be to particular individuals, it is impossible for boys who are exhausted by a whole day's physical toil to obtain either physical training or the necessary technical education. The "theory that boys can become errand boys," reports our Investigator, "for a year or two and then enter skilled trades cannot be maintained. Very few boys can pick up skill after a year or two of merely errand-boy work. . . . The great mass of them fall into the low-skilled trades or wholly casual labour." We have, therefore, come to the conclusion that, if we want to turn into trained and competent workmen the 300,000 boys who now annually in the United Kingdom start wage-earning at something or another, there is only one practicable plan. *We must shorten the legally permissible hours of employment for boys, and we must require them to spend the hours so set free in physical and technological training.*

We think that there would be many advantages in such an amendment of the Factory Acts and the Education Acts as would make it illegal for any Employer to employ any boy at all, in any occupation whatsoever, below the age of fifteen; or any youth under eighteen for more than thirty hours per week; coupled with an obligation on the employer, as a condition of being permitted to make use of the immature in industry, to see that the youth between fifteen and eighteen had his name on the roll of some suitable public institute giving physical training and technical education; and an obligation on the boy to attend such an institute for not less than thirty hours per week. This attendance might either be for five hours every day, in the morning or afternoon respectively, or for ten hours on alternate days, according to the convenience of employers in different industries; or, in order to suit the needs of agriculture, it might be concentrated, wholly or chiefly, in particular months of the year. It should at the same time be made obligatory on the Local Education Authorities to submit schemes for providing within a limited period the necessary institutions for the youths of their districts in whatever way was most suited to the local needs. Such a law would have various advantages:

(1) The employer would find it less advantageous to employ boys, even if he took them in double shifts, and paid them no more per hour than he did before, and he would consequently not be so anxious so to alter his processes as to substitute them for adult men. But (as the supply of boy labour would be halved) there would be a positive scarcity of boys, and their rate of wages per hour would probably rise, so that the employer would tend to employ, instead of boys, actually more adult men than at present.

(2) The youth, who now has even too much pocket-money, and gets, therefore, too soon independent of home, and too easily led into evil courses, would find his earnings reduced, perhaps not by half, but probably by one-third, and his leisure absorbed under discipline.

(3) At the Polytechnic it would be possible, in thirty hours a week, from fourteen to eighteen (or twenty-one) to put the youth through a course of physical training, under medical supervision, under which he would learn to swim, to row, to box, to ride, etc.; and it could be ensured that the adverse hygienic conditions of town life would be rectified.

(4) There would be possible, in the course of four or seven years' half-time at the trade school, an education of hand, eye and brain; a practical ability to use competently the ordinary tools; a knowledge of drawing, practical geometry, and workshop arithmetic; and even a groundwork of training in particular handicrafts; such as few even of duly indentured apprentices get. We need not try, or even desire, to convert every boy into a skilled engineer, cabinet-maker, or compositor. But we could make every boy, whatever his occupation, into a man of trained hand, eye and brain; disciplined, and good-mannered; of sound muscle and fully developed lungs; with a general knowledge of common tools and simple machines; able to read a plan and make a drawing to scale; ready to undertake any kind of unspecialized work, and competent, even if he does unskilled labour, to do it "with his head."

With regard to the need for extending, to boys between 14 and 18, something like the supervision and control exercised over them whilst at school, there is abundant evidence. At present, as in the past, it is mainly the "juvenile adult," between 16 and 21, who recruits our prison population. It is the absence of any system of control and organization for the employment of the young which is universally declared to be one of the principal causes of wrong-doing. "When a boy leaves school the hands of organization and compulsion are lifted from his shoulders. If he is the son of very poor parents, his father has no influence, nor, indeed, a spare hour, to find work for him; he must find it for himself; generally he does find a job, and if it does not land him into a dead alley at 18 he is fortunate. Or he drifts, and the tidy scholar soon becomes a ragged and defiant corner loafer. Over 80 per cent. of our charges admit that they were not at work when they got into trouble."

We have hitherto referred only to boys. But the problem of the girl is, from an educational standpoint, analogous. They all need the training of body and brain, hand and eye; they all need the instruction in the use of the household implements and tools; they all need the technical education that is necessary to produce competent housewives and mothers. Even if we regard the industrial work of girls as, for the most part, a "blind alley," destined to end at marriage, the need for their technical training in household duties becomes all the more imperative. They do not, and cannot, get such training before they leave the elementary school. The compulsory release of girls up to eighteen from industrial wage-earning for half their time, and their compulsory attendance at suitable educational courses, in which physical training and the various branches of domestic economy and household management (including how to rear a baby) would find place, offers, in our opinion, the best way of ensuring their adequate preparation for their duties as wives and mothers.

We should recommend these reforms even if they rested solely on their educational advantages. It is upon the proper physical and technical training of its youth that the nation has eventually to depend. But they present also the additional attraction that they would, we believe, arrest the tendency so to arrange industrial operations as to replace the labour of adult men and women by that of boys and girls. We do not think, in the face of the large number of the Unemployed and the Under-employed which our inquiry has revealed, that any objection can be made on the plea that the labour of immature boys and girls is indispensable to the nation's industry. One result of halving the effective labour force of boys and girls in industrial employment would, in fact, be to enable the National Labour Exchange to find places, at the time of "decasualisation," for at least as many men as the "Decasualisation of Casual Labour" and Suppression of Under-employment would leave on its hands.

(ii) *The Reduction of the Hours of Labour of Railway and Tramway Servants*

We look for a gradual reduction of the daily hours of labour in practically all industries. Just as the fourteen hours' day common in the eighteenth century gave way to the twelve hours' day of the opening of the nineteenth, and this again successively to the ten hours' day of a couple of generations ago, and to the nine hours' day of 1871, so we anticipate that, at no distant date, we shall regard as normal the eight hours' day already obtained in various industries. This, however, has, in our view, little bearing on Unemployment, and none at all on Under-employment. In most cases the improvement in industrial organization, the universal "speeding up" of work, and the diminution of those spells and intervals which, in the longer day, so greatly mitigated the severity of the toil, have resulted in the workers, in most manufacturing processes, at each successive reduction of hours, turning out practically as much product as before. Though the working hours have been reduced, the number of men employed has not thereby been increased. The social and economic advantage of the shortening of the working day, which we think it difficult to exaggerate, are to be found in the increased opportunities which it affords for recreation and self-improvement, and the duties of family life and citizenship.

In one great industry, however, that of the railway service, together with the allied omnibus and tramway services, the working day of nearly all the workers is still greatly in excess of what is socially desirable. The excessive hours of duty of engine-drivers and firemen, guards and porters, and tramway and omnibus drivers and conductors still amount, we regret to say, to a public scandal. It is not in the public interest that men should be on duty for twelve, fourteen, and occasionally even eighteen hours out of the twenty-four; or that they should resume duty after less than ten or twelve hours' interval. The failure of voluntary effort to obtain a reduction of hours led Parliament in 1893 to pass into law the Regulation of Railways Act, under which the Board of Trade was empowered, on being satisfied that the hours of labour of any railway servant were excessive, to require the railway company to submit a new and improved schedule of working hours. Under this Act, which has been slowly enforced by the

Board of Trade, a certain improvement has taken place in the course of the fifteen years, especially in the hours of signalmen in busy signal-boxes, who now usually enjoy an eight hours' day.

The hours of most grades of railway operatives are, however, under nearly all the companies, still excessive. The Board of Trade Returns do not now reveal the exact hours of duty of the railway men; and no account is taken of any instances of less than a twelve hours' day, which often means, not forty-eight, but eighty-four hours per week. Yet in the one month of October, 1907, no fewer than 113,490 cases were reported by the railway companies themselves of men who were kept on duty for more than twelve hours in the day. Even deducting the time spent in travelling home (which is, however, rightly paid for as time given to the employer's service), there were no fewer than 56,180 cases in which men were kept on arduous and responsible duty for thirteen hours or more in a day—some of them for fifteen and even for eighteen hours. That such excessive hours of duty are not really required by the exigencies of railway administration, or by the accidents of fog or breakdown, provided proper arrangements are made, is demonstrated by the fact that the Great Central Railway Company, in the same month of October, 1907, was able to report that scarcely any of its passenger train workers, and a tiny percentage only of its goods train workers had ever once exceeded twelve hours' duty.

The evil is not confined to the railway service. The great majority of tramway conductors and drivers in the United Kingdom still apparently work, not for forty-eight but for seventy, and occasionally as much as eighty or ninety hours per week; and even those directly in the services of the Municipal Authorities administering their own tramways usually work for twelve hours a day. The day's duty, too, is often made more harassing by being "split" between two turns, with an interval between, so that from start to finish the man is away from home for as much as sixteen or eighteen hours. The work of the omnibus drivers and conductors usually extends to eighty and even ninety hours per week.

Here there is no question of a new principle being involved. For the past twenty years the Board of Trade has intervened, in order to secure, by means of the powers deliberately entrusted to it by Parliament, shorter hours of labour for adult men. We think that the time has come when this intervention should become systematic, covering the whole field of the railway, tramway and omnibus services; and that those responsible for the administration of these services should be required to submit schedules providing that no man's ordinary duty should exceed, if not forty-eight, at any rate, as a maximum, sixty hours in any one week, or should be so divided as to deprive him of proper intervals for sleep, recreation, and the duties of family life.

This reform is advocated and required for its own sake. But such a reduction of the hours of duty of these classes of operatives would have the further advantage of actually increasing the number of men required in an occupation where employment is exceptionally stable and regular. If undertaken concurrently with the suppression of Under-employment, it would undoubtedly enable the National Labour Exchange to find places, not necessarily for the particular men thereby displaced, but for a number of men equivalent to a large proportion of the surplus labour thereby revealed and identified.

(iii) *The Withdrawal from Industrial Wage-Earning of the Mothers of Young Children*

We have seen that, of the 50,000 widows and deserted wives whom the Poor Law Authorities of the United Kingdom elect to maintain on Outdoor Relief, mainly because of their 135,000 children under fourteen, the vast majority are driven to engage in industrial work, notwithstanding their receipt of Outdoor Relief, because this is deliberately fixed at a rate inadequate for their support. It has long been the policy of the Local Government Board for England and Wales, as well as of that for Scotland, that Outdoor Relief or Aliment, where given at all, should always be adequate for the proper support of the family. It is obvious that, where there are young children, it is suicidal for the nation to drive the mother to earn money in industry, at the expense of so neglecting the children that they grow up, if they grow up at all, stunted, weak and untrained, and almost inevitably destined to recruit the ranks of the Under-employed and of Pauperism. Yet this, as we have seen, is what is happening to-day.

An analogous evil is taking place among the majority of the Unemployed and the Under-employed. Because the man's earnings cease, or are small and uncertain, the wife is driven to earn money at the laundry, or by "charing," by taking work out to be done at home in all the "sweated" trades, or in the thousand and one ways in which hard-driven women toil for a few shillings a week in London and other great cities.

Under a reformed administration such as we propose, the mothers of young children will not be driven to neglect their home duties by engaging in industrial work. If the widow, or other mother to whom Home Aliment is allowed, is not actually unfit to have the charge of her children, the Registrar of Public Assistance will, in accordance with the policy hitherto pressed in vain on the boards of Guardians, peremptorily see to it that the amount allowed to her is sufficient for the proper support of the family group. The children will be, in effect, "boarded-out" with their own mother; and it will naturally be a condition of such Home Aliment that she devotes her time and energy to their upbringing, and not to the industrial work which, with its concomitant neglect of the children, is as uneconomical to the nation as it is distasteful to every good mother. Similarly, when we get the Under-employed men, by the operation of the National Labour Exchange, regularly getting five or six days' work a week; and the Unemployed getting either prompt work or the provision that we shall presently describe—this, too, so far as made for the support of wife and children, being conditional on the mother giving her time and energy to her own children—the wives will, at any rate, not be driven to neglect their homes by engaging in industrial work in order to keep the household from starvation. There is, as we have seen, a consensus of testimony that it is the chronic Under-employment of the men, not any craving of the women to leave their home duties, that causes the greater part of the industrial work of wives and mothers. Concurrently with the operations of the National Labour Exchange for the Suppression of Under-employment, we may accordingly count on a considerable voluntary withdrawal of wives and mothers from industrial wage-earning; leaving, therefore, directly or indirectly, in the various re-arrangements of industry that will be taking place, many vacancies to be filled by men.

It is not, of course, suggested that the particular work heretofore done by the boys and girls, by the railway and tramway workers and by the mothers of families should be given to the particular men displaced by "decasualisation." What would happen would be that each employer would so re-arrange his employment of labour as to get his work done as conveniently as before, taking on, as additional hands, the most efficient men that he could obtain. These would leave vacancies which would tend to be filled by men who would otherwise have furnished the daily recruitment of the Under-employed that now goes on; or by the younger, the more energetic of those already in that great army. It is in this way that the total number of those at present Under-employed would be reduced to the number who could get fairly continuous employment. It is not necessary to imagine that the most demoralised and deteriorated man among the casual dock labourers would be able to become either a railway signalman, a telegraph messenger, or a shirtmaker.

(c) The Regularization of the National Demand for Labour

We have given prominence to the Absorption of Labour by the three desirable reforms that we have just described, apart from the usual expansion of industry, because the nation cannot be expected to undertake even so great an improvement as the Suppression of Under-employment, without adequate assurance that its industry would not thereby be crippled at times by lack of hands, or that openings could be found for the Casual Labourers who would be no longer required as such. But apart from preventing the weary and demoralising aimless hunt for work, and diminishing the present "leakage" of time between jobs, the National Labour Exchange will not prevent Unemployment, whenever the total volume of the business of the nation, and even of all the nations of the world, falls off in those periodical depressions of trade of which we have, as yet, no complete explanation. In the years 1826, 1839–42, 1847, 1857–8, 1867–9, 1878–9, 1884–7, 1892–5, 1903–5, and 1908–9 such cyclical trade depressions of general character have sent up the percentage of Unemployed workmen to three, four and even five times as many as in the better years. The proportion of Trade Union members in Unions paying Out of Work Benefit (as to whom alone there are yet any statistics), who retain their situations, falls from the 97 or 98 per cent. characteristic of good years, to 92 or even to 89 per cent. This means that something like a couple of hundred thousand skilled workmen in the United Kingdom find themselves, through no fault of their own, without work or wages, and unable, whatever their character or their efforts, for a prolonged period to get employment. At the same time all the various grades of unskilled and general labourers find their employment more than usually intermittent, and all the evils of Under-employment and of the seasonal fluctuations are intensified. The National Labour Exchange will be more than ever useful in these years of depression in demonstrating and accurately measuring the surplus of applicants over situations. But it cannot fill vacancies that do not exist. What is needed in the lean years, which we must expect to recur once or twice in every decade, though we cannot yet accurately predict their dates—what is required as much for the skilled men as for the labourers—is some means of keeping the demand for their services at a uniform level.

We think that the Government can do a great deal to regularize the aggregate demand for labour as between one year and another, by a more deliberate arrangement of its orders for work of a capital nature.

> In round numbers [testified our most distinguished statistician[1]] it may be estimated that 200,000 or fewer able-bodied adult males are out of work from non-seasonal causes one year with another, and have no sufficient resources, and that this number fluctuates between 100,000 in the best year, to 300,000 in the worst. . . . The economic and industrial problem is to re-arrange the demand for labour to the extent indicated by these numbers. . . . There is consequently a need, in the worst year, for wages to the extent of £10,000,000 to bring it to a level with the best, so far as these men are concerned; for the whole of the last ten years £40,000,000 would have sufficed. The annual wages bill of the country is estimated at £700,000,000. . . . Is it possible for the Government and other public bodies who employ labour in large quantities to counteract the industrial ebb and flow of demand by inducing a complementary flow and ebb; by withdrawing part of their demand when industry needs all the labour it can get, and increasing the demand when industry is slack? To have a useful effect this alteration would have to be commensurable with the sum named above [£40,000,000 in ten years].

We think that there can be no doubt that, out of the 150 millions sterling annually expended by the National and Local Authorities on works and services, it would be possible to earmark at least four millions a year, as not to be undertaken equally, year by year, as a matter of course; but to be undertaken, out of loan, on a ten years' programme, at unequal annual rates, to the extent even of ten or fifteen millions in a single year, at those periods when the National Labour Exchange reported that the number of able-bodied applicants, for whom no places could be found anywhere within the United Kingdom, was rising above the normal level. When this report was made by the Minister responsible for the National Labour Exchange—whenever, for instance, the Percentage Unemployment Index as now calculated rose above four—the various Government Departments would recur to their ten years' programme of capital outlay; the Admiralty would put in hand a special battleship, and augment its stock of guns and projectiles; the War Office would give orders for some of the additional barracks that are always being needed, and would further replenish its multifarious stores; the Office of Works would get on more quickly with

[1] Mr. A. L. Bowley, Reader in Statistics, London School of Economics, University of London.

its perpetual task of erecting new post offices and other Government buildings, and of renewing the worn-out furniture; the Post Office would proceed at three or four times its accustomed rate with the extension of the telegraph and telephone to every village in the Kingdom; even the Stationery Office would get on two or three times as fast as usual with the printing of the volumes of the Historical Manuscripts Commission, and the publication of the national archives. But much more could be done. It is plain that many millions have to be spent in the next few decades in rebuilding the worst of the elementary schools, greatly adding to the number of the secondary schools, multiplying the technical institutes and training colleges, and doubling and trebling the accommodation and equipment of our fifteen universities. All this building and furnishing work, on which alone we might usefully spend the forty millions per decade that are in question, is not in fact, and need not be for efficiency, done in equal annual instalments. There might well be a ten year's programme of capital Grants-in-Aid of the local expenditure on educational buildings and equipment. It requires only the stimulus of these Grants-in-Aid, made at the periods when the Minister in charge of the National Labour Exchange reports that the Index Number of Unemployment has reached the Warning Point, for these works to be put in hand by the Local Education Authorities all over the Kingdom to exactly the extent that the situation demands. At the same time the Local Authorities could be incited to undertake their ordinary municipal undertakings of a capital nature, whether tramways or waterworks, public baths or electric power stations, artizans dwellings or Town Halls, drainage works or street improvements, to a greater extent in the years of slackness than in the years of good trade. This, indeed, they are already tending to do; and to the great development of municipal enterprise in this direction, setting up a small ebb and flow of its own to some extent counteracting the flow and ebb of private industry, we are inclined to attribute the fact that the cyclical depressions of the last twenty years have been less severely felt in the United Kingdom than were those of 1878–9 and of 1839–42.

What we are proposing is not that the Government or the Local Authorities should start Relief Works. It is, indeed, the very opposite of the Relief Works for the employment of the Unemployed to which we have been accustomed:

A scheme of this kind [continues Mr. Bowley] would differ from a crude form of Relief Works in four important ways: (a) The work concerned would

be started before Unemployment became acute, say, when the Percentage Unemployed Index reached 4 per cent. (*b*) There would be no artificial demand
made for labour, only an adjustment in time of the ordinary demand. (*c*) The
Unemployed, as a class, would not be attracted, *for the demand would come
through ordinary trade sources*, and before there was any considerable dearth
of employment. (*d*) The wages paid would be measured only by the work
done, being contracted out on the ordinary commercial basis.

Such a scheme need involve no expenditure, save of thought and of fore-
thought; is of the nature of prevention rather than of cure; and in proportion
as the scale of its operation was sufficient would remove the principal legitimate cause of dissatisfaction of the genuine workman with industrial conditions.

It is, in fact, vital to this plan of Regularizing the Demand for Labour
that there should be no attempt to employ the Unemployed as such. The
men and women taken on would be picked out for employment, in the
ordinary way, because they seemed the most efficient at their trades, and
the most suitable for the service required. They would be taken on exactly
in the numbers, and in the proportions between grade and grade, as was
required for the most economical and efficient execution of the work. It
would be quite immaterial whether they were momentarily out of a job or
whether they relinquished other employment to take up what seemed a
better engagement. In short, whether the works put in hand are done by
direct employment (as at Woolwich Arsenal, the Army Clothing Factory
or the Government Dockyards), or put out to contract (as with some
warships, most of the buildings and stores, and all the furniture and printing), it is essential that they should be done *in the ordinary way*, by the
departments or contractors ordinarily concerned, and by the best of the
available workmen and labourers usually engaged in just those kinds of
work, taken on because their services are wanted, and without any regard
to whether or not they are "out of a job". They would have absolutely no
connection or contact with whatever provisions were made for the men in
want or in destitution. It is not the function of these enterprises to relieve
distress—that will, as we have presently to describe, be otherwise provided
for—but to prevent, long before they fall into distress, the two or three
hundred thousand good and efficient workmen from becoming Unemployed.

The works that the National Government or the Local Authorities
might, in this way, put in hand in the lean years of the trade cycle, need
not, of course, be confined to the kinds that we have mentioned, or to
those to which we have hitherto been accustomed. It has, in particular,

been pressed upon us by many witnesses that considerable schemes of Afforestation might advantageously be undertaken by the Government; and one estate in the West of Scotland has actually been acquired for that purpose. Moreover, the attention called to the loss of land by erosion of the coast at various points has led to proposals for Coast Protection and Land Reclamation, for which it has been suggested that "the Unemployed" could be engaged. These latter proposals are under the consideration of a separate Royal Commission, whose Report will doubtless show to what extent and under what conditions any such works could usefully be undertaken. It is, however, clear that, to the extent that it may be profitable for the nation to engage in either Afforestation or Land Reclamation, these enterprises should be undertaken, not as Relief Works for the Unemployed, but as public enterprises of national importance, valuable in themselves, but, as we should suggest, executed out of loans on a ten years' programme; and, within the decade, made to vary in volume, in such a way, as far as may be practicable, as to ebb and flow in a manner complementary to the flow and ebb of private industry. Both Afforestation and Land Reclamation have the advantage that they can be done in intermittent spells, the progress made and the staff employed being capable of graduation according to need. But neither Afforestation nor Land Reclamation can be done by men quite unskilled in these occupations. In both cases experience shows that the work is of a kind that is within the compass, if there is to be economy and efficiency, of particular classes of labourers, and of these classes only. It is work for which they have been more or less trained, and akin to that on which they are usually employed. It is these men who ought to be engaged for the work, whenever, in accordance with the Report of the Minister responsible for the National Labour Exchange, it is decided to undertake it, or to augment the staff upon it— not a heterogeneous crowd of men drawn from those who have applied for relief in the large towns. The work of planting trees, for instance, can best be done by the agriculturists out of work; and *so long as any such can be hired by the local superintendent of the plantation*, there is no reason why townsmen should be brought down to do it. To start making embankments and sea-walls with distressed tailors and bricklayers and clerks, when there are navvies looking for employment, is as great a wrong to the navvies (and as uneconomical) as it would be to take on the navvies at the Army Clothing Factory or to put them to build a new school. Each work, in short, should be undertaken, not by any Distress Committee or

Unemployment Authority, but by the particular Department requiring it; and should be executed by the best and most efficient of the men accustomed to that kind of work who can, at the time, be found and hired in the ordinary way. Under these conditions we think that the Board of Agriculture might well take its share with the other public Departments in regularizing the national demand for labour; and might always therefore have on hand extensive works of Afforestation and Land Reclamation, to be done out of loan, and executed on a ten years' programme, for which it would take on men, or place contracts, to greater or smaller extent each year, according to the Reports of the National Labour Exchange as to the state of the Labour Market.

It is an advantage of this method of executing the public enterprises of capital value which the nation requires during each decade, that it is actually cheaper than doing them, year by year, without thought of the Labour Market. For (what is usually forgotten) capital is Unemployed and Under-employed to at least as great an extent as labour. It is in the lean years of the trade cycle, when business is depressed, that most capital is Unemployed, and the Bank rate is at its lowest. It is, accordingly, just in the years that Government works are needed in order to keep up the National Demand for Labour that Government can borrow at the cheapest rate. The influence of this fact upon municipal enterprise has, in the last two decades, been most marked. It has, however, as yet scarcely affected the ordering of the national expenditure of a capital nature; partly, perhaps, because the Treasury book-keeping excludes, deliberately, anything in the nature of a capital account, and insists on regarding all expenditure within the year as chargeable exclusively to the income of that year. Yet to concentrate in the lean years most of the whole capital outlay of each decennium is clearly to reduce the cost of the works. This consideration enables us also to see that the undertaking of such works by the Government in the lean years does not, as is sometimes thoughtlessly alleged, cause as much Unemployment as it prevents. On the contrary, it actually increases the total volume of industry for the decade as a whole. It is objected that if the Government spends a pound on employing labour, it has to take that same amount from the taxpayer, who thereupon has necessarily to reduce his own expenditure on labour. But this is to ignore the fact that, in the years of trade depression, if the Government (which need not be subject to depression) sets the machine in motion, it may use, not the proceeds of taxes, but Unemployed floating capital, and mills and plants that are temporarily Under-employed, to employ the labour. If the Government, in years of depression, when no one else is willing to embark in new undertakings, borrows some of the capital that is lying idle and unused—offered, in fact, in vain at 2 or 3 per cent. per annum—in order to augment its own enterprises, it interferes with no taxpayer's employment of his coachmen or gardeners. Even those from whom the capital has been borrowed increase rather than decrease their personal expenditure. Thus there is in this way a real addition to industry. That which would otherwise have been idle is set to productive work. There is here, not merely a Regularization of the National Demand for Labour, but actually an increase, taking the ten years as a whole, over what would otherwise have been demanded. The interest and sinking fund on the loans raised in the lean years has, of course, to be met, but the nation has by that time the advantage of the new work; and the charge falls, moreover, largely on the years of good trade and high profits, when a curb on private expenditure is, from the standpoint of Regularizing the National Demand for Labour, a positive advantage.

(d) The Provision for the Unemployed

However effective may be the National Labour Exchange in getting men into continuous employment; however great may prove the opportunities of absorption afforded by limiting the labour of boys and the excessive hours of men; and however successful the Government may be in regularizing the National Demand for Labour, we cannot hope to escape having to make provision for a residuum of men and women who find themselves in distress from want of work. The measures that we have suggested will, we believe, go far to prevent unemployment; and they will certainly reduce the evil to manageable dimensions. Nevertheless there will be, at the outset, a considerable, and, at all times, a certain number of Unemployed, for whom (especially as there will be no Poor Law, and no other public agency dealing with able-bodied men) definite public provision must be made.

(i) *Trade Union Insurance*

We are impressed with the advantages which Trade Union organization offers in dealing with Unemployment. Where a Trade Union is highly organized and efficiently conducted, it possesses, in its branch meetings and its "Vacant Book," machinery for making known opportunities for employment, and for seeing that every unemployed member gets as quickly as possible into a new situation, that cannot be surpassed. With this machinery it can safely offer to give "Out-of-Work Benefit," and thus enable its members effectively to insure against Unemployment. But the cost is heavy, and has been found, so far, beyond the means of any but a small minority of the better paid artizans. The difficulty, too, of getting prompt information of all vacancies, and of ensuring that unemployed members really apply for them, has stood in the way of the payment of Out-of-Work Benefit by the trades in which Discontinuous Employment is the rule.

We propose that the State should help and encourage workmen to insure against Unemployment. We think that the plan now spreading throughout the Continent of Europe, of affording to Trade Unions a subvention from public funds, in order to assist them to extend their own insurance against Unemployment, is one that should be adopted in this country. Under what is called the Ghent system—instituted at Ghent in 1901; since adopted in nearly all (27) the principal towns of Belgium; and now in course of imitation in France (since 1905), Norway (since 1906), Denmark (since 1907), Belgium (since 1907), several Dutch towns, and by St. Gall (since 1905), Basle (since 1908), and Strassburg (since 1906)—a contribution is annually made to the Trade Union equal to something like half of the amount actually paid in Out-of-Work Benefit to members unemployed in the last completed year, apart from any strike or other collective dispute. This contribution from public funds to Trade Unions giving Out-of-Work Benefit has, to quote the words of the Board of Trade, "undoubtedly, in certain cases at least, been accompanied by a great development of Unemployed Benefits on the part of Trade Unions anxious to participate." What was before financially out of the reach of many of the Trade Unions has now become possible to them, with the result that a greater proportion of the workmen are protected from falling into distress from want of employment. "Insurance," reports the Board of Trade, "is thus encouraged both by the Trade Union motive of protecting the Standard Rate, and by the prospect of a bonus from without. Pressure to join a Trade Union is—at a price—converted by the Municipality into pressure to insure against Unemployment." We think that a similar inducement should be offered in the United Kingdom with a view, not only to helping the Trade Unions that already insure, but also to inducing the million other Trade Unionists, not at present enjoying this protection, to subscribe for Out-of-Work Benefit.

A further encouragement might well be afforded to the provident workman. As a large proportion of the situations in the skilled trades are not of the nature of casual employment, but do, as a matter of fact, last for a month or more (or could easily be so arranged as to do so), it would not be compulsory for these to be filled through the National Labour Exchange. It might even be desirable to make arrangements also for the shorter engagements and "casual" jobs of the skilled mechanics in such trades to be independently organised. It might be well to provide that where a Trade Union, giving out-of-work benefit, desired (perhaps in conjunction with an organisation of employers) to manage its own register of men unemployed and situations vacant, it would be permitted to do so in close connection with the National Labour Exchange, which would transfer to it at once any application notified by its members, or by the employers in that trade who were in the habit of dealing with the Trade Union, and not fill any such situations unless and until the special office for the trade failed to do so. In this way there would be secured, to those workers in any trade who had been provident enough to insure themselves against Unemployment, practical preference for the employment thus offered in that trade. This conjunction of the Trade Union register of unemployed workmen with the National Labour Exchange is, as we have already mentioned, coming to be a common feature in Germany, and is also working well in the London Labour Exchanges.

We have had it suggested to us that insurance against Unemployment might be universally extended if it were made compulsory. The idea of throwing upon the employers and workmen of particular trades, and through them on the consumers, the burden of the irregularity of employment in these trades has many attractions, but we cannot see that the universal and compulsory union of all the employers and all the workmen in an insurance fund is, even with Government aid, either practicable or desirable. It is worth notice that no such scheme has found a place in the elaborate proposals of the German Government for workmen's insurance; or has been adopted elsewhere. We do not see how, without the aid afforded by Trade Union organization, a Compulsory Insurance scheme could possibly be worked in such a way as both to provide for the "bad risks"—the men who, for one reason or another, are constantly falling into Unemployment—and yet to take care that these men embrace every opportunity of getting into situations. Moreover, these "bad risks" are, even under the sharp superintendence of a Trade Union, always contriving to draw, each year, their maximum Out-of-Work Pay, and thus to inflict a considerable loss on the insurance funds. The same men are continually "running out of benefit," and becoming ineligible for Out-of-Work Pay, long before they get into employment again; and hence requiring some other provision than any scheme of insurance can make. Moreover, the Trade Union can, and constantly does, exclude from its membership men who have not attained a certain degree of skill, or of regularity of conduct; exactly as a Friendly Society excludes men suffering from syphilis or phthisis, or any mortal disease. Even then insurance is beyond the reach of large sections of Trade Unionists. It would require a beneficent revolution to be effected both in the scale of remuneration and in the continuity of employment of the Casual Labourers of the great cities, and we think also, among the platers' helpers and other ship-yard labourers, and the builders' labourers, before their periods of recurrent Unemployment could be provided for by any insurance premium within their means, even with Government help. Seeing that these ill-paid labourers constitute nearly one-half of all the persons employed in their respective industries, we doubt whether any system of compulsory insurance, administered by a Government Department, could possibly provide for their great needs.

The case may be different if Compulsory Insurance is applied only to particular sections of workers or to certain specified industries, under carefully considered conditions. Any such plan, applicable only to a portion of the industrial field, has the drawback of not solving the problem of providing for the bulk of those in distress from Unemployment; for it would, of course, be the Casual Labourers, and generally the great army of the Under-employed, who would be omitted; and these form, as we have seen, the bulk of the applicants to the Distress Committees. Hence a plan of Compulsory Insurance for some classes of skilled artisans, or for the more regularly employed workers generally, could not be substituted, either for the existing provision under the Unemployed Workmen Act, or for any improvement on it. It could, at best, be only an adjunct to a comprehensive scheme of dealing with Unemployment. But such a scheme of Compulsory Insurance, even if partial, may be worth considering for its own sake. If the Government and the employers were financially interested in it, they would both have a motive, even if somewhat indirect and remote, for reducing Unemployment to a minimum. It seems to us clear, however, that two conditions would be essential. No such scheme could possibly be worked without a national organisation in the nature of a Labour Exchange, *to which all available vacancies were reported*; and to which all insured workmen out of Employment were required to apply for situations. Without machinery of this sort, it would never be possible for the administrators of the Insurance Fund to be sure that the workman claiming benefit was really unable to obtain a situation. The "bad risks" would, in any case, constitute a serious drain on the Fund; and without some means of ensuring that definite situations were offered to them, these "industrial malingerers" would eat it up altogether. In short, resort to the National Labour Exchange would have to be made legally compulsory, in the insured industries, both upon all employers having vacancies to fill, and upon all workers claiming Unemployed Benefit. The second essential condition would be some definition of the terms upon which a workman could be required to accept a situation offered to him, under a penalty of being refused the Unemployed Benefit towards which he had contributed. It is clear that an engineer or a carpenter could only be expected and required to accept a situation in his own trade, and upon the wages, hours and other conditions customary in the locality. For the Government Insurance Fund to refuse to pay the engineer or the carpenter the Unemployed Benefit towards which these workmen had contributed, merely because they had refused to accept situations in "unfair" establishments, at wages below the recognised Standard Rate, or for hours or under other conditions of labour contrary to the customarily recognised Common Rules of the industry, would be to provoke a storm of indignation; and, indeed, to deal a mortal blow at Trade Unionism itself. It is plain that the Unemployed Benefit could not be refused to a workman merely because he declined to accept a situation under unreasonable conditions. The conditions which a Government Insurance Fund would declare to be reasonable could, nowadays, hardly be other than what are commonly known as "Trade Union conditions"; namely, the rates of pay, hours of labour, methods of remuneration, and other conditions of employment which have been agreed to, for each locality, by the associations of employers and employed; and which, in the absence of such agreement, are, in practice, obtained by the members of the Trade Unions concerned. Thus, so far as the operations of the Government Insurance Fund extended, these so-called "Trade Union conditions" would, in effect, be compulsorily enforced on all establishments. Without these two essential conditions, a Compulsory Insurance scheme, even if limited to carefully selected sections of the wage-earners, would in our opinion, be financially impracticable, and inimical to Trade Unionism. In view of the difficulties which so great an extension of the principle of compulsion would present, we prefer to recommend the simpler plan, already successfully put in practice in other countries, which involves no compulsion at all; namely that of a subvention to Trade Unions providing Unemployed Benefit, such as we have already described.

(ii) *Maintenance under Training*

We have to face the fact that, make what arrangements we will, there will be, at all times and under any organisation of society, a residuum of men who will be found in distress from want of employment. That residuum will be greater or smaller in proportion to the appropriateness and the completeness of the organisation of the National Labour Exchange, the Suppression of Under-employment, the "dovetailing" of seasonal occupations, the measures taken for the Absorption of the Surplus, the Regularization of the National Demand for Labour and the development of Trade Union Insurance. It will, moreover, always wax and wane according to the changing circumstances of particular industries. But great or small, though the individuals will come and go, a residuum will always be there.

We may, however, confidently anticipate that the permanent residuum of men in distress from want of employment will differ very considerably, both in numbers and in composition, from the crowds that now embarrass the Distress Committees at every season of depression. The great bulk of these crowds—at least, one-half of the whole—consists at present of the Casual Labourers, and other members of the chronically Under-employed class; the suppression of which, as a class, is (as we have shown) not only possible but a necessary condition of any improvement whatsoever. When the National Labour Exchange has got thoroughly to work, and has "dovetailed" the jobs so as to provide practical continuity of employment; and when the surplus thereupon revealed and identified has been to a large extent absorbed by the measures that we have described, there is no reason to suppose that this part of the industrial army will furnish a larger contingent of persons in distress through Unemployment than other parts enjoying no higher remuneration do at present.

Another important element is to-day contributed by the building trades and other seasonal industries; and these, as we have seen, can be provided for, the better-paid sections by an extension of Trade Union Insurance and the labourers, to a large, and probably a steadily increasing, extent, by the operations of the National Labour Exchange in "dovetailing" employment as between trades having different seasons of slackness. Even the men now out of work through the great cyclical fluctuations of the nation's industry can, as we have shown, be to a great extent provided for by the measures to be taken for the Regularization of the National Demand for Labour, and by the great extension of Trade Union Insurance that this Regularization, the work of the National Labour Exchange, and a government subvention will have made possible. Thus, instead of whole sections and whole classes coming on our hands at every season of stress, what we shall have to deal with will be individuals of all classes.

The individual members of the permanent residuum of men in distress from Unemployment will be of the most heterogenous kinds and descriptions. There will be the man from Class I, who has fallen out of a permanent situation; who is uninsured because there was no Trade Union to which he could belong; whose savings have been exhausted by illness or other family misfortune; who bears a good character, but for whom the National Labour Exchange fails to find a place—perhaps because of his advancing years, or the lack of adaptability which is the result of his long and faithful service in one narrow groove. There will be the man from Class II, whose discontinuous employment has suddenly become so intermittent that nowhere in the United Kingdom can the National Labour Exchange find him a job; whose Unemployment is so prolonged that he "runs out of benefit" and exhausts his savings. Both these men may be suffering, probably unconsciously to themselves, from a change of process or of industrial organization, which is steadily and permanently enabling their particular service to be partly dispensed with—a case which is to-day that of various grades of boot and shoe operatives, that of the carpenters and bricklayers, and that of grooms and stablemen. And from all grades and sections of industry there will dribble down—we may hope, when chronic Under-employment and untrained Boy Labour are suppressed, to a smaller extent than at present—individuals of defective will, intelligence or training; of dissolute habits or irregularities of character; or of chronically weak physical health; together with all sorts of industrial "misfits," and, intermingled among them all, the constitutionally vagabond or "work-shy." It is indispensable, alike for social health, and for the success of all the other measures taken to deal with the Able-bodied, that the heterogeneous assortment of "Unemployed," whose existence we have been unable to prevent, should be definitely and adequately provided for. There must be no idea of deterring people from applying. It is, in fact, as essential for industrial well-being that every person in distress from want of employment should receive at once the Public Assistance appropriate to his need, as it is to Public Health that no sick person should go unprovided with medical attendance.

It will, we think, be clear that, for this heterogeneous assortment of individuals, there can be no question of "making work" or providing productive employment at wages. The steps taken by the Government for the Regularisation of the National Demand for Labour and the Absorption of the Surplus will, in fact, have already found employment, at their own trades, and at the Standard Rates of wages, for the men for whom any such work can be provided. To deliberately "make work" for the odds and ends of Unemployed tailors, jewellers, brickmakers, ironmoulders, clerks, handymen and hawkers—for each of them in his own trade, in his own town, at his own Standard Rate of Wages—is not only administratively impossible, but would actually have the effect of ousting from employment some other men of these trades. For, apart from the personal factor, the reason why Unemployment has fallen upon men of these particular trades, rather than upon others, is that the consumers' demand for their particular services, or for the products of their labour, happens to have temporarily or permanently diminished, relatively to the consumers' demand for other services or products. To increase the supply of waistcoats, jewellry, bricks and iron-mouldings, merely in order to give employment in trades which are already suffering from surplus stocks, would be a suicidal proceeding. As a matter of fact, the costliness and the impracticability of providing work "at his own trade" for each of the Unemployed Workmen has saved us from the dilemma. What is actually demanded, and what is occasionally provided in response to this demand, is "work which all can perform."

But it is a fallacy to assume that there is such a thing as work, in the abstract, or of an undifferentiated character. The work that is of any use to the world is always the doing of some specific service, which, however humble and nominally "unskilled," always needs a certain amount of training, experience, and even skill to perform efficiently. A favourite idea is to put the men to cultivate the land. But agriculture is, of course, a highly skilled and very hazardous trade. Even digging—which, however well done, produces no value unless directed by very expert knowledge— requires training to do it effectively, whilst the planting of trees, or the making of a road, an embankment or a sea-wall turns out, on experiment, to be a skilled occupation, of which the raw hand makes a sad botch. Repeated experience has proved, in fact, that there is no productive enterprise, even of the simplest character, which can be undertaken with-out actual loss by a mixed assortment of individuals of different grades of skill, of all sorts of antecedents, and, for the most part, without experience of the particular kind of work they are called upon to perform. In some respects, indeed, the more superior the men and the more specialized their former callings, the more wholly incompetent they prove at the "common work" which alone can be provided for them. Under these circumstances the men not only fail to earn their keep, which would under any form of provision have to be given them; in nearly every case they fail to produce even the cost of the necessary expert direction and super-vision, which is actual out of pocket expense to the community. Nor is it ever possible to arrive at any satisfactory standard of wages. The hetero-geneous crowd of men of different antecedents clearly cannot be paid the various Standard Rates to which they have severally been accustomed. If it is determined to pay them the usual Standard Rate for the common work to which they have been put, and to pay them in accordance with their achievements, this results in their earning a shilling or two a day; or less than they can exist on. But the costliness of this method of providing for the Unemployed, and the difficulty of finding any satisfactory scale of remuneration, do not, in our opinion, constitute the gravest objections to Relief Works. The first question, to our mind, is, how does this method of provision affect the men subjected to it? Does it make them more fit and better qualified to regain their places in the industrial world, or less fit and worse qualified? It is clear, of course, that adequate maintenance, with any sort of occupation, is better for a workman than starvation and idleness. But no one who has ever watched Relief Works, in any form, or under any administration, can be satisfied with the effect of this kind of provision on the men to whom it is given. The work itself is monotonous and uneducational in character, even when it is not positively detrimental to particular forms of manual skill. With a heterogeneous gang of men, taken on, not because they are used to the work, and can be expected to perform it up to any normal standard of speed or efficiency, but merely because they are in distress from Unemployment, it is invariably found impracticable to discover and to exact from every man the full amount of effort of which he is capable. Inevitably, even if unconsciously, the pace is set for all by the slowest, the least efficient, and often the least willing of the gang. This has a grave effect on the whole gang. Thus the men put on Relief Works are in no way improving themselves for resuming work at their own trades; they are not being trained to other occupations so that they might find work in new directions; and they are steadily being more and more habituated to work at a low standard of speed, a low standard of effort, and a low standard of efficiency, at an occupation which is already chronically over-supplied with workers. For the "common work" thus provided for the heterogeneous assortment of men from all trades always turns out to be the appropriate work of the navvy and "ground labourer." Why is it that the advocates of work for the "Unemployed" of all trades never see anything objectionable in depriving the navvy of some of the jobs on which he would otherwise have been employed? Why, when it is sought to set the Unemployed to work, and when it is discovered that this involves training of some sort, should we always exercise them and train them in the trade of the navvy, and thereby increase the number of competitors of the existing navvies? The position is made the more ridiculous in that it has been abundantly demonstrated that it is just this kind of mere muscular effort and physical strength for which there is, in the industrial world of to-day, a steadily diminishing demand. It is the man who pushes, who lifts, who carries, who drags, who is finding more and more of his employment superseded by the hoist and the pulley, by the grain elevator and the travelling crane, by the "grab" and the "Scotchman" and the "iron man"—in short, by steam or electrically driven machinery of one kind or another.

But Relief Works for the Unemployed represent only a counsel of despair, in a community knowing no better alternative. The reduction in the numbers of those in distress from Unemployment, brought about by the various preventive measures that we have described, will enable the community to deal with the individuals in distress, not by such "wholesale" methods as Relief Works, but, personally, one by one, after careful consideration of each case, by the treatment best calculated to enable him to resume productive employment.

The first requisite is that all persons in distress from Unemployment should be provided with maintenance, so that they and their families may

be kept in health and strength, and be prevented from the rapid deterioration to which they would otherwise be subjected. But this maintenance
must be merely preliminary to attempting to solve the particular "human
problem" that each man presents. What has to be discovered is why these
particular individuals, out of the 12,000,000 whom employers have willingly engaged, have been left stranded and unemployed; and how their
industrial efficiency can be increased so as to enable them to earn a livelihood. The first thing to be done is to "test" them, using the word in its
proper sense, not of seeking how to induce them to take themselves off
our hands, but of probing their capacity so as to find out the points at
which they are weak, and can be strengthened, and the faculties latent in
them which might be developed. No one can have watched the crowd of
applicants to a Distress Committee—the scores of narrow-chested men
under thirty, the emaciated and flabby men of all ages, the nerveless and
rheumatic men, the men with varicose veins or untreated hernia—without
realising how sadly "out of condition" are nearly all these "Unemployed,"
and how enormously their working power would be improved by mere
medical advice, hygienic regimen, and physical training. We have to test
their eyesight, their colour vision, their hearing, their hearts, their muscular power, the steadiness of their hands, in order to find out what particular exercises or remedies will increase their capacity. Nor must we stop
at mere physical improvement. In the rough and tumble of industrial
life, with its monotonous toil in narrow grooves, the adult workman tends
to leave dormant all but the one faculty required for his job. The man
who has dropped out of a situation which he has held for ten or twenty
years would probably have been equally efficient in any one of half a
dozen other ways, if he had not been led to adapt himself to the particular
line required by his employer. Now that he has lost that situation, and
no similar one can be found for him, what has to be done is to see which
of his undeveloped or dormant faculties can be stimulated and exercised.
But there are moral invalids as well as physical ones. The men who have
lost situations through irregularity of conduct of one kind or another
plainly need training in character, under the beneficent influence of continuous order and discipline. In short, whatever may have been the
economic or industrial cause that has necessitated a certain number of
the nation's workers standing idle—and this cause may often be no fault
of the workers themselves—it is inevitable that the *particular individuals*
who, in that crisis, find themselves the rejected of all employers should be

capable of improvement, either physical or mental, or in most cases both. Which of us, indeed, is *not* capable of improvement by careful testing and training? We can clearly best utilise the period of enforced Unemployment by placing these men in training, so that, when the National Labour Exchange eventually finds openings for them, they may return to work in better health, of more regular habits, and with awakened faculties of body and mind. As has been well said, "The capacity of the industrial system to absorb fresh labour is no doubt far from exhausted, but this capacity depends entirely upon the labour being of a sort to be absorbed, that is to say, being suited or able to become suited to the particular developments of the time."

The National Authority dealing with the Able-bodied requires, therefore, what we might almost term a Human Sorting House, where each man's faculties would be tested to see what could be made of him; and a series of Training Establishments, to one or other of which the heterogeneous residuum of Unemployed would be assigned. These Training Establishments might, some of them, be in the man's own town, so that he need not be separated from his home; though it would be a condition that he should attend with absolute regularity from morning to night. For the young unmarried man, it would probably be best to send him at once to a residential settlement in the country, where he would be free from the distractions of town life. But whether in town or country, it is essential to successful treatment that the training should take up the man's entire day. If he is not at a residential Colony, he will be required to be in attendance at 6 a.m., as he would be if he were in employment; and as the day's training will need to be diversified, and must include organised recreation of various kinds, his obligatory attendance will usually be prolonged until eight or nine at night. This is not the place for any detailed plans of the curriculum and the regimen of these Training Establishments; which would, indeed, have to be worked out for men of different ages, different weaknesses, and different needs. But we can foresee that carefully graduated physical exercises will play a large part; that men of definite trades can be given opportunities for improving their skill and enlarging the range of their capacity in those trades; that practically all men can usefully be taught mechanical drawing, and working to plan and to scale; that they can all usefully improve their mental arithmetic and their power of keeping accounts; that all men nowadays need to know the use of the common tools and how to run the simpler machines; that many men have a desire, at least, to try their hands at the cultivation of the land, and these might well be put to the farm and garden work; and, seeing that all men would be the better for the seaman's knowledge of how to cook, how to clean, and how to mend and wash, there is every reason why all the men should take their share of the necessary work of the establishment.

We think that the proposal of Maintenance under Training avoids the grave defects that characterise the devices of the Poor Law and the "Employment Relief" of the Distress Committees. It is, to say the least, quite as "productive" to the community, as the occupations afforded by the General Mixed Workhouse, or the Able-bodied Test Workhouse, or as any "work at wages" to which the "Unemployed" are now being set by the Local Authorities; whilst it is far more "productive" than these to the man himself. Moreover, it escapes the demoralising element of pretence that the men are earning their own livelihood and have therefore the right to receive wages and to spend them as they choose. It avoids the economic dilemma of how to "set to work" the Unemployed in productive labour without taking away other men's jobs. And it escapes the administrative difficulty of how to keep up the Standard Wage and work the Normal Day without lowering the standard of effort and attracting men from low-paid employment. It avoids even the industrial disadvantage of habituating men to kinds of effort—general labouring, or "ground work," stone-breaking or hand-grinding—of which there is already a large surplus on the market. There is nothing degrading or depressing in physical, mental and technical training; there is in it, indeed, a strong element of stimulus and hope, because it will fit the men to take better situations than they could without it. On the other hand, it is not agreeable to the "average sensual man" to surrender himself continuously to an ordered round of continuous training of any sort under hygienic conditions, with every faculty kept alert by varied stimuli, so as to produce the highest state of physical and mental efficiency of which he is capable. In short, Maintenance under Training, whilst more "eligible" in every sense than starvation in idleness, is less agreeable than the ordinary industrial employment at wages, in one's own occupation, with freedom to spend or mis-spend one's wages and one's leisure as is desired. Thus, the individuals whom distress from Unemployment throws upon our hands will, by this Maintenance under Training, be restored to full health and vigour and otherwise improved, instead of, as at present, being deteriorated. On the other hand we shall, as is essential, leave in full force, not only the incentive to take

employment and to keep it, but also the incentive to insure against Unemployment by joining an existing Trade Union, or forming one if none
actually exists.

In working out the details of this scheme of Maintenance under Training
with men of practical experience in connection with the treatment of the
Able-bodied and the Unemployed, we have come face to face with four
difficulties which will be urged as objections.

It is clear that Maintenance under Training will involve a greater expenditure per head than maintenance without training. But the grant of
mere maintenance—that is, unconditional Outdoor Relief—is plainly
impossible; and experience shows that both Relief Works and Workhouses are, as a matter of fact, with all the necessary plant and administrative expenses, themselves extremely costly, as well as extremely demoralising. It may, however, be admitted that the State could hardly undertake
to provide very elaborate forms of training for hundreds of thousands of
men. There can be no successful treatment of the Able-bodied unless they
are dealt with *individually*, man by man. We agree with General Booth
when he declares that he placed "Individual Reformation in the front in all
operations which have for their object the betterment of society. Any
effort at social reform that does not provide facilities for the regeneration
of the individual is, in my opinion, foredoomed to failure." Under the
proposals that we are making the numbers of the Unemployed will be
greatly reduced; and the ultimate residuum that must be maintained ought
not be be so numerous as to transcend our powers. And the training must
be adapted to circumstances. When the numbers in any one place become
large it may not be possible to afford much beyond the simpler forms of
physical training and elementary instruction, which can be inexpensively
provided for men in mass. The more specialized treatment must necessarily be adapted to individuals, or small groups of similar individuals,
which a National Authority could collect in particular establishments each
with its own special variety of training. There is no reason why these
should be more expensive per head than the Hollesley Bay Farm Colony.
It is, indeed, inherent in any form of provision which aims at improving
the quality of the material to be dealt with that some expense should be
involved. The question is whether there is any alternative really cheaper
to the nation.

It is objected that Maintenance under Training, although distasteful to
the average workman, will be found attractive to some, at any rate, of the

men; and that these will be constantly falling out of employment in order to resort to it. The Superintendent of every institution learns to recognise the docile man, with no vices and no initiative, who is inertly content with the day's routine, and who asks nothing better than to be allowed to go on for ever. Such men, at present, linger on indefinitely at Relief Works, or in the Labour Yard; and even in the Workhouse. It is, however, just one of the advantages of training, as it is of the skilled medical treatment of the sick in hospital, that it can be indefinitely adjusted so as to apply to each patient the exact stimulus required to call out his faculties. With what we may call the "industrial malingerer" there will be other remedies. With the co-operation of the National Labour Exchange he can be given successive chances of employment; and, after a certain number of trials, his repeated return will be a cause for his judicial commitment to a Detention Colony.

An entirely opposite objection is urged by others, namely, that Maintenance under Training will be so repellent to those in distress from Unemployment that they will put up with any hardship rather than submit to it. Many men are unconscious of personal defect, or shortcoming, or weakness of body or mind; and will be unable to understand why they should go into training. We all shrink instinctively from a searching medical examination; and we should shrink still the more from a testing of all our faculties. But, as a matter of fact, the difficulty is an imaginary one. Whatever may be our objection to medical and other examinations, this is not found, in any grade of life, to stand in the way of applying for what we want, whether it be an appointment in the Army, Navy, or Civil Service, or admission to the police force or the railway service. No man in distress, or whose family is suffering distress, will let a medical examination stand between him and adequate provision. And the medical examination and testing of faculties convinces every man of his need of training, in one respect or another, whilst the training itself soon brings home to him that he is susceptible of improvement. Yet we need force no man to come in, nor detain any unwilling subject. He has always the alternative of trying to earn his own living outside. The National Labour Exchange will, at any time, do its best to help him to get a place. So long as he commits no crime, and neglects none of his social obligations—so long as he does not fail to get lodging, food and clothing for himself and his family—so long as his children are not found lacking medical attendance when ill, or underfed at school—so long, indeed, as neither he nor his family ask or require any form of Public Assistance, he will be free to live as he likes. But directly any of these things happen, it will be a condition that the husband and the father, if certified as Able-bodied, shall be in attendance at the Training Establishment to which he is assigned. If he is recalcitrant, he will be judicially committed to a Detention Colony.

The final objection is that "the Unemployed" are not worth training; that they are, in effect, Unemployable, and incapable of being improved. We do not think that any instructed person can seriously assert that there are not, among those in distress from Unemployment, many men— probably, at present, many thousands of men—who are in every way eligible and suitable for training of one sort or another. But if there are none such, the first step is to ascertain and certify the defectiveness of the persons in distress in order that they may be segregated in appropriate institutions. We do nothing to test and discover which are really the Un-employable by offering tasks of work to halfstarved crowds demoralised by periods of Unemployment. The men in distress present every possible variety; and the preliminary examination and testing of faculties, along with subsequent observation under training, will be always weeding out the definitely Unemployable. It will be the rule that no man is to be re-tained in any Training Establishment unless it is believed that he can be made fit, at some time or another, to resume his place in industrial employ-ment. There will be room for experiment with different kinds of training, in different establishments, as well as in different opportunities of wage-earning. But there will inevitably be some hopeless cases. There will be men permanently incapacitated by physical defects, which cannot be cured, and which do not permit of their earning a living wage at any occupation whatsoever. Such men will, like those who fall ill during train-ing, have to be remitted to the Local Health Authority, where they will be appropriately provided for as we have described (Part I, Ch. V and VII). There will be men found to be so mentally defective—whether epileptic, feeble-minded, or chronically inebriate—as to be incapable of continuing in wage-earning occupation. These will be handed over to the Local Authority for the Mentally Defective (Part I, Ch. VI). There will be other men, adjudged capable in body and mind of earning a liveli-hood, but persistently neglecting or refusing to do so—whether as what we now know as Professional Vagrants, or as merely "work shy" and recalcitrant to discipline. These men will remain on the hands of the National Authority dealing with the Able-bodied; but they will leave the free Training Establishments and be judicially committed to a Detention Training Colony.

What is essential to the success of these Training Establishments is, not only the power of exclusion of those found to be mentally or physically hopeless, but also the stimulus of Hope. Every man in the establishment, staff as well as patients, must be always conscious that men enter with the prospect of improving their condition, and that, in fact, men are, after training, constantly passing out to better positions. It is therefore vital to these establishments to have the means of placing out the men whom they have found to be fit, or have made fit. This is one reason why the Training Establishments must be in the closest possible connection with the National Labour Exchange, and therefore under the same authority. They will receive constant advices from the National Labour Exchange as to what kinds of training are most in demand. They will be constantly passing individuals back to the National Labour Exchange, at this point or that, when there is any prospect of places being found for them. And when there is any great accumulation of men in the Training Establishments, who are, or who have been rendered, fit for employment, but for whom employment, owing to the depression in trade, cannot be found, it will be a case for representation to the other Departments of the Government that the time has come for putting into operation the action already described for Regularizing the National Demand for Labour.

There is, however, one special direction in the United Kingdom in which the Training Establishments will, we believe, constantly be able to place out some of their best men. Experience shows that a certain number of the best of the Unemployed—especially among our Class I—have a desire for country life; and can be successfully established on Small Holdings. The Board of Agriculture should, we think, be able to afford opportunities—possibly in connection with its works of Land Reclamation—for these selected men to settle on the land.

Finally, there is emigration to other parts of the British Empire, where labour of various kinds is in greater demand than in these islands. For men who desire to try their fortunes in Canada or South Africa, Australia or New Zealand, residence at one or other of the Training Establishments will afford, not only useful training, but also a valuable opportunity for proving whether the would-be emigrant has such qualities and capacities as warrant the belief that he can make a successful start in a new country.

There remains the Detention Colony, the existence of which, as a place to be avoided, is an indispensable element in any scheme of dealing with the Able-bodied. The Detention Colony, though it will be entered only upon commitment by a judicial authority, will not be a prison, or a convict settlement. It is essential that the men committed to it should not be regarded as criminals. For this reason it should not be administered by the Prison Commissioners, or be under the Secretary of State for the Home Department. It should remain, in fact, as merely one among the Training Establishments, under the Minister dealing with the organisation of the National Labour Market. The Detention Colony will be, in fact, merely a Training Establishment of a peculiar kind, which has necessarily to have the characteristic of compulsory detention. Its inmates are sent there to be treated for, and if possible cured of, a morbid state of mind, which makes them incapable of filling a useful place in the industrial world. The general lines of the appropriate regimen have been laid down by various experimental colonies in Switzerland and Germany, Holland and Belgium; but there is much yet to be done to adapt them for this country, and to work them out in detail. Enforced regularity of life, and continuous work, of a stimulating and not monotonous kind; plain food, with opportunities of earning small luxuries by good conduct and output of work; restriction of personal liberty; and power to those in charge to allow return to one of the ordinary Training Establishments on probation, as soon as ever it is believed that reformation has been effected—these features sufficiently indicate the outlines of the experiment. Repeated recalcitrance, and, of course, any assault on the persons in charge, would be criminal offences, leading to sentences of penal servitude in a convict settlement.

(E) THE MINISTRY OF LABOUR

It is, we think, clear that the whole of the elaborate organization that we have outlined for dealing with the various sections of the necessitous and destitute Able-bodied and of the persons in distress from want of employment must be the work, not of Local Authorities, having jurisdiction only over limited areas, but of a Department of the National Government. Whether we consider the fifty to eighty thousand Vagrants perpetually drifting, at the expense, one way or another, of the rest of the community, from North to South and from South to North, or the large Stagnant Pools of Under-employed Labour which make up so much of waterside Boroughs such as West Ham, it is plain that the problem, by its very nature, transcends the powers of even the ablest Local Governing

Body. The remedies are not within its scope. The network of Labour Exchanges must, it is obvious, be free to act, and to find situations for the Unemployed and to select men for employers, quite irrespective of their places of residence—or of business. The areas of the various Local Authorities, whether urban or rural, are usually very far from coincident with the geographical aggregations of manufactures and commerce. The Metropolitan area for business purposes already greatly transcends that of the Administrative County of London; and its Labour Market cannot be organised without including East Ham and West Ham, Walthamstow and Tottenham, Willesden and Ealing, Richmond and Croydon—not to speak of Chelmsford and Luton, Reading and Guildford, Erith and Tilbury. We could not possibly have independently governed Labour Exchanges for Manchester, Salford, Prestwich, Stockport, Hyde and Oldham; or for Liverpool, Birkenhead and Bootle; or for all the separate Counties and Boroughs that make up the busy and closely interlaced industrial districts of the Lower Clyde, Tyneside, the West Riding and the Black Country respectively. The various local branches of the Labour Exchange must be free, it is clear, to fill situations and to place men where they can, anywhere in the Kingdom, without the clogging influences of local preferences for finding work for local men, or "keeping all our herring in our own sea-maws." Moreover, it is essential that the Labour Exchange should work in the closest co-operation with the Associations of Employers and the Trade Unions; and these are organized without any regard for municipal or county boundaries, and are, indeed, to a great extent, national in scope. Any scheme of Government aid to Trade Union Insurance, dealing as it would with the great national trade societies, must clearly be national in its administration. Similarly, the Training Establishments, at which the ultimate residuum of Unemployed must be maintained whilst they are being tested and improved, are plainly beyond the capacity of the Local Authorities. Some kinds, like the Detention Colonies, will be few in number; possibly only one or two for each of the three Kingdoms. Of the others, the more highly specialized, providing particular kinds of training, or dealing with men in particular states of body or mind, must, like specialized hospitals, draw their patients from all over the country. Moreover, all these institutions must be in close and easy communication with each other, so that men can be transferred without any question of finance, from one to the other, being freely passed from grade to grade, and from training to training, according to their condition and their need. They must always be, too, in intimate touch with all the branches of the National Labour Exchange, acting constantly in conformity with its Reports as to the state of the Labour Market and its changing needs. But beyond all considerations of administrative efficiency of the Labour Exchange, Trade Union Insurance, and the Training Establishments, it seems to us essential to success that we should link up these measures of provision with the measures of prevention that are no less required for the absorption of the surplus and the mitigation of the recurrent fluctuations of Trade. The legislative restriction of Boy Labour and the legislative reduction of the hours of the railway and tramway servants need to be put into operation in concert with the operations of the Labour Exchange. It there is to be any Regularization of the National Demand for Labour, by means of a Ten Year's Programme of Government Works, to be started by the various Departments in the years of depression, it is clear that this action can safely be taken only on the advice of another Department of the Government. If the provision for the Unemployed were in the hands of the Local Authorities, each of them would be pressing the National Government to start the supplementary Government Works whenever its own local industry happened to be depressed, irrespective of the state of the Labour Market in the nation as a whole; and to start them, too, within its own area, for the convenience of its own Unemployed, irrespective of the national needs. The result would inevitably be that, in order to prevent the measure degenerating into the mere opening of local relief works, the Government would tend to disregard the representations altogether. For all these reasons, it is imperative, in spite of the difficulty of inducing the National Government to undertake an extensive new service, that the Local Authorities, whom we are already sufficiently burdening, should insist on being relieved, once and for all, of all duties relating to the Able-bodied and the Unemployed.

(i) *The Minister for Labour*

We propose that, in order to ensure complete ministerial responsibility, and the full and continuous control of Parliament over so important a branch of industrial organisation, the whole work should be entrusted to a Minister for Labour, who would naturally be a member of the House of Commons and included in the Cabinet. His Department would embrace three entirely new administrative services, namely, the National Labour Exchange, the Trade Insurance Division, and the Maintenance and Training Division. To these three Divisions, we should be disposed to add, by transfer, three existing branches of other Government Departments; so that the Ministry of Labour would consist of six separate and distinct Divisions, each under its own Assistant Secretary. We should transfer, in this way, to form a new Industrial Regulation Division, all the administration of the laws relating to hours, wages and conditions of employment, including the Factories and Workshops Acts, the Shop Hours and Truck Acts, and the Mines Regulation Acts, from the Home Office; and the Regulation of Railways Act, 1893, from the Board of Trade. The Labour Department of the Board of Trade would form the nucleus of a new Statistical Division, and the Emigrants' Information Office under the Secretary of State for the Colonies the nucleus of a new Emigration and Immigration Division.

It has been suggested that the Minister for Labour should be the President of a Board including representatives of employers and employed. We are entirely opposed to any such arrangement, as calculated to interfere with the control of Parliament, and the complete responsibility of the Minister to the House of Commons. Unless the Minister, and the Minister alone, is placed in a position to decide what is to be done, it will be difficult for Parliament to ensure that its views upon policy will not be thwarted by influences over which it has no control; and impossible for the House of Commons to hold the Cabinet in general, and the Minister for Labour in particular, responsible for the results of his administration. The place of representatives of employers and employed is on Advisory Committees, which should be either constituted permanently or convened from time to time as required, to make suggestions, offer criticism, and supply information, in connection with particular subjects; or even generally with regard to such branches of the administration as the working of the National Labour Exchange, the arrangements for insurance or emigration, or the organization of the institutions for training.

There would be many advantages in making the Department of the Minister for Labour responsible for the whole of the United Kingdom, as are the Treasury (with the Inland Revenue, Customs and Post Office); the Board of Trade (with its Mercantile Marine Offices and its Labour Department); and the Home Office (for Prisons and Factory Acts). We think, however, on the whole, that the work would probably be organized with less friction if separate Departments on similar lines were arranged for Scotland and Ireland respectively; under the responsibility of the

Secretary for Scotland, and the Lord Lieutenant and Chief Secretary for Ireland. We do not presume to suggest with what branches of the existing Scottish and Irish administration the new Department could be most conveniently associated.

(ii) *The National Labour Exchange*

It would be the first task of the Minister for Labour to organize, in every populous centre, one or more branches of the National Labour Exchange, and to convert them, as contemplated by the Unemployed Workmen Act of 1905, into a network of intelligence as to the demand and supply of labour. These local offices would naturally vary in size and organization. In London the Minister would find ready to hand, and would naturally take over, the system of Exchanges now administered by the Central (Unemployed) Body. In a few other towns the "Labour Bureau" or Employment Exchange run by the Municipality under the Unemployed Workmen Act is sufficiently distinct to be also taken over. But the National Labour Exchange must, from the outset, make it clear that it has nothing whatever to do with the relief of Distress from Unemployment, and must therefore carefully avoid connecting itself in the public mind with the registers of applicants to Distress Committees.

The Labour Exchange would, of course, not confine itself to filling situations in the ranks of casual employment, or from among those who had to be supported or assisted in one way or another. It would receive, and in every way encourage, voluntary applications from employers for labour of better grades, for durable situations; which it would do its best to fill from the best of those whom it had on its books, whether or not they were in distress, or even actually out of work. Its business, in short, is to find situations for all men who desire them, whether or not they are actually Unemployed, and quite irrespective to their affluence or their distress; and to find men for all the vacancies notified by employers, entirely without reference to whether the successful candidates are married or single, in want or not. Indeed, in Germany a large proportion of the applicants are men who have not yet left their situations, or employers who expect to have vacancies. The object to be kept in view is that the Labour Exchange should be used by everyone who needs its services, just as if it were a post office or a railway station. Hence, in all populous centres the Labour Exchanges should have premises in prominent positions, sufficiently large to allow of capacious waiting-rooms, and different entrances and exits: and also suitable rooms for the meetings of Associations of Employers and Trade Unions, whom it is desirable to encourage to use the Exchange. Experience would show how far it was desirable to develop separate Labour Exchanges for particular industries like that at present maintained by the Board of Trade for the mercantile marine which should presumably be transferred to the new department. In any case there should be, in each town, a Local Advisory Committee of representatives of the employers and of the Trade Unions, which should supervise the working of the Exchange; and which could supply, not only useful criticisms and suggestions, but also valuable information without which the institution can never achieve its full measure of success.

There will remain, after the Labour Exchange has met all the demands upon it, a residuum of men, who are demonstrably not wanted at that moment in that place. This "surplus labour" will be a varying amount from day to day. Some of it will be needed to meet the periods of increased demand for labour—the "wools" and the "teas" at the docks, the pressure on the railway companies at the holiday seasons, the extra postmen at Christmas, the "glut men" at the Custom House, the curiously regular irregularities of the printing and bookbinding trades, the increased demand in winter of the gas companies on the one hand and the theatrical industry on the other, the spring rush on painters and builders' labourers, on dressmakers, and trouser-finishers, and so on. But we shall be surprised to find how easy it will prove, after a year or two's experience, to forecast these requirements *for the town as a whole*; and, as we have suggested, how comparatively small is the variation in the aggregate volume of employment for unskilled and casual labour of one day or of one month, or of one season of the year, compared with another. What remains to be discovered is how far the different sporadic demands can be satisfied interchangeably by the undifferentiated labour that is available. Complete interchangeability of labour, and complete "dovetailing" of situations may, of course, even in the realm of casual unskilled labour not be possible. But probably it would become every year more practicable; and it will obviously be part of the training of the ultimate residuum of Unemployed to promote a more complete interchangeability; moreover, whilst it would be the policy of the Minister for Labour so to direct the operations of the National Labour Exchange as to bring about the "Decasualization of

Casual Labour," and the Suppression of Under-employment, and of the peculiar Discontinuity of Employment characteristic of the seasonal trades, this would have to be undertaken gradually and with caution. It could only proceed step by step with the arrangements for the Absorption of Labour that we have described, and with the organization of Training Establishments at which maintenance under training was provided for any person who might find himself without employment.

When the whole of the anticipated requirements of each town are provided for—and, of course, at all times as regards individual cases—it should be the duty of the various Labour Exchanges to communicate with each other as to the actual or anticipated requirements of other towns. Just as all the Labour Exchanges in one town would report, day by day, and even, telephonically, hour by hour, to a central office in that town, from which they would all be advised as to the localities where additional men were required, so the Labour Exchanges of all the different towns would report, at least once a day, to the Ministry of Labour as regards England and Wales, and to the corresponding Departments as regards Scotland and Ireland, stating: (a) What surplus labour they had; and (b) How much of it was not needed for the proximate local requirements; or on the other hand (c) What shortage of labour they had, or expected to have. Particular Labour Exchanges could then be put telephonically in direct communication with each other, either with a view to filling particular situations or with a view to an offer, to those labourers who were disengaged, of the chance of migration to the town in which additional labour of any particular sort was required. It might well be part of the help afforded by the State to make this mobility possible by advancing any necessary railway fares, in the form of special, non-transferable railway tickets, available only for the particular journey authorised.

(iii) *The Trade Insurance Division*

The Trade Insurance Division would, in the main, deal with finance and accounts. As we have explained we do not recommend any Government Insurance Fund to provide Out-of-Work Pay in competition with the Trade Unions. The Trade Insurance Division would prepare and administer the regulations under which the Government Subvention to the societies providing insurance against Unemployment was annually granted. It is not suggested that the Government should assume any

responsibility for the management, or the financial soundness of the societies to which it paid its subvention. Nor would the Government give any
undertaking as to the future; or come into contact with any individual
member. All that it would do, year by year, would be, in recognition of
the fact that certain voluntary associations had, by their system of Trade
Insurance, actually provided Out-of-Work Pay in the preceding year for
so many men, at such and such a cost, and thereby greatly relieved the
burden which the Unemployed cast upon the Government, to grant to such
societies amounts equal to some fixed proportion (not exceeding one-half)
of the sums thus already disbursed. This would merely involve the making
of an annual application by the Trade Union, supported by statistics from
its duly audited accounts, stating the particulars of all its Out-of-Work
Benefit for the preceding year. The Trade Insurance Division would, of
course, be entitled to make any inspection of books, or other investigation
necessary for satisfying itself that the application was, in all its details,
in accordance with the regulations. But there would be no control over
policy. The Trade Insurance Division would have no further power than
to withhold payment of its subvention in respect of any cases in which it
was not satisfied that the Out-of-Work Benefit had been granted only in
relief of members unemployed through slackness of trade.

The relations of the Trade Insurance Division with the Executive Committees of the different trade societies would be facilitated by the fact
that their connection would be entirely voluntary, and terminable at any
time. There is no advantage in pressing, still less in compelling, a Trade
Union to accept the subvention offered to it. It might be allowed, if it
chose, to remain as at present, paying its own benefits for its own members
exclusively from its own funds; or declining to take up Out-of-Work
Benefit.

(iv) *The Industrial Regulation Division*

We need not describe the function of this Division, of which the present
Factory Department of the Home Office and the analogous department of
the Board of Trade dealing with the hours of railway servants, would form
the most substantial part. We imagine that this department will be presently reinforced by the organization of boards of employers and workmen
to decide on the conditions of employment which should obtain in particular industries, and to get these embodied in new clauses of the Factory Act

or voluntarily agreed to by employers and workpeople. Some such industrial organization will become more than ever desirable in order to guide
the National Labour Exchange with regard to particular industries.

(v) *The Emigration and Immigration Division*

This Division would develop the office now maintained under the
Secretary of State for the Colonies, in close communication with the
responsible governments of other parts of the Empire. In particular it will
be constantly transmitting information to the Maintenance and Training
Division as to the qualities needed to make a man or woman fit to
emigrate with a prospect of success. But we anticipate that this Division
will not confine itself to overlooking the emigration of our citizens; it will
also supervise and, if necessary, check the immigration of alien labour.
When a National Labour Exchange has undertaken the responsibility of
finding situations for unemployed citizens, and a Maintenance and Training Division has undertaken to provide for those for whom situations
cannot be found, we do not think it likely that the community will
acquiesce in any indiscriminate invasion by necessitous foreign wage-earners at times when the home market is over-stocked. The principle of supervision has already been enacted by Parliament and we recommend that
the carrying out of this statute should be transferred to the Ministry of
Labour. With regard to the emigration of individuals to other parts of
the Empire, we think that the Division should consider the expediency of
making use of the organization of the various Colonial Governments and
Voluntary Associations.

(vi) *The Statistical Division*

The Statistical Division would work in close connection with the rest
of the Department. It would summarize and collate all the information
available with regard to the labour market, the temporary or permanent
depressions in certain industries, the level of wages and hours, and the
flow of labour in and out of the country. On this material it would be able
to calculate the beginnings of waves of depression or waves of inflation
with more certainty, and, we hope, with more practical result than the
Meteorological Department forecasts the weather. Upon these statistics
the Minister of Labour would inform the Ministers responsible for the
spending departments of the approaching scarcity or surplus of Labour in
particular trades or in the country at large. These statistics would be also

available to calculate insurance premiums, or to guide the Maintenance and Training Division in the determination of the kind of training required. Upon these statistics boards of employers and workmen might determine, subject to any statutory regulations, the hours and wages of particular occupations. Finally, on these statistics would be determined how far it was desirable to encourage emigration out of the United Kingdom, or permit immigration into it.

(vii) *The Maintenance and Training Division*

To this Division there falls the most difficult and perhaps the most important task, that of working out the *technique* of an entirely new departure, in which previous experience, whether under the Poor Law or under the Unemployed Workmen Act, offers but little beyond examples of what to avoid.

We see at once that there will have to be one or more spacious Receiving Offices in each considerable centre of population, to which able-bodied persons in distress from want of employment, or unable to get food or lodging, could apply for maintenance. Such persons would either apply spontaneously, or they might be referred or brought in by the police, or by the officers of the Local Health or Education Authorities. Their urgent wants would have to be met, as they have to be at present under the head of "Sudden or Urgent Necessity"; and they would then be medically examined, and their faculties tested, to see what could be done for them. The Receiving Office would promptly pass all its cases on to one Training Establishment or another; but it would plainly require to have a certain amount of cellular sleeping accommodation available for occupation by persons absolutely homeless, pending their removal. The officers of the Receiving House for the Able-bodied would naturally act in close concert with those of the Local Health Authority and Local Education Authority, all alike "searching out" destitution, and passing to one another the cases with which each was specially concerned—all destitute children, for instance, being instantly taken charge of by the Local Education Authority, and all sick persons in distress by the Local Health Authority.

We have explained, in the Scheme of Reform with which we concluded Part I. of this Report, how the various classes of the Non-Able-bodied would be taken charge of by several specialised statutory committees of the County or County Borough Councils—the children of school age by the Local Education Authority; the infants, the sick, the permanently incapacitated and the aged requiring institutional treatment by the Local Health Authority; the mentally defective of all kinds by the Local Authority for the Mentally Defective; and the aged in receipt of local or national pensions by the Local Pensions Authority. In order to avoid overlapping of assistance to different members of the same family, or to one and the same person by different Authorities or by private charity, as also to ensure that all necessary requirements are fulfilled, we have proposed that all forms of Public Assistance should be entered in a common Register for each County or County Borough; and that all proposals for the grant of Home Aliment by any Committee should be submitted for sanction to the local Registrar of Public Assistance. It is clear that the same course should be followed with all Public Assistance granted to the Able-bodied. The Superintendent of the local Receiving House for the Able-bodied would, in fact, stand in the same relation to the Registrar of Public Assistance as the various Local Authorities for the several classes of the Non-Able-Bodied.

From the Receiving Office the Able-bodied person in distress would be assigned to one or other of the Training Establishments according to the circumstances of his case. If he was a married man with a home, he would probably be directed to attend next morning at 6 a.m., at the Day Training Depot of his town or district, where his whole day would be taken up with the training appropriate to his needs; with good plain meals on the dietary prescribed by the Trainer. But he would return home at night. Day Training Depots of this kind will be required on the outskirts of all large towns though they will not all necessarily be on the same model. If there were dependent children at home, the Superintendent of the Receiving Office would have to apply to the local Registrar of Public Assistance (giving simultaneous notice to the officers of the Local Education Authority and Local Health Authority) for sanction to have Home Aliment paid. This would be charged to the Local Education Authority; and if that Authority was not satisfied with the home circumstances for the children, it could elect to take them into one of its residential institutions, or admit them to its Day Industrial School.

But the unmarried or homeless man would probably find himself assigned to one or other of the residential Training Establishments in the country. These Farm Colonies would be established as and where required. They would adopt different kinds of training and different types of regimen, according to the needs of their respective classes of inmates. Hence the Superintendent of the Receiving House would have to decide where each applicant could most appropriately be sent. He would bear in mind also the state of the local labour market, and whether it was expected that there would be an early increase in the demand. He would consider also the peculiar needs of each man, and where he was most likely to be benefited.

We have to consider the case of women as well as of men. There must, it is clear, be a Women's Side of the Receiving Office, under a female officer. The able-bodied woman applicant would be dealt with exactly on the same lines as the man; being assigned, if single and without children, or if homeless, to a suitable day or residential Training Establishment for women only. The woman with dependent children, and with a home which satisfied the minimum requirements of the Local Health Authority and Local Education Authority would receive (unless she was adjudged unfit to have the charge of the children) Home Aliment for their support from the Local Education Authority, subject always, in order to prevent over-lapping and infringement of economic conditions, to the sanction of the local Registrar of Public Assistance. Far from being provided with indus-trial employment, the mother with whom her children were thus "boarded out" by the Local Education Authority would be required to devote herself wholly to their care, on pain of having them withdrawn from her.

There remains the case of the Able-bodied wife, without dependent children, of the able-bodied man having a decent home, but yet in need of assistance. Usually the man would be assigned to the Day Training Depot, where he would have his food. For the wife, the Superintendent of the Receiving House would enquire from the Labour Exchange whether employment of suitable nature could be found, which would permit her to keep up the home. If not, he would apply to the local Registrar of Public Assistance for sanction for the grant of Home Aliment, out of national funds, to the woman herself. This should be made conditional on her taking such steps for her own self-improvement as the Local Women's Advisory Committee might suggest; including, probably, daily attendance at the nearest Domestic Economy School for further training in cookery, dressmaking and housekeeping.

The Maintenance and Training Division would, it is clear, be able to make great use, at each stage of its work, of voluntary helpers and volun-tary institutions. It would have its Local Women's Advisory Committees, and its volunteer visitors, who would look after the wives, and help with the women inmates of the Women's Training Establishments. In the establishment and management of these institutions, the Government might receive, too, a practically unlimited amount of voluntary help and co-operation. In this connection there would be a great opportunity for making use of the fervour and zeal of philanthropy and religion. The greatest results in the way of the reclamation and training of individuals have always been achieved by religious organizations. It would be wise for the State to make a greatly increased use (with proper inspection) of farm colonies and similar settlements and homes, conducted by religious and philanthropic committees, for such of the residuum as may be willing to be sent to them in preference to the Government establishments. It may well be that for all that important side of training that is implied in the strengthening of moral character, the building up of the will, the power to resist temptation, and the formation of regular habits, the most effective instruments are a degree of love and of religious faith that a Government establishment with a Civil Service staff may not always be able to secure. The Ministry of Labour would therefore be well advised to let the denominations and the philanthropists have all the scope that they can take, and only to establish such additional Government farm colonies as are found needful to supplement the private effort. This private effort could be subsidised by payments for each case, as has long been done for a whole generation in the reformatory schools, and is now being done in inebriate homes.

(F) "UTOPIAN?"

This elaborate scheme of national organization for dealing with the grave social evil of Unemployment, with its resultant Able-bodied Destitution, and its deterioration of hundreds of thousands of working class families, will seem to many persons Utopian. Experience proves, however, that this may mean no more than that it will take a little time to accustom people to the proposals, and to get them carried into operation. The first step is to make the whole community realise that the exil exists. At present, it is not too much to say that the average citizen of the middle or upper class takes for granted the constantly recurring destitution among wage-earning families due to Unemployment, as part of the natural order of things, and as no more to be combated than the east wind. In the same way the eighteenth century citizen acquiesced in the horrors of the contemporary prison administration, and in the slave trade; just as, for the first decades of the nineteenth century, our grandfathers accepted as inevitable the slavery of the little children of the wage-earners in mines and factories, and the incessant devastation of the slums by "fever." Fifty years hence we shall be looking back with amazement at the helpless and ignorant acquiescence of the governing classes of the United Kingdom, at the opening of the twentieth century, in the constant debasement of character and *physique,* not to mention the perpetual draining away of the nation's wealth, that idleness combined with starvation plainly causes.

The second step is for the Government to make a serious endeavour to grapple with the evil as a whole, on a deliberately thought-out plan. By the Unemployed Workmen Act of 1905, Parliament and the Nation have admitted the public responsibility in the matter. We may agree that the work of the Distress Committees has resulted in little. But the experiments of the last few years have definitely revealed the nature of the problem, and the lines on which it can be dealt with. *We have to report that, in our judgment, it is now administratively possible, if it is sincerely wished to do so, to remedy most of the evils of Unemployment*; to the same extent, at least, as we have in the past century diminished the death rate from fever and lessened the industrial slavery of young children. It is not a valid objection that a demonstrably perfect and popularly-accepted *technique,* either with regard to the prevention of Unemployment, or with regard to the treatment of the Unemployed, has not yet been worked out. No such *technique* can ever be more than foreshadowed until it is actually being put in operation. Less than a century ago the problem of dealing with the sewage of London seemed insoluble. Half a million separate private cesspools accumulated each its own putrefaction. To combine these festering heaps into a single main drainage system seemed, to the Statesmen and social reformers of 1820 or 1830, beyond the bounds of possibility. We now take for granted that only by such a concentration is it possible to get rid of the festering heaps and scientifically treat the ultimate residuum. In the same way, a century ago, no one knew how to administer a fever hospital; the eighteenth century "pesthouse" must, indeed, have killed more people than it cured. Yet it was only by establishing hospitals that we learnt how to make them instruments of recovery for the patients and of a beneficent protection to the rest of the community. And, to take a more recent problem, less than half a century ago, when millions of children in the land were growing up untaught, undisciplined, and uncared for, it would have sounded wildly visionary to have suggested that the remedy was elaborate organisation on a carefully thought-out plan. Could there have been anything more "Utopian" in 1860 than a picture of what to-day we take as a matter of course, the 7,000,000 children emerging every morning, washed and brushed, from 5,000,000 or 6,000,000 homes in every part of the Kingdom, traversing street and road and lonely woodland, going o'er fell and moor, to present themselves at a given hour at their 30,000 schools, where each of the 7,000,000 finds his or her own individual place, with books and blackboard and teacher provided? What has been effected in the organisation of Public Health and Public Education can be effected, if we wish it, in the Public Organisation of the Labour Market.

* * *

(Signed) H. RUSSELL WAKEFIELD
FRANCIS CHANDLER
GEORGE LANSBURY
BEATRICE WEBB